STRATEGY PROCESS

Strategic Management Society Book Series

The Strategic Management Book Series is a cooperative effort between the Strategic Management Society and Blackwell Publishing. The purpose of the series is to present information on cutting-edge concepts and topics in strategic management theory and practice. The books emphasize building and maintaining bridges between strategic management theory and practice. The work published in these books generates and tests new theories of strategic management. Additionally, work published in this series demonstrates how to learn, understand, and apply these theories in practice. The content of the series represents the newest critical thinking in the field of strategic management. As a result, these books provide valuable knowledge for strategic management scholars, consultants and executives.

This particular volume seeks to define the contours of the field of strategy process, and provides a deep understanding of how strategies are shaped, implemented and changed. Complementing strategy content research focused on finding winning strategy positions, the strategy process researcher aspires to learn how these winning positions are realized. Strategy content emphasizes attractive destinations, while strategy process involves the journey to get there. This journey has been haphazardly developed in part because not all strategy process researchers have a shared sense of the destination. While contributions have come from multiple disciplines, prior research has not provided the road to the desired destination, winning strategies, and superior firm performance. This book seeks to provide a road map to help integrate and cumulate the research on strategy process. It identifies several useful research streams where quality work is strongly needed. The framework provided in this book has been shared with researchers and practitioners belonging to the newly formed Strategic Management Society's Interest Group on Strategy Process, and at the mini-conference on strategy process research jointly sponsored by the Strategic Management Society, IMD, and the University of St Gallen. The authors in this book have used feedback from the conference and from the co-editors to develop thought-provoking and creative explorations of their topics. The book is an important reference for scholars and thoughtful executives interested in how strategies are realized.

Michael A. Hitt
Series Editor

Strategy Process

Shaping the Contours of the Field

Edited by

Bala Chakravarthy
Guenter Mueller-Stewens
Peter Lorange
Christoph Lechner

Blackwell
Publishing

MT

© 2003 by Blackwell Publishing Ltd
except for editorial arrangement and introduction © 2003 by Bala Chakravarthy, Guenter Mueller-Stewens, Peter Lorange, and Christoph Lechner

350 Main Street, Malden, MA 02148-5018, USA
108 Cowley Road, Oxford OX4 1JF, UK
550 Swanston Street, Carlton South, Melbourne, Victoria 3053, Australia
Kurfürstendamm 57, 10707 Berlin, Germany

First published 2003 by Blackwell Publishing Ltd

Library of Congress Cataloging-in-Publication Data

Strategy process : shaping the contours of the field / edited by Bala Chakravarthy ... [et al.].
       p.   cm. — (Strategic Management Society book series ; 3)
    Includes bibliographical references and index.
    ISBN 1–4051–0067–2 (hc : alk. paper)
    1. Strategic planning.   I. Chakravarthy, Bala.   II. Series
  HD30.28 .S7393 2003
  658.4′012—dc21

                                                              2002005034

A CIP catalogue record for this book is available from the British Library.

Set in 10 on 12 pt Galliard
by Ace Filmsetting Ltd, Frome, Somerset
Printed in and bound in the United Kingdom
by TJ International, Padstow, Cornwall

For further information on
Blackwell Publishing, visit our website:
htttp:/www.blackwellpublishing.com

2/19/04

Contents

List of Figures   vii
List of Tables   viii
List of Contributors   ix
Preface   xii

1   Defining the Contours of the Strategy Process Field   1
    *Bala Chakravarthy, Guenter Mueller-Stewens, Peter
    Lorange, Christoph Lechner*

2   Transforming the Firm through the Co-evolution of
    Resources and Scope   18
    Alvaro Cuervo-Cazurra

3   Change in the Presence of Fit: The Rise, the Fall, and the
    Renaissance of Liz Claiborne   46
    Nicolaj Siggelkow

4   Resources, Management Systems, and Governance: Keys
    to Value Creation   77
    Karen Schnatterly, Catherine Maritan

5   The Essence of Process: Effective Strategic Planning in
    Practice   97
    John C. Camillus

6   A Multilevel Analysis of the Strategic Decision Process and
    the Evolution of Shared Beliefs   110
    Mirela Schwarz

7   The Social Construction of Organizational Capabilities:
    A Multilevel Analysis   137
    *V. K. Narayanan, Benedict Kemmerer, Frank L. Douglas,
    Brock Guernsey*

8 The Conditioning and Knowledge-creating View:
   Managing Strategic Initiatives in Large Firms   164
   Martin W. Wielemaker, Henk W. Volberda, Tom Elfring,
   Charles Baden-Fuller

9 A Longitudinal Study of Organizational Learning,
   Unlearning, and Innovation among IJVs in a Transitional
   Economy   191
   Marjorie A. Lyles, Katalin Szabo, Eva Kocsis, Jeff Barden,
   Charles Dhanaraj, Kevin Steensma, Laszlo Tihanyi

10 Strategic Renewal Processes in Multi-unit firms:
   Generic Journeys of Change   208
   Henk W. Volberda, Charles Baden-Fuller

11 Shaping, Implementing, and Changing Strategy:
   Opportunities and Challenges   233
   Bala Chakravarthy, Guenter Mueller-Stewens, Peter
   Lorange, Christoph Lechner

Author Index   242

Subject Index   251

Figures

1.1	Going beyond the normative and synoptic views of strategy process	3
1.2	An integrative framework	5
1.3	Strategy dynamics	7
1.4	Stream A: adaptation to changes in the businesss context	9
1.5	Stream B: organizational context and performance	11
1.6	Stream C: context, process, and outcomes	13
2.1	Temporal and atemporal representations of the interactions among resource and activity dimensions	42
3.1	Performance landscapes	49
3.2	Change framework	51
3.3	Map of interactions among Liz Claiborne's choices in the early 1990s	59
3.4	Map of interactions among Liz Claiborne's choices in 1997	68
4.1	Value creation model	78
5.1	A framework for the study of strategic planning processes	102
6.1	Empirical evidence: interplay between the development of shared beliefs and the strategic decision process	117
6.2	Emergence of different belief patterns	120
6.3	Development of critical mass of supporters	124
6.4	Theoretical framework for the relationship between the development of shared beliefs and the strategic decision process	128
8.1	An integrative framework of initiatives	172
8.2	The relation between the resource approval and development processes	173
10.1	Generic renewal journeys of multiunit firms	213
10.2	One example of a development journey of strategic renewal	225
11.1	An integrative framework	235

Tables

1.1	Classification schemes for studying strategy process	4
1.2	Overview of the chapters	15
2.1	Standard for the evaluation of the accumulation of resources towards international best practices	24
2.2	Standard for the evaluation of the accumulation of activities	27
2.3	Evaluation of the transformation of dimensions of resources and scope at the beginning and end of the period under study	30
2.4	Individual transformation actions and their relationship to competitive advantage (CA)	36
3.1	Financial data for Liz Claiborne, Inc.	64
4.1	Measurement of variables	86
4.2	Descriptive statistics and correlations among the variables	88
4.3	Results of conditional logit estimation	89
7.1	Overview of organizational capability building process stages	149
7.2	Embedding speed: execution of individual processses vs. building organizational capability	154
A7.1	Interviewees	160
8.1	The initiatives investigated	177
9.1	Intercorrelation matrix for independent and control variables	197
9.2	Significance of the overall models	197
9.3	Coefficients for the models	198
10.1	Selection and adaptation	210
10.2	An inquiry into journeys of strategic renewal in multiunit firms	215
11.1	Overview of the chapters	237

Contributors

Baden-Fuller, Charles
City University
e-mail: *c.baden-fuller@city.ac.uk*

Barden, Jeff
Duke University
e-mail: *JBQ@duke.edu*

Camillus, John C.
University of Pittsburg
e-mail: *camillus@katz.pitt.edu*

Chakravarthy, Bala
International Institute for Management Development, Switzerland
e-mail: *chakravarthy@IMD.ch*

Cuervo-Cazurra, Alvaro
University of Minnesota
e-mail: *acuervo@csom.umn.edu*

Dhanaraj, Charles
Indiana University
e-mail: *dhanaraj@iupui.edu*

Douglas, Frank L.
Aventis Pharma, Frankfurt
e-mail: *frank.douglas@aventis.com*

Elfring, Tom
Vrije University, Amsterdam
e-mail: *telfring@fbk.eur.nl*

Guernsey, Brock
Quintiles Inc., Kansas City
e-mail: *brockguernsey@worldnet.att.net*

Kemmerer, Benedict
University of Kansas
e-mail: *bkemmerer@ku.edu*

Kocsis, Eva
Budapest University
e-mail: *kocsis.eva@ohg.bke.hu*

Lechner, Christoph
University of St Gallen
e-mail: *christoph.lechner@unisg.ch*

Lorange, Peter
International Institute for Management Development
e-mail: *lorange@imd.ch*

Lyles, Marjorie A.
Indiana University
e-mail: *mlyles@iupui.edu*

Maritan, Catherine
State University of New York at Buffalo
e-mail: *cmaritan@buffalo.edu*

Mueller-Stewens, Guenter
University of St Gallen
e-mail: *guenter.mueller-stewens@unisg.ch*

Narayanan, V. K.
Drexel University, Philadelphia
e-mail: *vnarayanan@worldnet.att.net*

Schnatterly, Karen
University of Minnesota
e-mail:kschnatterly*@csom.umn.edu*

Schwarz, Mirela
University of Southampton
e-mail: *mirela@socsi.soton.ac.uk*

Siggelkow, Nicolaj
University of Pennsylvania
e-mail: *siggelkow@wharton.upenn.edu*

Steensma, Kevin
University of Washington
e-mail: *steensma@u.washington.edu*

Szabo, Katalin
Budapest University of Economics
e-mail: *katalin.szabo@comp.bke.hu*

Tihanyi, Laszlo
Oklahoma University
e-mail: *ltihany@ou.edu*

Volberda, Henk W.
Erasmus University, Rotterdam
e-mail: *hvolberda@fbk.eur.nl*

Wielemaker, Martin W.
University of New Brunswick
e-mail: *wielemam@fac.fadmin.unb.ca*

Preface

Despite voluminous research, the process through which strategies are shaped, implemented, and changed remains ill understood. The old debates continue: Is strategy emergent or planned? Does it bubble bottom-up or is it set top-down? Is the process rational or political? Is strategy the work of a lone genius or the result of a collective, albeit more mundane, effort? Reconciling the varied and often contradictory findings into coherent guidelines for action has been difficult. Also, scholars who write about the process of strategic change seem disconnected from their colleagues who write about the relatively steady-state processes of protecting and extending an existing strategy. But what if change is frequent, as in many businesses? What then is the process of continuous change and renewal?

Business executives who are faced with the above dilemmas often seek the help of management consultants. While the consultants (as do some academics) may have insights on how to help a particular company, they often do not have the time or inclination to investigate these insights more rigorously. Clearly, there is an opportunity to strike several potent alliances: (1) among academics in order to undertake more ambitious research projects and to cumulate their findings, (2) between academics and business executives to engage in research that is actionable, and (3) between academics and consultants to develop deeper and more valid knowledge on the strategy process.

The purpose of this book is to set the stage for these potential alliances. We first need an organizing framework that defines the contours of the strategy process field. This book seeks to provide one. But it is just a first step, a "living" document that can form the basis for continuous refinement of the field's agenda. The ideas presented in the book have been discussed and debated at two different meetings over the past three years.

The SMS Meeting at Vancouver, Canada, October 2000

The first was a meeting called by Bala Chakravarthy, the newly designated Chair of the Interest Group on Strategy Process. Twenty-five strategy process researchers, management consultants and business practitioners met on the sidelines of the Vancouver conference of the Strategic Management Society (SMS). The purpose of the meeting was twofold:

◆ to identify the most important opportunities for research on strategy process.
◆ to identify the most effective ways of building a bridge between the academics (As), businesspeople (Bs) and consultants (Cs).

The group nominated the following as some of the more important opportunities for research:

◆ How do financial markets impact strategy making within firms?
◆ Can we not follow the trail of money (both resources to fund projects and personal incentives) through an organization to understand how strategy is made and implemented?
◆ Isn't an important part of the process, impression management? How does this link to a firm's realized strategy?
◆ How does a management team decide when, where, and how to diversify its market presence and competence base?
◆ How are dominant logics formed and changed in firms? How are they different from routines?
◆ How do firms generate, share, and use knowledge?
◆ Generic strategies are fine, but how does a firm migrate from one (say differentiation) to another (say cost leadership)? How does it create a hybrid? Or is this the proverbial hell of being stuck in the middle?
◆ How does an old economy firm move into the new economy?
◆ How do firms create value, capture value, and align their organizations internally to this value proposition?
◆ How do multiple levels of managers interact to shape, implement, and change strategy?
◆ How can we reconcile an often-bureaucratic process with creative individuals? If process cannot enhance creativity, can it at least nurture and not stifle creativity?
◆ How can risk be managed better in the strategy process?
◆ Is there an underlying craft to strategy making, implementation, and change? What are some of its salient features? How can the firm derive a "process advantage" from such a craft?

While the above list is offered with no priority ranking (the group could not agree on it), the simple consensus was clear. It is not enough to talk just about winning strategy positions, or attractive destinations that are discerned after the fact. It is high time to start addressing the more important questions of how do we know where to go, who should drive the journey, when and how? Addressing these and related questions is the mission of the Strategic Management Society's Interest Group on Strategy Process.

On the other important question of how do we bring academics, business practitioners, and consultants together in a grand alliance, the consensus of the Interest Group was to:

- build an electronic community,
- hold a smaller pre-conference at the annual SMS conference,
- agree to field joint sessions at the SMS conference,
- hold mini-conferences around the globe.

Taking to heart some of the suggestions from this first meeting, the editors of this book organized a mini conference on Shaping, Implementing and Changing Strategies at St Gallen, Switzerland, jointly sponsored by the Strategic Management Society, IMD and the University of St Gallen.

The IMD–St Gallen SMS mini-conference, May 2001

A select group of academics from all the major centres on strategy process research in Asia, Europe, and the United States were invited to the conference, as were several leading business executives and expert consultants to create a powerful melange of academics (A), businesspeople (B) and consultants (C). Sixty-four participants attended the St Gallen meeting.

The first day of the conference was centered around two panels. Each panel presentation was followed by small group discussions and a plenary debate on the ensuing reactions. The first panel was on "A Practitioner's View of Strategy Process Research." The panelists were: Jan Oosterveld (Philips), Dieter Heuskel (Boston Consulting Group), and Stephan Dyckerhoff (Cap Gemini Ernst & Young Strategic Consulting). The panel noted that what the practitioner needs are better insights than the current research offers on how to deal with industry breakpoints and anticipate emerging consumer needs. Heuskel pointed out that benchmarks are passé. What is needed are "bench breaking" strategies. How to sense new opportunities better is an important challenge for the practitioner. The panel also emphasized the need for more usable research on speeding up the strategy process and ensuring that it keeps the firm flexible. Dyckerhoff outlined a proprietary intervention technique (Accelerating Strategy Events or ASE) that his firm uses with clients to speed up their process. Oosterveld reminded the participants that static snapshots may bring back nostalgic memories; but these do not help with the life that lies ahead. He pointed out that the "Philips of tomorrow will be more Chinese and American than Dutch!!" While its heritage may be European, the company will have to be a major player in Asia and America if it has to prosper. "What is the next stage in Chandler's model of strategy and structural evolution?" he asked. The panel invited academics to work on the current pressing problems of the practitioner, and not to waste their talents researching trivial problems of yesterday.

The second panel was on "Making Strategy Process Research Both Relevant and Rigorous," The panelists were Yves Doz (INSEAD), Charles Lucier (Booz, Allen & Hamilton), and Howard Thomas (University of Warwick). Doz asked the participants to investigate seriously whether markets or hierarchies are better at allocating resources. If it is the former, what is the value added of the strategy process? He urged researchers to start conceptualizing the competitive advantages to a firm from its strategy process. Lucier noted that a successful consulting engagement offers the client at least a 10 percent improvement in its performance. He then asked the provocative question: "How would academic research stack up on a similar criterion?" Thomas went on to point out that good strategy process research must be multi-period, multi-level, multi-context, multi-actor and multi-disciplinary; if it has to catch reality that is in flight. The panel strongly agreed that we need stronger research paradigms. It urged academics to step up their theoretical contributions, and be creative in their use of methodologies. It suggested greater use of simulation and the borrowing of techniques that have worked in other disciplines like cognitive psychology. Above all, it urged academics to stop testing tired old ideas, to shun mindless empiricism.

On the second day of the conference, sixteen pre-screened research papers were presented in two tracks to ensure quality discussions on each. Nine of these papers were subsequently selected and developed for this book. The authors represent a roughly equal mix of established and starting academics; and Europe and North America based scholars.

The idea of the conference was not to end with something of a shared "declaration." That goal would have been unrealistic anyway. Rather, we focused on mapping the contours of the strategy process field. We started the process of sharing this map late last year at the first formal meeting of the SMS Strategy Process Interest Group in San Francisco. This book is an attempt to share the emerging consensus with a wider audience.

In putting this book together, we are indebted to many people. First, we are grateful to the authors for participating in such an "experimental project" and sharing their excellent work with the readers of this book. We have asked a lot of them and they have delivered gracefully each time. Second, we are thankful to the distinguished academics, management consultants and business practitioners, who not only gave us their encouragement but also participated actively on our panels and in our deliberations. Third, we deeply appreciate the enormous support that we have received from the Strategic Management Society for launching the Strategy Process Interest Group. We thank in particular Dan Schendel, whose idea it was to launch Interest Groups like ours within the society. Howard Thomas (past president of the society), John McGee (its present president), Jeremy Davis (the president elect), Jack Keane (the society's treasurer), made time to attend the St. Gallen mini conference. Jan Oosterveld, a senior executive at Philips and a SMS board member, brought to our meetings his refreshingly new perspectives as a thoughtful practitioner. Finally, we would like to acknowledge the efforts of the many who have helped with the production of the book itself. Mike Hitt, the society's Vice President for publications, gave us his enthusiastic support right from the early stages of this project. Rosemary Nixon and her excellent publishing team at Blackwell Publishing have been a pleasure to work with. Our own assistants, Stephanie Jacquat at IMD and Michaela Solterbeck at St Gallen, have helped in numerous ways. While we are thankful to many, the blame for any inadequacies in the book must rest squarely with us.

Bala Chakravarthy   *Guenter Mueller-Stewens*
Peter Lorange   *Christoph Lechner*
IMD   University of St Gallen
Lausanne, Switzerland   St Gallen, Switzerland

CHAPTER ONE

Defining the Contours of the Strategy Process Field

Bala Chakravarthy, Guenter Mueller-Stewens, Peter Lorange, Christoph Lechner

The label strategy process, to some, is an oxymoron. Strategy is about creativity and innovation, whereas process smacks of bureaucracy and control. It is true that the word process does carry with it some baggage. Perhaps "Shaping, Implementing and Changing Strategy" is a better label for the strategy process field. While labels are important, it is even more important to define the contours of a field devoted to shaping, implementing, and changing strategy.

Strategies, as we well know, are in part planned and in part emergent. But can a firm have no strategy at all? Inkpen and Choudhury (1995) examine three situations where a firm can be seen as having no strategy, that is, it is "strategyless." The first such is an attribution, valid or not, when a firm fails. External observers blame this failure on the inability of its top management to set a clear strategy for the firm. The second is one when the firm is in a transitional phase from one strategy to another. It may temporarily appear "strategyless." While the first two may be more in the eyes of the beholder, they also point to a third situation, where they suggest a deliberate attempt on the part of top management to create more flexibility and innovation by simply not setting strategies.

It is true that the sheer genius of top management is not enough to set a firm's strategies. In any large diversified firm, the enormity of this task is bound to exceed the cognitive capacities of top management. Strategies are better realized through the collective efforts of multiple organizational actors operating at many levels in the organization: functions, business units, and corporate. The shaping, implementing, and changing of strategies requires the paradoxical blend of top-down and bottom-up efforts, planned and emergent actions, autonomy and collectivism in both decision-making and action taking. The research on strategy process unfortunately has not always been open to these paradoxical blends.

A Historical Perspective

In his pioneering work on corporate strategy, Andrews (1971) proposed that there are two distinct phases to strategic management: "*formulation*" and "*implementation*."

While the emphasis in the formulation phase is on decision-making, the implementation phase deals with how to convert these decisions into actions and thus achieve a predefined goal. This classical view informed much of the early work on strategic planning and management control. Research in this tradition made the following assumptions:

1   Strategy process was regarded as a *sequence of clearly defined phases:* "formulation" and "implementation," or also referred to as "agenda building" and "decision, implementation, and control." Each phase involved multiple steps and included rationally justified instructions on what had to be done at every step.
2   *Decisions* were the relevant objects of analysis. Strategy formulation was perceived as a decision-making process, since it was through decisions that the agenda of the corporation was shaped and defined.
3   The formulation and implementation of strategies was an *active, goal-oriented process.* Strategies did not simply happen spontaneously nor were they just subjects of ex post rationalization, but were made explicitly and deliberately, prior to action.
4   This process was initiated and driven by *top management.* Strategies shaped the future of a corporation and therefore the responsibility for their formulation and implementation had to rest with top management. Middle and lower management participated in the ongoing process by providing the necessary information, serving as facilitators in both the formulation and implementation phases.
5   The possibility that corporations might not have a strategy at all was not dealt with, nor even considered.

Each of the above assumptions has been seriously challenged by more recent research. In contrast with the rather synoptic and normative view of strategy in the classical approach, Mintzberg (1987, 1994) offers four other perspectives on strategy that he calls *position, ploy, perspective, and pattern – in contrast with the other "p," plan.* Strategy as plan shows the firm how to get from its current to its targeted position. On the other hand, strategy as position refers to attractive destinations, markets and competitive positions that are particularly advantageous to a firm. Strategy as ploy refers to how a firm games the competitive context in its favour. Strategy as perspective refers to the firm's view of the world and its own place in it. Finally, strategy as pattern refers to configurations in the firm's stream of decisions or actions. Realizing strategy is not only a planned process but also an emergent one (Mintzberg and Waters, 1985). Consequently, there has been an increase in the number of descriptive studies on strategy process to counter-balance the earlier normative work. Recent research on strategy process has used more than one of the five Ps as a guide.

But, if strategy is an emerging pattern of decisions and actions, who gets to determine this pattern? According to Kirsch (1997), this has to be made by a collective within the firm and not by any external observer. An individual, usually a senior executive, often has a pattern that he or she prefers. But this individual preference may not necessarily be aligned with the views and actions of other executives in the company, not to mention the rest of the organization. Unless a common inter-subjective preference for a decision or action stream exists and is supported at least by members of the dominant coalition in a firm (its senior executives), Kirsch would argue that the pat-

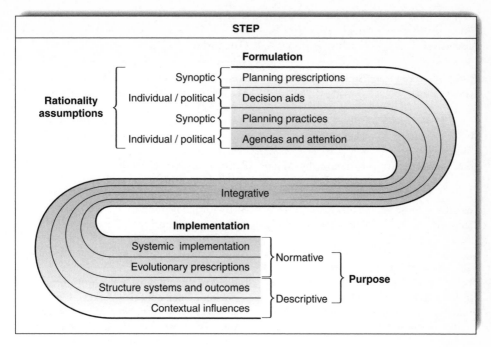

Figure 1.1   Going beyond the normative and synoptic views of strategy process
Source: Huff and Reger, 1987

tern does not constitute a strategy. Therefore, Kirsch suggests differentiating between individual strategies and corporate strategies. Strategy process is not an individualistic process, but a collective one. The political interplay of individual and collective interests has to be examined in order to understand strategy better. In studies where the object of reference is the chief executive officer only, it is clear that such methodological individualism leads to shortcomings in the understanding of strategy process (Willke, 1993; Weick, 1995).

Huff and Reger (1987) propose a wider frame to understand strategy process. They classify the research in the field using the three dimensions discussed above: (1) does the research deal with strategy formulation and/or implementation (the classical distinction), (2) was the purpose of the study normative or descriptive, and (3) was the theoretical frame of the researcher synoptic or individual/political? Using this classification scheme, they identified the nine "streams" of strategy process research (see figure 1.1) that were published in seven leading journals from 1981 to 1987.

Others have proposed different classification schemes. Some of these are shown in table 1.1. Useful as these schemes have been for distinguishing the work in the field, none has been helpful for integrating this research. Chakravarthy and White (2001) have recently provided a framework that attempts such integration.

Table 1.1 Classification schemes for studying strategy process

Dimension	Author(s)	Categories
Process phases	Andrews (1971)	Formulation, implementation
Types of processes	Garvin (1998)	Managerial (direction setting, negotiating, control)
		Organizational (work, change, behavioural)
Modes of strategy making	Hart (1992)	Command, symbolic, rational, transactive, generative
Research perspective	Chakravarthy/White (2001)	Rational: decision-making
		Political: resolving goal conflicts
		Evolutionary: action-taking
Research purpose	Huff/Reger (1987)	Normative, descriptive
Rationality of the researcher	Huff/Reger (1987)	Synoptic, individual/political
Assumptions about decision-making	Chakravarthy/Doz (1992)	Rational, bounded/rational, extra-rational
Unit of analysis of the research	Chakravarthy/Doz (1992)	Individual (in and outside the firm), firm, environmental context (markets, society)
Guiding assumptions of the research	Pettigrew (1992)	(1) embeddedness: studying processes across number of levels of analysis; (2) temporal interconnectedness: studying processes in past, present and future time; (3) a role in explanation for context and action; (4) a search for holistic rather than linear explanations of process; (5) a need to link process analysis to the location and explanation of outcomes.
Phenomena	Lechner/Mueller-Stewens (2000)	basic questions, phase-specific questions, cross-sectional questions

A Proposed Integrative Framework

We have modified the Chakravarthy and White framework based on the learning from the IMD–St Gallen SMS mini-conference (see figure 1.2). The framework is a composite of four distinct relationships: (1) the relations between competitive position, distinctive competencies, business context, firm performance and financial market evaluation, (2) the impact of decisions and actions on a firm's competitive position and distinctive competencies, (3) the influence of organizational context on the core elements of the strategy process, and (4) the dynamic equilibrium that top management keeps a firm in through its continuous redefinition of the relevant strategy dynamics for the firm.

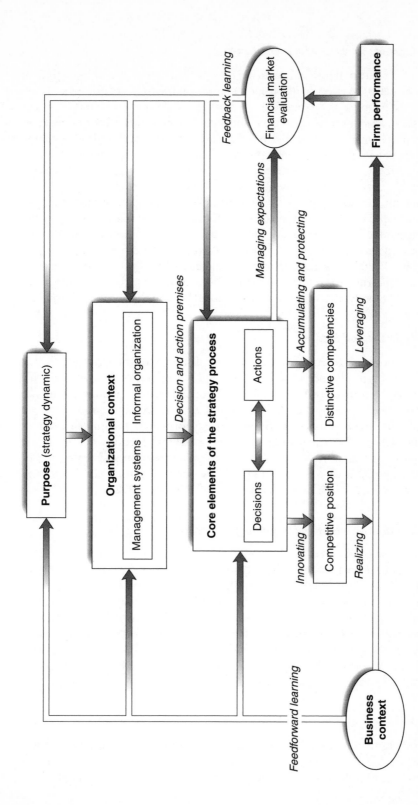

Figure 1.2 An integrative framework
Source: Adapted from Chakravarthy and White, 2001

Adapting to Changes in the Business Context

The first (the lower part of figure 1.2) visualizes how a firm's strategy and its distinctive competencies mediate the effect of its business context on the firm's performance (Porter, 1991). Investigating this relationship is normally the domain of strategy content researchers, but strategy process researchers must complement this work in important ways by discerning how new competitive positions are innovated and realized, and how distinctive competencies are accumulated, protected and leveraged. The purpose of strategy process research is to facilitate the realization of more innovative and defensible strategies. But process researchers have not always included a strategy outcome in their studies. When they do associate process characteristics with an organizational outcome, it is often financial performance. But, financial performance is but one input to how the financial markets value a firm. Managing the expectations of the financial markets is an equally important factor. Strategy process must be concerned both with a firm's performance and its effective communication to the financial markets. Moreover, it must respond to the concerns of the financial market by transforming the firm's organizational context and modifying its decisions and actions. We call this feedback learning.

Outcomes of decisions and actions

Decisions and actions are often viewed as the core elements of the strategy process, though their relative importance to a firm's strategy is a matter of some debate. We accept that strategy is realized through both emergent and planned actions that implement prior decisions. In turn, these decisions and actions are continuously revised based on feedback and feed-forward learning. Strategy formation and implementation are closely intertwined. The relationship, captured by the mid-section of figure 1.2, is between decisions and actions of a firm to: (1) the identification and realization of innovative new competitive positions and (2) the accumulation, protection, and leveraging of its distinctive competencies (Chakravarthy et al., 2002).

Organizational context and decision and action premises

The third relationship captured by the framework (the upper part of figure 1.2) is between the organizational context of a firm and how it shapes the premises for both decisions and actions within the firm (Chandler, 1962). Organizational context includes: (1) a firm's management systems, like structure, planning, control, human resources management (HRM) and incentive systems, and (2) its informal organization, including values, norms, culture, and leadership style. The importance of organizational context in the shaping of decision and action premises has been long recognized; and yet with rare exceptions like Bower (1970) and Burgelman (1983, 1996), there are very few studies of this important relationship.

Strategy dynamics

Time is an important dimension for all elements in figure 1.2. Firm performance, strategy, competencies, decisions, actions, business, and organizational contexts, all change over time and influence each other dynamically. The final component of the

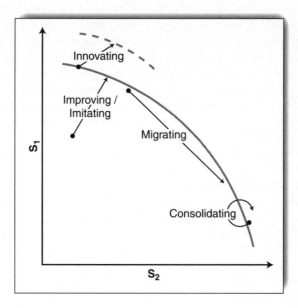

Figure 1.3   Strategy dynamics
Source: Chakravarthy and White, 2001

framework captures this dynamic interaction. Strategy content research has distinguished between three levels of strategy: business, multi-business, and multi-national, and offers a typology for each. The dimensions used to create these typologies reflect the key tensions inherent in any strategy: cost leadership vs. differentiation, vertical vs. horizontal integration, or national responsiveness vs. global integration. Figure 1.3 presents a two-dimensional strategy space (S_1 and S_2) capturing these tensions. The curved solid line represents a sort of strategy frontier, where those firms with the current best practice are positioned.

If a firm is not on the strategy frontier, improving/imitating advances the firm's strategic position toward the strategy frontier. Other firms on the strategy frontier, or those closer to it, provide the firm seeking improvement ready benchmarks to follow. Having reached the strategy frontier, a firm may start consolidating and maintaining this position by monitoring its competitors and making incremental improvements (Hammer and Champy, 1993), or it may seek to innovate. Innovating goes beyond established best practices and advances the strategy frontier (dashed line). Lastly, migrating involves a change in a firm's position along the existing frontier; for example, from differentiation to low cost. While this is a significant change, it differs from innovating. A firm migrating from one generic strategy to another has exemplars. The position it seeks is not new. Other firms, elsewhere along the strategy frontier, have already achieved this strategy and provide benchmarks. An innovator does not have this luxury. Nevertheless, both innovating and migrating are more risky than improving, imitating or consolidating. Firms opting for innovation and migration not only seek a different market opportunity, they are also willing to redo their competence base.

Defining the appropriate strategy dynamics for the firm is a key top management responsibility. In multi-business firms, more than one dynamic may be necessary. Different types of process may be required to drive the four strategy dynamics described in figure 1.3. For example, migrating from a differentiation to a cost leader business strategy, or changing from a local responsive to a globally integrated multinational strategy may both require rebalancing the power structure in the organization (Prahalad, 1975). On the other hand, consolidating a successful business or corporate strategy may be more of a rational process. The process should be similar for the same type of dynamic even across different levels of strategy.

Contrast this with the tendency to use generic strategies as outcomes in strategy process research. There is no reason to believe that the process required to deliver an *innovative* differentiation strategy should be any different from that required to deliver an *innovative* cost-leadership strategy. It is innovation that distinguishes the process and not the underlying generic strategy. Certainly, the cast of characters involved in decision-making and action taking will vary with the generic strategy pursued. For example, product developers and marketers may be more important to differentiation and procurement experts and operations managers may be more relevant to a cost-leadership strategy. But the process they follow will be guided more by the strategy dynamic that is being pursued and not the generic strategy under consideration or the level (business, corporate, or international) at which it is pursued. While the core elements of strategy process may be in the patterns of decisions and actions that are witnessed in a firm, these have to be tied closely to its strategy dynamics.

Integrative framework

The proposed framework clearly demarcates what the appropriate outcomes are for different types of research: financial performance; competitive position/distinctive competence; decisions/actions; or organizational/business context, depending on which of the four parts of the framework a researcher is interested in.

A Guide to the Papers

Nine papers were selected from those presented at the IMD–St Gallen SMS mini-conference on strategy process research. These are presented in this book from chapters 2 to 10. The papers are clustered into four streams using the framework proposed here (see figure 1.2).

A   Longitudinal research on how a firm adapts to changes in its business context (chapters 2 and 3)
B   Linking organizational context to firm performance (chapters 4 and 5)
C   Interaction between organizational context, process elements and competitive position/distinctive competencies (chapters 6–8)
D   Interplay between organizational context, process elements and performance (Chapters 9 and 10)

Stream A: longitudinal research on adaptation

In this stream (See figure 1.4), we selected two papers that examine longitudinally the stepwise development of a firm's new competitive position and competence platform, in response to a shift in its business environment. In Chapter 2, Cuervo-Cazurra describes how firms in Spain and Argentina in three different industries (paper, petroleum, and construction) have coped with deregulation and economic liberalization. Contrary to the assertions of the two main schools of strategy: the resource-based view and the activity-based view (or positioning school), neither the desired resources nor targeted position were predetermined. Rather, in the better performing firms resource accumulation and activity scope *co-evolved*, mutually influencing each other through a multi-phase process. The author concludes that the competitive advantage of a firm is more likely to be sustained when it pursues a co-evolutionary process rather than when it chooses a unidirectional process of transformation, where a predetermined resource or activity architecture drives change.

Three quartets of Argentinean and Spanish firms, each from a different industry, were selected for the study. In each quartet there were both high- and low-performing firms. This set up a nice experimental design. Cuervo-Cazurra measured resource accumulation in the 12 selected firms along eight dimensions (production team, human resources, organization, finance, technology, production supply network, and marketing) and competitive positioning along three dimensions (vertical integration, horizontal diversification, and internationalization). The study used structured interviews and company archives to collect its data, and an innovative qualitative analysis method to analyze the data.

Siggelkow, in chapter 3, presents the second study in this stream. He distinguishes between *fit-destroying* and *fit-conserving* environmental change by looking at the impact that they have on what he calls the "performance landscape." The quality of external fit or the appropriateness of the choices a firm makes given its business context, is represented by its height on the performance landscape. A peak on this landscape represents consistency among these choices, or internal fit. Further, the stronger the degree of interaction among a particular set of choices, the steeper the associated peak. Siggelkow visualizes environmental change then as changing the performance

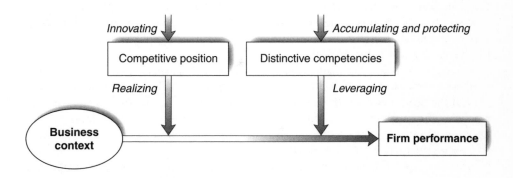

Figure 1.4   Stream A: adaptation to changes in the business context

landscape: the height, shape, or location of its peaks. In a fit-destroying change, the firm no longer occupies a peak, whereas in a fit-conserving change the firm still occupies a peak, but its height is now reduced. Using this performance landscape metaphor, the author goes on to describe the choices made at Liz Claiborne in the early 1990s in response to a changing business context. The company's external fit decreased, while there was no change in its internal fit. In the author's terminology, this meant that the company was challenged by a fit-conserving change. Top management reacted sluggishly, changing only partially its set of choices for activities in the value chain. A new leadership team that came in 1994 had to change the choices and reverse the ensuing slide in performance.

The Siggelkow study underscores the findings of Cuervo-Cazurra. Transforming a firm's activity set or resource pool is especially difficult if the environmental change is fit-conserving. The firm's inertia prevents it from scaling back from the performance peak it is occupying, even though the changing landscape keeps reducing the height of this peak progressively. The process of co-evolution, where resources and activity scope are changed iteratively, could be a way of breaking this inertia. While neither study helps us understand the processes of feed-forward and feedback learning (shown in figure 1.2) which are associated with this co-evolution, they point to important problems which are worthy of further study. It would be interesting, for example, to visualize how Cuervo-Cazurra's co-evolution would look on Siggelkow's performance landscape. Is co-evolution a dynamic process in the steady state or a transitional process to get to a steady state? How does co-evolution trade off internal for external fit? Why does it take a new management team to shake off a firm's inertia? What is the process of abandoning internal fit? How does a firm gather valid information on emerging new external fits? Can a firm not shape its business context to ensure the durability of its internal fit? How? By addressing the dynamics of strategy, the two papers take us beyond the common preoccupation of content researchers with static fits and cross-sectional studies. They generate a host of interesting research questions for the other streams which are described in this book.

Stream B: linking organizational context to firm performance

In this stream we present two papers that typify research that seeks to identify the enduring contextual factors that influence superior performance (see figure 1.5). While it is easy to criticize this stream of research for ignoring all of the other intervening variables in figure 1.2, it seeks to identify the *necessary* contextual characteristics without which superior performance is less likely.

In chapter 4, Schnatterly and Maritan analyze the reasons for differences in the market to book value (M/B) of otherwise comparable firms. Using the resource-based view of the firm, they posit three kinds of *intangible assets* as sources of this value gap: resources and capabilities, operational governance mechanisms and high-level governance mechanisms. They hypothesize that the stronger each of these intangible assets, the higher the market-to-book value of a firm.

However, reputation is not an organizational context element; rather, it is a distinctive competence of the firm. But the two governance variables in their study refer to a firm's management systems. These include: composition of the firm's board of directors, the

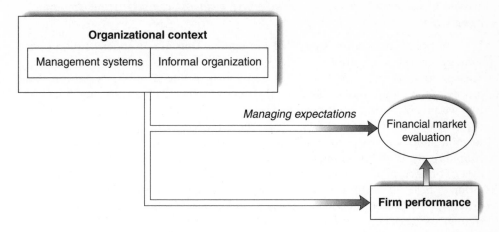

Figure 1.5   Stream B: organizational context and performance

structure of the compensation package for its CEO, accounting systems, policies, procedures, contingent pay for employees, and the use of teams or other liaison roles to facilitate communication. Using a content–context analysis methodology, the authors measured
each of their independent variables for 38 matched pairs of companies.

The study found that a firm's technical reputation was not a significant discriminator of market/book value (M/B). This is not surprising. Figure 1.2 would suggest
that competence influences performance, only in conjunction with a firm's competitive positioning. However, reputation did impact financial valuation in the study, as
figure 1.2 would have suggested. As for the organizational context variables, the results were mixed. The authors speculate why this was so in their chapter. While the
findings of the study may be disappointing, they at least point to the contingent nature
of the variables studied.

In chapter 5, Camillus reports on the distinguishing characteristics of the strategic
planning process in the "benchmark" companies that he studied. He suggests that all
planning systems can be examined under four phases: generation and prioritisation of
issues; generation of alternatives; evaluation of alternatives; and implementation and
communication. The study looks at 22 benchmark companies from Asia, Europe, and
North America that are known and accepted as "best-practice" companies in the field
of strategic planning. It contrasts their planning characteristics with that of 80 others.
Camillus found that the benchmark companies engaged in continuous improvement
of their planning processes, emphasized qualitative over financial analysis, integrated
strategic and business planning into a single cycle complementing these with an issue
management process, set stretch goals, developed detailed and specific action plans,
valued planning managers and emphasized good communication. Useful as this short
list is, Camillus does not offer a model of causation. Future studies can fill in the
missing links between organizational context and performance, as suggested by figure
1.2. By providing a shortlist of process characteristics to focus on, studies of this genre
help set the research agenda for the next stream.

Stream C: interaction between context, process elements, competitive position and competencies

Examining this interaction is essential for gaining a profound understanding of the strategy process (see figure 1.6). Three papers in the book fit this stream. In chapter 6, *Schwarz* looks at the impact of the shared beliefs in a team on its decision-making process. Using a grounded theory methodology, Schwarz chooses a single-field setting within a European multinational firm and carries out a two-year longitudinal in-depth field study. The triggering event for the study is the attempt of a service manager to communicate a new product idea to senior managers and to gain their support and commitment. In the beginning, each of them differed either in their valuation of the idea or on their perceptions of the service manager's ability to execute the idea. While group A believed both in the idea and in the manager, group B just liked the idea, group C only trusted the service manager, and group D was sceptical of both. Then, strategic debates between the "like-minded" took place. They exchanged their perceptions verbally and became aware of their similar attitude towards the new product idea and/or the service manager. By doing so, the previously invisible groups now became "visible." This in turn led to a meaningful debate on the idea and the likelihood of its realization, followed by the formation of a critical mass of supporters and the final decision to pursue the initiative. By elaborating how management teams go about making a strategic decision, Schwarz sheds light on how elements of a firm's organizational context shape decisions.

In the following chapter, Narayanan, Kemmerer, Douglas, and Guernsey, identify a six-stage process model for building "fast-cycle" capability in drug development and describe the triggers, challenges, drivers, transition mechanisms, key actors, micro-politics, and cognition required at each stage. The six stages they identify are: activation, articulation, mobilization, implementation, diffusion of routines, and retention of capability. The research design is based on a nested case study within one corporate setting, conducted over a three-year period and employing diachronic and synchronic analysis techniques. As the authors are interested in capturing the formation of a capability at the organizational level, they first observe six discrete drug development projects and then study their spillover effects at the organizational level. This innovative approach avoids the usual trap of inductively leaping from a single project on to the organizational level. The authors employ a social constructivist perspective for their study, showing how in the development of the desired capability, several compromises and adaptations had to be made by the actors involved. Building a new capability required the gradual transformation of the prevailing belief system. Together with the Schwarz study, this research points to the important interaction between belief systems, competitive positioning, and capability building.

In chapter 8, Wielemaker, Elfring, Volberda, and Baden-Fuller argue that the success of *strategic initiatives* depends on how supportive or hostile the organizational *context* is to that initiative. They further show that the *approval* of an initiative can be better supported by appropriate conditions when these are adjusted to the phase in which it is. The *phases* are defined with reference to the search for knowledge and resources in the development of an initiative: linking, interpreting, and integrating. Organizational *conditions* are measured by control and support systems, organizational form, administrative and incentive systems, and managerial roles. The study is done

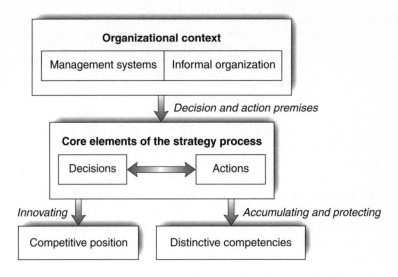

Figure 1.6   Stream C: context, process, and outcomes

using a multiple case study design. Twenty-five initiatives in three Dutch companies from different industries were analyzed in depth. This chapter provides an important complement to the studies on resource allocation by also focusing on how organizational context shapes the formation of an initiative and not just its approval.

Stream D: co-evolutionary interplay of context/process/outcomes over time

This is the most ambitious in scope of the three streams. We have included two chapters in this stream. In chapter 9, Lyles, Szabo, Kocsis, Barden, Dhanaraj, Steensma, and Tihanyi assess the relationship between the context, process, and survival of international joint ventures (IJVs) in Hungary. They further qualify survival as continuation as an IJV, absorption by the foreign parent, or by the Hungarian parent. The paper employs a mixed research strategy, following a quantitative analysis phase, with a qualitative phase. In phase one, 159 IJVs are analyzed. Using multinomial logit analysis, the authors examine the impact of learning, unlearning and innovation on the governance state of the IJV: bankruptcy, 100 percent foreign ownership, 100 percent Hungarian ownership or continuation as a joint venture. The authors report several important findings. Of interest here is their observation that when an IJV was learning well from the foreign parent and was also performing well, the Hungarian parent was more likely to stay engaged and seek the continuation of the IJV. This shows a symbiotic relationship between process, financial performance, and organizational context.

In phase two, the authors conducted in-depth interviews in four select Hungarian IJVs. They observe that only after a joint venture became familiar with the basic principles of operating in a market economy, knowledge transfer from the foreign parent could begin. The study points to the important role played by the informal organization in a firm in structuring its decision and action premises. Only after the IJV had absorbed the values and norms of a market economy, its decisions and actions could be modified based on the learning from its foreign parent. The study further goes on to suggest that transforming the IJV's management systems, including its organizational structure, core business systems, and managerial processes, may be a first step in changing its values and norms. Understanding the relationships between the formal and informal elements of a firm's organizational context is another important topic that needs further study.

Chapter 10 of the book, authored by Volberda and Baden-Fuller, addresses the broad question: How do large multi-unit firms renew? The authors take an evolutionary perspective on the development paths of a company and its business units. Based on the assumption that the survival of a company is best achieved when a firm is able to balance exploration and exploitation in its activities, they derive three generic ways to achieve the desired balance: (1) within each business unit; (2) through an appropriate portfolio of business units balanced at any point in time; and (3) through an appropriate portfolio of business units which may not be in balance at any given time, but is over a longer period. There are four different paths toward this balance: naive selection, managed selection, hierarchical renewal, and holistic renewal. Each is defined by the active or passive roles played by frontline managers and top management in the renewal journey. The authors do not tie their four renewal paths to the three generic ways of balancing exploration and exploitation that they posit. But there is a likely relationship.

The notion of strategy dynamics discussed earlier (See figure 1.3) maps well onto the concepts of exploration and exploitation. Volberda and Baden-Fuller correctly point out that the latter two have to be in balance. In fact there may be at least three different ways to achieve this balance, each appropriate to a different business context. Thus given the business context that a firm operates in, there are certain strategy dynamics that are vital for its renewal. Once these are determined, through the process of setting a firm's purpose, figure 1.2 would suggest that the firm's organizational context and process elements must be aligned to this purpose if sustained superior performance is to be expected. Both papers in stream D, that by Lyles et al. and Volberda and Baden-Fuller, suggest that this alignment has to co-evolve. Strategy process research has done well to move away from cross-sectional to longitudinal studies. Its next challenge is to move away from simple causal models to more complex co-evolutionary models that link purpose, context, process, and outcomes.

Summary

The nine chapters (chapters 2 to 10) are summarized in table 1.2. We see a broad spectrum of research topics and methodologies. This gives us a glimpse of how rich this field is, as well as its white spaces. Most of these papers used a qualitative research *methodology* due to the early stage of theory building in the field. Where a multiple or comparative case study approach was used, we find different sampling logics (matched pair design, industry quartets, etc.). The number of cases used in each study range from 1 to 38. Two papers combine comparative case studies with quantitative analysis.

Studies under streams A, B and D use firm performance as an outcome, but these

Table 1.2 Overview of the chapters

	2 Cuervo-Cazurra	3 Siggelkow	4 Schnatterly/ Maritan	5 Camillus	6 Schwarz	7 Narayanan et al.	8 Wielemaker et al.	9 Lyles et al.	10 Volberda/ Baden-Fuller
Research stream	A Longitudinal content research		B Linking organizational context to firm performance		C Interaction between organizational context and process elements			D Interplay of Context/ Process/Outcomes	
Research question	How do a firm's resources and activities (competitive position) co-evolve?	How is a firm's internal fit adapted to changes in its external environment?	How do features of a firm's organizational context and its resources impact its financial market valuation?	What are the few necessary features that all superior planning systems must have?	What is the impact of shared beliefs on strategic decision making?	What is the impact of managerial processes on capability formation?	How does the organizational context for an initiative vary with its development phase?	What is the relationship between learning/ unlearning and the four survival tax-onomies for an IJV?	How do large multiunit firms renew?
Methodology	Four cases, each in three different industries: paper, petroleum, and construction in Argentina and Spain. Language process method	A longitudinal case study of Liz Claiborne using archival data and field interviews	Thirty-eight matched pairs of companies with average and high M/B ratios. Qualitative data collection (SEC); discriminant analysis	Questionnaire and interviews in 22 high and 80 average performing companies	Longitudinal study of belief systems and decision-making in a European multinational firm	Longitudinal study of six projects in Marion Merrell Dow (MMD) on how fast-cycle capability was built in that firm	A field study on the conditioning and creation of 25 initiatives across three large Dutch companies with differing organizational contexts	A survey of 335 IJVs in Hungary, followed by multinomial logit analysis. Follow-up case studies on four IJVs in Hungary	Conceptual study
Study layout	Describes how resources (along 8 dimensions) and activities (along 3 dimensions) co-evolve	Addresses how a tight fit among a firm's activities affects its ability to react to external changes	Proposes three types of intangible assets: resources, management systems, and governance mechanisms	Suggests a four-phase process to study all planning systems	Examines the reciprocal relationship between shared beliefs and strategic decision process	Develops a six-stage model of capability formation	Proposes a three-phase development process and 4 context categories	Classifies four survival categories and measures their learning/ unlearning characteristics	Describes three generic renewal journeys and four co-evolutionary paths
Link to firm performance	Adaptation	Market valuation	Market/book ratio	"Best practice" in the eyes of experts	—	—	—	Firm survival	Firm survival
Theoretical perspective	Resource- and activity-based	Activity-based view	Resource-based view	Normative theory	Social constructivist	Social constructivist	Contingency theory	Knowledge management	Evolutionary theory

are variously measured as successful adaptation, survival, best practice or financial market valuation. Practitioners would prefer greater use of financial market measures in strategy process research. Only two studies oblige. The three studies under stream C did not use firm performance as an outcome variable and rightly so. The field needs to develop strong theories on how intermediate outcomes such as competitive position and distinctive competencies are developed, and on how the premises that drive actions and decisions are set. It was refreshing to see these authors avoid the mindless rush to throw in a firm performance measure that would have been inappropriate given the focus of their studies.

While we have tried to provide a road map of what is to come, we hope the reader will enjoy reading the nine excellent studies that follow in their entirety, and appreciate the creative ways in which these authors have approached difficult problems. After you finish reviewing these papers we will be back again in chapter 11 to offer some closing comments.

References

Andrews, K. 1971: *The concept of corporate strategy*, Homewood, IL.: Dow Jones-Irwin.

Bower, J. L. 1970: *Managing the resource allocation process*. Boston, MA: Harvard Business School Press.

Burgelman, R. A. 1983: A process model of corporate venturing in the diversified major firm. *Administrative Science Quarterly*, 28: 223–4.

Burgelman, R. A. 1996: A process model of strategic business exit: Implications for an evolutionary perspective on strategy. *Strategic Management Journal*, 17, 193–214.

Chakravarthy, B. and Doz, Y. 1992: Strategy process research: focusing on corporate self-renewal, *Strategic Management Journal*, 13, 5–14

Chakravarthy, B. and White, R. 2001: Strategy process: forming, implementing and changing strategies. In A. Pettigrew, H. Thomas, and R. Whittington (eds), *Handbook of strategy and management*. London: Sage, 182–205.

Chakravarthy, B. S., McEvily, S., Doz, Y., and Rao, D. 2002: Knowledge management and competitive advantage. In M. Easterby-Smith, and M. Lyles (eds), *Handbook of organizational learning and knowledge*. London: Blackwell Publishers, forthcoming.

Chandler, A. 1962: *Strategy and structure*. Cambridge, MA: MIT Press.

Garvin, D. A. 1998: The processes of organization and management. *Sloan Management Review*, 39 (4), 33–50.

Hammer, M. and Champy, J. 1993: *Reengineering the corporation*. New York: Harper Business.

Hart, S. 1992: An integrative framework for strategy-making processes. *Academy of Management Review*, 17, 327–52.

Huff, A. S. and Reger, K. R. 1987: A review of strategic process research. *Journal of Management*, 13, 211–36.

Inkpen, A. and Choudhury, N. (1995): The seeking of strategy where it is not: towards a theory of strategy absence. *Strategic Management Journal* 16, 313–23.

Kirsch, W. 1997: *Wegweiser zur Konstruktion einer evolutionären Theorie der strategischen Führung*. München: Kirsch Verlag.

Lechner, C. and Mueller-Stewens, G. 2000: Strategy process research: what do we know, what should we know? In S. B. Dahiya (ed.), *The current state of business disciplines*, Rohtak: Spellbound, 1,863–93.

Mintzberg, H. 1987: The strategy concept I: five P's for strategy. *California Management Review*, 30, 11-24.

Mintzberg, H. 1994: *The rise and fall of strategic planning.* Hertfordshire: Prentice-Hall.

Mintzberg, H. and Waters, J. A. 1985: Of strategies, deliberate and emergent. *Strategic Management Journal*, 6, 257–72.

Pettigrew, A. 1992: The character and significance of strategy process research. *Strategic Management Journal*, 13, 5–16.

Porter, M. E. 1991: Towards a dynamic theory of strategy. *Strategic Management Journal*, special issue, 12, 95–117.

Prahalad, C. K. 1975: The strategic process in a multinational corporation. Unpublished doctoral dissertation, Boston, MA: Harvard Business School.

Weick, K. E. 1995: *Sensemaking in organizations.* Thousand Oaks: Sage Publications.

Willke, H. 1993: Systemtheorie I: Eine Einführung in die Grundprobleme der Theorie sozialer Systeme, Stuttgart: UTB.

CHAPTER TWO

Transforming the Firm through the Co-evolution of Resources and Scope

Alvaro Cuervo-Cazurra

The analysis of the competitive advantage of the firm is at the core of strategic management. There is a large body of literature that analyzes the relationship between a firm's characteristics and its advantage over other companies, trying to identify the firm factors that are most likely to be associated with superior performance as the embodiment of its competitive advantage. This type of analysis has led to the division of the field into two camps: the resource-based view of strategy, which views resources and their underlying imperfections in input markets as the most important factors (Penrose, 1959; Wernerfelt, 1984), and the positioning school or activity-based view of strategy, which views activities and their associated imperfections in product markets as the most important factors (Ansoff, 1965; Porter 1980, 1985). This divide among researchers is not likely to be solved unless we understand the processes that link resources and activities by which companies arrive at their competitive advantage.

In this chapter the processes that firms followed in their effort to develop competitive advantage are analyzed. Companies facing radical changes in their institutional environment were studied; these companies confronted the challenges of regaining their competitiveness and developing a competitive advantage after environmental changes rendered previous strategies obsolete and altered the value of resources and activities. The analysis of this experimental setting serves to reveal teleological processes (Van de Ven, 1992) of company transformation as firms actively try to develop an advantage in the face of new competitive rules and rivals.

Since there is no clear theoretical lead to follow, an inductive study of comparative multiple-structured case studies was conducted in order to understand the processes and to establish causal relationships among variables (Yin, 1994), leading to the development of an empirically grounded theory (Eisenhardt, 1989). The transformations undertaken by three matched quartets of firms under conditions of discontinuous institutional environment change from three industries and two countries were studied. The comparison of companies in different industries and institutional settings facilitates the establishment of generalizable propositions (Chandler, 1990).

Based on the inductive analysis, it is argued that one way that companies regain their competitiveness is through the co-evolution of resources and scope, or the interactive evolution of resources and activities. Transformations in the resource set induce alterations in the activity set, which in turn lead to changes in the resource set, and so on, thus facilitating the development of a dynamic competitive advantage. This is a guided process that is only revealed through the analysis of longitudinal chains of events that link dimensions of resources – management, human resources, organization, finance, technology, production, supply, and marketing – to dimensions of scope such as vertical integration, diversification, and internationalization. This process integrates the dichotomy of strategy, based on either the resources of the firm or on its activities, into one dynamic perspective of strategy, where both resources and activities are the basis of the firm's behavior and, ultimately, of its competitive advantage.

The study contributes not only to theory but also to the development of management practice. Managers have to create and administer not only the resources and capabilities inside the company, but also the activities, markets, and geographies in which the firm competes, to achieve the competitive advantage that would assure the survival of the firm and lead to profitability. By viewing the development of resources and activities as part of a co-evolutionary process, they can gain a dynamic view of the interrelations among resources and activities as the sources of the transformation of the firm and its competitive advantage.

The rest of the chapter is organized as follows: the theoretical background and reasons for an inductive study are provided; the research design is presented; the results of the comparative case studies are discussed and the propositions that emerge from them are developed; finally, conclusions are provided.

Views of Strategy: Resources and Activities

There are currently two main views within strategic management on the source of the competitive advantage of the firm: the positioning school or activity-based view, which argues that the competitive advantage of the firm lies in its product-market positioning, and the resource-based view, which argues that the competitive advantage of the firm lies in its factor-market positioning.

Under the positioning school or activity-based view (Ansoff, 1965; Porter, 1980, 1985, 1991), the firm derives its competitive advantage from its position in the industry, sustained by barriers to entry (Bain, 1956) and barriers to mobility (Caves and Porter, 1977). The activities of the firm determine the position of the firm in the marketplace and ultimately its profitability; two generic strategies, differentiation or cost leadership, are used to achieve this. Following this approach, managers have to understand and select the industry that has the potential to provide monopoly rents, and choose either to be the leader in costs, or to differentiate the products of the firm. The source of superior profitability arises from imperfections in the product markets that enable the firm to obtain monopoly rents.

Under a resource-based approach (Penrose, 1959; Wernerfelt, 1984), the company is a bundle of resources. Among these resources, those that are rare, valuable, difficult to imitate, and difficult to substitute have the ability to sustain the competitive advantage of the firm (Barney, 1991) and the achievement of rents (Peteraf, 1993). Following this view, managers have to understand and select the resources that have the potential to provide rents to the firm and choose how to exploit those resources. The sources of abnormal returns emerge from imperfections in the factor markets that enable the firm to obtain Ricardian rents.

The two views suffer from problems that limit the constructive dialogue between them and the development of a dynamic theory of strategy. Within these two views, the achievement of competitive advantage tends to be discussed from a static viewpoint, since they are grounded in the economics literature, with its focus on equilibrium conditions and comparative statics. Hence, the dynamics are downplayed, which limits the interaction between the views. Thus a chicken-and-egg problem is created – which comes first, resources or activities, in determining the sources of the competitive advantage? On the one hand, resource-based view authors (such as Barney, 1986) argue that the activity-based view treats the firm as a black box and that the activities are based upon resources. Therefore, resources are the basis of competitive advantage. On the other hand, activity-based authors (for example, Porter, 1991) argue that the resource-based view neglects the environment of the firm and that only when the resources are applied to the activities is competitive advantage generated. Thus activities are the basis of the firm's competitive advantage.

Due to the division within existing theory and the lack of a dynamic view of the transformation processes that enable firms to develop a competitive advantage, an inductive study was undertaken to determine the relationship between resources and activities as part of the contextual transformation process of the firm. The use of an inductive study serves to develop a theory that explains the transformations and interactions between resources and activities, facilitates the identification of the process of transformation, and solves the chicken-and-egg problem of the sources of competitive advantage. In particular, the transformation of firms under conditions of radical changes in the institutional environment that induce the search for regaining their competitive advantage is analyzed. Hence, a teleological approach to the analysis of process (Van de Ven, 1992) is followed, where an analysis is undertaken of the transformation processes followed by firms facing the necessity of regaining their competitive advantage after radical changes in the competitive environment render previous strategies obsolete and force their transformation. This line of research falls under the broader field of research of strategy process, or the analysis of how effective strategies are shaped within the firm and then validated and implemented efficiently (Chakravarthy and Doz, 1992, p. 5); it focuses on the latter part of the realm of the firm, the efficient implementation of strategies. Moreover, it follows, to the extent possible, the five consistent guiding assumptions of strategy research processes (Pettigrew, 1992: 9): embeddedness, temporal interconnectedness, explanation of context and action, holistic explanations, and link to the location and explanation of outcomes.

Research Design

The experimental setting of firms facing radical changes in the institutional environment

The analysis of firms facing radical changes in the institutional environment serves as a natural experiment of the transformation of firms attempting to regain competitiveness. This analysis helps to reveal the processes by which companies develop their competitive advantage. The current chapter is not an analysis of firms under conditions of discontinuous institutional changes, but rather an analysis of the process of development of competitive advantage. Radical changes in the institutional environment, such as processes of economic liberalization, create the need for domestic firms to regain their competitive advantage. In general, companies protected from international competition by barriers to trade or governmental regulation become accustomed to lower levels of competitive pressure and have fewer incentives to become competitive at international levels. The discontinuous institutional environment changes created by governments as they open and integrate their economies into free-trade areas and liberalize and deregulate industries alter the basis and rules of competition and the type and number of competitors. The alteration of the competitive environment, in turn, renders previous strategies obsolete and alters the strategic value of resources and activities upon which the strategies were built. Thus, the radical changes in the institutional environment force firms to alter their strategy (Baden-Fuller and Stopford, 1991) and develop their resources (Geroski and Vlassopoulos, 1991; Helfat, 1997; Sharma and Vredenburg, 1998) in order to survive the transformations and regain their competitiveness in the face of new competitive conditions and incoming competitors.

The environment of the firm influences both the level of development of resources and the firm's set of activities. In a closed and regulated environment, firms are subject to constraints in the form of limitations on the resources controlled or the activities undertaken. These can include governmental regulation limiting the resources that firms can own or the use of resources in activities, government ownership of resources limiting the availability of resources to firms, or the government being the main client, which influences the development of activities to governmental specifications. There also exist limitations in the number or type of competitors, such as government regulation constraining the number of firms and/or number of competitors, or governmental protection shielding domestic firms from international competition. These constraints reduce the level of competitiveness of the firm in two ways. First, resources and activities are below optimal, since firms do not have the freedom to control resources or undertake activities as desired, and, second, firms lack any incentive to achieve higher levels of competitiveness, since companies are protected from competitive pressures.

Radical changes in the institutional environment such as deregulation, liberalization, or economic opening and integration, remove the constraints on the control and use of resources, activities undertaken, and the number and type of competitors, forcing the transformation of firms. The rapid changes in the basis of competition force firms to attempt to regain their competitiveness in the face of incoming international competitors with higher levels of competitiveness, and to alter the set of activities they undertake to adapt to and benefit from the changing environmental conditions. The removal of environmental constraints on the control and use of resources makes possible an upgrade in resources, as firms enjoy higher degrees of freedom with regard to how they can operate. It also makes possible an alteration in the activity set of the firm, in order to best make use of the resources the firm has and take advantage of the opportunities that open up in the environment. Moreover, incumbents face not only the possibility but also the incentive to alter their resources and activities to meet the new environmental demands that result from the transformation of the competitive conditions. Thus, the study of firms subject to radical changes in the institutional environment serves as a natural experiment to analyze the processes of development of the competitive advantage.

Case selection

The companies studied are three matched quartets of firms in the petroleum, paper, and construction industries in Argentina and Spain that operated under conditions of radical changes in the institutional environment. I chose to analyze firms from different industries and countries in order to achieve a degree of generalization (Chandler, 1990).

Argentina and Spain, the countries selected, are two late-industrializing countries that followed similar macroeconomic transformations, evolving from a closed, regulated economy with high state intervention in the 1950s to 1970s, towards an open and integrated economy in the 1990s, with a transition period in the 1980s.

The firms were chosen from three industries subject to different competitive pressures (Prahalad and Doz, 1987) to facilitate the generalization of results across industries: petroleum firms are subject to pressures for global integration, construction firms are subject to pressures for local responsiveness, and paper firms are subject to both.

The firms were chosen from the largest domestic firms in terms of sales in the 1980s, using the rankings of two long-established business magazines, *Mercado* in Argentina and *Fomento de la Producción* in Spain. Only domestic companies were chosen since subsidiaries of multinational enterprises are subject to different processes of resource development, as they can draw resources from the resource set of the parent firm (Bartlett and Ghoshal, 1989). The companies selected were matched by similarity in initial conditions before discontinuous institutional environment changes, rather than by their success at the end of the period or behavior in dimensions of resources or activities. This was done to increase external validity (Leonard-Barton, 1990) through the use of different data-points (McPhee, 1990), reduce selection biases, and study both high and low performers, thus facilitating the understanding of strategic success (Barnett and Burgelman, 1996). The petroleum companies selected were the leading state-owned and private firm in each country; the paper companies selected were similar large family-owned firms; and the construction companies selected were part of similar leading family-owned business groups. Despite the care taken in the selection procedure, the companies chosen are still subject to the selection bias of having survived discontinuous institutional environment changes.

The companies selected are the following: in the petroleum industry, the Argentinean YPF and Perez Companc and the Spanish Repsol and Cepsa; in the paper industry, the Argentinian Papel Argentina and Zucamor and the Spanish Unipapel and Papel España; and in the construction industry, the Argentinean Sideco Americana and BRH, and the Spanish FCC and ACS. Some of the names were disguised at the request of the managers.

Data sources

The sources of data are both documents and interviews. Annual reports, industry analyzes, periodicals, and public and company archival data formed the basis for the construction of the case studies of the contextual evolution of firms since their creation until the beginning of 1998. The analysis of written materials from the period enables the identification of the actions taken by the firm and the reasons and expectations at that point in time. After this, semi-structured interviews with managers at the executive and intermediate levels, with former managers, with directors, and with industry experts served to complete the case studies and obtain additional information. The interviews were undertaken during two three-month stays in Argentina and Spain in 1998. The number of people interviewed per company varied from four to twelve, with the following areas represented: (1) strategic management–general management, (2) production–operations–technology, (3) finance, (4) organization–human resources, and (5) marketing-sales. Interviews lasted between thirty minutes and four hours, and, in many cases, several interviews were conducted with key informants.

The ex post rationalization of the process that inductive studies face was addressed in two ways: empirically and theoretically. First, to avoid the ex post rationalization of the process by the sources of data, that is, managers, the annual events used by firms in their transformation were analyzed from written sources, identifying what the firm expected to obtain at that point in time; the chain of events in the transformation of the activity was then followed to reveal the interactions among resources and scope. Once the contextual transformation of the firm was understood, the interviews were used to collect additional information and clarify obscure areas. Second, to avoid the ex post rationalization of the process from a theoretical point of view, a full analysis of the motives and processes of transformation of activities is provided, first as single events and then as chains of events.

Case analysis

For the analysis of the processes of transformation of firms, events in eight dimensions of resources and three dimensions of scope were recorded in chronological order from the date when the company faced the radical changes in the institutional environment at the industry level until the end of 1997, and their interactions studied. The analysis of events facilitates the understanding of processes (Van de Ven and Poole, 1990), in particular which resources are developed and how. Events are separated into causes and consequences (Van de Ven and Poole, 1990) in order to establish the causality process, and into design and non-design (Glick et al., 1990) in order to establish purpose.

Events in resources are defined as discrete actions on a dimension of the resource set. I classify resources into eight dimensions to analyze their transformation, which are based on previous classifications (Collis and Montgomery, 1997; Grant, 1995; Itami, 1987; Porter, 1980) and selected because they are commonly considered to form the basis for firms' strategy. The dimensions studied are: (1) the management team or the executives that run the firm, where their educational and professional backgrounds, language capabilities, and international experience are examined; (2) human resources, focusing on education, training, and reward systems; (3) organiza-

Table 2.1 Standard for the evaluation of the accumulation of resources towards international best practices

	1	2	3	4	5
Management	Local managers Local language Local degrees No international experience	Local managers Local language Local degrees Some international experience	Local managers Some foreign languages Some foreign degrees Some international experience	Local and some international managers Foreign languages Some foreign degrees International experience	Local and international managers Foreign languages Foreign degrees International experience
Human	Local personnel Local training Local language Seniority based	Local personnel Local training Some foreign languages Some incentives	Local personnel Some international training Some foreign languages Some incentive payments	Local personnel and some foreigners Some international training Some foreign languages Incentive payments	Local and foreign personnel International training Foreign languages Incentive payments Performance focus
Organization	Centralized information Single decision-maker Unitarian	Centralized information Few decision-makers Functional	Information systems Multiple decision-making Functional with departments (mixed)	Decentralized information Decentralized decision-making Multidivisional	Decentralized information Decentralized decision-making Matrix
Finance	Internally generated Bank loans Family ownership and control of board	Loans in local capital markets Bank loans Family control	Equity in local capital markets Loans in international markets Family and some market control	International capital markets No investment rating of debt Small family influence	International capital markets Investment rating of debt Market control Independent board
Technology	Local technology Local machinery	Buy international technology Some local technology Local benchmarking	Adapt international technology to local conditions Regional benchmarking	Adapt international technology to local conditions Some technology development International benchmarking	International technology Develop technology and obtain royalties International benchmarking

Production	Inefficient Low quality	Efficient Quality	Efficient Local quality standards	Efficient ISO9000	Efficient ISO9000 ISO14000
Supply	Full integration In-house services and support functions	Full integration External support functions	Some subcontracting of activities	Large subcontracting	Large subcontracting Strategic management of supply chain
Marketing	Market relationships Price competition Traders	Market relationships Price competition Some services Distributors	Additional services Some loyal clients Distributors	Additional services Loyal clientele Reputation Management of distribution	Integration with clients Reputation Service competition Strategic managment of distribution chain

tion, specifically information systems, decision-making processes, and organizational structure; (4) finance; that is, the access to external sources of capital, both local and international, the rating of debt, and the ownership structure; (5) the origin, development, and benchmarking of technology; (6) production processes, where efficiency in manufacturing and the achievement of quality and environmental standards are examined; (7) the supply network, where the degree of subcontracting and relationships with suppliers is examined; and (8) marketing, specifically the relationships with clients and distributors.

A set of standards is developed for evaluating the accumulation of resources over time (table 2.1). The standards reflect requirements for operating in increasingly competitive environments, which increasingly incorporate a degree of international competition, rather than reflecting the internationalization of dimensions of resources, as discussed in other studies (Toulan, 1997). The standards are developed based on interviews with managers and industry specialists using the Delphi method, establishing different levels of requirements for operating in an increasingly demanding marketplace. The standards used represent the commonalities across industries and are independent of the industries and countries in which firms compete. These standards were chosen in order to allow comparison and generalization. This procedure results in a coarse grading of competitiveness, which in other studies can be more finely graded and adjusted to the conditions of specific industries. External indicators are used instead of the assessment of the competitiveness of the firm's resources by either researchers or managers in order to reduce biases in the evaluation of resources.

Events in scope are defined as discrete actions on a dimension of the activity set. The scope of the firm is studied in three dimensions that are commonly discussed in the literature, but that have previously been analyzed separately: 1) vertical integration, focusing on the integration of activities that are part of the value chain and that could be performed by independent firms; 2) horizontal diversification, that is, the expansion into related or unrelated activities outside the value chain; and 3) internationalization, the firm's expansion into other countries. Table 2.2 presents the standards used for evaluating the accumulation of activities in the firm. The standards were developed following the same procedure used for evaluating resources.

The transformation of each firm was analyzed in three phases in order to facilitate the analysis of processes. First, a case study on the contextual transformation of the firm since its inception until 1998 was constructed, allowing an understanding of historical background, transformation, and environmental influences.

Second, events were charted in the eight dimensions of resources and the three dimensions of scope, from the date when the company faced radical changes in the institutional environmental at the industry level, changes that were induced by the transformations at the country level, until 1997. This was done to allow an understanding of the transformation of the firm in detail; the stated reasons for the event, the action, and the expected implications were recorded. The starting dates for the analysis of petroleum firms are 1989 for Argentinian companies and 1984 for Spanish companies, since this is when the petroleum industry was deregulated, and restrictions on the ownership of productive assets, prices, and entry of new and foreign competitors were lifted. For paper firms, the starting dates for comparison are 1989 for Argentinian firms and 1986 for Spanish firms, since this is when the paper industry began to

Table 2.2 Standard for the evaluation of the accumulation of activities

	1	2	3	4	5
Integration	Single segment in value chain	25 percent connected segments	50 percent the value chain	75 percent of chain	Full value chain
Diversification	No diversification Single activity	Some small related activities, less than 10 percent revenue Main activity	Important diversification, more than 10 percent revenue Defining activity and complementary ones	Related and unrelated diversification, more than 30 percent revenue Group of related activities and unrelated ones	Large diversification, more than 50 percent revenue Unrelated diversification No defining activity
International- ization	Local market No foreign revenues Single country	Exports Less than 10 percent foreign revenues 1–2 countries FDI	Sales offices More than 10 percent revenues 1 region FDI	Production centres More than 30 percent foreign revenues 2 regions FDI	Production centres More than 50 percent foreign revenues More than 2 regions FDI

open to international competition, which included the liberalization of acquisition of firms and of imports, as well as the lifting of restrictions on the operation of companies. Finally, for construction firms, the starting dates for comparison are 1987 for Argentinian firms and 1989 for Spanish firms. This is the point at which demand conditions were altered, as the main client of construction firms, the state, altered the basis of contractual relationships from construct–transfer to construct–operate–transfer.

Third, the actions of transformation of the firm were mapped, noting the relationships among dimensions of resources and dimensions of scope, and grouping them by their common images using the KJ or language process method. This method was developed in the field of ethnology for analyzing qualitative field data (Kawakita, 1991) and later applied in the field of quality management (Center for Quality of Management, 1995; Detert, Schroeder, and Mauriel, 2000; Shiba, Graham, and Walden, 1993). The KJ or language process method is a tool for organizing qualitative data by abstracting and grouping statements based on their common images.

The KJ method was applied to the analysis of the field data on firm transformation as follows. First, the individual actions in resources and scope recorded in the second phase of the data analysis were transferred onto sticky notes. Second, actions were grouped by their common image by abstracting from the stated action. Third, the common elements of the grouped actions were recorded; this served as the basis for the analysis of the motives for transformation of individual activities. Fourth, the sequence of events in each of the actions was collected. Fifth, as with the individual actions, these sequences of actions were grouped by their common image by abstraction. Finally, the common elements among sequences of actions were recorded; this allowed an analysis of the processes of transformation of resources and scope.

This procedure reveals the reasons and transformation processes of activities and their relationships with the resources of the firm. The analysis of the actions taken by firms in their transformation is presented by, firstly, providing the "why" of the events and chains of events that enabled the transformation of the companies. The processes used in the transformation of the events and chains of events, and their connections to the development of a competitive advantage, are then identified. Once the actions, reasons, processes, and impact on competitive advantage have been identified, their implications for the development of a dynamic theory of strategy are discussed. This process enables the development of testable propositions.

Transformation Processes of Resources and Activities

The transformation processes that enabled firms to develop their competitive advantage can be analyzed by studying the changes of dimensions of resources, the alteration of dimensions of activities, and the interactive transformation of both resources and activities. Table 2.3 presents a summary of the firms' transformation over the period of analysis, based on the standards of accumulation of resources and activities presented in Tables 2.1 and 2.2. The analysis of the changes of dimensions of resources independently of activities is discussed in another study (Cuervo-Cazurra, 1999), where it is argued that transformation of the dimensions of resources is done through the use of alternative methods of resource development – purchase of resources, link to a firm to obtain resources, or internal development of resources – based on their capacity to provide a rapid upgrading of resources, with purchase facilitating a rapid and large upgrade, link permitting rapid and medium upgrades, and internal development facilitating rapid and small upgrades. Moreover, the use of these methods evolves over time; purchase and link are used more intensively at the beginning of the discontinuous institutional environment changes when companies have to catch up, and internal development is used more intensively later on when firms have already caught up and now have to develop a competitive advantage. Regarding the transformation of the dimensions of activities, after the discontinuous institutional environment changes, firms slightly increase and then reduce their vertical integration, augment their related diversification, increase and then decrease their unrelated diversification, and expand their internationalization (Cuervo-Cazurra, 2001). The transformation of the scope is subject to limitations in the management of a complex set of diverse activities, with dimensions of scope evolving through paths that reflect this limitation (Cuervo-Cazurra, 2001). Finally, the transformation and interactions among dimensions of resources and activities leads to the co-evolution of resources and scope (see table 2.3); this is discussed more extensively in this chapter.

The analysis of the relationships between resources and activities is presented as abstractions from the actual events in the form of stylized descriptions rather than the particular actions taken by the firms. This abstraction process enables the development of an empirically grounded theory and propositions. To do this, the transformation processes of resources and activities are examined in two parts. In the first part, individual events are studied, and their motives and processes are analyzed. These transformation events are grouped into three clusters representing different transformation actions: the event may be associated with the entry in a new activity, with the exit from an activity, or with the development of an ongoing activity. In the second part the full chain of events comprising the action is studied. This longitudinal approach serves to analyze processes of interactions among resources and activities that are missed in the simple causal links of the single event transformations.

Individual transformation events: motives, processes, and competitive advantage

Motives for entry in a new activity

The analysis of the motives for the entry into new activities revealed by the events can be grouped into two classes: either the desire to take advantage of opportunities and make money in the new activity, or the need to protect current activities that are rent generators. On one hand, the firm enters a new activity to take advantage of an apparent opportunity that appears before it in the form of: (1) investing in a project that will lead to a quick profit, (2) using resources that are already developed in the firm and that could be transferred and used profitably in the new activity, but that cannot be separated from the firm, either because it is not physically possible or because the firm would lose value if they were separated, or (3) finding an alternative source of growth, if its current activities have limited capacities for expansion because of its dominant control of the activity. On the other hand, the firm can enter a new activity to protect

Table 2.3 Evaluation of the transformation of dimensions of resources and scope at the beginning and end of the period under study

Firm	Year	Resource							Scope			
		Management	Human resources	Organization	Finance	Technology	Production	Supply	Marketing	Integration	Diversification	Internationalization
YPF	1989	1	1	2	1	1	1	1	1	4	2	2
	1997	4	4	4	5	4	5	4	4	5	3	4
PC	1989	2	2	2	3	3	2	1	2	2	5	1
	1997	3	3	4	3	3	5	2	4	5	4	3
Repsol	1984	1	1	2	1	3	2	1	1	4	2	2
	1997	4	3	4	5	4	4	2	4	5	3	4
Cepsa	1984	2	2	2	3	3	2	1	2	4	3	3
	1997	4	3	4	3	4	5	2	4	5	3	4
Papel Argentina	1989	1	1	2	3	2	1	2	2	2	3	2
	1997	1	2	2	3	2	2	2	3	5	2	2
Zucamor	1989	1	1	2	1	2	2	1	2	5	2	1
	1997	4	4	3	3	3	4	5	5	3	2	2
Unipapel	1986	1	1	2	1	2	2	1	2	3	2	1
	1997	3	3	3	3	4	4	3	5	3	4	2
Papel España	1986	2	1	2	1	2	2	1	1	4	3	3
	1997	4	2	2	3	3	4	3	3	4	1	3
BRH	1987	1	1	2	1	2	2	1	1	5	2	2
	1997	3	3	3	3	3	4	3	2	4	5	3
Sideco	1987	1	1	2	1	2	2	1	1	5	1	1
	1997	4	4	3	3	3	4	5	4	1	5	3
ACS	1989	2	2	3	1	3	2	3	2	5	2	1
	1997	3	3	4	3	4	4	3	3	5	4	3
FCC	1989	1	1	2	1	2	2	2	2	5	3	1
	1997	3	3	4	3	4	4	3	3	5	4	3

Numbers refer to the standards presented in tables 2.1 and 2.2.

current activities. In this case, the firm is either aiming to reduce the impact of the cycles in revenues by conducting a new activity not subject to the same variance in earnings, or attempting to support current activities and internalize necessary operations, such as supply or marketing, because there are no firms which can provide the company with the products and services necessary for its operations, or because environmental changes create uncertainty that induces the control of necessary inputs.

Process of entry in a new activity
The processes of entry into the new activity vary depending on the objective the firm is pursuing and the conditions it faces. Expansion to take advantage of an opportunity to make money is done as an investment with a partner that provides the resources necessary to operate the new activity, where the company acts as a financial investor. Entry into an activity to use existing excess resources or to achieve growth is done by evaluating the need for complementary resources in the new activity. This leads, in many cases, to the use of existing resources, primarily management, technology, and finance, while acquiring complementary resources that are needed to operate in the activity, primarily production but also marketing, by buying a company, or sharing the activity with another firm, especially when it lacks technology. In some cases the firm decides to operate alone, especially when it has the necessary knowledge and distribution, meaning that only production need be added. In this case, the entry in the new area is initially done on a small scale. As the operation grows and appears successful, the scale is expanded through acquisition. The process of entry into an activity to protect current operations, in the case of the reduction of cycle impacts, is done through the acquisition of a share in another company whose earnings are less subject to the cyclical variations of the current operation. In the case where current operations are supported by the internalization of other activities, entry depends upon physical collocation of the activities. On the one hand, activities that do not need the collocation can be obtained through the acquisition of a share in another company that will support current activities. On the other hand, activities that need the collocation are done through the internal investments, which, additionally, facilitate the interactions among activities.

Developing competitive advantage through entry into the new activity
Although theoretically one would expect that the different motives for entry into the activity would have the ultimate objective of increasing competitive advantage, not all of them are directly linked to competitive advantage. Some of them are only related indirectly while others are not related to competitive advantage at all, but only to firm profitability. Below, the way in which different motives are associated with different methods of developing competitive advantage is explored in more detail.

First, in the case where the entry is undertaken to benefit from an opportunity to make money, the firm is not attempting to achieve a competitive advantage and associated rents, but rather to improve the profitability of the operations, which can support the development of other areas where the competitive advantage is achieved. Second, in the case where the entry is undertaken in order to capitalize upon an opportunity to use existing excess transferable resources, the profits come from the use of resources already developed in alternative settings, thus increasing the return on the initial investment. The rents accrue to the company if the resources are unique to the firm, thus leading to a potentially profitable extension of activities, and if the firm manages the new activity profitably, which might be challenging if it needs complementary resources to succeed in the new activity. Third, when the firm enters an activity in search of an avenue of growth because of dominance in its original activity, it is enjoying a competitive advantage and rents from the dominance of the activity, and the new activity undertaken might not lead to rents unless the firm has resources that can be transferred to the new activity or the company can achieve a dominant position similar to the one it is enjoying already. Fourth, the entry into a new activity to protect current activities from the influences of cycles is not done directly in search of a competitive advantage, but rather to stabilize the profitability of the firm over time. Finally, entry into a new activity to protect current activities by supporting them through the internalization of the activity is not conducive to competitive advantage, but to the protection of the competitive advantage and the associated rents from being either shared with other firms on which the company depends or from being dissipated by interruptions in the relationship on which the company depends.

In summary, not all the reasons for entering into a new activity are related to the achievement of a competitive advantage in a direct manner, as is usually assumed in the literature. Moreover, the different motives for entry can be ranked by the competitive advantage the firm was attempting to achieve, a ranking that is absent in other studies that analyze the motives separately. The entry undertaken to make use of resources in a new activity, which is traditionally discussed in the literature (Chatterjee and Wernerfelt, 1991; Penrose, 1959), is likely to lead to the development of competitive advantage. The search for growth and avoidance of cycles might lead to the development of a competitive advantage if the firm enters a growing or counter-cyclical activity where it can transfer existing resources, and manage the activity successfully. These two reasons are likely to be related to the development of short-term profitability, depending on the success of the operation, but not to a competitive advantage and the associated sustained long-term profitability. Finally, the entry into a new activity to support current activities is not likely to lead to any inherent increase in profitability or competitive advantage in itself, but it will prevent the disappearance of existing competitive advantage from existing activities. Therefore, the following relationship between actions and competitive advantage is proposed:

- *Proposition 1*: Actions of entry into new activities are related differentially to the development of a competitive advantage and associated rents.
- *Hypothesis 1a*: Entry into a new activity to use existing resources is more likely to be associated with the development of a competitive advantage than entry in search of growth or the reduction in the impact of cycles.
- *Hypothesis 1b*: Entry into a new activity to use existing resources, entry in search of growth, and entry to reduce the impact of cycles are more likely to be associated with the development of a competitive advantage than entry to support current activities.
- *Hypothesis 1c*: Entry to take advantage of an investment opportunity is more likely to be associated with (short-term) profitability than with competitive advantage.

Motives for exit from an activity

The analysis of the events reveals several motives that explain the exit from an activity. First, the firm seeks to exit an activity after it has redefined its strategy and activity set in the face of new environmental conditions, thus exiting activities in which it does not need to be present, which are primarily changes in supply or complementary products. Second, the firm might be forced to exit activities for the following reasons: (1) because it is not competitive, for example because of inefficiencies in production in the face of a new competitor, and because it has limited finance to invest in the modernization of the operation; (2) because it lacks necessary complementary resources, such as distribution, to be competitive in the activity, and cannot solve these deficiencies in the face of existing competition; (3) because it faces serious financial problems, forcing it to exit some profitable activities and sell them as an instrument to reduce its leverage; or (4) because changes in the environment, either institutional or technological, lead to the disappearance of the market and the firm has no alternative area where it can use the resources. The third possible motive for a firm exiting a strategy is that some of the activities have a predetermined schedule, and once the objective is accomplished the firm exits. Finally, a company might exit an activity when a buyer appears and provides a valuable offer to the company that induces it to sell.

Process of exit from an activity

The process of exit varies depending on the motive for exiting, but a common process can be identified. Once the firm has decided to exit the activity, the next step is to attempt to make the exit profitable. In order for it to be profitable, the company has to be able to transfer the activity to a potential buyer, which requires the separation of the resources associated with the activity. These can include not only tangible resources such as production facilities, but also intangible resources such as brands and client lists. Once there is a clear legal separation of the activity from the firm, which in some cases requires the creation of a separate legal entity, the company must search for a buyer. If the activity cannot be transferred because the resources associated with it cannot be grouped as an independent entity, the firm separates those resources that can be sold independently (machinery, land) and sells them. In this case, it loses the value of the intangible resources associated with these tangible resources. The exit from the activity benefits the firm not only because it provides finance in exchange for the resources transferred, but also because it liberates for other uses those resources that are not transferred, such as management, human resources, or production capacity.

Whereas the separation and sale of resources might be straightforward in the case of redefinition of the strategy, it is only undertaken as a last resort in the case of a forced exit. In these cases, the company first tries to obtain resources and solve the problem by negotiating with other firms the access to needed resources, such as finance from banks or technology from a partner. The firm exits only if it cannot access external resources to complement the lack thereof in the company. In the case where a firm exits an activity with a predetermined objective, the activity is closed when this objective is achieved, as has already been programmed. Finally, the exit from an activity because of the acceptance of a purchase offer first requires the evaluation of the expected future of the activity, including additional developments and requirements from the company versus the actual payment it will receive. In the case where the firm sells, it might keep a small participation in order to benefit from the increase in future value, or maintain a contractual relationship in order to avoid losing investments in intangible assets or marketing outlets.

Developing a competitive advantage through exiting an activity

While exiting an activity has traditionally been associated with a failure, and thus its relationship with competitive advantage has not been analyzed, we can establish relationships between exit and competitive advantage, albeit indirect ones. On one hand, exiting an activity reduces limitations to existing competitive advantage provided by other activities and resources. On the other hand, exiting an activity liberates resources that can be used in other activities, thus promoting the development of competitive advantage in other areas. Besides these generic considerations, the different motives for exit may be related to competitive advantage on different levels. Exit due to the redefinition of strategy is more likely to be associated with competitive advantage, since the firm has broken away from the inertia of change and is willing to proactively achieve a competitive advantage. A forced exit might be an indication of deeper problems in the firm, and maybe of an overall lack of competitive advantage, especially when it has financial difficulties; however, this is not necessarily the case when a technological or institutional change altered the prospects for profitability. Exit due to an objective being accomplished and exit due to the acceptance of a purchase offer might not be considered failures, but rather an indication of successful operations and an underlying advantage for the firm. This leads to the following proposition:

- *Proposition 2*: Exit from activities is related differentially to the development of a competitive advantage and associated rents.
- *Hypothesis 2a*: Exit due to accomplishment of objectives or exit due to acceptance of purchase offer are more likely to be associated with the existence of competitive advantage in the firm than exit due to redefinition of strategy.
- *Hypothesis 2b*: Exit due to accomplishment of objectives, exit due to acceptance of purchase offer, or exit due to redefinition of strategy are more likely to be associated with the existence of competitive advantage in the firm than forced exit.

Motives for development of an ongoing activity

The transformation of the company is done not only through the entry into or exit from activities, but also through the development of ongoing activities. The inductive analysis revealed two main motivations for the transformation of the ongoing activities: (1) improvement in efficiency to face new competitive conditions and incoming competitors; and (2) control over certain activities in order to achieve nation-wide dominance, in order to face the entry of international firms.

Process of transformation of an ongoing activity

The processes to transform current activities in order to achieve efficiency are based on the use of cost reduction programs and investments in improvements. Alliances or contracts with other firms, primarily foreign, are used to obtain the production and organization technology necessary to reduce costs. The cost reduction programs are in many cases accompanied by restructuring of relationships among activities, separating some of them into independent firms that are later either spun off to increase the efficiency of the activity by introducing competition, or discarded as the firm redesigns its strategy. Efficiency is also achieved by increasing the scale of the operation, either by acquiring production or marketing facilities of other firms, or by investing in the development of current facilities. Processes to control activities and achieve a dominant position in certain aspects of the industry, such as becoming the sole producer or possessing the deepest distribution network, are primarily done through the acquisition of other firms or parts of firms, such as the production facilities or the distribution network, which were sold by firms that could not withstand the competition.

Establishing a competitive advantage through the development of existing activities
The transformation of ongoing activities is associated with different types of rent generation mechanisms. The improvement of efficiency to increase competitiveness is associated with the development of a competitive advantage based on one of two factors: the possession of resources that are valuable, rare, difficult to substitute, and difficult to imitate (Barney, 1991), providing Ricardian rents, or the development of innovative capacity, creating Schumpeterian rents. The transformation of the firm to control certain aspects of the activity is related to the achievement of a competitive advantage based on either the control of resources needed by other firms, which generates Ricardian rents, or the creation of barriers to entry, which creates monopoly rents. However, not all sources of competitive advantage are equally sustainable. The competitive advantage generated by control over activities is more likely to lead to competitors' substituting the necessary resource. This can be done either by using an alternative resource, which may exist in the country or be brought in from elsewhere in the case of control over necessary inputs, or by bypassing the barrier to entry via acquisition of incumbent firms. However, competitive advantage based on the firm's efficiency is only likely to be undermined through the achievement of efficiency by competitors, or by technological change, which in general is not in the hands of a single firm but of the technological and social community (Rosenkopf and Tushman, 1994). This leads to the following proposition:

- *Proposition 3*: The actions that lead to the development of ongoing activities are differentially related to the sustainability of competitive advantage.
- *Hypothesis 3a*: The competitive advantage acquired by the transformation of an ongoing activity through the achievement of efficiency is likely to be more sustainable than the competitive advantage acquired by the transformation of an ongoing activity through the control of the activity.

The previous discussion is summarized in table 2.4, which presents the reasons for the actions, their relationship to competitive advantage, the conditions for success, and an abstraction of the steps undertaken in their development. Although the analysis of individual events generates only partial understanding of the interactions between resources and scope over time because of the temporal limits, it nevertheless serves as the base for analyzing longitudinal processes, while providing additional insights into the relationship between transformation processes and competitive advantage. On one

Table 2.4 Individual transformation actions and their relationship to competitive advantage (CA)

Actions	Motive	Relationship to CA	Conditions for success	Process (steps)
Entry	Invest	Neutral, but positive on performance	Select project and partner	Selection of project, investment
	Use resource	Very positive	Use excess transferable resources, obtain complementary resources	Identification of excess transferable resources, selection of area of application, identification of needed complementary resources, selection of source of complementary resources (purchase, link, internal development), integration of resource set
	Growth	Potentially positive	Use excess transferable resources if possible	Identification of growth area, identification of resources needed to operate, selection of source of resources (firm, partner, acquisition), integration of resource set
	Reduce impact of cycle	Potentially positive	Use excess transferable resources if possible	Identification of area with counter-cyclical performance, identification of resources needed to operate, selection of source of resources (firm, partner, acquisition), integration of resource set
	Protect	Positive	Have existing CA that is protected	Identify area that might be or is creating a potential problem, identify alternative sources of resources, select method of control of resources (partner, acquisition, internal development), integrate new activity with ongoing activities
Transformation	Improve efficiency	Very positive	Have finance for investment plan that improves efficiency	Realize need for improvement of efficiency, identify program of cost reduction, identify missing areas with limited knowledge on cost reduction and obtain necessary external knowledge (consultant, partner), obtain financial resources for investment, invest in the solution of production inefficiencies investing in the development of human resources, rethink value-added chain and, if necessary, spin-off activities, control processes and achieve production efficiency (ISO programs), redefine relationships with clients and establish service contracts, rethink organization processes and determine efficiency program for organization

Exit	Control operation	Very positive	Achieve control of operation and avoid substitution or bypassing of control	Identify area that is crucial for operation in country and who controls it, assess presence of firm in the area, expand internal operation while acquire operations of competitors, either the firm or the activity
	Redefinition of strategy	Positive	New strategy build on strength	Identify strategy in the new environment, identify relationships among activities, assess value of activities for firm and competitiveness of activity in relationship to other suppliers, assess potential dependence on activity if independent, separate activity as a independent entity, spin-off or sell
	Forced exit because lack of competitiveness	Negative	Failure. Firm lacks competitiveness in the activity from which it exits and not in all its activities	Realize lack of competitiveness in activity not solvable with further investments, neither alternative avenues of transformation likely to result in successful operation, stop investment process, separate activity, search for buyer and sell, or close if no buyer is found
	Forced exit because lack of finance	Negative	Failure. Firm lacks financial resources to continue investing	Realize need for financial resources over time is above the availability of resources, separate and reorganize activity while looking for a buyer, sell
	Forced exit because of financial problems	Very negative	Large failure. Firm faces financial problems that hampers overall C.A.	Realize financial problem can be solved via the sale of activities and associated resources, separate the activity, renegotiate with the debtors for exchange of debt for operation, transfer operation and solve financial problems
	Forced exit because changing environment	Neutral	Understand change in environment and find buyer for resources	Realize competitive problems arise from change in technological or institutional conditions, identify potential transformations of activity, attempt transformation or separate activity and search for buyer and sell
	End of life	Neutral	Successful completion of project	Attain desired objective for project of complete predetermined schedule, close operation as programmed
	Purchase opportunity	Positive	Embedded in it as there is buyer for operation	Receive purchase offer, evaluate future requirements from activity and needs to develop additional resources, as well as financial condition of company versus offer; if offer appears more valuable, separate activity and sell

hand, the analyzes of entry motives reveals the existence of a ranking between motives according to their relationship with competitive advantage; this ranking is absent in other studies that analyze individual motives. On the other hand, the analysis of exit motives indicates that they are not always signs of failure and a lack of competitive advantage, as commonly suggested. In fact, quite the opposite is true: some of them indicate existence of a competitive advantage, and can be ranked accordingly. Finally, the analysis of the motives for the changes in ongoing activities also reveals a ranking of competitive advantage, this time based on the sustainability rather than the degree of competitive advantage.

The complete transformation cycle: processes, interactions, and competitive advantage

In this section the longitudinal transformation of the actions of the firm is explored in order to provide a complete analysis of the process of change and examine the interactions between resources and scope. Instead of analyzing individual events, the chain of events that creates the cycle of change is studied, from entry and progression to exit.

Processes of transformation in the transformation cycle
The processes of transformation in the cycle vary initially with the motives for entry and later with the progression in the environmental conditions, which might lead to the exit. Their analysis reveals diverse relationships between resources and activities, and the existence of enabling and constraining factors that influence the progression of the transformation and the outcome. First, the entry in a new activity driven by an opportunity for investment leads to the use of resources, primarily finance, which are invested with a partner who provides the necessary knowledge and production and marketing skills. The operation progresses over time, the partner managing the operation and the firm acting as an investor. The firm withdraws if it encounters problems by selling its participation. A successful operation can continue its development over time if there is no pre-specified completion. It can reach an end when its objectives are accomplished and, hence, it is closed in the predetermined manner. Alternatively, the firm might be presented with a purchase offer from another firm and decide to sell, or it might need to obtain financial resources, and decide to sell its participation to recover some funds.

Second, in the case of entry into a new activity based on existing resources, the firm has developed resources for internal use, usually to improve the efficiency of ongoing operations, and finds itself with the opportunity to use its excess resources, especially technology but also production and marketing, which were created by the previous development of resources (Penrose, 1959). The firm enters the new activity by complementing its existing resources with additional resources, usually through internal development of the complementary resources, especially production and marketing; however, it may also use a partner or consultant to obtain the necessary production and organization technology. As the company progresses in the new activity, it undertakes actions to improve its efficiency, thus investing in the development of resources, both initial resources transferred from the original activity and complementary ones. Meanwhile, as the activity progresses and improves, the firm might find that it requires additional inputs, which might induce it to enter new activities to support the expansion, since it wants to ensure the distribution of the product from the new activity. This induces it to expand its distribution network, either extending the existing network or, if the new products are too different, developing a parallel distribution network. In this manner, as the transformation of the activity progresses, the development of resources to improve the activity serves as the basis for further extensions into other activities that complement the new activity, which leads to the development of existing and additional complementary resources for them, and so on. If the new activity becomes successful, the company usually redefines it as strategic, which draws more resources. In case of a high level of success, the firm might eventually start reducing its original activity and move towards the new one, thus leading the transformation not only of the activity, but of the whole firm.

However, this transformation process requires that the new activity be successful, which in some cases might be hampered by the lack of financial resources to continue growing in the new activity, a financial constraint that might induce the firm to accept purchase offers or search for a buyer. In this case, the exit from the activity provides the firm not only with finance, but also with a set of developed resources, which can then be used to enter a new activity and start the process again, if the new activity requires fewer financial resources than the previous one. This interactive process does not automatically lead to success. The new operation can be unsuccessful if the firm, even when using a partner, does not manage to develop the necessary complementary resources that will sustain its development, especially marketing knowledge and distribution, thus leading to the eventual exit from the activity through sale to another firm, if possible, or closure. In this case, although apparently a failure, the company might benefit from the development of resources that can be used in the original operation, especially technology and knowledge.

Additionally, the success of the operation might be hampered because technological or institutional changes alter the value of the opportunity. This induces firms to either exit the operation or try to continue it by searching for alternative uses in a growth area for the resources deployed in the operation, either within the partnership or with another firm, a search that might start another process of successful transformation.

Third, the search for a source of growth, which can be the outcome of the need to find an alternative use for a resource developed in an unsuccessful area or of the fact that the firm has achieved dominant market position and further growth would be very difficult or legally problematic because of antitrust concerns, or the search for an activity that reduces the impact of business cycles, lead to similar processes of entry. The likelihood of success increases if there are resources that the company can use in the new area, and the firm can add value from the transfer of its own resources while the new area provides a source of revenue. Alternatively, the company can try to enter a new area where it cannot apply its own resources but can obtain access to resources through the acquisition of an ongoing concern. In this case, the purchase process of the particular firm will determine the success of the operation, not only because it selects a target company that already has a developed competitive advantage, but also because the price paid for the firm and the source of finance for the operation might place a burden on the firm that can lead to the failure of the operation.

Finally, when the company wants to protect its ongoing activities, it enters a new activity that supports its current activities, such as supply or marketing. This is usually done through the acquisition of another firm or part of it; the firm operates and improves it, until changes in the environment lead to the redefinition of the value of the activity and induce the exit, and the firm sells its participation. It might also search for ways of reducing the impact of business cycles on the firm, which leads to investment in other firms but not to their management, since the company does not have the resources to do this, but will benefit from the financial flows.

Interactions between resources and scope in the transformation cycles
These longitudinal processes reveal the existence of interactive relationships between resources and scope that are missed in the analysis of single events, interactive relationships that are termed co-evolutionary here. The analysis and stylized description of single events in entry or exit performed in the previous subsection lend support to the common views of unidirectional relationships between resources and scope, where either changes in resources drive the transformation of activities, or changes in activities drive the transformation of resources. However, the mapping of the actions undertaken over time and the analysis of the processes of transformation reveal the intimate interactions among resources and activities, showing how the transformation of one influences changes in the other and vice versa in an interactive and sequential, rather than simultaneous, manner. Here these interactive relationships between resources and scope are termed co-evolutionary. This use of the term differs from the way in which it is used by other authors, who define coevolution as the simultaneous, and implicitly automatic, evolution of two hierarchical variables (Baum and Singh, 1994, p. 379). Although the co-evolution of resources and scope can be performed simultaneously, the process is not necessarily automatic, but can also be guided (Lovas and Ghoshal, 2000).

The co-evolutionary process of transformation of the firm through the interactive evolution of resources and scope is not a fully automatic process. Unlike other co-evolutionary processes between organizations and their environment (Baum and Singh, 1994; Rosenkopf and Tushman, 1994; Van de Ven and Garud, 1994), the co-evolution of resources and scope within the firm requires a guided transformation (Lovas and Ghoshal, 2000), not only to set the process in motion, but also to increase its likelihood of success. The co-evolutionary process needs to be managed to facilitate the interactive transformation of both resources and activities towards the development of competitive advantage. The development of resources can be the starting point of a co-evolutionary process, where the company uses the resources developed in its current activity to enter a new activity where it can obtain additional returns from those resources. However, at the same time the entry into the new activity requires the development of complementary resources that will enable the achievement of the initial potential competitive advantage granted by the driving resources. The development of these complementary resources feeds back into the original activity, thus improving it, and might lead to the extension into additional activities, and so on. Alternatively, the coevolutionary process can also start with the entry into a new activity that provides the firm with a position. As the firm operates in the new activity, it develops the necessary resources, either by internal development, acquisition or transfer from a partner; once these resources have been developed, they can serve not only to reinforce the resources of the original activities but can also extend the activities of the firm into new realms. In this manner, the co-evolutionary process enables the interactive transformation of both resources and scope towards the achievement of competitive advantage, which, ultimately, can be attributed to neither the possession of the resources nor the positioning in the activity, but to their interaction. This coevolutionary process can be managed from the beginning, though the success of the process is revealed over time as the firm develops resources and activities interactively and the environment reveals the value of the actions taken by the firm.

Alternatively, the firm could choose to follow unidirectional relationships between resources and scope, or limit the relationships and the co-evolutionary process of transformation. For example, the company might choose to focus on improving existing resources and limit their relationships with its activities, thus leading to a unidirectional improvement in resources that are not applied to the transformation of the activities but that support the development of the competitive advantage of the firm. Alternatively, the company could enter a new activity and not undertake the transformation in resources, for example by being granted an ongoing activity that is legally protected from competition, and thus does not have an impact on the firm resources, but nevertheless develops the firm's competitive advantage.

Figure 2.1 is the visual representation of the three alternative interactions between resources and activities that facilitate the transformation of the firm: the unidirectional resource-based transformation in which resources enable the development of activities, the unidirectional activity-based transformation in which activities drive the changes in resources, and the bidirectional co-evolutionary transformation in which resources and scope induce each others' transformation. In it, it is not only the direction of the main thrust of change that is highlighted, but also the time component in the relationship. In the activity-based transformation, the main change occurs first in activities; this later leads to changes in resources. In the resource-based transformation, the primary change appears first in resources; this leads to changes in activities. The co-evolutionary transformation can be represented either by feedback loops that highlight the interactive evolution of resources and scope, or by using a temporal representation that highlights the interaction of resources and scope over time and their managed nature.

The full transformation cycle and competitive advantage
The analyzes of sources of competitive advantage in single events assume the creation of rents from one action, but do not explore interactions over time, which can also generate rents. Thus, the sources of rents can arise not only from the initial action, which is either resource-based or activity-based, but also from the co-evolutionary interactions among resources and scope. In the former case, the sources of rents are maintained as long as the resources or activity that sustain the rents are protected. In the latter case, the sources of rents may come not only from sustaining the initial sources of rents, either in resources or activities, but also from the interactive development of other sources of rents in resources and activities, or the co-evolutionary interaction. The co-evolution of resources and scope enables companies to regain their competitive advantage by exercising effort on both resources and their upgrade and activities and their control. Both become a source of competitive advantage, and their

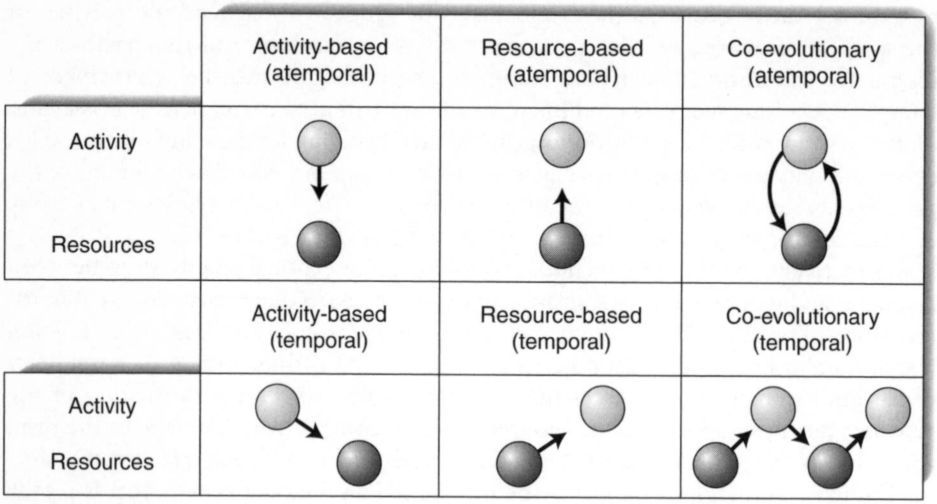

	Activity-based (atemporal)	Resource-based (atemporal)	Co-evolutionary (atemporal)
Activity **Resources**			

	Activity-based (temporal)	Resource-based (temporal)	Co-evolutionary (temporal)
Activity **Resources**			

Figure 2.1   Temporal and atemporal representations of the interactions among resource and activity dimensions

interaction becomes a third source of competitive advantage. This is more difficult for competitors to imitate and reduce, not only because there is no single action to take but rather a set of interrelated actions, thus creating a causal ambiguity (Lippman and Rumelt, 1982), but also because the coevolution of resources and scope reinforces the competitive advantages provided by the resources and activities and is in itself a sources of competitive advantage as it enables the firm to manage its transformation as the environmental conditions progress, in the spirit of dynamic capabilities (Teece, Pisano, and Shuen, 1997). Therefore, it is proposed that:

♦ *Proposition 4*: The co-evolutionary processes of transformation are more likely to be associated with a more sustainable competitive advantage than the unidirectional processes of transformation.

Conclusions

The analysis of firms' longitudinal transformation in their quest to achieve a competitive advantage reveals processes that have been missed in previous single-event studies: the co-evolution of resources and scope, or the interactive evolution of resources and activities. This analysis extends the work of Penrose (1959) by uncovering alternative motives for transformation and the three different transformation processes followed by firms. The co-evolution of resources and scope complements previous literature on coevolution across different levels of analysis by focusing on the level of the firm and studying the co-evolution of internal variables: resources and activities. Other studies have focused on the co-evolution between internal and external variables, such as the firm and its environment (Baum and Singh, 1994; Van de Ven and Grazman, 1999), technology and organizations (Rosenkopf and Tushman, 1994), firm capabilities and industry (Levinthal and Myatt, 1994), or innovations and institutions (Van de Ven and Garud, 1994). However, the coevolution of resources and scope differs from these interactions, as it is a managed process rather than an automatic one (Lovas and Ghoshal, 2000).

The proposition that the co-evolution of resources and scope is superior to a unidirectional approach, either resource-based or activity-based, expands the strategic management literature by providing a basis for understanding the process of company transformation, linking the resource-based view (Barney, 1991; Penrose, 1959) and the positioning argument (Ansoff, 1965; Porter, 1980) within a single dynamic view of company transformation, where resources and scope are two sides of the same coin (Wernerfelt, 1984). In a dynamic analysis of company evolution, both resources and scope are a source of competitive advantage as they are interdependent and co-evolve.

Note

This paper is based on my thesis at the Sloan School of Management, Massachusetts Institute of Technology, which was awarded the 2000 Free Press Best Dissertation Award of the Business Policy and Strategy Division of the Academy of Management. My special gratitude goes to the thesis committee, Arnoldo Hax, Donald Lessard (chair), Scott Stern, and Eleanor Westney, for their comments and suggestions. Additionally, the comments of Xavier Castañer, Bala Chakravarthy, Annique Un, participants at the Strategic Management Society Mini-Conference and the Academy of Management Annual Meeting, and anonymous reviewers helped improve previous versions of the paper. Special thanks also go to Professor Alvaro Cuervo García, Professor Enrique Yacuzzi, and Dr Raul Casa for their introduction to numerous managers, and to Carlos Lac-Prugent, Nestor Braidot, Viviana Brunatto, and Lucia Repetto for facilitating the logistics during the field research in Argentina. Most importantly, I thank the managers, entrepreneurs and owners who graciously shared with me their experiences and views. The financial support of "la Caixa" and the Massachusetts Institute of Technology is gratefully acknowledged. All errors remain mine.

References

Amit, R. and Schoemaker, P. J. H. 1993: Strategic assets and organizational rent. *Strategic Management Journal*, 14, 33–46.

Ansoff, H. I. 1965: *Corporate strategy: an analytic approach to business policy for growth and expansion*. New York: McGraw-Hill.

Baden-Fuller, C. W. F. and Stopford, J. M. 1991: Globalization frustrated: the case of white goods. *Strategic Management Journal*, 12, 493–507.

Bain, J. 1956: *Barriers to new competition*. Cambridge, MA: Harvard University Press.

Barnett, W. P. and Burgelman, R. A. 1996: Evolutionary perspectives on strategy. *Strategic Management Journal*, 17, 5–19.

Barney, J. B. 1986: Strategic factor markets, expectations, luck, and business strategy. *Management Science*, 32, 1231–41.

Barney, J. B. 1991: Firm Resources and Sustained Competitive Advantage. *Journal of Management*, 17, 99–120.

Bartlett, C. A. and Ghoshal, S. 1989: *Managing across borders: the transnational solution.* Boston, MA: Harvard Business School Press.

Baum, J. A. C. and Singh, J. V. 1994: Organization–environment coevolution. In J. A. C. Baum and J. V. Singh (eds), *Evolutionary dynamics of organizations,* Oxford: Oxford University Press, 379–402.

Caves, R. E. and Porter, M. E. 1977: From entry barriers to mobility barriers: conjectural Decisions and contrived deterrence to new competition. *Quarterly Journal of Economics,* 91, 241–61.

Center for Quality of Management 1995: *The language processing method (LP): a tool for organizing qualitative data and creating insight.* Cambridge, MA: Center for Quality of Management.

Chakravarthy, B. and Doz, Y. 1992: Strategy process research: focusing on corporate self-renewal. *Strategic Management Journal,* 13 (summer special issue), 5–14.

Chandler, A. D. 1990: *Scale and scope: the dynamics of industrial capitalism.* Cambridge, MA: The Belknap Press of Harvard University Press.

Chaterjee, S. and Wernerfelt, B. 1991: The link between resources and type of diversification: theory and evidence. *Strategic Management Journal,* 12, 33–48.

Collis, D. J. and Montgomery, C. A. 1997: *Corporate strategy: resources and the scope of the firm.* New York: Irwin.

Cuervo-Cazurra, A. 1999: Methods and timing to develop resources. Paper presented at the Iberoamerican Academy of Management Biannual Meeting, Madrid, Spain.

Cuervo-Cazurra, A. 2001: Evolution and limitations of scope after market liberalization. Paper presented at the Academy of International Business Annual Meeting, Sydney, Australia.

Detert, J. R., Schroeder, R. G., and Mauriel, J. J. 2000: A framework for linking culture and improvement initiatives in organizations. *Academy of Management Review,* 25, 850–63.

Eisenhardt, K. M. 1989: Building theories from case study research. *Academy of Management Review,* 14, 532–60.

Geroski, P. and Vlassopoulos, T. 1991: The rise and fall of a market leader: frozen foods in the UK. *Strategic Management Journal,* 12, 467–78.

Glick, W. H., Huber, G. P., Miller, C. C., Doty, D. H., and Sutcliffe, K. M. 1990: Studying changes in organizational design and effectiveness: retrospective event histories and periodic assessments. *Organization Science,* 1, 293–312.

Grant, R. M. 1995: *Contemporary strategy analysis: concepts, techniques, applications,* 2nd edn. Cambridge, MA: Blackwell.

Helfat, C. E. 1997: Know-how and asset complementarity and dynamic capability accumulation: the case of R&D. *Strategic Management Journal,* 18, 339–60.

Itami, H. 1987: *Mobilizing invisible assets.* Cambridge, MA: Harvard University Press.

Kawakita, J. 1991: *The original KJ method.* Tokyo: Kawakita Research Institute.

Leonard-Barton, D. 1990: A dual methodology for case studies: synergistic use of a longitudinal single site with replicated multiple sites. *Organization Science,* 1, 248–66.

Levinthal, D. A. and Myatt J. 1994: Co-evolution of capabilities and industry: the evolution of mutual fund processing. *Strategic Management Journal,* 15 (winter special issue), 45–62.

Lippman, S. A. and Rumelt, R. P. 1982: Uncertainty imitability: an analysis of interfirm differences under competition. *Bell Journal of Economics,* 13, 418–38.

Lovas, B. and Ghoshal, S. 2000: Strategy as guided evolution. *Strategic Management Journal* 21, 875–96.

McPhee, R. D. 1990: Alternate approaches to integrating longitudinal case studies. *Organization Science,* 1, 393–405.

Penrose, E. 1959: *The theory of the growth of the firm*. Oxford: Basil Blackwell.

Peteraf, M. A. 1993: The cornerstones of competitive advantage: a resource-based view. *Strategic Management Journal*, 14, 179–91.

Pettigrew, A. M. 1992: The character and significance of strategy process research. *Strategic Management Journal*, 13 (winter special issue), 5–16.

Porter, M. E. 1980: *Competitive strategy*. New York: Free Press.

Porter, M. E. 1985: *Competitive advantage*. New York: Free Press.

Porter, M. E. 1991: Towards a dynamic theory of strategy. *Strategic Management Journal*, 12 (winter special issue), 95–117.

Prahalad, C. K. and Doz, Y. L. 1987: *The multinational mission*. New York: Free Press.

Rosenkopf, L. and Tushman, M. L. 1994: The coevolution of technology and organization. In J. A. C. Baum and J. V. Singh (eds), *Evolutionary Dynamics of Organizations*. Oxford: Oxford University Press, 403–24.

Sharma, S. and Vredenburg, H. 1998: Proactive corporate environmental strategy and the development of competitively valuable organizational capabilities. *Strategic Management Journal*, 19, 729–53.

Shiba, S., Graham, A., and Walden, D. 1993: *A new American TQM: four practical revolutions in management*. Portland, OR: Productivity Press.

Teece, D. J., Pisano, G., and Shuen, A. 1997: Dynamic capabilities and strategic management. *Strategic Management Journal*, 18, 509–33.

Toulan, O. 1997: Adaptation to environmental shocks: internationalisation responses to market liberalization in Argentina. Unpublished dissertation. Cambridge MA: Sloan School of Management, Massachusetts Institute of Technology.

Van de Ven, A. H. 1992: Suggestions for studying strategy process: a research note. *Strategic Management Journal*, 13 (summer special issue), 169–88.

Van de Ven, A. H. and Garud, R. 1994: The coevolution of technical and institutional events in the development of an innovation. In J. A. C. Baum and J. V. Singh (eds), *Evolutionary dynamics of organizations*. Oxford: Oxford University Press, 425–43.

Van de Ven, A. H. and Grazman, D. H. 1999: Evolution in a nested hierarchy: a genealogy of twin cities health care organizations, 1853–1995. In B. McKelvey and J. A. C. Baum (eds), *Variations in organization science: in honor of Donald T. Campbell*. Thousand Oaks, CA: SAGE, 185–209.

Van de Ven, A. H. and Poole, M. S. 1990: Methods for studying innovation development in the Minnesota Innovation Research Program. *Organization Science*, 1, 313–35.

Wernerfelt, B. 1984: A resource-based view of the firm. *Strategic Management Journal*, 5, 171–80.

Yin, R. K. 1994: *Case study research: design and methods*. Thousand Oaks, CA: Sage.

CHAPTER THREE

Change in the Presence of Fit: The Rise, the Fall, and the Renaissance of Liz Claiborne

Nicolaj Siggelkow

We have seen a remarkable upsurge of interest in the concepts of interaction and fit. Within the management and organization literatures, the notion of fit has a long-standing tradition. In particular, the internal fit between the strategy and the structure of the firm (e.g., Learned, Christensen, Andrews, and Guth, 1961; Chandler, 1962) and the external fit between the structure and the environment of the firm (e.g., Lawrence and Lorsch, 1967; Pennings, 1987) have received much attention. During the late 1980s and 1990s, originally spurred by analyzes of Japanese manufacturing methods, researchers revived the topic of fit. The emphasis shifted to studying internal fit at a very fine-grained level of analysis. The importance of replicating entire systems of practices, including production, supply, and human resource policies, rather than single elements, was recognized (e.g., Jaikumar, 1986; MacDuffie, 1995). Expanding the concept of fit beyond manufacturing, and ascribing to it a central role in strategy formulation, Porter (1996) stressed the importance of mutually reinforcing activities in creating and sustaining a competitive advantage. Over the same time period, economists as well have become interested in the issues of fit and interdependence among firm choices and have started to create mathematical frameworks that allow rigorous modeling of at least certain types of mutually reinforcing interactions (e.g., Milgrom and Roberts, 1990, 1995).

The common theme of these approaches is that to understand the performance of a firm, one must analyze the firm as a *system* of interconnected choices: choices with respect to activities, policies and organizational structures, capabilities, and resources. Internal fit among choices can lead to a sustainable competitive advantage because it makes imitation difficult (Porter and Rivkin, 1998; Rivkin, 2000). However, the implications of tight fit on the sustainability of a competitive advantage given environmental change are ambiguous. On the one hand, "firms may have difficulty navigating a changing environment not only because the changes in the environment negate the value of the organization's assets, but also because a tightly coupled organization may have difficulty adapting to such changes" (Levinthal, 1997, p. 936). Tight coupling requires a firm to modify many choices simultaneously, an inherently difficult task (Nadler, Shaw, and Walton, 1994). On the other hand, tight fit raises the incentive for management to optimally configure and adjust all of its choices. Since each choice influences the payoff of many other choices, the marginal payoff to adjusting each choice in response to some external change is increased in the presence of tighter fit (Porter, 1995). Moreover, tight fit can make a firm more sensitive to environmental change (Weick, 1976). Changes are quickly detected, since the repercussions are felt in multiple areas in the firm.

This article presents a new framework for thinking about the relationship between fit and organizational inertia when a firm is confronted with environmental change. As part of the framework, a new classification scheme for environmental changes is developed. In line with the more recent literature on fit, I examine fit at a very detailed level of analysis – at the level of individual activity choices. To illustrate the framework, I present a longitudinal study of how a firm has created a system of tightly interconnected activity choices, and how the firm responded (or failed to respond) to environmental changes. In particular, I study the developmental journey of Liz Claiborne, the largest US manufacturer of women fashion apparel, from its inception in 1976 to late 1997. I analyze the initial success of Liz Claiborne, the environmental changes it faced in the early 1990s, its first responses, and its subsequent actions in the late 1990s.

Literature Review and Change Framework

Before I examine the historical journey of Liz Claiborne, it will be helpful to briefly review the literature on organizational change that is concerned with changes in systems of interconnected choices. Following the review, I present a new framework for thinking about the relationship between fit and organizational responses given different types of environmental changes.

Logically prior to any theory about *changes* of systems of interrelated parts, is the notion that internal fit should not be thought of as pairwise associations between variables, but as gestalts, or configurations, describing sets of elements and their inter-relationships (Drazin and Van de Ven, 1985; Khandwalla, 1973; Miller, 1986; Miller and Friesen, 1984; Nadler and Tushman, 1992). Whereas the term "fit" is used in the literature on configurations to describe the internal relationship among activities, in the contingency literature the term is used to describe the relationship between a firm's choices and its environment. To gain clarity on the concept of fit, I suggest making the distinction between *internal fit* among activities – that is, whether a firm has a coherent configuration of activities – and *external fit*, that is, the appropriateness of the configuration given the environmental conditions facing the firm.

Building on the idea that firms consist of systems of interrelated parts, Miller and Friesen (1982) analyze the change processes of these systems. They hypothesize and empirically find that quantum changes (changes in many attributes over a short period of time) yield better performance than piecemeal incremental approaches. Following a similar line of thinking, Tushman & Romanelli (1985) propose that firms follow a developmental path best described by a punctuated equilibrium model of organizational evolution. Firms engage in incremental changes during most of their history, yet sporadically undergo relatively rapid and fundamental transformations (Gersick, 1991). Empirical support of this developmental pattern has been provided by Tushman, Newman, and Romanelli (1986), Pettigrew (1987), and Romanelli and Tushman (1994).

Intimately tied to the process of change is the issue of inertia that firms display. For the purpose of our discussion, I will focus on factors that may cause senior management to fail to respond to environmental changes. Hambrick and Mason (1984) propose a helpful framework for understanding management inertia. In short, managers are thought of as having mental maps that influence both the information they perceive and the way they process it. As a consequence, managers, especially those with long tenure, may be unable to "unlearn" outdated views of the world (Nystrom and Starbuck, 1984). Past success, in particular, reinforces and eventually ossifies mental maps, leading to increased inertia (Murmann and Tushman, 1997). Studies have shown that past success leads to a reduction in information processing (Miller, 1993) and an increased belief that environmental changes are not going to affect the organization negatively (Milliken, 1990). Moreover, past success can lead to the accumulation of slack resources, which reduce the perceived need to change (Milliken and Lant, 1991), and to the creation of a strong organizational identity or culture. Both past success and strong organizational identities have been found to increase the belief in the organization's relative invulnerability to environmental changes (Milliken, 1990; Miller, 1994).

In sum, a variety of psychological reasons has been described in the literature as leading to firm inertia. In the following framework, I develop a link between the work on inertia and the previously described literature on fit. As described by Tushman and Romanelli, inertial forces lead firms along a process of convergence to a specific configuration of strategic position and organizational form. The value of this process has been previously analyzed with respect to two different environmental conditions: stability and turbulence (Miller, Lant, Milliken, and Korn, 1996; Tushman and Romanelli, 1985; Tushman and Rosenkopf, 1996). As long as the environment is relatively stable, convergence, and hence inertial forces, have been found to be beneficial. However, in turbulent environments inertial forces are a liability.

Rather than distinguishing between stable and turbulent environments, the following framework characterizes changes in the environment in terms of their impact on internal and external fit. This characterization scheme can offer new insights into the mediating role that fit plays in the relationship between environmental changes and the ensuing changes (or inertia) at the firm level. In particular, the framework points toward the difficulty of managers' perceiving and reacting to environmental changes that *leave the internal fit among the elements within a firm's set of choices intact, yet decrease the value of the set of choices as a whole, that is, destroy external fit.*

For the following discussion, the notion of a "performance landscape" is useful. The concept of a performance or fitness landscape was first developed in the realm of evolutionary biology by Sewell Wright (1932). The concept has been further developed and formalized by Kauffman (1993) and has found application in, for instance, studies of organizational adaptation (Levinthal, 1997), organizational variety (Westhoff, Yarbrough, and Yarbrough, 1996), and the difficulty of imitating complex strategies (Rivkin, 2000). In our context, the performance landscape is a multi-dimensional space

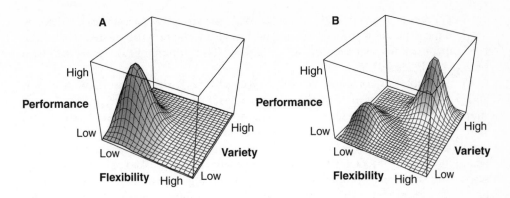

Figure 3.1(a)   Performance landscape (1900s)
The Ford production system (low flexibility, low variety) provides high performance.

Figure 3.1(b)   Performance landscape (1980s)
The Japanese production system (high flexibility, high variety) provides better performance, while the value of the Ford production system has decreased.

in which each dimension represents the values of a particular choice that a firm can make, and a final dimension indicating the resulting performance value. For illustration, consider a simple example in which a firm can make only two choices: the breadth of product variety and the flexibility of the production set-up. Imagine the breadth of product variety is on the x-axis, the degree of flexibility is on the y-axis, and the ensuing performance is on the vertical z-axis. The performance landscape maps each pair of variety and flexibility onto a performance value (see figure 3.1(a)). Similarly, for each set of N choices, the performance landscape would attach a performance value to it in a $N + 1$ dimensional space.

Performance landscapes provide a suggestive way to illustrate the concepts of internal and external fit. External fit, that is, the appropriateness of a set of choices given environmental conditions, is represented by the height of a particular point on the landscape. Environmental conditions encompass all factors that affect the relative profitability of a firm's set of choices, including competitors' actions, customer preferences, and available technologies. As shown in figure 3.1(a), certain combinations of flexibility and product variety lead to higher performance than other combinations. Measures of external fit include absolute and relative profitability measures, such as return on investment or the difference between the firm's profitability and its industry's average profitability. More informal assessments of external fit could include an identification of the inherent tradeoffs that the current set of choices entails coupled with an evaluation of the costs of these tradeoffs given the current environmental conditions.

Consistency among choices, that is, internal fit, is represented by a peak in the landscape. We say a set of choices is consistent if changing any single choice (and not changing any other choice) would lead to a decline in performance. On a landscape, when a firm chooses to change one of its choices, it moves along a single dimension from its existing position. If any such move leads to lower performance, the firm has a consistent set of choices or perfect internal fit. At the same time, if it is the case that any single-dimension move from its existing position leads the firm to a lower point on the landscape, it means that the firm sits on a peak. Thus internal fit is represented by a peak in the landscape.

Two examples of consistent sets of choices are the Ford mass-production system and the Japanese lean manufacturing system (Milgrom and Roberts, 1990). In our simple two-dimensional example, the mass production system is represented by low variety and low flexibility, whereas the lean production system is represented by high variety and high flexibility (see figure 3.1(b)). Note, the choices of product variety and flexibility not only interact with each other (causing a multi-peaked performance landscape), but they are also complementary, or reinforcing. The higher the level of product variety, the higher the marginal benefit of increasing manufacturing flexibility, and vice versa. A firm with a high degree of internal fit tends to display many such complementary choices that have been resolved in a consistent manner. (In the example above this would imply that high flexibility is adopted together with high product variety, or low flexibility is adopted together with low product variety). This notion of internal fit is consistent with Miller's suggestion that "the fit among the elements of an organization may be evidenced by the degree to which strategy, structure and systems complement one another" (Miller, 1996, p. 511). The shape of each peak contains further information: the stronger the degree of interaction among a particular set of choices, the steeper the associated peak. This feature results from the fact that in systems with strong interactions, the performance penalties for misalignments are particularly high because the value of many activities is affected.[1]

Environmental changes can be thought of as changing the landscape: the height, shape, or location of peaks changes, new peaks arise, and so forth (Levinthal and Siggelkow, 2001). For instance, in the early 1900s, with the information and production technologies available at the time, the choice of "low variety–low flexibility" could be implemented very efficiently: the Ford production system represented a high peak in the performance landscape, while the "high variety–high flexibility" choice was technologically very difficult (or even infeasible) to implement for high-volume production, thus, it represented a very low point on the performance landscape (figure 3.1(a)). By the 1980s, choosing high variety with high flexibility had become technologically feasible; moreover, it provided substantial advantages in the marketplace. The landscape had changed: the value of the Ford production system had declined, while a new peak, the Japanese production system, had arisen and formed a higher-performing set of choices (figure 3.1(b)).

For a firm that occupies a peak, environmental change can affect both external and internal fit. Logically, we can distinguish four cases, which are depicted in figure 3.2.

1   *No change*: If neither external nor internal fit is affected, the environmental change has no relevance to the firm in question.
2   *Detrimental fit-destroying change*: If both external and internal fit are affected, the firm finds itself at a lower elevation (lower external fit) and located away from a peak (lower internal fit).
3   *Benign fit-destroying change*: In this case, the firm's performance has not decreased, yet internal fit has been compromised by the environmental change.

External fit

Internal fit		No change	Change
	No change	No change	Fit-conserving change
	Change	Benign fit-destroying change	Detrimental fit-destroying change

Figure 3.2   Change framework

4   *Fit-conserving change*: While internal fit has not been affected, external fit has de-creased. In other words, the environmental change has left the internal logic of the firm's system of choices intact while decreasing the appropriateness of the system as a whole.

In sum, with *fit-destroying* change the firm no longer occupies a peak; with *fit-conserving* change, the firm still occupies a peak, the height of which has declined, however. The distinction between these two types of changes is important, since firms' reactions to them can differ significantly. After fit-destroying change, a firm will at-tempt either through local, incremental search, or through long-range search to change its activities in order to climb onto a new peak. A firm might react quickly in such a situation, since both its financial performance has deteriorated (in the case of detri-mental fit-destroying change), and internal misfits can be identified. In other words, it is clear that something should be done, and at least some clues as to what should be done might exist, since various elements are misaligned. Moreover, for changes that only nudge a firm away from a peak, one can hypothesize that a firm with a high degree of internal fit reacts faster than a firm with a loosely coupled system. Since peaks are steeper for firms with high internal fit, their incentive to find realignment is large. On a smaller scale, the lean production line is a good example of tight fit leading to fast response. The absence of inventory (or work-in-process) between individual work-stations creates a tightly coupled system. A problem at any work-station is detected very quickly, as the entire line comes to a halt. In addition, incentives to improve each individual production step are high, since the cost of stopping the entire line is large (Womack, Jones, and Roos, 1990).

The situation is different, however, in the case of fit-conserving change: even though the firm's financial performance has declined, no obvious misfits can be detected be-cause the internal logic of the old system remains intact. In this situation, a firm can react in three ways:

1   *Playing the old game*: The firm does not change anything. It keeps its old system of choices, which still displays internal fit, though creating suboptimal performance. Graphically, the firm stays on its old, lower peak.
2   *Playing an incomplete game*: The firm changes single elements in its system of choices with the consequence of an even further performance decline; the firm moves incrementally away and down from its peak.

3 *Playing a new game*: The firm changes a whole range of its elements and locates on a new and higher peak.

The first two reactions, though destructive, are easily defensible, as managers continue to rely on their old mental maps. Within the landscape metaphor, the term mental "map" is particularly apt: the mental map can be thought of as a manager's map of the performance landscape. In *playing the old game*, managers continue to rely on previously successful practices and choices. Moreover, managers may rightly point out that any incremental change would lead to a performance decline. This is the result of their systems already being fully aligned. In a sense, firms are held captive by their existing systems – they have fallen into a competency trap (Levinthal, 1992; Levitt and March, 1988).

Managers choosing the option of *playing an incomplete game* feel compelled to act, since performance has declined. Yet, in this case, incremental changes only lead to further performance declines. For instance, the American automobile industry recognized that the height of the peak associated with their production system had decreased, even though the internal logic of the mass-production system was still intact. Yet, by copying only individual elements of the Japanese production system, the American automobile industry played an incomplete game for many years that did not generate the hoped-for benefits (Hayes and Jaikumar, 1988). In sum, after fit-conserving change, local search and incremental adaptations are not effective.

Only through the third reaction, *playing a new game*, i.e., a comprehensive rearrangement of a large part of its system of choices, can a firm achieve a significant performance improvement. Graphically, the firm locates itself on a new peak. Such an approach is, however, very difficult to undertake. It requires that managers perceive the systemic nature of the needed changes. Moreover, they need to be willing to act on a broad scale, potentially contradicting some of their past actions. Thus, they have to overcome both their own behavioral "blind spots" (Zajac and Bazerman, 1991) and establish internal legitimacy for their actions (Suchman, 1995). In addition, this broad set of changes has to be implemented successfully – a difficult undertaking as discussed in the organizational ecology literature on "core changes" (Hannan and Freeman, 1984; Singh, House, and Tucker, 1986). Lastly, these changes have to take place over a short period of time for the firm not to experience large performance deficits caused by misfits during the transition period (Miller and Friesen, 1982, 1984). As a result, managers of firms with tightly-coupled activity systems face a formidable task – structurally, cognitively, and psychologically – if they are to respond successfully to fit-conserving environmental change.

The following case study illustrates the change framework. After providing a methodological note on the case research, I present a brief sketch of Liz Claiborne's history followed by an analysis of Liz Claiborne's success. I describe Liz Claiborne's choices within five important stages along its value chain: design, production and distribution, the selling process to retailers, the presentation of its merchandise, and marketing. The section concludes with a description of the internal fit within Liz Claiborne's set of choices and a map displaying the interaction among the choices. To use the terminology of the framework, I establish that Liz Claiborne was located on a peak. Moreover, I show that the system of choices had high external fit given the environmental conditions at the time, that is, Liz Claiborne's chosen peak was high. The environmental factors considered are customer taste and demand, retailers' requirements, and the available technology.

In the second section, I describe how these three environmental factors changed in the early 1990s. In other words, Liz Claiborne's performance landscape was shifting. More specifically, Liz Claiborne faced fit-conserving change. The internal logic of its system remained intact, yet the external fit of its system decreased. Moreover, a new peak, which involved a host of different choices with respect to distribution and production, had arisen. The company's management responded to the fit-conserving change by playing an incomplete game: Liz Claiborne attempted to partially change its set of choices with the consequence of a further performance decline.

In the third main section, I use the same five categories of choices (design, production and distribution, the selling process to retailers, the presentation of its merchandise, and marketing) to systematically describe the actions, beginning in 1994, of Liz Claiborne's new leadership team, which eventually moved Liz Claiborne to a new peak. This section concludes with another map, displaying the particular choices and the interactions among them. In the last two sections, I further discuss the framework and outline future research opportunities.

Methodological note

The data for the case study were obtained from several primary and secondary sources. Over a period of one and a half years, between 1996 and 1997, personal interviews, ranging from one hour to several hours, and shorter follow-up telephone interviews were conducted with members of Liz Claiborne's management team. Interviewees included the CEO, the CFO, the vice president for corporate planning, and several division presidents. The tenure at Liz Claiborne of the interviewees ranged from one year to ten years. After completing the fact gathering from secondary sources (about nine hundred articles about Liz Claiborne in trade journals and magazines, in addition to security analysts' reports) and company documents (annual reports, filings with the Securities and Exchange Commission such as 10Ks, and documents provided by management), a several-hour interview was conducted with one of the founders of the company (Jerome Chazen). Early drafts of the case study were circulated among members of Liz Claiborne's management in addition to Chazen, all of whom provided additions and corrections on factual data in the case. Subsequent discussions with industry experts were used to confirm the outlined changes, in particular those occurring at the industry level.

Brief Historical Overview

Founded in 1976 with a starting capital of $250,000, Liz Claiborne reached revenues of $116 million in 1981, the year it went public. Five years later, the company became part of the *Fortune 500* list, the first company started by a woman (the designer Liz Claiborne) to do so. In 1989, *Fortune* reported that Liz Claiborne had achieved the highest average return on year-end equity during the 1980s among all *Fortune 500* industrial companies: 40.3 percent. In 1991, Liz Claiborne's sales surpassed the $2 billion mark for the first time and its stock price reached record heights: in May of that year, an investment of $10,000 in shares bought at the initial offering had a market value of over $610,000 (see table 3.1 for financial data).

Beginning in 1992, however, problems in Liz Claiborne's performance surfaced. Its sales stagnated and its net income declined. Over the next three years, Liz Claiborne's market capitalization dropped from $3.5 billion at the end of 1992 to $1.3 billion at the end of 1994. In 1994, Paul Charron, the former executive vice president of VF Corporation, was hired, and he became the new CEO at Liz Claiborne one year later. The implementation of a series of operational and marketing changes led to a marked increase in net income and to a renaissance of Liz Claiborne's stock. By May 1997, Liz Claiborne was trading close to a record high, giving it a market capitalization of $3.2 billion.

Liz Claiborne's Rise

How was Liz Claiborne able to achieve its remarkable success in its early years? To summarize, in the late 1970s, Liz Claiborne identified a growing customer group (professional women) and created a new market segment (a segment between moderate and designer sportswear). Unlike the designers of many fashion houses, Ms. Claiborne designed apparel to fit the actual shapes of her customers. She made a mark on the apparel industry with the pronouncement that "the American woman is pear-shaped" (Hass, 1992). Moreover, Liz Claiborne pioneered overseas production for fashion items, thereby allowing it to offer its apparel at lower prices. Lastly, the practice of presenting the lines of apparel as collections within which customers could mix and match made shopping for career clothes easier. As a result, the company garnered the loyalty of customers, who considered Ms. Claiborne to be a personal friend, whose taste they could trust when it came to purchasing career clothes (Belkin, 1986). In the words of Paul Charron, Liz Claiborne's CEO, for an entire generation of professional women, Ms. Claiborne provided the imprimatur on clothes acceptable to wear in the workplace.[2]

In the following sub-sections, I will describe in detail Liz Claiborne's positioning and the choices its management took with respect to five stages of the company's value chain: design, presentation of its merchandise, the selling process to retailers, marketing, and production/distribution choices. In the concluding paragraph of this section, I will illustrate the internal and external fit of these choices.

Liz Claiborne's positioning in a growing niche

Liz Claiborne took full advantage of the change in the demographics of the American workforce. In 1960, only 21.9 million American women were employed. By 1990, 53.5 million American women were working, making up 45 percent of the US workforce. In the mid-1970s, as this process was unfolding, the professional woman did not have much choice with respect to career clothing. There was a large void between the classic dark-blue suit (made, for instance, by Evan-Picone) and the haute couture of, for instance, Carol Horn. Ms. Claiborne, who had spent 16 years as a women's sportswear designer at Youth Guild, a division of Jonathan Logan, was aware of this increasingly expanding niche (Bratman, 1983). In 1976, after Youth Guild closed, Ms. Claiborne decided to pursue this opportunity together with her husband Arthur Ortenberg, a former consultant in the apparel industry. Within the first months they recruited Leonard Boxer, who had apparel production expertise and connections to overseas suppliers from running production at Susan Thomas Inc., and Jerome Chazen, who knew the marketing side of the women's sportswear industry. With this team of industry experts, Liz Claiborne enjoyed some upfront trust in the industry. Department stores knew Ms. Claiborne's design skills and were willing to give her coveted floor space (Bratman, 1983). In its first year, Liz Claiborne was already generating $2.2 million in sales and operating with a profit.

Design choices

In 1980, Ms. Claiborne described her offerings as "classic enough that a woman can wear them for several years. They aren't moderate in price, but aren't exorbitant, either'" (Ettore, 1980). In her first collections, no item sold for more than $100. Although the clothes did not fit the formal "dress for success" mold, they were not too far-out to be worn to the office. At the same time, customers perceived the moderately priced Liz Claiborne label as competing against top designers whose clothes cost more than twice as much (Byrne, 1982).

Ms. Claiborne had two goals in mind. She wanted to provide high value to her customers, and she wanted to make shopping easier (Bratman, 1983). It turned out that both could be achieved by an innovative kind of "color-by-the-numbers fashion" that saved customers both time and anxiety (Traub and Newman, 1985). Ms. Claiborne designed clusters of skirts, shirts, blouses and sweaters that could be mixed and matched. More precisely, each season's line comprised four to seven concept groups, each of which consisted of a balance of items such as blouses, shirts, skirts, and pants. Within each concept group, the mix-and-match design was practiced – that is, each group told a different "color story." Customers could put together an outfit not only in terms of the total look but also in terms of size, by choosing different sizes for tops and bottoms, thereby avoiding the need for alterations. Moreover, sizes were the same across styles, and colors never changed: navy blue remained the same navy blue, so that a jacket bought in one year would match a skirt or blouse bought two years before.

Presentation choices

From the beginning, Liz Claiborne focused on selling its merchandise in large department stores. In 1994, Liz Claiborne's products were offered in more than 9,500 locations in the US and Canada, yet its four largest customers (Dillard's, May, Macy's, and Federated Department Stores) accounted for 44 percent of its sales. For the end-customer to reap the benefits of Liz Claiborne's mix-and-match design, it was important that the collection be presented together and not split up. Hence, Liz Claiborne pushed for a new presentation format at its retailers. While department stores had been traditionally organized around classifications, such as blouses and pants, Liz Claiborne required a dedicated space to present its entire collection. Liz Claiborne was actually not the first company that tried to convince retailers to present an entire collection. Chazen had learned that Evan-Picone had put together a small collection of very classic merchandise and had received small, dedicated areas from department stores. By and large, however, "retailers were not sure what to do with these collections and were looking for a complementary resource which would allow them to enlarge the floor space dedicated to collection presentation."[3] Consequently, retailers were willing to listen to Chazen when he tried to convince them to present Liz Claiborne's merchandise as a collection.

To help retailers with the presentation of the collections, Liz Claiborne distributed "Claiboards" or "Lizmap diagrams" that included sketches, photos, and text showing how merchandise should be displayed in groups. Other innovations included simple measures such as naming the groups and attaching these names to hangers, thus allowing customers to quickly see which pieces of apparel belonged to each group. Moreover, a dedicated staff supported the retailers: Over twenty consultants traveled throughout the country to ensure that clothes and displays were arranged in department stores correctly. These consultants were also engaged in product information seminars for the department stores' sales personnel. In addition, 150 retail specialists who were employed by the stores in which they worked yet received training from Liz Claiborne helped with merchandise presentation, provided instruction for sales help and relayed customer feedback to Liz Claiborne's headquarters (Better, 1992).

Creating dedicated areas for Liz Claiborne merchandise was a first step toward gaining control over product presentation. Beginning in 1987, Liz Claiborne took its efforts towards product presentation one step further. In Jordan Marsh's flagship store in Boston, Liz Claiborne opened its first store-within-a-store. The 7,200 square foot "LizWorld" shop housed Liz Claiborne's full range of merchandise: Liz Collection, LizSport, LizWear, dresses, accessories, shoes, hosiery, eyewear and fragrance. Within the next few years, Liz Claiborne set up over two hundred concept shops within department stores. Moreover, since these shops increased business for retailers, Liz Claiborne successfully argued for the department stores' covering the costs for these concept shops. Liz Claiborne's Accessories division copied the presentation format and introduced its first concept shop within a department store in 1990. The shop featured a full range of handbags and small leather goods, while Liz Claiborne's latest fashion looks – fully accessorized – decorated the walls.

Selling process

Since Liz Claiborne believed its merchandise had the greatest impact if presented as a collection, it rejected orders from department stores that were not willing to present the Claiborne line the way Liz Claiborne saw fit. For instance, stores always had to buy a proper ratio of tops that matched its order of bottoms (Belkin, 1986). Moreover, buyers were required to purchase an entire concept group, i.e., they could not pick and choose among the garments shown.

Along with its emphasis on large, upscale department stores, Liz Claiborne never had a road sales force, making it the only leading garment house in the country that functioned without one (Birmingham, 1985). Retailers who wanted to look at the new Liz Claiborne line had to come to the showrooms in New York,[4] where they were welcomed by an 80 to 90 person sales force who won the title of "America's Best Sales Force" from *Sales & Marketing Management* magazine in 1987. Its centralized selling location enabled Liz Claiborne to establish relationships at a higher level than would otherwise have been possible. As Chazen explained: "On the road a salesman is lucky if he sees the buyer. But when retailers come to New York, top management often comes to see the market" (in: Skolnik, 1985). As a result, although store buyers still placed the orders, every major store president in the country visited Liz Claiborne several times a year and met with Liz Claiborne's management.

Liz Claiborne not only demanded the purchase of entire groups, but enforced also a rigid non-cancellation policy: if spring merchandise did not sell well in stores, retailers could not cut previous orders for the summer line (Better, 1992). The company created further leverage by pursuing a strict production policy of manufacturing about 5 percent less merchandise than there was demand (orders) for (Hass, 1992). This policy had two effects. First, it increased Liz Claiborne's sell-through (percentage of clothes that were sold at full price), which some industry observers pegged at 75 percent as compared to an industry average of 50 percent (Deveny, 1989). Second, the policy created a climate of fear among its retailers, giving Liz Claiborne a credible weapon with which to ensure that its desires such as those with respect to retail presentation, were met.

Customer contact and marketing

Despite being a company that had originally no direct retailing contact with its end-customers, Liz Claiborne sought feedback from them. Its consultants and retail specialists talked to customers daily, and they also arranged, during so-called "LizWeeks," in-store events for career women, such as full-blown fashion shows in which 25 to 30 outfits were shown, and "breakfast clinics" during which women had the chance to see the newest collection and to shop before they went to work. In total, Claiborne sponsored over a hundred in-store events each month across the country.

In addition, Liz Claiborne established a point-of-sales data collection system in 1985. Its Systematic Updated Retail Feedback (SURF) system provided management with details on clothes sold in 16 representative stores around the country (Skolnik, 1985).

Owing to its high name recognition and extensive coverage in the editorial pages of many fashion magazines, Liz Claiborne was able to refrain from running expensive corporate advertising campaigns. Moreover, the absence of splashy, "fantasy-driven" advertising campaigns fit well with Liz Claiborne's image as a "trusted friend." It presented all its products in co-op ads, produced in conjunction with local department stores.

Production and distribution choices

Since its inception, Liz Claiborne had contracted out the production of its merchandise. Moreover, it was one of the first big apparel makers in the 1980s to outsource production across the globe – mainly into Taiwan, Hong Kong, and South Korea. In its first year of operation, Liz Claiborne had used domestic manufacturers exclusively but encountered problems. The domestic suppliers were inflexible and unwilling to work with Liz Claiborne's new designs. Since Leonard Boxer had experience in apparel assembly in the Far East, he started to move production overseas. In 1982 Liz Claiborne was still sourcing about 50 percent of its merchandise domestically, but by 1994 only 14 percent of its merchandise was produced in the US. Liz Claiborne had contracts with over 500 suppliers in 38 countries, with most of its suppliers being situated in China, South Korea, Sri Lanka, Hong Kong, and Indonesia. Twenty-four percent of its purchases were manufactured by its ten largest suppliers, with none of its suppliers accounting for more than 5 percent.

While it provided some support to contractors, it did not engage directly in production. In 1992, Liz Claiborne opened its first major production enterprise, a 270,000 square foot plant in Augusta, Georgia, that annually turned out 500,000 to one million pounds of cotton circular-knitted fabrics (jerseys, fleeces, and other types). One advantage of local production lay in response time: this factory was able to fill an order in 20 to 25 days, as supposed to the 60 days Liz Claiborne's Asian suppliers required.

Liz Claiborne also differed from its competitors with respect to how often it offered its merchandise to its retailers. The apparel industry was used to a four-season buying cycle. Liz Claiborne, however, "invented" two more seasons, pre-spring and pre-fall to let stores buy six smaller inventory batches of fresh merchandise instead of four larger ones. While reducing inventory costs for the stores, this choice also helped Liz Claiborne's suppliers, who operated more efficiently with two extra cycles filling their slack periods. In addition to offering two more collections, Liz Claiborne offered the collections later than its competitors, with the intent that clothes appropriate for the current season be available in the stores. Thus, instead of delivering fall goods in July, the company would ship them in late August and September. In other words, Liz Claiborne offered a new season every two months, with, for instance, the clothes delivered in January and February intended to be sold and worn during February and March.

Internal and external fit

As described in the previous sub-sections, Liz Claiborne's goal of dressing the professional woman with products that provided high value was implemented through a series of choices that particularly suited its strategy. To systematize the analysis, Liz Claiborne's choices were grouped into five categories: design, presentation, selling, marketing, and production/distribution. Figure 3.3 summarizes the choices within each category and displays the interactions among the choices. The following discussion elaborates on several of the interactions indicated in figure 3.3, showing the high internal fit among Liz Claiborne's choices. A discussion of external fit is provided in the second half of this section.

Liz Claiborne's mix-and-match design could only be appreciated if the entire collection was presented together. Hence, it was important (and valuable) to push for a collection rather than a classification presentation. It should also be noted that once a collection presentation was in place, the returns to a mix-and-match design were increased. Thus, formally, collection presentation and mix-and-match design were complementary (Milgrom and Roberts, 1990).[5] The collection-presentation format was supported by a host of other choices, such as concept shops, LizBoards, retail associ-

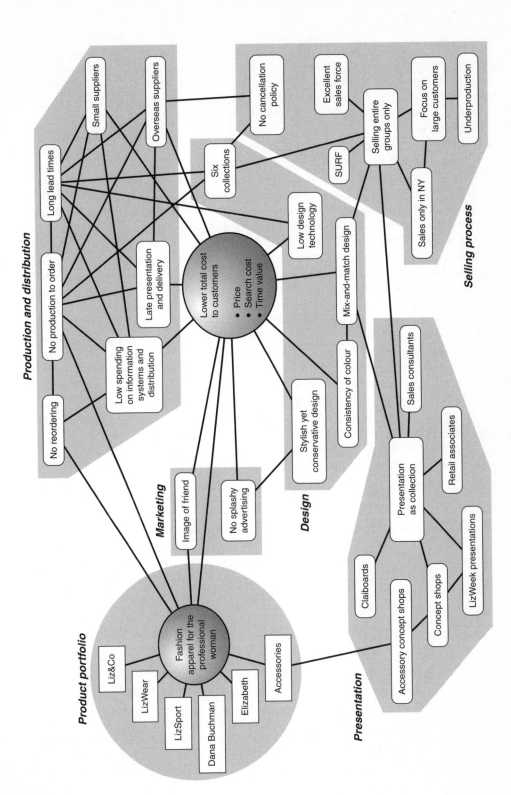

Figure 3.3   Map of interactions among Liz Claiborne's choices in the early 1990s

ates, sales consultants, and LizWeek department store presentations. Again, a complementarity existed: the value of these activities was increased by the presence of a collection presentation, while at the same time, the value of the collection presentation was increased by the support activities. Similarly, the apparel could provide its "mix-and-match value" only if the department store carried the full collection.

In this light, one can understand Liz Claiborne's strict policy of selling only complete groups to its customers. An incidental effect of this requirement was that end-customers always saw a full collection in the department store, which strengthened confidence in the brand and increased its perceived value. A consequence of this vending policy with respect to Liz Claiborne's sales organization was that Liz Claiborne had to focus on large buyers. In addition, success with such an inflexible order policy necessitated a high level of trust in its customers. Liz Claiborne's decision to sell only in its New York show room addressed these concerns. On the one hand, senior department store management would come to New York to establish the required trust. On the other hand, the lost customers (those not willing to pay for the trip to New York) were small customers who were not able to buy a full line anyhow. The trust level was further bolstered by an expert sales force and its SURF system, which provided a closer contact with end-customers than most other apparel designers could offer at the time. Lastly, Liz Claiborne's decision to offer six collections a year alleviated the inflexibility of being required to buy full lines, since a larger number of lines was offered. The ability to choose from six lines also lessened the impact of the no-cancellation policy, because each order was smaller than would have been the case with four lines. The no-cancellation policy, in turn, made long-term planning possible, which was important for Liz Claiborne's overseas sourcing strategy. Since its overseas supply system implied longer lead-times and inability to react quickly to demand changes, a steady demand was beneficial. In return, Liz Claiborne could provide high value (and achieve high margins), owing to the lower production costs of its overseas suppliers.

Since Liz Claiborne focused on large buyers, there was a potential risk of being squeezed by its retailers. By following a strict underproduction policy, however, the company retained leverage over its retailers. Moreover, this strategy had beneficial side-effects. By producing slightly below demand, the sell-through was increased, which meant that Liz Claiborne merchandise was less frequently on sale (or was on sale in lower quantities). This in turn fortified the company's "every-day value" claim.

It is important to note that Liz Claiborne's set of choices involved tradeoffs. Its decision to use mainly suppliers located in the Far East and to invest little in design, distribution, and information technology all helped to keep costs down, yet led to three disadvantages: (1) it generated long lead times between the start of the design to the delivery of the finished product, (2) retailers could not reorder, and (3) no merchandise could be made to order.

In evaluating the severity of these disadvantages, the *external fit* of Liz Claiborne's set of choices becomes apparent. All the disadvantages were alleviated by external factors: customer demand, retailers' requirements, available technology, and competitors' strengths. First, the impossibility of reordering was not crucial, since Liz Claiborne faced high customer demand mainly for fashion apparel that was not reordered anyway. Second, the health of Liz Claiborne's primary retail channel, department stores, was relatively solid during the 1980s. As a consequence, department stores were not (yet) concerned with reducing inventory which would have put pressure on Liz Claiborne to offer reordering. Third, the information and design technology that would allow an efficient reordering system coupled with shortened design cycles was only in its early stages of development. As a result, there did not exist a feasible alternative set-up (in other words, a different peak) with which competitors could attack Liz Claiborne's position. Yet, imitating Liz Claiborne, i.e., trying to climb the same peak and competing on the same terms, was very difficult, because the entire system of choices would have to be duplicated. Consequently, Liz Claiborne enjoyed a strong competitive position that enabled it to easily sell the majority of its output. In turn, with such "guaranteed demand," long lead times and no production-to-order did not pose a problem.

In sum, Liz Claiborne's choices showed high internal fit and – given the environmental conditions at the time – high external fit: in the 1980s, Liz Claiborne had positioned itself on a high peak in the performance landscape. However, during the late 1980s and early 1990s, changes in customer demand, retailers' economic health, and technological advances reduced the external fit of this coherent system: the height of Liz Claiborne's peak started to decrease while a new peak arose in the performance landscape.

Liz Claiborne's Fall

Changes in customer demand and product portfolio

By the early 1990s, the trend towards "casualization" of the workplace had picked up momentum – a development that Liz Claiborne had first underestimated.[6] More and more companies allowed their employees to dress casually, yet customers could not find an attractive assortment of Liz Claiborne apparel to fulfill this need. Liz Claiborne eventually responded to this shift in customer demand and increased its offerings in the casual and more basic categories. In addition, in May 1992, Liz Claiborne acquired for $31 million Russ Togs, Inc., which had filed for Chapter 11 protection the previous November. Russ Togs manufactured moderately priced women's sportswear under the Russ Togs and The Villager labels. The acquisition was intended to take Liz Claiborne into national and regional chain department stores and the moderate areas of traditional department stores.

While these shifts in its product portfolio appeared to be natural responses to changes in customer demands, the shift in the product portfolio had far-reaching consequences: the company increased its number of apparel categories in which reordering had become a convenience offered by many competitors, yet it was not set up to efficiently offer reordering.

Changes in the retail channel

During the late 1980s and early 1990s, the industry of Liz Claiborne's main distribution channel, that is, traditional department stores, underwent wrenching change. Several hostile takeovers and leveraged buyouts stretched the liquidity of many department store chains, often to the point of bankruptcy. Prominent examples of this development included Federated Department Stores, which filed for Chapter 11 protection in January 1990, R. H. Macy, which declared bankruptcy in January 1991, and Carter Hawley Hale, which filed for bankruptcy protection in February 1991. As a result, department stores tried to save cash wherever they could.

First, the stores cut down the retail support they provided to their vendors. For instance, much less attention was spent on the presentation and restocking of goods on the department store floor. Liz Claiborne, being accustomed to having retailers pay for concept shops and presentation support, failed to compensate for this deficit. Since careful presentation of Liz Claiborne's apparel as a collection was essential to its value proposition, the deterioration of shop-floor presentation was particularly detrimental for the company.

Second, department stores demanded larger discounts from their vendors. Similar to its unwillingness to pay for retailing support, Liz Claiborne refused to cut prices.[7] Past success had created a belief of infallibility coupled with a tinge of hubris at Liz Claiborne, as it has at many other successful companies (Miller, 1994). In 1989, Jay Margolis, the highest executive at the firm after the remaining founders, proudly proclaimed: "We like to think of ourselves as the IBM of the garment district" (Deveny, 1989). Liz Claiborne's strong internal culture – the company directory still listed its employees alphabetically by first name – had created a belief in the organization's near invulnerability to environmental changes (Milliken, 1990). Moreover, negative performance was frequently attributed to external factors rather than to internal problems, another common pattern in firms responding to downturns (Ford, 1985). A former Claiborne executive commented as follows: "If the product didn't sell, it was always someone else's fault. The buyer didn't show it right, or it wasn't delivered the right way" (in: Caminiti, 1994). Yet, Liz Claiborne's apparel, with sagging sales and with lower margins for its retailers than other vendors' apparel provided, became less attractive to department stores and received even less attention and, eventually less floor space.

Third, to alleviate their liquidity problems, department stores aggressively pursued inventory reduction. Increasingly, they demanded that manufacturers offer an option to reorder items, so they could avoid buying in bulk and having to store merchandise in their stock-rooms.

The old peak declines and a new peak arises

In addition to the retailers' demand for reordering, Liz Claiborne faced new competitors who employed a different production paradigm which allowed them to offer reordering efficiently. Improvements in information-, design-, and production-technology, as well as the spread of standards in bar coding and point-of-sales terminals, had made short reordering cycles, shorter design cycles, and partial production-to-order economically feasible (Abernathy, Dunlop, Hammond, and Weil, 1995). In other words, technological changes had created a new peak in the performance landscape that required a different set of choices. For instance, Jones Apparel, one of Liz Claiborne's strongest new competitors, sourced 55 percent of its products domestically, as compared to 14 percent for Liz Claiborne (D'Innocenzio, 1994). This sourcing strategy in addition to heavy investments in design technology allowed Jones to react quickly to new trends in the marketplace.

At the same time, with the demands of retailers and customers shifting, Liz Claiborne's set of choices, although still internally consistent, had become less appropriate to the environment. The company's disadvantages, in particular the long design cycles, and lack of reordering and production-to-order, had become more costly. Whereas in the 1980s these disadvantages were small, given Liz Claiborne's product portfolio, the requirements of retailers, and the high costs of a lean production model, the disadvantages had grown in the 1990s: the relative height of Liz Claiborne's peak had declined.

Playing an incomplete game

In 1991, faced with increasing demands from retailers for reordering, Liz Claiborne initiated a reordering program for items in its casual division. The company's management followed the path described in the change framework as *playing an incomplete game*: Liz Claiborne changed single elements in its activity system with the consequence of a further performance decline. The firm moved down from its local peak to even lower performance.

The only elements of "quick response" – as these reordering programs became known in the apparel industry – that Liz Claiborne implemented were to enable department stores' buyers to submit their orders electronically and to promise to fill orders within two weeks. On the production side, no changes were made. The company produced a warehouse full of merchandise and sold it as orders came in. Since inventory costs had never entered Liz Claiborne's profitability measurements, the inefficiency of this reordering process remained financially hidden.[8] Moreover, past success had created a "buffer" of $300–$500 million in cash and securities on Liz Claiborne's balance sheet (see table 3.1). With this buffer, Liz Claiborne never experienced the liquidity problems that could have resulted from having funds tied up in inventory. Slack resources had reduced the necessity for Liz Claiborne's management to act upon this inefficiency – a common pitfall of past success (Milliken and Lant, 1991).

In addition, allowing department store buyers to place orders (rather than having a vendor-driven continuous replenishment program) caused large swings in the volume of orders, which in turned meant that either orders went unfilled or inventory was increased even further. Moreover, department store buyers whose allotted purchasing budget was exhausted often would not reorder at all – even styles which had been sold out – thus leaving popular styles out of stock.

As figure 3.3 illustrates, the choice of "no-reordering" was intimately tied to many other choices Liz Claiborne had made. Simply offering reordering to retailers without making further changes in the system as a whole was bound to create problems. As Hammond (1993) outlines, partial production-to-order and a shortened product development cycle are necessary if a company is to pursue a quick-response strategy efficiently. Otherwise, inventory at the manufacturer starts to accumulate. However, Liz Claiborne's lead times were nine months, about three months longer than lead times of some of its competitors (D'Innocenzio, 1994). Figure 3.3 is also helpful in identifying the reasons for Liz Claiborne's long design-to-market cycle: the location of most of its suppliers in the Far East, the small size of its suppliers who did not invest in (information) technology that would have reduced cycle times, and its small investments in technology, such as CAD systems that could reduce time-to-market. As this

Table 3.1 Financial data for Liz Claiborne, Inc. (all figures in millions except EPS and share price)

	1996	1995	1994	1993	1992	1991	1990	1989	1988	1987	1986	1985	1984	1983	1982	1981
Sales	2,217	2,081	2,163	2,204	2,194	2,007	1,729	1,411	1,184	1,053	813	557	391	228	160	116
growth	6.5%	−3.8%	−1.9%	0.5%	9.3%	16.1%	22.5%	19.2%	12.4%	29.5%	46.0%	42.3%	71.1%	42.9%	37.0%	46.0%
COGS	1,341.1	1,290.9	1,407.7	1,452.4	1,364.2	1,207.5	1,030.8	841.7	758.3	655.6	502.2	341.7	243.8	144.7	109.6	76.2
Gross margin	39.52%	37.99%	34.92%	34.10%	37.82%	39.84%	40.38%	40.35%	35.95%	37.74%	38.23%	38.65%	37.69%	36.73%	31.50%	34.76%
SG&A	641.7	600.5	604.4	568.3	507.5	471.1	393.1	321.9	255.5	194.7	146.3	97.3	66.3	40.1	27	18.2
SG&A/sales	28.94%	28.85%	27.94%	25.78%	23.13%	23.47%	22.74%	22.81%	21.58%	18.49%	18.00%	17.47%	16.94%	17.53%	16.88%	15.58%
NI	155.7	126.9	82.9	126.9	218.8	222.7	205.8	164.6	110.3	114.4	86.2	60.6	41.9	22.4	14.1	10.2
growth	22.7%	53.1%	−34.7%	−42.0%	−1.8%	8.2%	25.0%	49.2%	−3.6%	32.7%	42.2%	44.6%	87.1%	59.2%	37.9%	64.5%
NI/sales	7.02%	6.10%	3.83%	5.76%	9.97%	11.10%	11.90%	11.67%	9.32%	10.86%	10.60%	10.88%	10.71%	9.79%	8.79%	8.73%
EPS	2.15	1.69	1.06	1.56	2.61	2.61	2.37	1.87	1.26	1.32	1.00	0.71	0.50	0.27	0.17	0.13
ROE	15.3%	12.8%	8.4%	13.0%	21.9%	24.5%	28.9%	26.9%	24.1%	32.0%	34.8%	37.2%	40.1%	34.7%	34.2%	38.1%
Cash+securities	528.8	437.8	330.3	309.2	425.6	471.5	431.8	372.9	278.3	160.4	104	56.2	19	11.2	na	na
Inventory	349.4	393.3	423	436.6	385.9	322	265.7	198.2	168	156.4	114.9	72.8	73.4	34.2	21.3	na
Inv. days	95.1	111.2	109.7	109.7	103.2	97.3	94.1	85.9	80.9	87.1	83.5	77.8	109.9	86.3	70.9	0.0
LT debt	1	1.1	1.2	1.3	1.4	1.6	15.1	15.6	14.1	14.5	0	10	0	0	0	0
D/E	0.10%	0.11%	0.12%	0.13%	0.14%	0.18%	2.12%	2.55%	3.08%	4.06%	0.00%	6.15%	0.00%	0.00%	0.00%	0.00%
Market value	2,796.8	2,064.9	1,335.0	1,844.1	3,495.0	3,610.6	2,581.8	2,109.8	1,509.1	1,434.4	1,844.0	1,035.4	539.2	357.0	194.6	97.3
Share price	38.63	27.50	17.00	22.63	41.63	42.25	29.75	24.00	17.25	16.50	21.38	12.13	6.38	4.25	2.33	1.22

example illustrates, incremental changes in a tightly coupled system rarely lead to the desired result. Not until a new management had changed a whole series of choices in the design, distribution, and production set-up, moving Liz Claiborne to a new peak, did performance improve.

Liz Claiborne's Renaissance

In 1994, with Liz Claiborne's sales declining and net income plummeting by 35 percent, Paul Charron was hired as new Chief Operating Officer. Charron had previously worked for Procter & Gamble and General Foods, and had most recently been EVP at VF Corporation, the manufacturer of Wrangler and Lee jeans. In 1995, Charron replaced Chazen as CEO, while Chazen remained chairman of the company. This position was also taken on by Charron in 1996, when Chazen retired.

Beginning with his tenure as CEO in 1995, Charron pursued three avenues of change within Liz Claiborne: first, a revitalization and modernization of choices within presentation and design that had become neglected over the previous years. Second, a shift in Liz Claiborne's product portfolio. Third, a wide-ranging restructuring of the company's production and distribution set-up.

Revitalization of presentation and design

In 1995, Charron created, under the name "LizEdge," a new in-store marketing department. The company hired 125 sales associates, each responsible for in-store presentation of better sportswear in four locations. At the same time, Liz Claiborne started to install new in-store fixtures (LizView) in department stores around the country. By April 1997, 200 LizView shops had been installed, with plans to add another 400 by the end of 1997. Similar to the success in the mid-1980s with the LizWorld shops, sales increased an average 19 percent after shops had been installed. In addition to providing the new fixtures, the firm began a training program (Liz & Learn) that provided sales support and incentives for department store salespeople.

To obtain a better understanding of the marketplace, Charron commissioned a study on the characteristics and shopping behavior of Liz Claiborne's customers. One of the study's findings was that customer confidence about picking outfits had risen considerably. While in the early 1980s Liz Claiborne's function had been to show what apparel was suitable for the workplace, customers now asked to be presented with options. In the words of Charron, the customer "has gained confidence to 'put it together' by herself if she is provided with cues."[9] These insights were taken into account in designing the new LizView in-store display units.

Another finding of the consumer study was that a typical customer played a large number of "roles" during the day (professional woman, soccer-mom, and so on) without having much time to change clothes. Hence, versatility of apparel and the ability to dress up or down quickly (for example, by adding accessories or changing a top) were valued very highly. As a result, Liz Claiborne strengthened its efforts to allow its customers to mix-and-match across divisions (between LizSport and LizWear, for example).

To ensure that colors were held constant across collections and groups, designers of all units were required to use the same color card. Moreover, meetings among the designers from all the company's businesses were held on a regular monthly schedule; previously, they had met haphazardly.

Changes in product portfolio

For the long term, Charron was concerned that the current trend in retailing, the decline of the department stores and the rise of the discount stores such as Wal-Mart, would continue. Concurrent with the consolidation in the retail market, he expected a consolidation in the apparel supply market. As noted, prior to Charron's arrival, Liz Claiborne had acquired Russ Togs, Inc. The sales of this division, called the "Special Markets Unit," increased to $112 million by the end of 1994 (partly inflated by sell-offs of excess inventory) and decreased to $77.3 million by the end of 1996. Charron decided to enlarge this unit. His vision was to have a different Liz Claiborne brand for every retail channel and every price point: the Russ label for the "budget" segment (to be sold at stores like Wal-Mart), The Villager, and a new brand, First Issue, intended for the "moderate" segment (to be sold, for instance, at Sears); another new brand, Emma James, for the "upper moderate" segment (to be sold at stores like Federated Department Stores); the traditional Liz Claiborne Collection and the casual lines, including LizWear, for the "better" segment (to be sold, for example, at Dillard's); and the successful Dana Buchman line for the "bridge" segment (to be sold, for instance, at Saks Fifth Avenue).[10]

In order to increase general brand awareness, national brand advertising was increased substantially. Using model Niki Taylor as the centerpiece of its advertising strategy, Liz Claiborne tried to rejuvenate its image, which had grown stale, especially in the eyes of the new generation of professional women. In addition to the public media campaign the company made a statement within the fashion industry by opening a 19,000 square foot flagship store at 650 Fifth Avenue at the end of 1994.

Production and distribution changes

While the new initiatives with respect to presentation consisted mainly of the modernization of previous choices, fundamental changes occurred in the way Liz Claiborne orchestrated its production and distribution. In 1995, Charron announced a comprehensive program, LizFirst, which was geared toward increasing efficiency. Its goals were to reduce excess inventories by 40 percent, cut cycle time by 25 percent, and reduce SG&A by $100 million over three years. Two ways in which Liz Claiborne sought to fulfill its goals were to reduce the number of suppliers by half and to shift 50 percent of its production to the western hemisphere. By concentrating production within larger suppliers who could afford and were willing to invest in information and production technology, and by moving production closer to the region of retail, cycle times could be shortened.

Liz Claiborne also switched back to four instead of six production and design cycles. With six seasons, that is, a two-month delivery period, none of the merchandise could be made to order. With four seasons, the three-month delivery period allowed the company to produce at least some items to order for the third month of a season. Liz

Claiborne also started with some of its clients a vendor-based restocking system, or "retail inventory management" program (LizRim), in which Liz Claiborne automatically replenished basic merchandise (mainly jeans, slacks, and shorts) to prior negotiated inventory levels at department stores. This system dramatically lowered stock-outs and kept inventory levels at department stores small, without causing huge production and order swings for Liz Claiborne.

One of the pioneers of such a vendor-based system had been Procter & Gamble (in co-operation with Wal-Mart). Later, VF Corporation and Haggar were among the first to adopt a similar system in the basic apparel industry. Charron's prior work experience at Procter & Gamble and VF Corporation provided him with valuable knowledge about the activities needed to support a successful implementation. At Liz Claiborne, the program was spearheaded by the casual wear division, whose new president had been recruited by Charron from Haggar in December 1994. Charron also brought further expertise in-house by hiring a new chief information officer, who had previously been an executive vice president for business systems/logistics at a leading apparel retailer, and a new senior vice president for manufacturing and sourcing who had a background in low-cost private label manufacturing.

By 1997, LizFirst showed good results: excess inventory had been cut by 47 percent from 1994 levels, its retail management program was in 1,200 stores, operating expenses had been reduced by $82 million, and cycle time in certain key processes had been cut by 40 percent. Moreover, the number of factories Liz Claiborne used had been cut by half.

Internal fit on a new peak

Following the structure of figure 3.3, figure 3.4 depicts Liz Claiborne's choices as of 1997 in the five categories of design, presentation, selling, marketing, and production/distribution and displays the interconnections between the choices. The locations of the five categories on the maps have been kept approximately constant to facilitate comparison of the choices between the two points in time.

We find a familiar cluster of reinforcing choices dealing with the strengthening of the retail presentation. As noted above, Liz Claiborne was rejuvenating its former successful formula: mix-and-match design coupled with a careful presentation strategy involving, among other features, new displays and sales associates. The main changes within these categories were that mix-and-match was extended across divisions and that Liz Claiborne, rather than the retailers, paid for the presentation support.

The largest number of new choices clustered around Liz Claiborne's new reordering process (LizRim), and around the system to allow partial production-to-order. Whereas the presentation support was mainly geared towards Liz Claiborne's traditional better sportswear, LizRim was designed to fulfill the requirements of mass-merchants that would carry its budget brands. However, because of its large size, the Liz Casual division, which belonged to the better sportswear division, was initially accounting for the largest use of LizRim. By keeping out-of-stock positions low, LizRim reinforced efforts with respect to the renewed presentation format—the best trained salespeople and most cleverly designed display units could not sell merchandise that was out of stock.

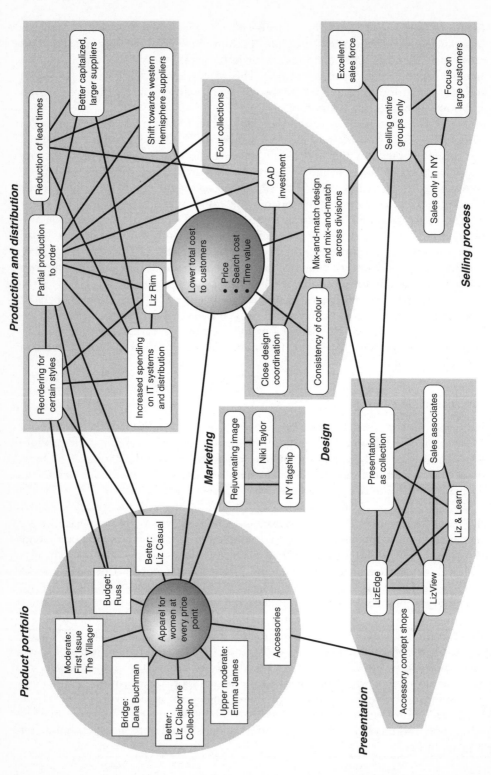

Figure 3.4   Map of interactions among Liz Claiborne's choices in 1997

Discussion

Why had Liz Claiborne's old management been unable to respond to the environmental changes, a common finding for declining organizations (Cameron, Whetten, and Kim, 1987)? The analysis presented above suggests that a major contributing factor was that Liz Claiborne's management faced fit-conserving change. Environmental changes had decreased the value of a part of Liz Claiborne's set of choices (in particular choices concerning production and distribution). Small, incremental changes – exploring the local neighborhood of the current position – no longer sufficed. At the same time, larger, systemic changes lay outside the mental maps of existing management. Different mental maps of the changed performance landscape were required to move Liz Claiborne to a new performance peak.

The purpose of the framework developed in this chapter was to explore how fit influences the link between environmental changes and ensuing firm change. To this end, I suggested that a useful distinction could be made between environmental changes that affect external and/or internal fit. Whereas environments have been differentiated in the existing literature in terms of stability and turbulence – a distinction based on the unpredictability and frequency of performance landscape changes – I instead suggest classifying environmental changes with respect to the impact they have on the landscape. The framework thus offers an alternative and complementary classification. With this classification, the effect of environmental change on firms can be described as fit-destroying and fit-conserving—a useful distinction, since managers react differently to these two types of changes. Managers will have a particularly difficult time reacting to fit-conserving change because the internal logic of the existing system of choices remains intact.

The argument outlined in this chapter finds a parallel in the conceptual approach of Henderson and Clark (1990) who study a particular type of environmental change (a technological innovation) and its effect on incumbent firms. They suggest that rather than distinguishing between incremental and radical innovations (thus measuring the magnitude of change), it is useful to classify innovations with respect to their impact on interactions within existing product-systems. Analogously, I argue for the classification of environmental changes according to their impact on internal and external fit, rather than by their frequency. The new distinction Henderson and Clark (1990) introduce is whether an innovation changes architectural knowledge (how parts interact) or component knowledge (how parts work). This distinction allowed Henderson (1993) to explain the inertia of incumbent firms facing innovations in the photolithographic alignment equipment industry. Similarly, it is hoped that the framework proposed here and the distinction between fit-conserving and fit-destroying change will provide a new lens through which the impact of environmental changes on firms with high internal fit can be better understood.

In addition to a framework concerning environmental change, I believe that the maps of the firm's choices and their interactions can provide a helpful tool for understanding the structural requirements of change in a system with tight internal fit. For instance, in the present case, Liz Claiborne wanted to offer reordering. As figures 3.3 and 3.4 illustrate, the choice of whether or not to offer reordering was tied to many other choices. Figure 3.3 can be used to predict the changes that were necessary to implement an efficient reordering process. Directly affected were the previous choices to keep spending low on information and distribution technology and the decision not to produce any apparel to order. One could call these "first-order" changes. However, to produce some merchandise to order, other choices had to be changed: part of the supplier base had to be shifted to the western hemisphere, the number of collections had to be reduced to four (which had implications for the design process), the delivery dates had to be moved up in time to allow information gathering early in the season for production delivered late in the season, and lead times had to be reduced. In turn, to reduce lead time, increased investments in design technology, and a shift to larger, better capitalized suppliers who could invest in information and production technology had to follow. Thus, not only first-order, but also second- and third-order changes were necessary. The mapping of choices and their interactions as in figures 3.3 and 3.4 make these ripple effects clearly visible. At the same time, these maps point out those choices that did *not* have to be changed. For instance, the presentation format, which was mainly connected to the design concept of mix-and-match, was not affected by changes in the production set-up.

Future Research Directions

The framework outlined in this chapter provided a new link between the issues of organizational adaptation and internal fit. Specifically, I suggested a link between the structural interdependencies among an organization's choices and the ability of the organization's management to respond to different types of environmental changes that affect the interdependencies in different ways. This chapter is clearly only a first step to unraveling this complex relationship.

Consider, for instance, the issue of how managers create and update their mental maps. How do managers form representations of complex, interdependent systems, such as their firms and their associated strategies? What consequences arise from these simplified representations? While Gavetti and Levinthal (2000) and Siggelkow (2002b) have started to shed some light on the consequences of simplified or faulty representations, much more work needs to be done, especially on the question of how managers update their mental maps. The concepts of first-order and second-order learning (Watzlawick, Weakland, and Fisch, 1974; Lant and Mezias, 1992) might become helpful in this regard. First-order learning is an incremental, conservative process that is geared towards sustaining the current condition. Second-order learning involves the unlearning of prior premises, and the developing of new frames and new interpretive schemes (Bartunek, 1984).[11] In our terminology, first-order learning can be thought of as updating the mental map around the local neighborhood of the current position. In contrast, second-order learning is a broader scanning of the landscape resulting in a changed mental map that recognizes new peaks. How can managers switch successfully between first-order and second-order learning when environmental changes necessitate such a switch yet offer little cues that such a switch is required, as occurs with fit-conserving change? It appears that incumbent managers frequently cannot perform such a switch, and that organizations have to rely on "importing" new mental models through executive succession (Greiner and Bhambri, 1989; Lant, Milliken, and Batra,

1992; Virany, Tushman, and Romanelli, 1992) and replacement of entire management teams.[12]

While managerial action is shaped by the cognitive representations held by managers, actions are also influenced by the organizational context in which managers have to make their decisions. Elements of organizational structure, such as hierarchical communication channels and incentive systems, often do interact (Rivkin and Siggelkow, 2002) and can help or impede a firm to respond to environmental changes depending on the degree of internal interdependency and type of environmental change. The interplay between organizational structure, the degree of interdependency among a firm's choices, and managers' processes to create representations of these highly complex systems is likely to be a fertile ground for future research efforts. Using the terminology of the strategy process framework proposed by Chakravarthy and White (2002), such work would link elements of the organizational context to the decision and action premises of managers, while evaluating the resulting decisions and actions taking the characteristics of the business context of the respective organization into account.

The issue of organizational adaptation in response to environmental change raises the question of how a firm can move from one configuration to another configuration – and the current article throws some light on this question. How a firm develops its configuration in the first place is left unsaid, however, pointing to a broad, largely unexplored, issue of organizational development. Firms are not born with fully elaborated systems of choices as depicted in figures 3.3 and 3.4. While a substantial amount of research has developed a series of typologies for different types of configurations (for example, Burns and Stalker, 1961; Miles and Snow, 1978; Mintzberg, 1979), the possible paths towards configurations have received much less attention, as lamented, for example, by Miller (1996) in his review of progress in the literature on configurations (for one of the few attempts to address this issue, see Siggelkow, 2002a).

Closely related to the question of patterns of development is the question concerning the motors behind development. What are the drivers that propel a firm along a particular trajectory and what are the consequences of different drivers? The work by Van de Ven (for example, Van de Ven and Poole, 1995) makes admirable strides towards addressing these issues but still leaves open many avenues for further research.

Common to all the possible research directions outlined above is an emphasis on dynamics. While the notion of "fit" is an inherently static concept (as it is measured at a given point in time), the dynamic issues surrounding fit are of both theoretic and practical importance. The payoff to carefully conducted research on these issues promises to be high. At the same time, though, the challenges are formidable. Different methodological approaches are likely to be called for. One important direction of deepening the research is to drill down further into the organizations, to the level of individual decisions and accompanying decisions processes and cognitive frames. This work would require an even deeper immersion, an even finer level of detail as provided, for example, in the current study of Liz Claiborne. Such work is likely to be feasible only for issues with tightly defined timeframes as researchers might be able to observe such processes first-hand at an organization. For other issues, such as the general organizational development towards a configuration – a process which may take decades – this methodology is likely to be infeasible. In these cases, recourse to archival material, interviews, and other information that can help triangulate gathered information might be the only possible approach (see, for instance, the discussion of "historical ethnography" by Vaughan (1996)).

Lastly, while inductive, well-grounded empirical process research will yield intriguing new insights, conceptual work and formal modeling will continue to be important complementary research approaches. A useful balance needs to be struck between initially unguided field-based research that is open to a broad range of findings, and more theory-driven research. In particular, as we attempt to move research from a small number of in-depth observations to larger samples, only a joint-effort of induction (to identify possible variables) and deduction (to identify the crucial variables from the large set of possible variables) is likely to be successful.

Notes

This chapter is an extended version of a paper published under the same title in the *Academy of Management Journal*. Reprint permission was granted by the Copyright Clearance Center, Inc. I would like to thank Kim Cameron, Giovanni Gavetti, Pankaj Ghemawat, Bruce Kogut, Daniel Levinthal, Johannes Pennings, Michael Porter, Daniel Raff, Jan Rivkin, Harbir Singh, Sidney Winter, and participants at the 1999 Strategic Management Society Meeting, Berlin, and the 2001 Strategic Management Society Mini-Conference on Strategy Process, St. Gallen, for their helpful comments. Any remaining errors are mine. Financial support by the Division of Research of the Harvard Business School and the Reginald H. Jones Center for Management Strategy, Policy and Organization at the University of Pennsylvania is gratefully acknowledged.

1   For formal models of performance landscapes with these features see Kauffman (1993).
2   Personal communication with Paul R. Charron, February 30, 1997.
3   Personal communication with Jerome Chazen, October 7, 1997.
4   Until 1990, all of Liz Claiborne's (domestic) sales were performed through its New York showroom. In order to reach smaller specialty stores, Liz Claiborne decided to open two small showrooms in Atlanta and Dallas in 1990 and 1992. However, in these showrooms only dresses, accessories, jewelry and Liz & Co. better casual knitwear was displayed. The traditional sportswear was not shown, since the minimum orders were too high for most specialty stores.
5   Two elements A and B are complementary if the marginal benefit of A increases with the level of B, and vice versa. This concept can be extended to non-continuous cases as long as A and B and their combinations can be ordered (Milgrom and Roberts, 1990).
6   Personal communication with James Lewis, President Liz Claiborne Casual, February 30, 1997.
7   Personal communication with Jerome Chazen, October 7, 1997.
8   Personal communication with James Lewis, President Liz Claiborne Casual, February 30, 1997.
9   personal communication with Paul R. Charron, February 30, 1997.
10   personal communication with Paul R. Charron, February 30, 1997.
11   Fundamentally related are the concepts of single- and double-loop learning discussed by Argyris and Schön (1978).
12   Liz Claiborne's experience is no exception. By 1993, the year prior to Charron's arrival, Liz Claiborne's top management team consisted of Chazen and a group of eight executives who had been with the 17–year-old company on average eight and a half years. In 1994, Charron, an outsider with experience in the new production paradigm who was not men-

tally tied to the old system, was hired. Moreover, Charron aggressively changed the composition of Liz Claiborne's top management team by hiring further expertise from outside and promoting younger managers from within. At the end of 1995, the top six managers had an average tenure of four years (the median was one and a half years). Similarly, from the extended top management group in 1993, which consisted of 25 managers (all managers from the vice president level up), only eight were left among the top 28 managers in 1995 (Dun & Bradstreet, various years; Liz Claiborne 10K, various years).

References

Abernathy, F. H., Dunlop, J. T., Hammond, J. H., and Weil, D. 1995: The information-integrated channel: a study of the US apparel industry in transition, *Brookings Papers: Microeconomics*, 7, 175–246.

Argyris, C. and Schön, D. A. 1978: *Organizational learning*. Reading, MA: Addison–Wesley.

Bartunek, J. M. 1984: Changing interpretive schemes and organizational restructuring: the example of a religious order, *Administrative Science Quarterly*, 29, 355–72.

Belkin, L. 1986: Redesigning Liz Claiborne's empire, *New York Times*, May 4, 1.

Better, N. 1992: The secret of Liz Claiborne's success, *Working Woman*, 17 (4), 68.

Birmingham, J. 1985: Claiborne's men, *Daily News Record*, May 28, S11.

Bratman, F. 1983: Liz Claiborne and a landmark, *New York Times*, February 27, 6.

Burns, T. and Stalker, G. M. 1961: *The management of innovation*. London: Tavistock.

Byrne, J. 1982: Liz, tailor, *Forbes*, January 4, 286.

Cameron, K. S., Whetten, D. A., and Kim, M. U. 1987: Organizational dysfunctions of decline, *Academy of Management Journal*, 30, 126–38.

Caminiti, S. 1994: Liz Claiborne: How to get focused again, *Fortune*, January 24, 85.

Chandler, A. D., Jr 1962: *Strategy and structure: chapters in the history of industrial enterprise*. Cambridge, MA: MIT Press.

Chakravarthy, B. S. and White, R. E. 2002: Strategy process: forming, implementing and changing strategies. In A. Pettigrew, H. Thomas, and R. Whittington (eds), *Handbook of strategy and management*, London: Sage, 182-205.

Deveny, K. 1989: Can Ms. Fashion bounce back?, *Business Week*, January 16, 64.

D'Innocenzio, A. 1994: Jones, Claiborne tussle for turf, *Women's Wear Daily*, March 23, 8.

Drazin, R. and Van de Ven, A. H. 1985: alternative forms of fit in contingency theory, *Administrative Science Quarterly*, 30, 514–39.

Ettore, B. 1980: Spotlight working woman's dressmaker, *New York Times*, July 6, 7.

Ford, J. D. 1985: The effects of causal attributions on decision makers' responses to performance downturns, *Academy of Management Review*, 10, 770–86.

Gavetti, G. and Levinthal, D. 2000: Looking forward and looking backward: cognitive and experiential, *Administrative Science Quarterly*, 45, 113–37.

Gersick, C. J. G. 1991: Revolutionary change theories: a multilevel exploration of the punctuated equilibrium paradigm, *Academy of Management Review*, 16, 10–36.

Greiner, L. E. and Bhambri, A. 1989: New CEO intervention and dynamics of deliberate strategic change, *Strategic Management Journal*, 10, 67–86.

Hambrick, D. C. and Mason, P. A. 1984: Upper echelons: the organization as a reflection of its top managers, *Academy of Management Review*, 9, 193–206.

Hammond, J. H., 1993: Quick response in retail/manufacturing channels. In J. Hausman and R. Nolan (eds), *Globalization, technology, and competition*, Boston: Harvard Business School Press, 185–214.

Hannan, M. T. and Freeman, J. 1984: Structural inertia and organizational change, *American*

Sociological Review, 49, 149–64.

Hass, N. 1992: Like a rock, *Financial World*, February 4, 22.

Hayes, R. H. and Jaikumar, R. 1988: Manufacturing's crisis: new technologies, obsolete organizations, *Harvard Business Review*, 66 (September–October), 77–85.

Henderson, R. M. 1993: Underinvestment and incompetence as responses to radical innovation: evidence from the photolithographic alignment equipment industry, *RAND Journal of Economics*, 24, 248–70.

Henderson, R. M. and Clark, K. B. 1990: Architectural innovation: the reconfiguration of existing product technologies and the failure of established firms, *Administrative Science Quarterly*, 35, 9–30.

Jaikumar, R. 1986: Postindustrial manufacturing, *Harvard Business Review*, 64 (6), 69–76.

Kauffman, S. A. 1993: *The origins of order: self–organization and selection in evolution.* New York: Oxford University Press.

Khandwalla, P. N., 1973: Viable and effective organizational designs of firms, *Academy of Management Journal*, 16 , 481–95.

Lant, T. K. and Mezias, S. 1992: An organizational learning model of convergence and reorientation, *Organization Science*, 3, 47–71.

Lant, T. K., Milliken, F. J., and Batra, B. 1992: The role of managerial learning and interpretation in strategic persistence and reorientation: an empirical exploration, *Strategic Management Journal*, 13, 585–608.

Lawrence, P. R. and Lorsch, J. W. 1967: *Organization and Environment.* Boston: Harvard Business School Press.

Learned, E. P., Christensen, C. R., Andrews, K. R., and Guth, W. D. 1961: *Business policy: text and cases.* Homewood: Irwin.

Lee, M. 1994: Weaving their way home, *Washington Post*, August 25, B9.

Levinthal, D. and Siggelkow, N. 2001: Linking the old and the new: modular and integrated adaptation to the internet. Working paper, Wharton School, University of Pennsylvania, Philadelphia.

Levinthal, D. A., 1992: Surviving Schumpeterian environments: an evolutionary perspective, *Industrial and Corporate Change*, 1, 427–43.

Levinthal, D. A. 1997: Adaptation on rugged landscapes, *Management Science*, 43, 934–50.

Levitt, B. and March, J. G. 1988: Organizational learning, *Annual Review of Sociology*, 14, 319–40.

MacDuffie, J. P. 1995: Human resource bundles and manufacturing performance: organizational logic and flexible production systems in the world automobile industry, *Industrial and Labor Relations Review*, 48, 197–221.

Miles, R. E. and Snow, C. C. 1978: *Organizational strategy, structure and process.* New York: McGraw–Hill.

Milgrom, P. R. and Roberts, J. 1990: The economics of modern manufacturing: technology, strategy, and organization, *American Economic Review*, 80, 511–28.

Milgrom, P. R. and Roberts, J. 1995: Complementarities and fit: strategy, structure, and organizational change in manufacturing, *Journal of Accounting and Economics*, 19, 179–208.

Miller, D. 1986: Configurations of strategy and structure: towards a synthesis, *Strategic Management Journal*, 7, 233–49.

Miller, D. 1993: Some organizational consequences of CEO succession, *Academy of Management Journal*, 36, 644–59.

Miller, D. 1994: What happens after success: the perils of excellence, *Journal of Management Studies*, 31, 325–58.

Miller, D. 1996: Configurations revisited, *Strategic Management Journal*, 17, 505–12.

Miller, D. and Friesen, P. H. 1982: Structural change and performance: quantum versus piece-meal–incremental approaches, *Academy of Management Journal*, 25, 867–92.

Miller, D. and Friesen, P. H. 1984: *Organizations: A Quantum View*. Englewood Cliffs, NJ: Prentice-Hall.

Miller, D., Lant, T. K., Milliken, F. J., and Korn, H. J. 1996: The evolution of strategic simplicity: exploring two models of organizational adaptation, *Journal of Management*, 22, 863–87.

Milliken, F. J. 1990: Perceiving and interpreting environmental change: an examination of college administrators' interpretation of changing demographics, *Academy of Management Journal*, 33, 42–63.

Milliken, F. J. and Lant, T. K. 1991: The effect of an organization's recent performance history on strategic persistence and change, *Advances in Strategic Management*, 7, 129–56.

Mintzberg, H. 1979: *The Structuring of Organizations*. Englewood Cliffs, NJ: Prentice-Hall.

Murmann, J. P. and Tushman, M. L. 1997: Organizational responsiveness to environmental shock as an indicator of organizational foresight and oversight: the role of executive team characteristics and organizational context. In R. Garud and P. R. Nayyar, and Z. B. Shapira (eds), *Technological Innovation*, New York: Cambridge University Press, 260–78.

Nadler, D. A., Shaw, R. B., and Walton, E. A. 1994: *Discontinuous change*. San Francisco: Jossey–Bass.

Nadler, D. A. and Tushman, M. L. 1992: Designing organizations that have good fit: a framework for understanding new architectures. In D. A. Nadler, M. S. Gerstein, and R. B. Shaw (eds), *Organizational architecture*, San Francisco: Jossey–Bass, 39–56.

Nystrom, P. C. and Starbuck, W. H. 1984: To avoid organizational crises: unlearn, *Organizational Dynamics*, 12 (spring), 53–65.

Pennings, J. M. 1987: Structural contingency theory: a multivariate test, *Organization Science*, 8, 223–40.

Pettigrew, A. M. 1987: Context and action in the transformation of the firm, *Journal of Management Studies*, 24, 649–70.

Porter, M. E. 1995: Positioning tradeoffs, activity systems, and the theory of competitive strategy. Working paper, Harvard Graduate School of Business Administration, Boston.

Porter, M. E. 1996: What is strategy?, *Harvard Business Review*, 74 (6), 61–78.

Porter, M. E. and Rivkin, J. W. 1998: Activity systems as barriers to imitation. Working paper 98–066, Harvard Business School, Boston, MA.

Rivkin, J. W. 2000: Imitation of complex strategies, *Management Science*, 46, 824–44.

Rivkin, J. W. and Siggelkow, N. 2002: Balancing search and stability: interdependencies among elements of organizational design. Working paper, Wharton School, Philadelphia, PA.

Romanelli, E. and Tushman, M. L. 1994: Organizational transformation as punctuated equilibrium: an empirical test, *Academy of Management Journal*, 37, 1141–66.

Siggelkow, N. 2002a: Evolution toward fit. *Administrative Science Quarterly*, 47, 125–9.

Siggelkow, N. 2002b: Misperceiving interactions among complements and substitutes: organizational consequences. *Management Science*, 48, 900–16.

Singh, J. V., House, R. J., and Tucker, D. J. 1986: Organizational change and organizational mortality, *Administrative Science Quarterly*, 31, 587–611.

Skolnik, R. 1985: Liz the wiz: Liz Claiborne Inc., *Sales and Marketing Management*, 135, 50.

Suchman, M. C. 1995: Managing legitimacy: strategic and institutional approaches, *Academy of Management Review*, 20, 571–610.

Traub, J. and Newman, M. 1985: Behind all of the glitz and glitter, *Smithsonian*, 16, 30.

Tushman, M. L., Newman, W. H., and Romanelli, E. 1986: Convergence and upheaval: managing the unsteady pace of organizational evolution, *California Management Review*, 29 (1), 29–44.

Tushman, M. L. and Romanelli, E. 1985: Organizational evolution: a metamorphosis model of convergence and reorientation, *Research in Organizational Behavior*, 7, 171–222.

Tushman, M. L. and Rosenkopf, L. 1996: Executive succession, strategic reorientation and performance growth: a longitudinal study in the US. cement industry, *Management Science*, 42, 939–53.

Van de Ven, A. H. and Poole, M. S. 1995: Explaining development and change in organizations, *Academy of Management Review*, 20, 510–40.

Vaughan, D. 1996: *The Challenger Launch Decision*. Chicago: The University of Chicago Press.

Virany, B., Tushman, M. L., and Romanelli, E. 1992: Executive succession and organization outcomes in turbulent environments: an organizational learning approach, *Organization Science*, 3, 72–92.

Watzlawick, P., Weakland, J. H., and Fisch, R. 1974: *Change: principles of problem formation and problem resolution*. New York: Horton.

Weick, K. E. 1976: Educational organizations as loosely coupled systems, *Administrative Science Quarterly*, 21, 1–19.

Westhoff, F. H., Yarbrough, B. V., and Yarbrough, R. M. 1996: Complexity, organization, and Stuart Kauffman's The Origins of Order, *Journal of Economic Behavior and Organization*, 29, 1–25.

Womack, J. P., Jones, D. T., and Roos, D. 1990: *The machine that changed the world*. New York: Rawson.

Wright, S. 1932: The roles of mutation, inbreeding, cross–breeding and selection in evolution, *Proceedings, Eleventh International Congress of Genetics*, 1, 356–66.

Zajac, E. J. and Bazerman, M. H., 1991: Blind spots in industry and competitor analysis: implications of interfirm (mis)perceptions for strategic decisions, *Academy of Management Review*, 16, 37–56.

CHAPTER FOUR

Resources, Management Systems, and Governance: Keys to Value Creation

Karen Schnatterly, Catherine Maritan

The dramatic rise and subsequent fall in stock market values during the past few years has generated a lot of interest in the question of what if anything, underlies the stock market valuations of corporations' equity. Since the late 1970s, there has been a decline in the association between stock prices and key financial statement variables, such as earnings, cash flow and book value (Lev and Zarowin, 1999). During the same period, the proportion of market value of publicly traded firms represented by their book values decreased from 95 percent to 28 percent (Boulton et al., 2000). In other words, 72 percent of what the stock market is valuing is not represented on companies' balance sheets. If as Teece (1998) argues, the rapid expansion of goods and factor markets has left intangible assets as the main basis of competitive differentiation in many industries, then understanding if and how these intangibles serve as drivers of value is important to understanding how firms compete.

Strategy scholars have long recognized the importance of intangibles such as firm resources, capabilities and organizational routines to creating firm value (Barney, 1986, 1991; Dierickx and Cool, 1989; Peteraf, 1993) but because intangible assets are by their nature difficult to value, little strategy research has addressed their valuation. Researchers in accounting (e.g. Lev and Sougiannis, 1996,1999), finance (e.g. Chauvin and Hirschey, 1993; Lev, 1999) and marketing (e.g. Park and Srinivasan, 1994) also recognized this difficulty. However, they have addressed only very specific issues relating to their fields, for example research and development, advertising, and brand strength.

In the study reported here we attempted to capture a relatively wide range of intangible assets and evaluate their contributions to firm value. We draw on the resource-based view of the firm to define categories of resources and capabilities. Perhaps more unexpectedly, we also draw on the corporate governance literature and organization theory for guidance on defining certain types of management systems or capabilities.

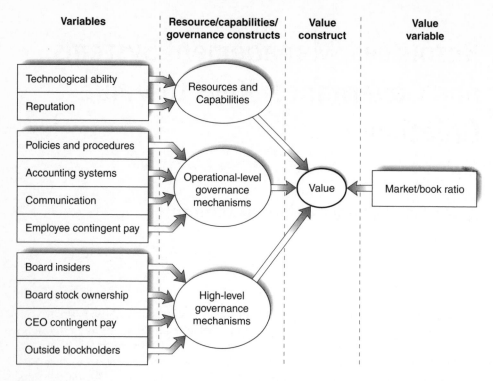

Figure 4.1   Value creation model

Theory and Model

Since intangible assets are in general not valued on a balance sheet, the difference between the book value and the market value of a firm can in simplest terms be interpreted as representing the value of intangible assets.[1] These intangibles consist of: (1) the firm's resources and capabilities such as accumulated knowledge, skills and reputation, (2) its internal operational-level governance mechanisms such as management systems and coordination mechanisms, and (3) the external governance of the firm including its ownership structure, composition of the board of directors and executive compensation. A higher ratio of market-to-book value would imply that a firm has more value created by its resources, capabilities, and governance mechanisms. Although as discussed below, both internal and external governance mechanisms may be viewed as organizational capabilities, we separate them from resources and capabilities because they are treated separately in the literature. We investigate the relationship between intangible assets and firm value based on the model depicted in Figure 4.1.

Resources and capabilities

Possession of unique or superior resources or capabilities may lead to sustainable competitive advantage, or superior value. The resource-based view of the firm sees firms as heterogeneous. It is resources that drive this heterogeneity, and the differential use firms put them to that drives performance differences (Peteraf, 1993). The investigation of the impact of resources and capabilities on firm performance is difficult due to their tacit nature. In previous empirical studies researchers typically have developed context-specific measure for single industry settings (e.g. Henderson and Cockburn, 1994; Miller and Shamsie, 1996) or have used more general proxies such as research and development intensity and advertising intensity as suggested by Mahoney and Pandian (1992).

Our study followed the second approach and used general proxies since one of our objectives was to use measures that are applicable across multiple industries, but, in contrast to previous work, we used a relatively large number of variables intended to capture a more comprehensive set of resources and capabilities. We recognize that this is still a very incomplete inventory of resources and capabilities; however, this study was largely exploratory and represents an initial attempt to investigate the contribution of intangibles to value, so we elected to begin with a limited set of variables within each of several broad categories.

Technology

Superior technological ability is a resource that can drive firm heterogeneity. This technological ability can also translate into intellectual property rights protected by patents. Both the ability itself and the patents are intangible assets. The firms in our sample compete in technology-intensive industries that typically make use of patents. We used two variables to capture this dimension. First, and most coarse is R&D intensity which Mahoney and Pandian suggest is "a reasonably effective proxy for capturing an enterprise's endowment of unique knowledge possessed by individuals and teams within the organization" (1992, p. 367) and has been used in this way in empirical research (Bierly and Chakrabarti, 1996; DeCarolis and Deeds, 1999).

However, R&D intensity is a coarse measure that does not directly capture the nature, quality or expected benefits of a firm's technology investment. Also since many innovative activities particularly for small companies, are not classified as R&D, patent-based measures may represent the only available information about the value of innovation for some firms (Deng et al., 1999). Therefore, we also used a patent-based indicator of technological ability. There is a well-established economics literature that has studied patent citations as indicators of knowledge flows (Griliches, 1981; Pakes, 1985) and a developing strategy literature that uses patent-based measures as indicators of technological capabilities (Henderson and Cockburn, 1994; DeCarolis and Deeds, 1999; Ahuja, 2000). In a study of technology-intensive industries, Deng et al. (1999) found the strength of the companies' patent portfolios, based on the citation of their patents by other patents subsequently granted, were positively associated with future stock returns and market-to-book value ratios.

To demonstrate that a new patent is novel, useful and not obvious, substantial details about an innovation must be disclosed in a patent application. Such disclosure may include sufficient detail to provide opportunities for competitors to imitate the firm's innovation or to develop a competitive response to the innovation thereby substantially reducing its value and its potential to contribute to competitive advantage. For that reason, firms may choose to not patent some or all of their technological innovations. To control for the effects of this choice it is important to capture an indication of a firm's patenting policy.

Reputation

The reputation of a firm is also an intangible asset (Hall, 1993) that can be seen as an overall perception of the company's accomplishments and prospects (Szwajkowski and Figlewicz, 1999). It includes the perception of the firm's interactions with its stakeholders: customers, employees, community, competitors, suppliers, environment and owners. *Fortune* magazine publishes an annual survey of corporate reputation that has been used by management researchers to assess the relationship between reputation and financial performance (e.g., Fombrun and Shanley, 1990; Fryxell and Wand, 1994). However, the *Fortune* survey includes only the largest firms and we are interested in a broader sample. Therefore, we used the awards and honors a firm has publicly received as a proxy for its reputation.

The resource-based view of the firm holds that superior resources and capabilities, such as technological capabilities and firm reputation, drive heterogeneity among firms, leading to value creation and superior performance. We therefore hypothesize that:

- *Hypotheses 1*: Firms that have greater resources and capabilities will have higher market-to-book value than firms that do not.

Governance

Corporate governance is concerned with oversight and control of the activities of a firm. Much of the governance research in the management literature concerns high-level monitoring and incentive issues such as ownership structure, CEO and board of directors' stock ownership, board structure and compensation, and executive compensation. These mechanisms serve to mitigate the effects of the agency problems that arise due to the separation of ownership and control. However, there exists another type of corporate governance mechanism that operates internally, at a lower level within the firm to deal with agency problems that may exist between senior management and lower-level employees. We label these mechanisms "operational-level" to reflect the organizational level at which they operate and differentiate them from "high-level" governance mechanisms that concern the board of directors and ownership issues.

Operational-level governance

Operational-level governance mechanisms comprise management systems that constitute the "organizational rules of the game" (Fama and Jensen, 1983, p. 13) and provide operational support. Examples include control systems such as formal policies and procedures and accounting systems, coordination systems such as communications mechanisms, and incentive systems such as employee compensation plans. Although they have not explicitly been characterized in this way in the literature, these operational-level governance mechanisms can be thought of as organizational capabilities. Superior control, coordination, and compensation systems that better mitigate the agency problem for one firm relative to its competitors may contribute to competitive advantage. While there has been extensive study of high-level governance issues by finance, accounting and organizational scholars, there has been far less research on operational-level governance mechanisms. However, the organization theory literature identifies some important internal governance constructs.

Management control is the broad term that is related to the budgeting, planning and reporting systems in a firm. It gives managers a way to incorporate top-level decisions into departmental activities and to assess whether strategies are influencing organizational performance. Daft and Macintosh (1984) found that management control systems consist of strategic and operating plans, periodic statistical reports, and policies and procedures specifying guidelines, rules, and job descriptions. Dissemination of policies throughout the organization, training, clearly defined responsibilities, and formalized procedures are examples of strong control systems and are expected to increase communication with and improve monitoring of employees.

Drawing from systems theory, communication can be viewed as a system binder that facilitates internal stability and control (Almaney, 1974). Frequency, informality, openness and density contribute to the intensity of communication. "[M]ore intense communications patterns create greater information processing capacity" (Gupta and Govindarajan, 1991, p. 778) and information processing can overcome some organizational ambiguity (Daft and Lengel, 1986), thereby mitigating potential agency problems. Vertical communication is important in multi-unit organizations. The internal structure in multi-unit organizations is not homogenous throughout the organization (Ghoshal and Nohria, 1989). There are different approaches to integrating this corporate differentiation through the existence of liaison roles, task forces, corporate meetings and management transfers which facilitate communication between corporate headquarters and subsidiaries (Martinez and Jarillo, 1989; Gupta and Govindarajan, 1991; Hoskisson et al., 1993). Inter-unit communication is also a key mechanism for achieving coordination and integration of different subsidiaries. Lateral relations such as joint work in teams, task forces and meetings facilitate communications (Martinez and Jarillo, 1989; Hoskisson et al., 1993; Ghoshal et al., 1994). Other examples are job rotation and management development programs.

Contingent pay for employees also serves as an operational-level governance mechanism. When an employee stock ownership system has meaningful equity, information and influence, it produces psychological ownership, which leads to a bonding or integration of the employee-owner with the organization (Pierce et al., 1991). A second form of contingent pay is gainsharing. Gainsharing is a collective contract that encourages mutual monitoring of agents' behavior within a work unit (Welbourne et al., 1995). The benefits are lower labor costs, high productivity, good product quality (Schuster, 1984), and improved employee attitudes (Hatcher et al., 1989).

Operational-level governance includes accounting systems, policies, and procedures, communication within the firm, and contingent pay for employees. These mechanisms fundamentally move information throughout the firm. As such, the greater the presence of these mechanisms, the greater the value impact will be to the firm. We therefore hypothesize that:

◆   *Hypothesis 2*: Firms that have stronger operational-level governance will have higher market-to-book values than firms that do not.

High-level governance
High-level oversight and control, what is traditionally thought of as corporate governance in the management literature, can also be viewed as a type of organizational
capability. A firm with superior monitoring and incentives that reduce and/or mitigate the effects of the agency problem, which in turn creates value, may have a competitive advantage over rivals.

An effective board is successful at monitoring and motivating the management of
the firm. There is some sense that a board dominated by outsiders might be a key
factor in making a board more effective. The use of outside directors may be a signal
for better quality of information (Fama, 1980; Watts and Zimmerman, 1990; Anderson
et al., 1993). Outsiders may focus more on financial performance measures, which is
an important component of monitoring (Fama and Jensen, 1983; Johnson et al., 1993),
and may act on that information, as boards dominated by outsiders are more likely to
dismiss CEOs following poor financial performance (Warner et al., 1988; Weisbach,
1988). Finally, outsiders may also contribute a breadth of knowledge not otherwise
available (Vance, 1983). Stock ownership by directors may signal a vigilant board, and
therefore more effective governance as it can be seen as an incentive to fulfill control
responsibilities (Mizruchi, 1983; Shleifer and Vishny, 1986; Tosi and Gomez-Mejia,
1989; Beatty and Zajac, 1990; Kosnik, 1990).

Another high-level governance mechanism is concentration of ownership which reflects a potential exercise of control by holders of large blocks of shares. Monitoring
management is costly so there must be sufficient financial reward to do so. Therefore,
depending on the difficulty of monitoring, there will be some percent of ownership
where monitoring to protect wealth provides a benefit to the blockholder (Alchian
and Demsetz, 1972; Schleifer and Vishny, 1986; Holderness and Sheehan, 1988;
Agrawal and Mandelker, 1990). This monitoring may have performance implications;
however the empirical evidence is mixed. For example, Hill and Snell (1989) found a
positive relationship between ownership concentration and productivity while Demsetz
and Lehn (1985) found no relationship between ownership concentration and profits.

CEO compensation has been widely seen as a way to appropriately align the CEO's
interests with those of the shareholders by linking the CEO's pay to firm performance.
This alignment can be achieved through contingent compensation contracts (Baiman,
1990). Ferris, et al. (1998) find that firms that have announced a long-term performance plan have higher return on equity following the announcement. This increase is
primarily attributable to improved profit margins, suggesting that there may be a performance effect to contingent compensation.

Strong high-level governance means the board functions efficiently because it is
independent; there is contingent compensation for the CEO; block holders are present;
and board members own stock. The board has the ultimate responsibility for monitoring the CEO and the firm. As such, when high-level governance is strong, the firm
should have better oversight, and will be more efficient and effective. This will generate positive value. We therefore hypothesize that:

♦   *Hypothesis 3*: Firms that have stronger high-level governance will have higher mar-
    ket-to-book values than firms that do not.

Methods

Sample

To assess the contributions of resources, capabilities, and governance mechanisms to firm value, we examined pairs of similarly sized firms competing in the same industry, one with a high market-to-book value ratio and one with an average market-to-book value ratio. An important feature of this research is that the resource and governance measures were designed to be general and applicable across multiple industries. However, there are industry-specific characteristics that may affect the levels of some of our measures. By using a matched pair design we can control for industry-specific characteristics by the sample construction. For example, one of our variables is technology strength which captures how influential or important a company's technology is. This measure is calculated from the frequency with which its recent patents have been cited in all US patents subsequently granted, or its citation impact. Citation impact varies by industry due to differences in practices and technology types; therefore, the definition of superior technology strength is industry-dependent. For example, typically there is more citing of recent patents in telecommunications than in pharmaceuticals (Narin, 2000; *Technology Review, 2001*). Through our matched pair design we made comparisons between competitors and not against an absolute measure or cross-industry composite. There are also industry-specific characteristics that directly affect our dependent variable. By matching on industry we could define high and average market-to-book ratios relative to industry norms and subsequently combine observations across industries.

To identify our sample, we wanted to begin with a set of firms with unambiguously high market-to-book ratios. We first generated an initial multi-industry list of firms in the COMPUSTAT database with market-to-book value ratios exceeding 9.0 based on 1995 figures. We then calculated the mean market-to-book ratio for the primary industry in which each of those firms competed, based on four–digit SIC codes. Firms whose market-to-book ratio was at least 1.5 standard deviations above the industry mean were retained as "high-value" firms. We matched these high-value firms based on size (primarily in terms of assets and secondarily in terms of sales) and product market scope, with firms having market-to-book ratios close to the means for their industries. Although SIC codes were used as an initial screen, these industry definitions can be very broad for some codes and include firms that do not compete in the same product markets. Therefore, our definition of "industry" was further refined for the purpose of matching. The actual matching was conducted based on a careful reading of 10K reports so that firms in a pair competed in similar product markets. Our final sample comprised 38 pairs of high- and average-value firms in multiple industries. Because of our initial screening criterion for high-value firms, all of our pairs compete in technology-intensive industries such as pharmaceuticals, biotechnology, medical equipment, and computer equipment.

Data collection

We collected data for each firm's resources, capabilities and governance mechanisms depicted in figure 4.1. All data were collected for 1995. Current technological resources/capabilities were measured by R&D intensity and a patent-based measure of technology strength, both of which have been used previously in accounting and technology management research (e.g., Deng et al., 1999; Hicks et al., 2001). The patent data were acquired from CHI Research Inc., which has for many years conducted patent analysis for the National Science Foundation. Technology strength is an indicator of quality of the firm's patent portfolio calculated from the number of times a company's most recent five years of patents are cited in the current year relative to all the patents in CHI's database, and the number of patents granted to the company in the current year. To adjust for situations in which a firm's the technology strength is low due to a policy of not patenting rather than having patents that are not cited, we introduced a patenting policy control. Based on content-context analysis of annual reports and 10K statements as described below, we defined a 0–1 dummy variable to indicate when a firm has a stated policy of not patenting either all of its technology or its most important technologies. The firm's investment in reputation was measured by the number of awards and honors it received in the current year as mentioned in the current annual report and 10K statement. An example of an award that would be counted is the Baldrige National Quality Award while a recognition such as membership in the *Fortune 500* would not be counted.

Two categories of governance mechanisms were measured. The high-level board and ownership governance mechanisms were captured by the ownership structure of the firm, the composition of the board of directors, and the structure of the CEO's compensation package. These data were collected from proxy statements filed with the SEC. Operational-level governance mechanisms considered were the strength of the accounting system and the policies and procedures, presence of teams, or other liaison roles to facilitate communication, and contingent pay for employees. Operational-level governance variables were measured using qualitative data derived from what we call content-context analysis of company annual reports, 10K's and proxies.

Because our method of qualitative data collection and analysis is somewhat unusual, it is described here in some detail. Electronic versions of the SEC filings of annual reports, 10K's and proxies were imported into QSR NUD*IST 4 qualitative data analysis software. For the accounting system, policies and procedures, communication and patenting policy measures, we developed dictionaries of terms related to each construct and searched the documents for occurrences of those terms. For example, for policies and procedures the dictionary included the terms "policy, policies, procedure, duty, duties, manual, training, process, document." The complete list of search terms with the variables to which they relate are contained in appendix 4.1.

We use the term content-context analysis to differentiate our approach from typical applications of content analysis in which the frequency of a word contained in a text is counted. We analyzed words in their contexts. For each occurrence of a search term, the 10 lines of prior and 10 lines of subsequent text were saved along with the line in which the word appeared. The 21 lines of text retrieved for each occurrence of all relevant terms were saved for the particular variable being measured. The set of saved references were then reviewed to eliminate irrelevant material. There are two main types of material defined as irrelevant. The first is uses of the search terms in ways that do not relate to the constructs in our model. For example, the term "document" appears in the title of each of the SEC filings searched and is not being used in reference to a policy or procedure. The second is reference to a search term contained in a paragraph about a construct that we captured through separate measure. For example "policy" may appear in a paragraph referring to an employee profit-sharing program. Since employee contingent pay is a separate variable, that reference would also be found in the contingent pay search. Therefore, it would be discarded as irrelevant in the policies and procedures search. Once the irrelevant material was discarded, the remaining references were read with each reference in context and scored on a scale. For example, in the case of "policies and procedures" which is scored on a 1–7 scale, a score of 1 was assigned for only a basic, general reference to the existence of policies, a score of 4 was assigned to evidence of comprehensive, understood procedures in one division and a score of 7 was assigned to evidence of clearly defined organizational responsibilities and communications throughout the company. Each company was coded with the highest score that was obtained from the set of documents. The scoring schemes are listed in Appendix 4.1.

The selected search words and assigned strengths are theoretically informed. Because judgement was involved, both researchers agreed upon the dictionaries and we checked our coding for inter-coder reliability on a random sample of documents. The absence of established measures for the operational-level governance constructs makes it difficult to establish construct validity for our dictionaries and scales beyond grounding them in the literature. The measure for patenting policy is not literature based; however, there is evidence that patenting practices can vary by industry (Narin, 2000; Hall and Ziedonis, 2001). We also verified the use of different practices in different industries with a consultant who specializes in patenting and intellectual property protection.

Market values will be strongly affected by profitability; therefore, we controlled for this factor using the average of the three previous years' return on sales. See table 4.1 for a description of the constructs, variables and measures.

Analysis

Since we are interested in which resources, capabilities and governance mechanisms contribute to firm value, we used a discriminant technique to determine which of our variables differ between the high-value and average-value firms in our pairs. Although we could have used ANOVA for each of our variables, we wanted to test the variables as a system. We therefore used a logit model. We chose logit over discriminant analysis because of its less stringent requirements for data normality (Press and Wilson, 1978). Because of our sample design we used a conditional binomial logit model that takes into account the grouping of the data into matched pairs (Hosmer and Lameshow, 1989). A conditional logit model differs from a standard binomial logit model in that since the data are grouped, the likelihood is calculated relative to each group, that is, a conditional likelihood is used. We can therefore explicitly compare the members of a given pair rather than pools of high value and average value firms that overall represent the same set of industries and firm sizes. Stata 5.0 econometric software was used to estimate the model.

Table 4.1 Measurement of variables

Construct	Components	Measurement
Value (dependent variable)	Market-to-book ratio	• COMPUSTAT data • Converted to 0–1 dichotomous variable for high and average MV/BV firms based on matched pairs for analysis
Resources and capabilities	Technological ability	• R&D intensity (R&D/sales) – from 10K • Technology strength from CHI Research data • Patenting policy control: 0–1indicator variable for policy of not using patents or not patenting most important technology based on content analysis of SEC filings[a]
	Reputation	• Scale: number of honors or awards won in the year[a]
Operational-level governance	Policies and procedures	• Scale 1–7: based on content analysis of SEC filings for mentions/descriptions of internal controls, budget, formal procedures, job descriptions[a]
	Accounting systems	• Scale 1–7: based on content analysis of SEC filings for mentions/descriptions of strength of accounting system, control procedures[a]
	Communication	• Scale 1–7: based on content analysis of SEC filings for mentions/descriptions of meetings, conferences, retreats, communication, interaction, contact, feedback, job rotation, teams[a]
	Employee contingent pay	• Scale 1–6: based on content analysis of SEC filings for mentions/descriptions of bonus, profit sharing, stock plan[a]
High-level governance	Board insiders	• Fraction of board members who are employees or ex-employees of the company – from proxy statement
	Board stock ownership	• Fraction of total stock owned by Board – from proxy statement
	CEO contingent pay	• Fraction of CEO total compensation that is stock based contingent compensation – from proxy statement
	Outside block holders	• 0–1categorical variable for blockholder with minimum 5% of common equity and not an employee or inside director of the company – from proxy statement
Control	Profitability	• Average 3-year return on sales – from 10K

[a] Indicates a measure we developed based on content-context analysis of company SEC filings.

Results

Table 4.2 presents descriptive statistics and a correlation matrix for the sample. Technology strength is positively and significantly related to policies and procedures, contingent pay for employees and past performance. R&D intensity is positively related to communication and negatively related to profitability. Patenting policy is positively associated with reputation, communication, board insiders and profitability. Policies and procedures is positively related to employee contingent pay, and communication is positive and significant with the accounting system. Insiders on the board is positively related to board ownership and past performance, and negatively related to outside block holders. Board ownership is negatively related to CEO contingent pay and outside block holders. The correlations between the governance mechanisms was expected, as many of these mechanisms substitute or complement each other (Rediker and Seth, 1995). For example, greater board ownership and CEO contingent pay are negatively related. The more stock a board owns, the less necessary it is to pay the CEO through large options contracts, for example.

Table 4.3 presents the results of the conditional logit model estimation. Our explanatory variables do discriminate between the high value and average value firms quite well. Our model controls for industry and firm size by construction, and we include a control for past performance, so it is clear that the market does indeed recognize differences in these intangible assets and values them accordingly (model significant at $p < 0.01$ level). However, only some of our specific hypotheses are supported.

Hypothesis 1 is only partly supported. We eliminated R&D intensity in our final model, as we had several missing observations that further reduced an already small sample.[2] Technology strength is not significant in the model even after controlling for firm policies of not using patent protection. This finding is surprising given the emphasis on the value of knowledge-based assets in both the resource-based strategy literature and the popular press, and our sample of technology-intensive companies. A possible explanation for this finding is that the firms are very closely matched with regard to asset size and product scope that their stock of technological resources may indeed be similar. This result does not necessarily mean that technological resources are not important, just that they do not differ significantly between high and average value firms. In this analysis, we compared high-value companies to average value companies, not low-value ones. Perhaps, if the comparison was made with below average value firms, the gap in technological resources may be more pronounced. Alternatively, the market may not be rewarding investments in technology to as great a degree as generally believed. The other resource variable testing hypothesis 1, reputation, was a significant discriminator ($p < 0.01$) indicating that the market rewards positive reputations. This makes intuitive sense, as we operationalized reputation as number of honors or awards. For example, an award such as an industrial design award signals that peers see the quality of the firm's product or process which in turn can be interpreted as a positive signal for future value creation. However, an alternative explanation for the result could be that that high-value firms are disproportionately awarded honors simply because of their relative value ranking.

Three of the operational-level governance variables serve as effective discriminators. Stronger policies and procedures are associated with higher-value firms while more

Table 4.2 Descriptive statistics and correlations among the variables

	Mean	Standard deviation	1	2	3	4	5	6	7	8	9	10	11	12	13
1 R&D intensity	8.58	59.72	—												
2 Technology strength	5.07	16.75	−0.02	—											
3 Patenting policy	0.51	0.50	−0.15	−0.11	—										
4 Reputation	1.64	1.23	−0.08	−0.00	0.19†	—									
5 Policies and procedures	2.43	1.39	−0.05	0.32*	0.08	0.11	—								
6 Accounting systems	2.11	1.15	−0.10	0.14	0.04	0.09	0.10	—							
7 Communication	1.93	1.19	0.20†	−0.14	0.23*	0.18	0.11	0.20†	—						
8 Employee contingent pay	2.74	1.08	0.01	0.23*	0.18	0.15	0.29*	0.12	0.10	—					
9 Board insiders	0.343	0.155	−0.17	−0.12	0.21†	0.07	0.08	−0.00	0.00	0.07	—				
10 % board stock ownership	0.156	0.168	−0.02	−0.00	0.13	0.07	0.12	0.02	−0.01	0.01	0.37**	—			
11 CEO contingent pay	0.492	0.433	0.11	−0.10	−0.13	−0.04	0.10	0.17	0.06	0.02	−0.10	−0.19†	—		
12 Outside block holders	0.618	0.489	0.09	−0.05	0.10	−0.10	−0.15	0.05	0.05	0.09	−0.31**	−0.59**	0.19	—	
13 Profitability	−618.0	2,504.25	−0.35*	−0.29**	0.21†	0.11	−0.03	−0.02	0.04	0.14	0.20†	0.12	0.05	−0.13	—

† p < 0.10; * p < 0.05; ** p < 0.01.

Table 4.3   Results of conditional logit estimation

Variable	Coefficient estimate	P-value
Technology strength	0.0064	.861
Patenting policy	−1.2851	.216
Reputation	1.2723*	.023
Policies and procedures	1.6690*	.013
Accounting systems	−0.7589*	.031
Communication	−1.0373*	.047
Employee-contingent pay	−0.6263	.186
Board insiders	2.2838	.356
Board stock ownership	−10.8976†	.061
CEO-contingent compensation	−2.8549†	.064
Outside blockholder	−0.1884	.906
Profitability	0.0003	.193

N = 76, Log likelihood = −12.73; Chi^2 (d.f. = 12) = 27.22; Prob. > Chi^2 = 0.0072; pseudo R^2 = 0.52;
† $p < 0.10$; * $p < 0.05$; ** $p < 0.01$

extensive communications mechanisms and stronger accounting systems are present in lower-value firms. This only somewhat supports hypothesis 2, as we hypothesized that all these mechanisms support higher value. The sample and method control for size and industry, so this is to say that, of firms of similar size and scope, the firm with the weaker accounting system has the higher relative value or that the firm with the stronger accounting system does not have as high a value. A possible explanation for this finding is that an accounting system that is *too* strong may be a signal of excessive bureaucracy that hampers innovation (Burns and Stalker, 1961). Alternately, as we have mentioned before, there is complementarity and substitutability between governance mechanisms, and we may be seeing the result of substitution among policies and procedures and communication and accounting systems. The negative coefficient on communication is counterintuitive in addition to being opposite our hypothesized direction. It may be that much of the benefits to communication are being captured in the policies and procedures variable, and formal communication beyond that might be seen as a sign of excess bureaucracy that hampers innovation and therefore value creation. With excessive bureaucracy, too rigid an adherence to formal reporting mechanisms may impede the objectives of the organization as there is goal displacement, and means become ends in themselves (Merton, 1958); however, the significant positive result for policies and procedures would appear to contradict that explanation. A possible alternative explanation for the negative relationship between both accounting systems and communication and value could simply be that high-value firms may not require such strong formal accounting systems or communications mechanisms.

Of the high-level governance variables, only CEO contingent compensation and board ownership are significant but they are negatively related to value, contrary to hypothesis 3. In other words, the more a CEO is compensated with stock-based contingent pay and the more stock the board owns, the less likely the firm is to have high value. This result is puzzling. The board ownership finding may be capturing risk aversion on the part of the board. If risk taking is necessary for superior performance, boards with extensive ownership may be reluctant to allow the firm to take risky actions. Similarly, the CEO compensation finding may be capturing the CEO's risk aversion as well, again, assuming risk taking is necessary for superior performance. As the insiders variable is not significant, this finding indicates that insiders are not any worse at monitoring the performance of the firm as outsiders. The implication is that the idea of outsiders as superior monitors is not supported.

Discussion and Limitations

Although strategy scholars have long recognized the importance of intangible assets to value creation and competitive advantage, little work has attempted to explicitly calculate their contribution to a firm's value. Our study represents an initial attempt to empirically evaluate the relative contribution of different categories of intangible assets to firm value. We use variables from theory and previous research to create a model of what comprises resources, capabilities and governance and how they are associated with firm value. Since there has not been much research to date that has empirically examined this question, the selection of variables used was theoretically guided and largely exploratory.

Our finding that high value firms look very different from average value firms is significant. The key variables that discriminate between these firms are reputation, policies and procedures, communication, accounting systems, board ownership and CEO contingent pay. Interestingly, a stronger reputation and stronger policies and procedures are associated with high value firms, while more communication, stronger accounting systems, more board ownership and more CEO contingent pay are associated with average value firms.

It is important to recognize that our study design precludes making any claims regarding causality. Although we hypothesize based on theoretical arguments from the literature, that the resources, management systems, and governance mechanisms drive value creation, we can only test for association. As discussed in the previous section, there are plausible alternative explanations for the reputation, accounting systems, and communications results that argue high value drives the level or strength of the resources and governance mechanisms. Tracking changes over time may help us to at least partially untangle the issue of causality.

We used only a limited set of measures as we were constrained by our sample size. Since the governance mechanisms especially are likely to be complements or substitutes, being able to include a fuller set of variables may better explain the valuation differences. With additional degrees of freedom we would be able to add governance variables such as blockholder types, management stock ownership, CEO tenure, and debt policy (as an indicator of external monitoring). We would also be able to directly investigate substitution effects through the incorporation of interaction terms. Additional controls could include company age and type of founding. Since some of the unexpected management systems results might be explained by the degree of bureaucracy and its affect on innovation, measures of internal organizational structure such as layers of management might be included.

Our study used high-value and average-value firms. We may get very different results if we study high- versus low-, or even average- versus low-value firms. Additionally, because of this sample construction, we cannot really say is these phenomena are linear. Our unexpected results might be due to non-linearity. For example, our hypotheses assume that stronger accounting systems and communications are better. However, the negative result may not indicate the inverse relationships. It may be that too strong an accounting system or too much formal communication is bad for high value, but so may be too weak an accounting system or too little communication. There may be optimal levels. Similarly, very high as well as very low stock ownership by the CEO and board members may destroy value. This possible non-linearity was not addressed in the study.

It is important to note that our dependent variable is based on stock market values and we are therefore capturing market perceptions of value creation. We are assuming that the stock market is efficient and market valuations reflect actual value creation. Although we cannot measure market valuations of individual resources, management systems and governance mechanisms, through our analysis were have identified which variables effectively discriminate between high- and average-value firms. We interpret their relative effectiveness as discriminators as indications of the importance of these intangible assets to market value.

Similarly, we also make assumptions about some of our explanatory variables, specifically those that are derived from the text of documents. Although our content-based measures were developed from the literature, the validity of these measures as indicators of underlying constructs depends on the accuracy and completeness of the statements made by company managers in the SEC filings. We cannot test for accuracy or completeness; however, given our significant results, we are comfortable that the text presents a reasonable representation of the company activities which we tried to capture.

In this study we have provided some quantification of a subset of resources, management systems and governance mechanisms, all of which can be thought of as strategy process elements, and some insight as to which of them are associated with high market-to-book valuations. In particular, the notion of operational-level governance mechanisms used in this study provides some new insights based on management systems, practices, and processes not well studied in the context of value creation. Although we did not directly observe firm processes, we measured proxies for their existence and level or strength, and linked those attributes to the quality of a performance outcome. The successful development of these process measures using secondary data is encouraging because strategy process research typically requires primary, often proprietary, internal data. There may be many other variables that can be captured and measured using our approach, facilitating large scale, multi-industry studies of strategy process.

In light of the stock market's behavior during the last several years and the debate about whether or not we are in a "new economy," the results of our study might provide some direction for better understanding how strategy process, in the form of resources, management systems and governance mechanisms, matters.

Appendix 4.1

Patenting policy

Does the company rely on patents to protect technology or processes? *Search terms:* patent, copyright, secret, proprietary.

0 They patent technology.
1 They do not patent any technology or do not patent important technology.

Policies and procedures

How well do people know their job, what to do, etc.? Where are lines drawn? *Search terms:* policy, polices, procedure, duty, duties, manual, training, process, document.

1 only basic (e.g., "activities include") or procedures with little relevance to operations,
2 brief mention (e.g., "product development process" without any specifics),
3 discussion of systems or mention of examination of process (e.g., "due to potential future growth we will need to adjust the following systems"),
4 evidence of comprehensive understood policies in one division or function(e.g., quality assurance),
5 policies communicated throughout company, selection, training,
6 well-defined organizational responsibility,
7 clearly communicated organizational responsibility, formalized procedures, training to update.

Accounting systems

Search terms: accounting, internal, audit.

1 provides reasonable assurance,
2 evaluates costs vs. benefits,
3 internal auditor evaluates and reports on adequacy and effectiveness, emerging accounting issues,
4 new control procedures implemented, based on recommendations,
5 systematic review and modification of procedures,
6 communication throughout company, selection, training, development of qualified personnel,
7 6, above, plus more procedures, including code of conduct, organizational responsibility.

Communication

Cross-company communication, opportunity for formal and informal interaction and communication. *Search terms:* meeting, conference, retreat, contact, feedback, rotation, interaction, cross, liaison, team group.

1   no mention, or mention, but large generic team, or only TMT,
2   mention of use of small teams, or large group, remote locations,
3   cross-functional teams, product development, or sales groups or smaller, with lim-
    ited responsibility,
4   mid-level, limited cross-cooperation,
5   team structure, products with management/strategy focus,
6   limited teams, careful selection, full participation, training, or managers with open
    doors and rotating meetings, or rotating managers,
7   6, above, plus teams rotate across function or geography, or cross-functional man-
    agement teams.

Employee contingent pay

Search terms: ESOP, employee stock, employee benefit, bonus, profit sharing, retention, promotion, discount, incentive, commission, pension.

1   employee savings plan/basic retirement plan,
2   options to key employees or 401K and post retirement benefits to all,
3   options to key employees and 401K and post retirement benefits to all,
4   promotion from within,
5   bonus or profit sharing available to all,
6   options or stock possible to all.

Notes

1   There are of course some intangible assets reported under current US accounting standards
    such goodwill and the cost of acquiring assets such as patents and trademarks; however,
    these are generally acknowledged to capture only a portion of the value of intangibles and
    only for those firms that make acquisitions through purchase. A second and more impor-
    tant exception is software development which has been recognized as a special case and has
    its costs capitalized once technological feasibility is determined.
2   We estimated several models including R&D intensity using the resulting smaller sample.
    In none of them was R&D intensity significant. We opted, therefore, for the larger sample
    model. Results are available upon request.

References

Agrawal, A. and Mandelker, G. N. 1990: Large shareholders and the monitoring of managers:
    the case of anti-takover charter amendments. *Journal of Financial and Quantitative Analysis,*
    25 (2), 143–61.
Ahuja, G. 2000: The duality of collaboration: inducements and opportunities in the formation
    of interfirm linkages. *Strategic Management Journal,* 21, 317–43.
Alchian, A. A. and Demsetz, H. 1972: Production, information costs, and economic organiza-
    tion. *American Economic Review,* 62, 777–95.
Almaney, A. 1974: Communication and the systems theory of organization. *Journal of Business
    Communication,* 12 (1), 35–43.

Anderson, D., Francis, J. R., and Stokes D. J. 1993: Auditing, directorships and the demand for monitoring. *Journal of Accounting and Public Policy*, 12, 353–75.

Baiman, S. 1990: Agency research in managerial accounting: a second look. *Accounting, Organizations and Society*, 15, 341–72.

Barney, J. B. 1986: Strategic factor markets: expectations, luck, and business strategy. *Management Science*, 32, 1,231–41.

Barney, J. B. 1991: Firm resources and sustained competitive advantage. *Journal of Management*, 17, 97–120.

Bierly, P. and Chakrabarti, A. 1996: Generic knowledge strategies in the US pharmaceutical industry. *Strategic Management Journal*, 17 (S2), 123–35.

Boulton, R. E. S., Libert, B. D., and Samek, S. M. 2000: A business model for the new economy. *Journal of Business Strategy*, 21 (4), 29–35.

Burns, T. and Stalker, G. M. 1961: *The management of innovation*. New York: Oxford University Press.

Chauvin, K. W. and Hirschey, M. 1993: Advertising, R&D expenditures and the market value of the firm. *Financial Management*, 22 (4), 128–40.

Daft, R. L. and Lengel, R. H. 1986: Organizational information requirements, media richness and structural design. *Management Science*, 32, 554–71.

Daft, R. L. and Macintosh, N. B. 1984: The nature and use of formal control systems for management control and strategy implementation. *Journal of Management*, 10, 43–66.

DeCarolis, D. M. and Deeds, D. L. 1999: The impact of stocks and flows of organizational knowledge on firm performance: an empirical investigation of the biotechnology industry. *Strategic Management Journal*, 20, 953–68.

Demsetz, H. and Lehn, K. 1985: The structure of corporate ownership: causes and consequences. *American Economic Review*, 93, 1, 155–77.

Deng, Z., Lev, B., and Narin F. 1999: Science and technology as predictors of stock performance. *Financial Analysts Journal*, 55 (3), 20–32.

Dierickx, I. and Cool, K. 1989: Asset stock accumulation and sustainability of competitive advantage. *Management Science*, 35, 1,504–11.

Fama, E. F. 1980: Agency theory and the theory of the firm. *Journal of Political Economy*, 88, 288–307.

Fama, E. F. and Jensen, M. C. 1983: Separation of ownership and control. *Journal of Law and Economics*, 26, 301–26.

Ferris, S. P., Kumar, R., Sant, R., and Sopariwala, P. R. 1998: An agency analysis of the effect of long-term performance plans on managerial decision making. *Quarterly Review of Economics and Finance*, 38 (1), 73–91.

Fombrun, C. and Shanley, M. 1990: What's in a name? Reputation building and corporate strategy. *Academy of Management Journal*, 33, 233–25.

Fryxell, G. E. and Wand, J. 1994: The *Fortune* corporate "reputation" index: reputation for what? *Journal of Management*, 20, 1–14.

Ghoshal, S., Korine, H., and Szulanski, G. 1994: Interunit communication in multinational corporations. *Management Science*, 40, 96–110.

Ghoshal, S. and Nohria, N. 1989: Internal differentiation within multinational corporations. *Strategic Management Journal*, 10, 323–37.

Griliches, Z. 1981: Market value, R&D and patents. *Economics Letters*, 7, 183–7.

Gupta, A. K. and Govindarajan, V. 1991: Knowledge flows and the structure of control within multinational corporations. *Academy of Management Review*, 16, 768–92.

Hall, B. and Ziedonis, R. 2001: The patent paradox revisited: an empirical study of patenting in the US semiconductor industry, 1979–1995. *Rand Journal of Economics*, 32 (1): 101–28.

Hall, R. 1993: A framework linking intangible resources and capabilities to sustainable competitive advantage. *Strategic Management Journal*, 14, 607–18.

Hatcher, L., Ross, T. L., and Collins, D. 1989: Prosocial behavior, job complexity, and suggestion contribution under gainsharing plans. *The Journal of Applied Behavioral Science*, 25 (3), 231–49.

Henderson, R. and Cockburn, I. 1994: Measuring competence? Exploring firm effects in pharmaceutical research. *Strategic Management Journal*, 15 (S2), 63–84.

Hicks, D., Breitzman, A., Olivastro, D., and Hamilton, K. 2001: The changing composition of innovative activity in the US: a portrait based on patent analysis. *Research Policy*, 30, 681–703.

Hill, C. W. L. and Snell, S. A. 1989: Effects of ownership structure on corporate productivity. *Academy of Management Journal*, 32, 25–46.

Holderness, C. G. and Sheehan, D. P. 1988: The role of majority shareholders in publicly held corporations: an exploratory analysis. *Journal of Financial Economics* 20, 317–46.

Hoskisson, R. E., Hill, C. W. L., and Kim, H. 1993: The multidivisional structure: organizational fossil or source of value? *Journal of Management*, 19, 269–99.

Hosmer, D. W., Jr and Lameshow, S. 1989: *Applied logistic regression*. New York: John Wiley & Sons.

Johnson, R. A., Hoskisson, R. E., and Hitt, M. A. 1993: Board of director involvement in restructuring: the effects of board versus managerial controls and characteristics. *Strategic Management Journal*, 14 (S1), 33–51.

Kosnik, R. D. 1990: Effects of board demography and directors' incentives on corporate greenmail decisions. *Academy of Management Journal*, 33, 129–50.

Lev, B. 1999: R&D and capital markets. *Journal of Applied Corporate Finance*, 11 (4), 21–35.

Lev, B. and Sougiannis, T. 1996: The capitalization, amortization and value-relevance of R&D. *Journal of Accounting and Economics*, 21(1): 107–39.

Lev, B. and Sougiannis, T. 1999: Penetrating the book-to-market black box: the R&D effect. *Journal of Business Finance and Accounting*, 26, 419–49.

Lev, B. and Zarowin, P. 1999: The boundaries of financial reporting and how to extend them. *Journal of Accounting Research*, 37, 353–85.

Mahoney, J. T. and Pandian, J. R. 1992: The resource-based view within the conversation of strategic management. *Strategic Management Journal*, 13, 363–80.

Martinez, J. I. and Jarillo, J. C. 1989: The evolution of research on coordination mechanisms in multinational corporations. *Journal of International Business Studies*, 20, 489–514.

Merton, R. K. 1958: *Social theory and social structure*. Glencoe, IL: Free Press.

Miller, D. and Shamsie, J. 1996: The resource-based view of the firm in two environments: the Hollywood film studios from 1936 to 1965. *Academy of Management Journal*, 39, 519–43.

Mizruchi, M. S. 1983: Who controls whom? An examination of the relation between management and boards of directors in large American corporations. *Academy of Management Review*, 8, 426–36.

Narin, F. 2000: Assessing Technological Competencies. In J. Tidd (ed.), *From knowledge management to strategic competence: measuring technological, market and organizational innovation*, London: Imperial College Press, 155–95.

Pakes, A. 1985: On patents, R&D, and the stock market rate of return. *Journal of Political Economy*, 93, 390–409.

Park, C. S. and Srinivasan, V. 1994: A survey-based method of measuring and understanding brand equity and its extendibility. *Journal of Marketing Research*, 21, 271–88.

Peteraf, M. A. 1993: The cornerstones of competitive advantage: a resource-based view. *Strategic Management Journal*, 14, 179–91.

Pierce, J. L., Rubenfeld, S. A., and Morgan, S. 1991: Employee ownership: a conceptual model of process and effects. *Academy of Management Review*, 16, 121–44.

Press, S. J. and Wilson, S. 1978: Choosing between logistic regression and discriminant analysis. *Journal of the American Statistical Association*, 73, 699–705.

Rediker, K. J. and Seth, A. 1995: Boards of directors and substitution effects of alternative governance mechanisms. *Strategic Management Journal*, 16, 85–99.

Schuster, M. 1984: Cooperation and change in union settings: problems and opportunities. *Human Resource Management*, 23 (2), 145–61.

Shleifer, A. and Vishny, R.W. 1986: Large shareholders and corporate control. *Journal of Political Economy*, 94 (3, 1), 461–88.

Szwajkowski, E. and Figlewicz, R. E. 1999: Evaluating corporate performance: a comparison of the *Fortune* reputation survey and the Socrates social rating database. *Journal of Managerial Issues*, 11 (2), 137–54.

Technology Review. 2001. The TR patent scorecard. 104 (4), 48–51.

Teece, D. J. 1998: Capturing value from knowledge assets: the new economy, markets for know-how, and intangible assets. *California Management Review*, 40 (3), 55–79.

Tosi, H. L., Jr and Gomez-Mejia, L. R. 1989: The decoupling of CEO pay and performance: an agency theory. *Administrative Science Quarterly*, 34, 169–90.

Vance, S. C. 1983: *Corporate leadership: boards, directors and strategy*. New York: McGraw-Hill.

Warner, J. B., Watts, R. L., and Wruck, K. H. 1988: Stock prices and top management changes. *Journal of Financial Economics* 20 (1, 2), 461–93.

Watts, R. L. and Zimmerman, J. L. 1990: Positive accounting theory: a ten year perspective. *The Accounting Review*, 65 (1), 131–56.

Weisbach, M. S. 1988: Outside directors and CEO turnover. *Journal of Financial Economics*, 20 (1,2), 431–61.

Welbourne, T. M., Balkin, D. B., and Gomez-Mejia, L. R. 1995: Gainsharing and mutual monitoring: a combined agency–organizational justice interpretation. *Academy of Management Journal*, 38, 881–99.

CHAPTER FIVE

The Essence of Process: Effective Strategic Planning in Practice

John C. Camillus

Introduction and Research Objectives

The process of strategic planning has evolved over the years from the synoptic processes recommended and employed in the 1960s (Steiner, 1969; Ansoff, 1991) through "logical incrementalism" (Quinn, 1980; Camillus, 1982) to innovative (Gilmore and Camillus, 1996) and contextually relevant exercises (Camillus, Sessions, and Webb, 1998; Campbell 1999). Rapidly changing concepts of process and the complexities associated with defining and measuring organizational success make it difficult to arrive at normative generalizations regarding characteristics that make processes effective. Process studies that are descriptive rather than normative are consequently easier to conduct (Rajagopalan, Rashid, and Datta, 1993). These descriptive studies are undoubtedly of great value. They offer insights and alternatives to systems designers who seek to develop processes that are tailored to the needs of individual organizations (Chakravarthy and Doz, 1992). Nevertheless, normative guidelines that possess wide if not universal relevance are obviously invaluable to designers of planning processes and systems. With this understanding, this chapter seeks to accomplish three related objectives:

1   Identify elements of strategic planning processes that are universally applicable and relevant regardless of organizational and situational characteristics.
2   Describe innovative practices in strategic planning that offer alternative approaches for consideration by designers of planning processes and systems.
3   Suggest normative guidelines based on practices that are perceived to be effective by organizations that employ them.

Methodology

To achieve these three objectives, this chapter draws on, integrates, and presents the findings of five studies of the practice of strategic planning conducted from 1995 through 2000. The American Productivity and Quality Center (APQC) conducted four of these studies and the Hong Kong Productivity Council (HKPC) conducted the fifth. The author served as "subject matter expert" (SME) with responsibility for designing these five studies and interpreting the findings. The fifth study, conducted by HKPC replicated the final (fourth) study conducted by the APQC, with a focus on Asian organizations.

The five studies, in total, looked in depth at 22, carefully selected ("target") organizations. The selection process employed in identifying these target organizations is described later. Information about the planning practices of the target companies and their executives' perceptions about the effectiveness of these practices was gathered through the use of questionnaires, semi-structured interviews and site visits.

The findings of these studies were immeasurably enriched by the involvement, guidance, interpretations, and perspectives of representatives of approximately eighty ("sponsoring") organizations. The sponsoring organizations, in addition to providing the funding to conduct the studies, were involved in:

♦ selecting target companies,
♦ reviewing the design of questionnaires and interview protocols,
♦ debriefings after site visits, and
♦ extended "knowledge transfer sessions" involving groups of both target and sponsor organizations.

Furthermore, they provided detailed information about their own strategic planning practices that helped identify and illuminate distinctive approaches adopted by the target companies.

Focus of the studies

Each of the five studies had a particular focus:

1 state-of- the-art practices,
2 strategic planning in highly dynamic environments,
3 the changing role of planning managers and departments,
4 strategy implementation in USA/Europe, and
5 strategy implementation in Hong Kong/PRC.

The process of strategic planning was an explicit research topic in all five of the studies, and descriptions of the process were gathered using similar questions in all five studies.

Four to six target organizations were carefully selected for each of these studies. The selection process was as follows:

1 An initial list of possible target companies was generated by the research depart-

ments of the APQC for the first four studies, and by the research department of HKPC for the fifth. These organizations were identified by a search of academic and practitioner journals for descriptions of relevant, interesting, unusual, or effective planning practices. Additional possible target companies were suggested by the SME.

2   Detailed information, including financial performance, from published sources was gathered about the companies in this initial list. Potential target companies that were below average in financial performance in their industries were eliminated from further consideration.

3   Personnel in the planning function in each of the remaining organizations were identified, using APQC's and HKPC's extensive membership and the SME's contacts.

4   Screening questionnaires relating to each study's focus areas were sent to the target companies. In addition the APQC/HKPC study manager and/or the SME contacted the potential target organization personnel by phone to obtain a richer understanding of their practices.

5   Based on the research, the responses to the screening questionnaire and the telephone interview, the SME prepared a matrix of possible organizations and their fit with and potential value for the study's focus areas.

6   Representatives of the sponsoring organizations met in a group with the study manager and the SME to discuss the SME's analysis and recommendations and rank the potential target companies.

7   Based on these rankings the final list of target companies was identified.

The target organizations for the five studies were from North America, Europe and Asia. The list of target organizations is provided below:

1   ABB–CE
2   Alcoa
3   Appleton Papers
4   CNA
5   Frito–Lay
6   Halliburton Energy Services
7   Honeywell
8   Hospital Authority of Hong Kong
9   John Deere
10 Merrill Lynch Credit Corporation
11 Methodist Healthcare System
12 National Semiconductor
13 PPG
14 Royal Dutch/Shell
15 Siemens
16 Silicon Graphics
17 Sprint
18 Sterling Chemicals
19 USAA

20   Whirlpool
21   Xerox (China)
22   Xerox (USA)

It bears mention that the target companies selected were relatively high performers in their industries at the time of selection. As noted earlier, organizations that were below average performers in their industries in financial terms, were eliminated as part of the screening process. There was a consensus among the individuals selecting the target organizations that performance at the time of selection was neither necessary nor sufficient to add validity to the conclusions of the studies. However, good performance was seen to be desirable as it was expected to enhance the credibility of the findings with one user group – the top management of the sponsoring organizations.

Data collection

Data were collected from the sponsoring organizations as well as the target organizations. Identical detailed questionnaires were applied to both sets of organizations. In addition, protocols were developed for interviews that were conducted in the course of a site visit with each of the target organizations. The site visit also involved presentations by and discussions with the target organization's planning managers and line executives. The site visit team included the SME, study managers from APQC/HKPC and a group of representatives of the sponsoring organizations. Oral debriefings were conducted immediately after the site visit followed by written observations by the site visit team about the learning that had taken place and insights that had been developed.

Data analysis

The data derived from the questionnaires were employed to compare the practices of the target companies with those of the sponsoring companies. They also gave rise to an understanding of the commonality of the practices among the target companies. A typical profile or template was evident with respect to certain practices adopted by the target companies. The existence of such common design decisions and practices suggested the possibility of normative conclusions.

Statistically, and not surprisingly given the selection process, in all the studies the target companies were found to be significantly different and superior to the sponsoring companies in terms of the perceived effectiveness of their planning practices (Kendall Rank Correlation Coefficient, $p < 0.05$). The other significant differences in practices were therefore considered to be prima facie of interest, as they are associated with the differences in perceived effectiveness between target and sponsoring companies.

The analyzes of the questionnaire data and the findings from the site visits were discussed in detail in day-long to two-day-long "knowledge transfer sessions" involving the target and sponsoring companies as well as the study managers and the SME. The knowledge transfer sessions were more in the nature of a dialogue rather than a one-way communication from the target to the sponsoring organizations. This dialogue reflected the main reason why the target companies agreed to participate in the studies, which was their desire to better understand and improve their own systems. Even the site visits reflected this motivation as target companies consistently asked for evaluations and observations from the representatives of sponsoring companies and from the SME regarding their practices. The practices of the target companies were employed as a launching pad for discussions between knowledgeable practitioners to lead to a mutually and accepted understanding about logically defensible, experientially validated and potentially effective planning practices.

The findings and guidelines included in this chapter have therefore benefited, in a structured and methodical fashion, from the inputs, observations, and critical review of literally dozens of planning executives from the target and sponsoring companies. The rationale underlying each of the findings has essentially been generated or accepted by a significant group of mangers engaged in strategic planning.

Limitations of the Methodology

A key limitation of this research is that there is no statistically supported association, let alone correlation, and certainly no demonstrated causal relationship between the planning practices that were recommended and traditional "objective" measures of organizational success. The findings are supported only by the fact that:

1   These practices were followed by organizations that perceived their planning systems to be relatively and significantly more effective in contributing to organizational effectiveness than the planning systems of a larger group of sponsoring organizations, and
2   These practices were accepted as conceptually credible or logically defensible by practicing managers.

A further limitation is that the findings are not all derived from a single set of organizations but from five different sets, albeit employing the same methodology and with consistency of concepts and frameworks supported by the involvement of the same SME.

The Process Framework

The twenty sponsoring organizations involved in the first of these studies developed a framework, which guided the description and analysis of strategic planning processes in all five of the studies. Recognizing the great diversity in approaches and practices employed in strategic planning, the managers representing these organizations sought to identify the elements common to all strategic planning processes. The intent was to develop a framework that was broad enough to allow acceptance and understanding on the part of all of the target and sponsoring organizations, and yet that was detailed enough to provide meaningful and practical guidance to those seeking to improve their practice of strategic planning.

The framework is of significance in multiple ways:

1   It is presumed to apply to strategic planning processes in all organizations. It is intended to reflect elements that are common to all strategic planning processes regardless of their unique tailoring to individual organizational characteristics. It consequently allows comparison of processes across organizations, which is essential for meaningful generalizations or guidelines to be developed.

2   As a corollary of the above point it can be argued that the elements identified in the framework represent required components of formalized strategic planning activity.

3   At the same time, the framework necessarily is parsimonious given that the components identified are common to diverse contexts.

4   Having been developed by practicing planning executives, the framework was created with the intent of providing guidance regarding the effective design of planning processes. The taxonomy of components maps onto the executives' process design choices.

In short, if the four points made above are valid, it follows that the framework captures what can reasonably be described as the practical essence of the strategic planning process.

The elements of this organizationally relevant, practice-oriented, presumably parsimonious but conceptually comprehensive framework were the focus of the studies and, since they were identified as common to all the organizations, provided for the possibility of rich and comparable information. The framework that was developed is diagrammed below in figure 5.1.

The backbone of the framework is the central sequence starting with "Generation and Prioritization of Issues" and ending with "Implementation and Communication." This sequence appears to be a variant of classic problem-solving models. Control is

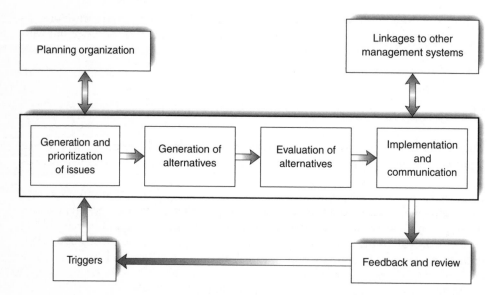

Figure 5.1   A framework for the study of strategic planning processes

built into the framework through the "Implementation and Communication" step and, of course, the "Feedback and Review" step. The stimuli or motivations for engaging in strategic planning are labeled "Triggers" and these triggers are linked to the control-oriented feedback and review component. The planning process cannot just happen and needs to be managed by a "Planning Organization" of some kind. Finally, the planning process cannot exist in isolation and "Linkages to Other Management Systems" – such as operational planning, capital budgeting, research and development, human resources and information technology – are needed.

The remainder of this chapter describes the findings of the studies regarding the distinctive characteristics of strategic planning processes in the target companies.

Target Company Practices

All the findings listed below possess the following characteristics:

1   The consensus of the executives participating in the study is that they reflect effective practices.
2   These practices of the target companies were significantly different ($p < 0.05$, employing non-parametric tests such as the Kendall τ and the Kruskal–Wallis ANOVA) from the practices of the sponsoring organizations, unless otherwise indicated.

The findings regarding key elements of the strategic planning process framework are discussed below.

Triggers

The triggers, that initiated strategic planning exercises, which were considered included:

1   the calendar,
2   deviations from expected performance outcomes,
3   changes in regulation or legislation,
4   developments in technology,
5   changes in the competitive situation,
6   changes in customer requirements,
7   changes in management.

The target companies were clearly different in their use of triggers in comparison to the sponsoring organizations. Not only were the differences significant in (non-parametric) statistical terms, but they also merit consideration by process designers because the target organizations evaluated the effectiveness of their strategic planning systems significantly more highly than the sponsoring organizations. This difference in perceived effectiveness is an important basis for viewing the practices of the target organizations to be of value in providing guidelines for improving the practice of strategic planning.

The dominant trigger for the sponsoring – less effective group of – organizations was the calendar. Changes in regulation, legislation, technology and customer requirements were not cited as reasons for triggering a strategic planning exercise. Strategic planning for these organizations could reasonably be inferred to be primarily time-triggered, a matter of routine. Target organizations on the other hand reported responding to each and every listed trigger. Less than 50 percent of their planning exercises were triggered by the calendar.

The overall thrust of the data was that strategic planning exercises in target organizations were issue-triggered. Related data indicated that issue identification was notably reliant on environmental scanning activities. Aspects of the strategic planning processes in target organizations appeared to be similar to the issue management systems, described by Ansoff (1991).

Issue generation and prioritization

The practices of target organizations were markedly different from those of sponsoring organizations in this regard. Both target and sponsoring organizations gave equal importance to external and internal issues. However, target organizations in comparison to sponsor organizations, gave much more importance to:

1 "vision" than the "market" as a source of issues,
2 line management than staff in identifying issues,
3 anticipated futures than the past as a basis for assessing issues.

Target companies were strongly and consistently oriented toward the future and their aspirations as the focus of their planning activities. Relatively, the target organizations were more concerned about past performance and current customers.

Not surprisingly, environmental scanning was relied on upon twice as much by target organizations, when compared to sponsoring organizations, as a technique for identifying issues.

Alternative generation

In this element of the process, there was no significant difference between the target and sponsoring organizations. Both groups relied on brainstorming, assignments to individuals, focused taskforces and cross-functional teams. Target organizations displayed a noticeably (though not statistically significant) greater reliance on teams and taskforces than did the sponsoring organizations.

Alternative evaluation and selection

A distinctly different pattern was evident between the criteria employed by the sponsoring organizations and those preferred by the target organizations. The target organizations gave greater importance to *market-based, financial* measures such as:

◆ EVA,
◆ shareholder value, and
◆ risk-adjusted rates of return.

In contra-distinction the sponsoring organizations gave greater importance to *internal, accounting* measures such as:

◆ profit/contribution,
◆ ROI, and
◆ cash flow.

The use of EVA and market-based measures rather than traditional accounting measures of profitability is indicative of the higher performance aspirations and contemporary character of the practices employed by target organizations. The emphasis on EVA and related measures reflect two characteristics of target organizations that were observable in all of the studies. These organizations utilized stretch goals as a device for motivating out-of-box thinking and higher performance. They also engaged in continuous improvement of their planning processes and techniques.

Implementation and communication

This phase of the process proved to be a rich source of guidelines. The most significant findings were:

◆ Target organizations gave more importance to business-unit strategies than to corporate strategies. The reverse was true for sponsoring organizations.
◆ Action plans and enablers were emphasized by target organizations. In general, target organizations explicitly required a detailed specification of the actions and programs to be undertaken to implement strategy.
◆ Changes in strategy were closely and explicitly linked to changes in organizational structure in target organizations.
◆ Communication was identified as the closest thing to a "magic bullet" for ensuring the effectiveness of both planning and implementation. Not surprisingly, both target and sponsoring organizations employed a wide range of communication mechanisms. One target organization's corporate planner went so far as to suggest that the most important indicator of the quality of planning at the divisional level was the extent of involvement of the divisional president and senior management in communicating the plan to personnel at all levels in the division.
◆ Face-to-face communication involving senior executives was rated as by far the most effective mode of communication, regardless of context, culture or industry.
◆ Target organizations placed emphasis on widely sharing their strategic plans within their organizations.
◆ Target organizations demonstrated innovativeness in developing communication forums and methods. Some of the forums and methods noted were websites, direct access to senior managers, regularly scheduled times and locations where senior managers would be available for discussions, hotlines to address rumors, and

regular open houses to promote social exchanges.

♦   The growing importance of online communication to accomplish a variety of tasks from scheduling though training to updating plans was explicitly recognized.

Planning organization

Planning departments tended to be lean in all the organizations. Consequently, it was not surprising to find innovative approaches such as "virtual planning teams" employed by target organizations to handle the workload. Planning managers also worked closely with other staff departments to accomplish their tasks.

Close relationships with staff departments responsible for "quality management" were noticeably widespread. In some target organizations close relationships with the human resource function were observed.

Planning managers played a wide variety of roles and were often employed as consultants by operating units in areas such as issue analysis and facilitation of group meetings.

Planning managers in target organizations were accorded significant roles. They are perhaps best described as *consiglieres* to senior management.

An unusual approach in one target organization was the use of two separate planning departments at the corporate level. One was charged with working with the divisions to help them develop better plans. The other analyzed and critiqued the divisional plans, alerting the top management to questions that needed to be raised. Separation of these two functions was intended to enhance the effectiveness with which these two responsibilities were executed.

The planning personnel in target organizations expressed the opinion that careful and thorough management of the planning process throughout the organization was important. In one organization the corporate planner scheduled planning meetings two years in advance, with the CEO issuing a memorandum detailing the timings and agendas, indicating that attendance by listed participants was mandatory and was to take precedence over other activities!

Planning executives in the target companies expressed and demonstrated their commitment to constantly reviewing and improving their systems. Their willingness to participate in the studies was compelling evidence of this commitment.

Linkages to other management systems

Except for "incentives and compensation," the differences between target and sponsor organizations were not statistically significant. Linkages to business plans, the capital budget, financial budgets, R&D, and information technology were all viewed as effective.

In the case of compensation and incentives, the target organizations indicated a level of effectiveness almost twice as high as that of the sponsoring organizations. The careful and explicit cascading of strategic goals to operational targets at lower levels helped target organizations link incentives to strategic performance at multiple levels.

Feedback and review

One of the most interesting findings was that target companies included their planning processes as part of formal performance reviews. A hierarchy of formal assessment was employed, ranging from performance through strategy, then the design of the planning process and, finally, to organizational structure. Thus, regularly scheduled reviews of performance also addressed needed improvements in planning processes and techniques. Issues of needed changes in strategy and in organizational structure were also raised at these reviews.

A continuous improvement philosophy with regard to planning processes was observed, supported by the formal use of quality management tools. For instance one organization had projects in place to reduce the "cycle time" of key planning processes.

Conclusion

The simple process framework developed by a group of planning managers and line executives proved to be a powerful analytical tool in helping identify practices and process designs that offer the promise of contributing to greater organizational effectiveness. The simplicity of the framework permits it to be of wide relevance in addition to providing needed focus and comprehensibility to a diverse and complex set of activities.

While this chapter focuses on process design, it is difficult to divorce it from issues relating to content. Two strongly evident content orientations in target organizations appear to have major implications for process design.

First, target organizations gave the greatest importance to "qualitative" factors when conducting the analysis necessary to develop plans. Strategic thinking received 50 percent of the total efforts and time devoted to planning. "Quantitative" but non-financial factors (such as market share) were next in importance. Financial analysis was given the least amount of time and effort. Financial performance was recognized to be of critical importance; however, it was believed that strategic thinking was what contributed to financial performance. To focus thinking and analysis on strategy rather than just numbers, some target companies placed stringent limits on the number of pages in plans and the number of minutes in presentations that could be devoted to financial analysis. In contrast, sponsoring organizations devoted the majority of their time and attention to financial analysis.

Second, target organizations displayed a pronounced orientation toward detailing the actions and "enablers" that would support their strategy. Sponsoring organizations placed relatively less emphasis on actions and required less specificity and detail in the description of the actions.

To summarize, the trends in process design displayed by the target organizations were:

- Multiple triggers for initiating a planning cycle.
- A movement towards "issue management" and away from routine exercises at prespecified intervals.

- ◆ Creative, out-of-box thinking, motivated by stretch goals, strongly emphasizing qualitative analysis and factors over financial analysis and numbers.
- ◆ An action orientation, focusing on "enablers" and providing specificity and detail regarding how strategic goals will be achieved.
- ◆ Future-oriented and vision-driven issue generation
- ◆ Generation of alternatives that are
  — innovative
  — specific and detailed, and
  — externally oriented.
- ◆ A greater use of electronic modes of communication and intranets for providing instructions and training, and for recording, communicating and updating plans
- ◆ A greater reliance on team-based processes.
- ◆ A stronger linkage between performance and incentive compensation.
- ◆ Increasingly significant roles for planning executives including those of
  — catalyst
  — top management advisor
  — process and technical consultant
  — integrator of business unit strategies
  — educator in analytic and strategic thinking.
- ◆ Integration of the planning activity and outcomes with other components of the management system
- ◆ Recognition of communication as both a key foundation and a consequence of effective planning

An intriguing observation is that in both the target and sponsoring organizations the distinction between traditional strategic and business planning processes appears to be getting blurred. Activities and analyzes that would in the 1980s be considered "strategic" and conducted less frequently than annually are now integrated into the annual business planning process. On the other hand, organizations appear to be increasingly engaged in activities that are more in the nature of issue management rather than an episodic "strategic planning" activity conducted every three to five years with annual updates in the intervening years. Issue management is conducted on an ongoing basis in response to emerging issues. Thus, instead of separate strategic and business planning cycles, organizations engage in annual plans that integrate traditional strategic and business planning. This integrated cycle is complemented by a continuous scanning activity coupled to an issue management process.

Finally, the target organizations' emphasis on continuous improvement of the planning process is indicative of a future in which new, innovative and ever-changing processes will characterize the practice of planning in organizations.

References

Ansoff, H. I. 1991: Strategic management in a historical perspective. *International Review of Strategic Management*, 2, 1, pp. 3–69.

Camillus, J. C. 1982: Reconciling logical incrementalism and synoptic formalism: an integrated approach to designing strategic planning systems. *Strategic Management Journal*, 3, 3, 277–83.

Camillus, J. C., Sessions, R. T., and Webb, R. 1998: Visionary action: strategic processes in fast-cycle environments. *Strategy and Leadership*, 26, 1, 20–4.

Campbell, A. 1999: Tailored, not benchmarked: a fresh look at corporate planning. *Harvard Business Review*, 75, 2, 41–50.

Chakravarthy, B. S. and Doz, Y. 1992: Strategy process research: focusing on corporate self-renewal. *Strategic Management Journal*, 13 (special issue), 5–14.

Gilmore, W. S. and Camillus, J. C. 1996: Do your planning processes meet the reality test? *Long Range Planning*, 29, 6, 869–79.

Quinn, J. B. 1980: *Strategies for change: logical incrementalism*. Homewood, IL: Irwin.

Rajagopalan, N., Rasheed, A. M. A., and Datta, D. K. 1993: Strategic decision processes: an integrative framework and future directions. In P. Lorange, B. Chakravarthy, J. Roos, and A. Van de Ven (eds), *Implementing strategic processes: change, learning and cooperation*. Cambridge MA: Blackwell, 274–312.

Steiner, G. A. 1969: *Top management planning*. London: Macmillan.

CHAPTER SIX

A Multilevel Analysis of the Strategic Decision Process and the Evolution of Shared Beliefs

Mirela Schwarz

Introduction

In recent years the strategic management literature has shown an increasing interest in executive cognition and its impact on strategic processes and outcomes (e.g. Gioia and Chittipeddi, 1991; Hambrick, 1988; Huff, 1990; Starbuck and Milliken, 1988; Walsh et al., 1988; Wiersema and Bantel, 1992). Most researchers contributing to this body of work argue that executive beliefs have a strong impact on strategic choices and actions and can influence the firm performance (e.g. D'Aveni and MacMillan, 1990; Day and Lord, 1992; Fiol, 1989; Priem, 1994; Thomas et al., 1993).

Research linking beliefs to organizational processes and suggesting that demographic characteristics are surrogates of beliefs (e.g. Finkelstein and Hambrick, 1990; Hambrick and Mason, 1984; Priem, 1994), found important relationships between executives' demographic characteristics and firm performance (Norburn and Birley, 1988; Smith et al., 1994), strategic orientation (Chaganti and Sambharya, 1987), innovation (Bantel and Jackson, 1989), diversification strategies (Song, 1982) and decision-making processes (Hitt and Tyler, 1991; Melone, 1994).

Studies exploring the impact of individual or shared beliefs of decision-makers showed that beliefs may influence the quality of decisions, the decision performance of executives, the timing of strategic response, the trust and risk attitude among decision-makers and the co-ordination of strategic choices and activities (Barr and Huff, 1997; Hambrick and Mason, 1984; Hitt and Tyler, 1991; Melone, 1994; Schwenk, 1984, 1995; Walsh et al., 1988). Evidence from field studies for the impact of shared beliefs on strategic decision process is less extensive (e.g. Hage and Dewar, 1972; Narayanan and Fahey, 1990).

In order to examine the effect and role of executive beliefs on organizational processes and in particular on the strategic decision process, it is important to understand the factors and processes influencing the beliefs held by executives (Walsh, 1995). So far, there has been an interesting array of studies discussing the factors influencing executive beliefs (Gray et al., 1985; Hambrick and Mason, 1984; Harris, 1994; Sproull, 1981) supported by empirical studies (Hambrick et al., 1993; Hauenstein and Foti, 1989; Ireland et al., 1987; Markoczy, 1997; Walker, 1985; Walsh, 1988). However, a gap remains in our understanding regarding how and to what extent the development of shared beliefs influences the strategic decision process or is influenced by the strategy development process itself.

This research first examines the factors involved in the development of shared beliefs among executives during the strategy development process and aims to contribute to the limited existing field studies in this area. Further, this research aims to carry out a multilevel analysis by examining the relationship between the development of shared beliefs among decision-makers and the strategic decision process. This chapter provides a new theoretical framework exploring the relationship of these two processes.

In the following the relevant literature is reviewed and the qualitative research approach applying grounded theory methodology for analyzing the empirical field data is discussed. Then, the research findings are presented providing an empirical case and a new theoretical framework for the development of shared beliefs and its relationship with the strategic decision process.

Literature Review

Individual and shared beliefs

The basic concept of belief and other related concepts (such as frames, mental models, schemata) have been useful in the strategic cognition research concerning the understanding of executives' interpretations of their complex environment during the strategy development process (Gioia and Sims, 1986; Kelly, 1955; Minsky, 1975; Rumelhart, 1980; Walsh, 1995; Weick and Bougon, 1986).

Beliefs are defined in this study as the "understanding that represents credible relationships between objects, properties, and ideas" (Sproull, 1981, p. 204). Beliefs are viewed in general as attributes of individuals and in order to achieve agreement concerning strategic choices and actions among executives,[1] there is a need for shared beliefs.

In the strategy development process individuals may continue to have different beliefs and interpretations, but they also may share beliefs with others (Bougon et al., 1977; Hodgkinson and Johnson, 1994). It is these shared beliefs among decision-makers which provide the basis for co-ordinated activity during the strategic decision process, for social processes, for formation of interest groups, and for implementing new policies (Gilbert, 1989; Kelly, 1955; Kuhn, 1970; Haas, 1992).

This concept of shared belief is supported by work on *shared understanding* (March, 1991), *cognitive consensuality* (Gioia and Sims, 1986), and *shared strategic frames* (Huff, 1982) within organizations. This chapter follows the argument that executives share similar beliefs and understanding with others in order to develop the basis for agreed choices and actions (Bougon et al., 1977; Hodgkinson and Johnson, 1994) during the strategy development process.

Influencing executive beliefs

Two major streams of research are evident in the strategic cognition literature on factors and processes influencing beliefs. The first stream of research examined the influence of functional related issues on belief (e.g. Beyer et al., 1997; Dearborn and Simon, 1958; Hambrick and Mason, 1984; Starbuck and Milliken, 1988; Waller et al., 1995; Walsh, 1988). Most researchers contributing to this body of work take the position that the functional experience of executives, the functional position an executive holds and functional related information concerning the functional role and position have an impact on the development of shared beliefs.

These findings are supported by psychological researchers who argue that executive beliefs are influenced by the requirements and expectations of their functional roles and are likely to be influenced by information relevant to their functional position and goal (Fiske and Taylor, 1991; Janis and King, 1954; Lord and Foti, 1986; Watts, 1967). Further research illustrates that the belief of organizational members is shaped by authority figures and peers who reward performing according to functional roles (Tetlock, 1983; Wortman and Linsenmeier, 1977).

The second stream of research emphasizes that social related processes and factors have a stronger impact on the development of beliefs than functional related issues (Chattopadhyay et al., 1999; Daft and Weick, 1984; Falcione et al., 1987; Gioia, 1986; Krackhardt and Kilduff, 1991; Salancik and Pfeffer, 1978; Weick, 1995). This body of research argues that existing beliefs are influenced by social information processes, social interaction, shared sense-making, and verbal and non-verbal communications. Evidence from field studies for the strong impact of social influences on the development of shared beliefs is less extensive (e.g. Thomas and McDaniel, 1990; Walker, 1985).

Another important issue in shaping beliefs is the fact that some team members have a stronger impact on fellow executives' beliefs than others. The reasons for this are explained by similarities in demographic characteristics such as functional background, age, tenure, and life experience which have an impact on behavior, style of non-verbal communication, and the inclination towards social interaction among executives (e.g. Byrne, 1971; Hambrick et al., 1993; Kulik and Ambrose, 1992; Smith et al., 1994). This body of research suggests that executives who show similarity with regard to certain demographic characteristic, tend to interact more strongly and effectively with one another and may, therefore, shape each others' beliefs to a greater extent than will other team members with lower levels of similarity.

Other dimensions which influence the development of shared beliefs are environmental issues such as market situation and trends, organizational issues such as size, structure, strategy, and financial success (Chattopadhyay et al., 1999; Barr and Huff, 1997). This research acknowledges that environmental and organizational factors may shape the development of executive beliefs.

This research highlights the fact that beliefs, in particular about new strategic ideas, are subjective and appear in different patterns. It is this subjectivity and the evolution of different belief patterns that this chapter suggests accounts for much of the influence on the strategic decision process.

Strategic decision processes and the impact of executive beliefs

The strategic decision process has been an important research topic as it examines the essential factors, resources, and decisions which influence the future of an organization (e.g. Eisenhardt and Zbaracki, 1992; Huff and Reger, 1987; Mintzberg et al., 1976; Rajagopalan et al., 1993; Schwenk, 1995).

The definition of the strategic decision process adopted in this research accepts the view identified in earlier studies that the process consists of three major phases: problem/issue identification, development, and selection (Mintzberg et al., 1976; Frederickson, 1984). These three phases have been shown to have subphases and possible interruptions, to be interrelated, and sometimes to return to earlier phases.

The strategic decision process involves continuing occurrence of strategic discussions and debates (Eden and Ackermann, 1998; Schwarz and Nandhakumar, 1999; von der Heijden, 1996). The major issues and processes involved in these debates are: organizational learning (Fiol and Lyles, 1985; Hedberg, 1981; Lucas and Ogilive, 1999; Shrivastva, 1983; Parkhe, 1991) and knowledge sharing (e.g. Nonaka and Takeuchi, 1994; Sanchez and Mahoney, 1996; Spender and Grant, 1996; von Krogh et al., 1997).

There are many factors which influence the strategic decision process. This study focuses on how the development of shared beliefs is influenced and influences the strategic decision process. The strategic literature shows evidence that shared beliefs strongly influence strategic choices and actions (e.g. D'Aveni and MacMillan, 1990; Day and Lord, 1992; Fiol, 1989; Priem, 1994; Thomas et al., 1993). It has been argued that shared beliefs during the strategic decision process provide the basis for agreed choices and actions (Bougon et al., 1977; Hodgkinson and Johnson, 1994). Research linking beliefs to organizational outcomes and suggesting that demographic attributes are surrogates of belief (Finkelstein and Hambrick, 1990; Hambrick and Mason, 1984) found that there are linkages between executive demographic attributes and decision-making processes (Hitt and Tyler, 1991; Melone, 1994).

Variations in beliefs held by executives may create disagreement concerning strategic issues during the strategic decision process (Lant et al., 1992). Miller, Burke, and Glick (1998) demonstrated that cognitive diversity among executives influence negatively the comprehensiveness of examination of strategic issues and long-term planning activities. Other studies have identified that a number of potential cognitive biases may influence strategic decision-makers (Barnes, 1984; Bazerman, 1998; Schwenk, 1984; Walsh et al., 1988). Cognitive biases may contribute to a reduced quality of strategic choices and decision (Walsh et al., 1988). Barr and Huff (1997) found that belief and stress influence the timing of strategic responses. Furthermore, it has been argued that trust and the risk attitude among decision-makers are influenced by shared beliefs (e. g. Sworder, 1995; Hitt and Tyler, 1991). There exist only limited empirical studies investigating the effect of executive beliefs on the strategic decision process (e.g. Hage and Dewar, 1972; Narayanan and Fahey, 1990). Hage and Dewar (1972), for example, illustrated that decision-makers believing in the value of change led more innovative organizations. Narayanan and Fahey (1990) demonstrated that executive beliefs relating to factors influencing sales and profits were differed in successful and unsuccessful organizations within the same industry.

These studies confirm the important influence of belief on the strategic decision process, which may ultimately have an effect on the firms' performance and future direction. While the importance of the effect of shared beliefs on the strategic decision process has been recognized, more insight into the role of beliefs on the strategy development process is needed (Chattopadhyay et al., 1999; Barr and Huff, 1997). To date, there are no field studies specifically exploring the relationship between the development of shared belief and the strategic decision process. The purpose of this chapter is to provide a multilevel analysis of these two processes leading to the development of a theoretical framework by drawing on data generated from the in-depth field study.

Research Methodology

The research approach adopted in this chapter is based on grounded theory methodology (Glaser and Strauss, 1967; Martin and Turner, 1986; Straus and Corbin, 1990) with the aim of developing a descriptive and explanatory theory of the development of shared beliefs during the strategic decision process. This methodology has been efficiently used in strategy process research (e.g. Gioia and Chitipeddi, 1991; Grundy and Johnson, 1993).

Grounded theory supports the development of a theoretical interpretation of a phenomenon while at the same time grounding such interpretation in empirical data (Martin and Turner, 1986). This approach facilitates "the generation of theories of process, sequence, and change pertaining to organisations, positions, and social interaction" (Glaser and Strauss, 1967, p. 114). Using grounded theory methodology, this research seeks to develop a context-based, process-oriented description and explanation of the development of shared beliefs and its role during the strategic decision process.

Research context and data sources

This longitudinal in-depth field study was carried out from June 1997 till December 1999 in a multinational company (SO: pseudonym for the firm's name) in Europe, which produces and provides substations and electrical networks purchased by utility companies.

The research started with the appointment of a new service manager who initiated a new product idea and the beginning of the strategic decision process. By the time the on-site research ended the new product was already implemented and the outcomes were observable. The field site provided a good example of a strategic decision process and of transparently observable changes in the organization's strategy which affected the products and services as well as their markets and customers (Pettigrew, 1990).

The newly appointed service manager started to meet with customers on a regular basis in order to receive information concerning the customers' satisfaction. The customers expressed a demand for outsourcing in-house service activities and services, with the aim of enhancing the lifespan of the substations. During these discussions the service manager came up with a new product idea for the service department. He thought of providing services which would include a feasibility study of the existing substation and customer sites, resulting in an analysis of future service requirements for enhancing the lifespan. Based on this, SO would develop a customized service plan for the customer, detailing the service, time, and resources required, together with costs and benefits. His idea was to sell all these activities in one product package. He initiated a market and customer survey in order to receive confirmation for such a product package. The customer and market survey confirmed the demand for this new product and showed that existing competitors did not offer such a service. These results reinforced the manager's belief that there was an opportunity successfully to introduce the new product.

The service manager first communicated his new product idea to organizational members of the service department. The majority of members of the service department perceived the idea positively and were looking for an increase in their responsibilities and career opportunities. With the support of the members of the service department the manager presented the concept of the new product to the CEO. The CEO's response was reserved, as his main concern was the reaction of other senior managers within the organization. The service manager did not inform the senior managers throughout the organization, because he outlined the importance of implementing the strategy immediately, before "all the politics started." During a previous restructuring of the firm the CEO had experienced great difficulties with the senior manager of sales. He explained that he was "not interested in fighting another battle with some of the senior managers." The CEO insisted that the service manager ought to carry out discussions with other senior managers. He hoped that the service manager would take over the task of obtaining a compromise agreement from other senior managers and promised him a special financial bonus for his efforts.

The analysis of the research findings focuses on the process whereby the service manager communicated his new product idea to senior managers, attempting to convince them of the idea and to achieve the commitment of the majority of senior managers for its implementation. The analysis of how the strategy development process was initiated was explored in detail in another paper (Schwarz and Nandhakumar, 1999).

This study involved a variety of engaged data-gathering methods (e.g. Nandhakumar and Jones, 1997; Silverman, 1993) involving unstructured and semi-structured interviews, observations and documentation reviews. From June 1997 to December 1998 interviews and observations were carried out at regular intervals of two weeks every two months. This was followed by a period of distant observation of outcomes and follow-up interviews with organizational members involved in the strategic decision process from December 1998 till December 1999.

During the field study the researcher had access to the main participants, formal and informal meetings, existing minutes and documentation highlighting some of the historical, processual, and contextual issues relevant to the strategic decision process. In addition, the interviews emphasized both individual and shared interpretations of key participants concerning actions, events, views, beliefs, aspirations, motives (Pettigrew, 1992). For every interview and observed event, such as formal and informal meetings and conversations, extensive notes have been taken supplemented with some tape-recorded and transcribed material.

The aim of the data collection process was to gather field data which is processual (with a focus on action and structure over time), pluralist (varying views of different actors), historical (historical reconstruction of ideas, actions and constraints) and contextual (Pettigrew, 1992). The researcher agreed to use all empirical data confidentially by, for example, changing names of the firm and interviewees. The interviewees had the opportunity to read the transcribed interviews and observation notes as well as the results of this research.

Data analyses

The data was analyzed using the techniques of grounded theory (Glaser and Strauss, 1967), which provided guidelines for the classification of and commentary on qualitative data. The first phase of the analysis involved an analytical technique of reading and rereading field notes and identifying possible concepts evolving out of the empirical findings, which is called the *open coding process* (Strauss and Corbin, 1990). These identified concepts were put together and organized in possible categories or main headlines with meaningful labels. This is known as *axial coding* (Strauss and Corbin, 1990), a technique of connecting related sub-categories in order to develop a more comprehensive and coherent scheme.

Maintaining the categories with the concepts was an iterative process. From the beginning of the research process, new concepts were continually being added and sometimes categories were reconstituted under different labels. This approach helped in organising and analysing the field notes. The iteration between field data and main concepts ended when enough categories and associated concepts had been identified. This stage was achieved when no additional concepts and categories evolved out of the existing empirical data. The developed categories and concepts explain the development of shared beliefs and its relationship to strategic decision process. Glaser and Strauss (1967) refer to this process as *theoretical saturation*. No claim is made that the concepts and interactions are comprehensive and complete.

The next stage of the analysis moved on to a more theoretical level, where the data was analyzed from a theoretical perspective aiming to develop a theoretical conceptualisation of the development of shared beliefs and its role during the strategic decision process. The developed framework is presented in the discussion section.

Overall, the research aim was not to confirm hypotheses, but to offer a description of events and actions and also to allow a different approach to illustrate the role of shared beliefs during the strategic decision process

Research Findings

The process of the development of shared beliefs and its relationship with the strategic decision process, developed from the field study, is depicted in figure 6.1. The figure presents the main concepts that emerged from the grounded theory analysis and indicate how they interact with each other. The following analysis does not claim to consider a complete list of issues and identification of concepts and interactions. Figure 6.1 aims to illustrate in simple terms the complex interactions, influences, events, and

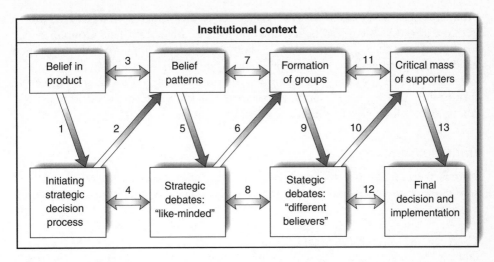

Figure 6.1   Empirical evidence: interplay between the development of shared beliefs and the strategic decision process

actions which occurred during the development of shared beliefs and the strategic decision process. Starting on the left side, figure 6.1 will be discussed briefly.

The development of shared beliefs among senior managers and the strategic decision process were influenced by their institutional context. This context reflects the firm's corporate strategy, organizational structure, customers and competitors. At SO, the service manager developed a new product idea and communicated his belief in its success to the senior managers initiating the strategic decision process (arrow 1). In response to this, the senior managers developed different views and beliefs concerning the new product idea and the manager's ability to implement it (arrow 2). The articulation and formulation of the different beliefs and views reinforced the service manager's belief in the new idea (arrow 3). The senior managers started to discuss and to exchange knowledge concerning possible policies, procedures and operations amongst the "like-minded" (arrow 5). These discussions stimulated the generation of new ideas with regard to the implementation of the product (arrow 4). The debates in turn influenced the beliefs of senior managers by reinforcing or changing their initial beliefs leading to formation of different groups sharing similar beliefs (arrow 6). The emergence of groups reinforced or changed the beliefs of individuals. This in return had an effect on the bonding of the formed groups (arrow 7). The formation of groups sharing similar beliefs led to resistance, conflict of interests and discussions between the groups (arrow 9). This resulted in an organizational learning process whereby the exchange of knowledge helped to develop the product idea further. During this learning process there was a general tendency to go back to earlier discussion topics and combine new information with existing ones (arrow 8). The discussions and actions carried out by senior managers influenced the opinions of organizational members who were uncertain in their beliefs (arrow 10). This in turn affected the development of a critical mass of senior managers sharing the same belief in the success of the product. The critical mass of senior managers led to the formation of a powerful group who reinforced its members' beliefs and confidence (arrow 11). This group of senior managers paved the way for the final decisions to realise and implement the developed product idea with detailed policies, procedures, and operation (arrow 12–13).

In the following section, the institutional context of SO and the analysis of the relationship between the development of shared beliefs and strategic decision process (figure 6.1) will be discussed in more detail.

Institutional context

As depicted in figure 6.1, the issues of environmental and organizational context had an important influence on the development of shared beliefs and the strategic decision process.

Corporate strategies and structure

During the period from 1995 till 2000 the substation manufacturer SO has been committed to improving revenues and profitability, both of which were strongly monitored and controlled by headquarters. In addition, there was an interest in increasing the involvement and activities of the local businesses overseas and decreasing the cost of SO's current west European operation. SO was organized in functional areas, such as purchasing, planning, and engineering, sales, marketing, and finance. The installations of substations were conducted in project teams involving local offices overseas. The service of substations included warranty and replacement of spare parts.

The majority of senior managers participating in the following strategic decision process had spent about fifteen to twenty years with the firm and sometimes came from other areas of the business of the international electronics manufacturer. They possessed working experience in at least two different functional areas and all of them had substantial overseas working experience. In 1997 the company appointed a new service manager who had already been with the company for twenty years and who had worked mainly in the installation of substations overseas.

Customers

The customers of SO were typically large energy providers. Service was carried out after the construction and sale of the substation. Service activities were viewed as a way to maintain customers and obtain follow-on contracts. The customers perceived the after-sales service as a major competitive advantage of substation providers in the bidding phase.

Competitors

SO competed with large multinational substation manufacturers, which in general belong to multinational electronic organizations. The firm attempted to differentiate itself by its customer relations, customized financial deals and services. SO had earned a reputation for reliability and good quality. While facing stronger competition from other firms, in particular from South East Asia, SO was still one of the leaders in the substation business. The service had in the past been perceived as "the lower end" of the sales department, as relatively unimportant. In the 1990s, the perception of service changed to that of a major critical success factor in the industry in order to achieve new contracts.

Interplay between the development of shared beliefs and the strategic decision process

Initiating the strategic decision process

The newly appointed service manager had launched a new service product for changing the current service business that had not yet been offered on the market. The new strategic ideas called for restructuring and the establishment of a new service organisation equal to other functional units within the organisation. He believed in the success of the new product ideas and, encouraged by the company's CEO, communicated his new product idea and his belief in the success of the idea to the senior managers in the company. He communicated his belief through formal and informal meetings and discussions throughout the organization. By communicating and articulating the new service idea the service manager initiated the strategic decision process.

Emergence of different belief patterns

The service manager's communication of the new idea led to the emergence of different beliefs and views among senior managers (figure 6.2). Two major patterns of beliefs emerged as a result of initiating the strategic decision process. The first pattern focused on beliefs in the success of the new product idea. The new idea was perceived to be important for the success of the company in terms of providing a possible competitive advantage in the industry. The second pattern concentrated on beliefs concerning the manager's ability to implement the new product idea. These two major belief patterns held by individual senior managers arose in different combinations.

The emergence of different belief patterns resulted, at this stage of the strategic decision process, in four main "invisible" groups sharing similar belief pattern. The majority of senior managers were not immediately aware that others held a similar combination of belief patterns. The "invisible" groups sharing similar beliefs did often not know of each other and did not yet exchange and discuss their beliefs.

The first "invisible" group (A) shared the same belief in the success of the new product and in the manager's ability to realise it successfully. Those managers who believed in the idea were influenced by their own business and industry experience, which was very often cross-functional and combined with overseas working experience. Individual senior managers evaluated the new product idea by relying on their understanding of the market and the customer situation as well as on their functional knowledge and expertise. Senior managers' belief in the service manager's ability was based on their judgement of his work experience, managerial experience and personality (described by one executive as "persistent, confident, enjoying taking risks with a high energy level").

The second "invisible" group (B) believed that the new product would not be successful and did not believe in its success and importance for the organization. However, long-term acquaintance together with close working and social relationships with the service manager contributed to their belief that he was able to implement the new product successfully.

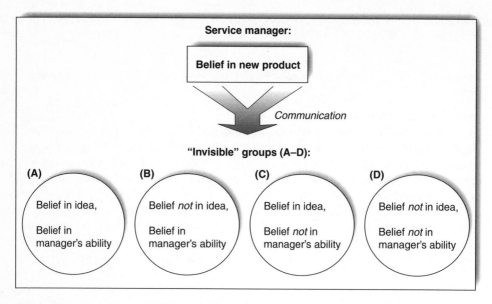

Figure 6.2   Emergence of different belief patterns

The third "invisible" group (C) believed in the success of the idea, as their own functional experience and current functional positions made them aware of the importance of such a service product. However, they did not believe in the manager's ability to implement it. They recognized his controversial political position within the organization and doubted his ability to implement it.

The fourth "invisible" group (D) believed neither in the success of the idea nor in the manager's ability. Here, the current political position had an impact on the belief of senior managers. For example, the senior manager of sales perceived the new service product as a threat to his sales department and to his own position. He explained that:

> I can't allow them [service department] to get direct access to our customers, that would undermine our position within the whole company and also with the customers. In addition, I have at least 6–10 people who are only dealing with spare part delivery of retrofit jobs [exchange of big parts of the substation], whom I would have to make redundant . . . I believe that the new service strategy will damage rather than be beneficial for our substation business.

Individual senior managers made comments and remarks concerning the new product, which reflected their beliefs. Those who articulated their beliefs were mainly from the first "invisible" group (A). This exchange reinforced the service manager's belief and allowed him to pursue the idea further. He explained that "these people know the business and, therefore, I know that their judgement is accurate. I know it is a good idea and now we are going to fight it through."

However, at this stage of the strategic decision process the majority of senior managers did not articulate and exchange their views and beliefs. As one manager pointed out

I wanted to hear more about the new product, especially I wanted to hear about the financial implications for our business. In fact, I already believe that this is a good idea, but I am not sure that the service manager would be the best person to implement it. However, I prefer to have more information before I express my views and beliefs publicly.

Strategic debate amongst the "like-minded"

Throughout the organization individual senior managers started to exchange their views and beliefs concerning the new product idea and the manager's ability to implement it. This exchange occurred in the form of meetings, discussions, and interactions at formal and informal events. Very quickly these exchanges came to concentrate mainly amongst individuals sharing similar beliefs. As one senior manager explained

> I talked mainly to the senior manager of finance, because he thinks in the same way as I do. At this stage I didn't want to be forced to talk about this issue with somebody who comes with a totally different view. At the moment, I am mainly trying to understand how this new product idea might affect our business, my department, and my position.

The exchange of beliefs, opinions, and knowledge occurred amongst individuals sharing similar beliefs due to insecurity. At this stage, hardly any conflicting discussions occurred due to uncertainty about the complexity of the new service product.

The strategic debates amongst the "like-minded" created an atmosphere of "save knowledge transfer and exchange" and also a way to "learn more about the idea" without being "exposed to saying something wrong" and "forced to make up my mind about this new product" as stated by several senior managers. One senior manager pointed out that he felt more encouraged to think creatively because

> I felt safe amongst the people who think like me and are on the same wave-length . . . this helped me to think out of the box, to be creative without having the fear to be judged or be rejected. For me, it's easier to come up with new ideas when I feel understood by my colleagues.

However, a few individuals felt less encouraged to think and participate creatively during the debates, as explained by one manager

> at this stage of the discussion I felt "paralyzed." . . . I was not able to come up with new ideas. I had this feeling of being overwhelmed by the beliefs and ideas of my colleagues. My mind was blocked and I needed to distance myself from it in order to think about it . . . Nobody was really challenging the idea – it was like they already agreed to it.

The service manager acknowledged that senior managers participated differently during the debates. He pointed out that

> I need to give to those who are quiet more time to open up and to talk about their views. I have to find a way to break their silence . . . maybe it would help to bring them together with people who totally refuse our ideas . . . The others who freely exchange ideas and

come up with new ones seem to be in a wonderful "bubbling" process. I have to make sure this process doesn't stop or slow down.

The strategic debates among the "like-minded" sharing similar beliefs either changed or reinforced the current beliefs of group members. This process started the evolution of group bonding among the individuals.

The first group (A) started to identify weaknesses and strengths of the new product by discussing the possible policies, procedures, and operations which it would be necessary to establish. The debates initiated and stimulated the strategic thinking process and supported the knowledge sharing and learning process amongst these managers. These exchanges led to an enhancement of the initial product idea. The senior managers extended elements of the idea, came up with new elements with regard to policies, operational issues, or revised ideas and identified more clearly the strengths and weaknesses of the initial product. As one organizational member explained

after weeks of discussion, I now feel more comfortable in discussing my understanding and views of the pros and cons of the new service product with colleagues with a different view.

Senior managers belonging to group (B) discussed the political implication of the new idea and the possible weakness and strengths of the new product.

At this stage of the strategic decision process, members of group (C) and (D) focused their debates and exchange of knowledge on political issues such as conflict of interests and loss of power. There was a general feeling that these discussions were "not important . . . and we don't want to participate in it, because we don't buy the idea and won't support it" as described by one of the managers.

The duration of strategic debates under the "like-minded" was carried out over a period of three months discussing, balancing out the arguments, understanding the situation, but also discussing the political implication of a new service product. Fortunately, at that time the competitors were in a similar position to SO and did not provide any innovation in the service area to their existing and potential customers. SO was in the fortunate position to carry out time consuming discussion with adverse consequences. At this stage, timing in the strategic decision process was not perceived to be crucial.

Formation of groups sharing similar beliefs

After some months of discussions, articulation, and exchange of beliefs it was apparent which senior managers had similar or dissimilar beliefs. The formulation and communication of individuals' beliefs led to the emergence of "visible" groups. At this stage of the development of shared beliefs the new idea was outlined in terms of policies, operations, and resources.

During the strategic debates, discussions, and meetings the beliefs of the first group (A) who shared the belief in the idea and in the manager's ability were reinforced. Their confidence in their own beliefs and views grew as well as their trust in their own judgement and in those sharing similar beliefs.

The second group (B) showed strong beliefs in the manager's ability which was influenced by long-term social and working relationships with the service manager, but they were not convinced of the idea. As a result of the previous strategic debates individual members of this group started to develop an interest in the new product idea and showed more openness and willingness to discuss it. The organizational learning process among these individuals led to a greater awareness of the perceived benefits and disadvantages of the new product. Individual managers changed their belief and became supporters of the ideas.

The third group (C) believing in the idea, but not in the manager's ability was at the beginning not confident in expressing their support for the new idea. Their belief that the service manager would not be able to implement it influenced their belief in the idea so far that their responses, reactions, decisions and behavior were rather reserved and partially resistant. They still distrusted the service manager.

The senior managers belonging to group (D), not believing in the new product and the manager's ability to implement it focused on planning actions against the manager and discussing how to damage his position. The discussions were focused on power distribution rather than on the content of the strategic ideas.

During this process individual senior managers took over the beliefs of a trusted colleague. For example, the senior manager of planning, an old friend of the service manager, was more open to the manager's idea due to his social relationship. He trusted the service manager's judgement, "even if the ideas were not totally convincing."

In addition, individual senior managers' beliefs were influenced by relationships based on power. This affected the beliefs held by individual managers who were concerned about conflicts and decided to adjust their views and beliefs toward a more powerful perceived manager. At SO, the senior manager of sales was considered to be a powerful man within the organization. As one senior manager explained "It was known that anybody who had a different view to him would get into trouble. Therefore, I thought it would be wise to support his views and beliefs."

The establishment of the four *visible* groups was supported by the previous formation of "*invisible*" groups and the strategic debates amongst the "like-minded." The group formation reflected senior managers with similar belief patterns. The events and action either reinforced or changed their beliefs. The beliefs of senior managers were influenced, changed or reinforced in different speeds and by different reasons. Overall, it was not clear when exactly individuals joined the "visible" groups. Two senior managers did not express and exchange their beliefs and views. Their participation and contribution to the discussions did not make it clear to which "visible" group they belonged to. They remained in one of the "invisible" groups.

Strategic debate between "different believers"

After the formation of the visible groups sharing similar beliefs, the first two groups of senior managers (A) started to initiate formal and informal meetings, and discussion with other groups. During these encounters they debated the different issue of the content, context, and realization of the new service idea, but also politics, loss of power and conflict of interests among senior management (figure 6.3). The first group (A)

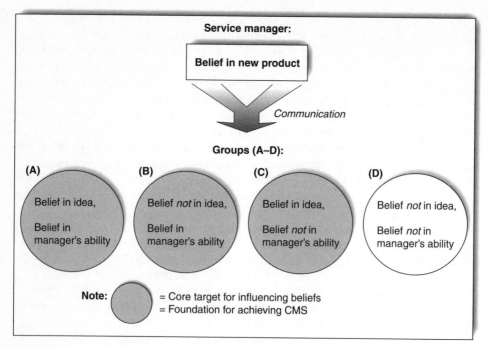

Figure 6.3   Development of critical mass of supporters

discussed their positions in a confident manner. Like the service manager they were convinced of the success of the idea. They realized that they needed the commitment and agreement of the other executives to start with the implementation.

Members of this group organized and initiated the meetings across the different groups. First, they approached the group (B), as they assumed that due to the social relationship with the service manager they would be more open and willing to discuss the strategy in greater detail. This group was perceived to be an important target group for receiving further support. Those organizational members who initially believed in the manager's abilities were influenced in their belief in the new product. The discussion between these "different believers" were dominated by different opinions and led to an interesting, stimulating and creative debate resulting in the improvement of the existing strategic ideas. One senior manager belonging to group (B) described the process as

> at the beginning the discussions started very slowly. Well, at least we all had the same opinion concerning the service manager's ability which made the actual discussion much easier . . . it was less emotional and we knew we stand on the same side. Then, knowing that we agree at least on something (the service manager) we started to challenge each other view. There were so many differing and opposing ideas that at the beginning it looked impossible to come to a conclusion. However, at the end we achieved enhancing the existing strategy with much better ideas.

Then, members of groups (A) started to discuss with group (C) their views and beliefs. At the beginning the discussions led often to a "heated debate" concerning the service manager's ability and personality. At this stage, the different opinion were perceived "hostile" and "pointless." Then, the service manager involved some middle managers of the service department to work, analyze and discuss the ideas with these senior managers. Individual senior managers were impressed by their working experience, determination, and knowledge of the market situation. First, this reduced their disbelief in the service manager and, second, supported their belief more strongly in the idea. This helped to convince individual members of this group (C) of the value of the idea as one senior manager explained

> During the discussions, meetings, I listened to all this . . . First, I was convinced this is all nonsense. But when I attended the twentieth meeting or so, suddenly when one of the service middle managers explained the implications on the resources and operations from their point of view, suddenly, I could see where it was going . . . and it all made sense.

These individuals started to distance themselves from those who were totally against it. They started to interact with supporters of the ideas to get more information. This, in turn, helped them to get engaged in content-related discussion rather than political discussion.

In this process of discussing the idea with different groups sharing different beliefs, members of group (A) used tactics of persuasion and negotiation in order to convince other senior managers, outmanoeuvre in politics, or achieve a compromise. Tactics of persuasion and negotiation were perceived to be important in influencing the beliefs and views of other senior managers and to create a critical mass of supporters amongst senior managers. In addition, group (A) used their old network to include organizational members from middle management to achieve a greater circle of supporters.

Finally, senior managers belonging to group (D) were perceived, as stated by one senior manager of group (A), as a "hopeless case." The different opinions during the discussions created stronger resistance amongst members of groups (D) and partly (A). The debates led to no new or improved ideas. Most of the critics' contributions and remarks were politically motivated and partially related to the disagreement among senior managers. The members of group (A) perceived the debates with group (B) as more creative than with other groups (C + D). The discussions with group (B) led to more new and improved ideas than with the other groups due to their similar belief in the service manager.

Senior managers of group (A) made a conscious decision to slow down the pace of the strategic decision process in order to achieve enough commitment and consensus. As a result of the debates with the different groups, members of group (A) adjusted the original idea, incorporated new suggestions, left out controversial issues, reformulated and changed the content. This improved the quality of the product ideas, the developed strategic choices and decision and finally, the whole strategic decision process.

The spatial closeness of senior managers also had an impact on the formation of shared beliefs and the strategic decision process. For example, the senior managers of engineering (Group C) and the service manager were located in the same part of the building and used the same lift and stairs to get to their offices. At this stage of the development of shared beliefs and of the strategic decision process the two senior managers were more willing and open to discuss the strategic issues and their beliefs while meeting up in the lift and on the stairs. With time they felt more willing to exchange opinions, as, for example, the senior manager of engineering explained "I felt more relaxed, I could joke about it and actually, sometimes, I received some valuable information from the service manager who I regarded as the 'enemy'."

Development of critical mass of supporters

The CEO of SO initiated the idea of developing a critical mass of supporters (in the following "CSM") by encouraging and partly pressuring the service manager to discuss his ideas with other senior managers.

At this stage of the development of shared beliefs and the strategy development process the first three groups (A, B, C) developed into a CMS. The strategic debate between "different believers" involved the interaction between different groups (A-D) which influenced senior managers in becoming more receptive to the content of and arguments for the new idea. This helped members of group (B) to understand more clearly what is involved in the new product which opened up their understanding and views. They could see more clearly the benefits and disadvantages of the new service product. Senior managers belonging to group (D) started to neglect their disbelief in the service manager's ability as they saw the increasing number of senior managers accepting the new product idea. The interaction during these strategic debates enhanced their existing belief and views.

Members of group (A) presented the foundation basis for the CMS, which pushed the discussion, analysis and exploration of the new product. The second and third group were the core targets for achieving the CMS. As a result of the debates, interactions, social and informal meetings the CMS developed similar beliefs into the success of the idea proposed initially by the service manager. The formation of shared beliefs among these senior managers led to the formation of trust among them.

The CMS group was not an institutionalized unit, rather it was an informal network which represented a certain number of decision-makers sharing the same belief about the success of a strategic idea. The critical number indicated that the group of supporters was politically strong enough to proceed with the implementation of the strategic decision as they have enough weight and supporters throughout the organization who would accept their decision. The new group demonstrated commitment and involvement throughout the strategic decision process. Their role was, as one organizational member stated "to start an 'avalanche,' a snowball that rolls down the mountain and gets bigger and bigger."

The CMS influenced the quality of the strategic decision process. The exchange of knowledge, the acceptance of the elaboration of the idea and the willingness to accept a better analysis was greater. As the group was based on shared belief they were more likely to share their knowledge and to be tolerant of each others' views.

The CMS proved to be a key success factor in gaining acceptance and commitment for the idea throughout the organization and strongly influenced the final decision for implementation among senior managers. Their interaction was continuously influenced by trust and tactics of persuasion and negotiation.

Final decision and implementation

Finally, the strategic debates led to a new service strategy for the substation company and a new independent organizational unit (profit centre). The new service strategy included a range of new service products which have not been provided before. The new strategy was implemented by the new organization with new infrastructure, resources, and capital provided by the parent company and international headquarters. This enabled the company to approach new customers which were so far serviced by competitors. Sales and profits in the service business increased to 100 percent in the following year.

The CMS was essential for the final decision and implementation. The members had enough power to make quick decisions with regard to implementation and to break up resistance in individual departments throughout the organization. The CMS took over the role of communicating the new product idea and demonstrated their strong commitment to it, which in turn discouraged certain political groups (for example, group D) opposing the new product.

With time the CMS was perceived throughout the organisation as a strong political group and the majority of organizational members, middle managers and some senior managers decided to accept their judgement because they saw no other way. Although resistance continued even after widespread commitment to the new service product CMS pushed the changes through.

The research findings depicted in figures 6.1, 6.2, and 6.3 described the content and processess of the development of shared beliefs and its relationship with the strategic decision process which were experienced by senior managers during the strategy development process at the field study SO. The relationships illustrated are not deterministic; they may be different in another organization, with a similar or different context.

Discussion

It is important to understand the impact of senior managers' beliefs on the strategic decision process, as they may influence organizational processes and ultimately organizational performance (e.g. Day and Lord, 1992; Priem, 1994; Thomas et al., 1993). No previous study has yet explored empirically how the relationship between the development of shared beliefs influences or is influenced by the strategic decision process. This research has presented the findings of a grounded theory study and has developed a theoretical framework for conceptualizing the interplay between these two processes.

Theoretical framework for the relationship between the development of shared beliefs and the strategic decision process

The theoretical framework explains the empirical situation and captures relationships and interactions between the main concepts of the grounded theory analysis. The core concept emerging out of the analysis is the *critical mass of supporters* (CMS), the main theme of the proposed framework (figure 6.4).

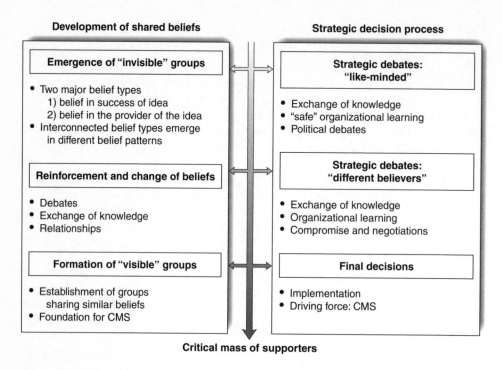

Figure 6.4   Theoretical framework for the relationship between the development of shared beliefs and the strategic decision process

The framework presented in figure 6.4 provides one way of anticipating, explaining, and evaluating the development of shared beliefs and its relationship with the strategic decision process. The framework developed here does not claim to provide a complete list of concepts and interactions. The context in which the development of shared beliefs and the strategic decision process occur and interact is the institutional one. The institutional context reflects the environment, structure, strategy, and culture of an organization.

The process of developing shared beliefs consists of three major phases: the emergence of "invisible" groups, the reinforcement and change of individual beliefs, and the formation of "visible" groups sharing similar belief patterns. The emergence of "invisible" groups at the beginning of the strategic decision process leads to the establishment of two major interconnected belief types. The first type is belief in the potential success of a strategic idea. The second is belief in the ability of the proposer of the idea to carry it through to implementation. These two belief types emerge simultaneously in different combinations amongst decision-makers. These shape the strategic decision process and create the context for the formation of "visible" groups sharing similar beliefs. The members of the "invisible" group share similar beliefs in a tacit way, which is not explicitly articulated and exchanged. Individuals may stay in the "invisible" group and not proceed through the suggested stages. The reinforcement and change of individual beliefs is shaped by debates, exchange of knowledge and relationship based on power and social networks. Organizational members demonstrate different speed in proceeding through these three stages and different reasons for joining the "visible" group. The establishment of groups sharing similar beliefs lead to the formation of visible groups and provide the foundation for the development of a critical mass of supporters.

The strategic decision process illustrates two major strategic debates occurring at different stages: strategic debates amongst the "like-minded" and strategic debates between the "different believers." The first stage consists of strategic debates amongst decision-makers sharing similar beliefs which stimulate the organizational learning and knowledge-sharing process amongst these decision-makers. In addition, political debates emerge focusing on conflict of interests. Some individual organizational members feel encouraged to think creatively amongst "like-minded" with similar beliefs. Others feel hindered in thinking creatively. During the strategic debates between "different believers" the process of organizational learning and sharing of knowledge is spread to other groups, in particular to those with dissimilar beliefs. Organizational members show different degrees of creativity in formulating and discussing ideas due to similar and dissimilar beliefs. Individual participants feel encouraged to think more creatively when faced with different opinions and beliefs. Such debates involve compromises and negotiations. These two type of strategic debates lead to the final decision of implementing the strategic idea. The implementation process is shaped and guided by the critical mass of supporters.

The iterative process between the development of shared beliefs and the strategic decision process leads to the evolution of the critical mass of supporters (CMS), the main theme proposed by this framework. In the context of this study, the CMS is understood as a certain number of decision-makers sharing the same belief about a certain strategic idea. Their belief is aided by commitment, motivation, and will together with dedication concerning the successful implementation of strategic idea. The level of "critical mass" indicates that the group is large and powerful enough to make and implement strategic decisions. A certain number of these decision-makers are vital to communicate the ideas, to convince and persuade other executives and organizational members and to implement the strategic decisions with all their implications. During the strategic decision process the CMS apply tactics of negotiations and politics in interaction with other decision-makers in order to achieve a greater number of supporters. The tactics chosen are different for each group with different belief patterns. At the end of the strategic decision process the CMS are the key drivers in the decision-making process and strategy implementation.

This research supports the argument that both functional and social related issues influence the development of shared beliefs. Some evidence from this field study confirms the view that social related issues such as social interaction, social information processing, and shared sensemaking have a stronger influence on the development of beliefs than functional issues (Chattopadhyay et al., 1999; Daft and Weick, 1984; Falcione et al., 1987; Gioia, 1986; Salancik and Pfeffer, 1978; Weick, 1995).

Although the factors influencing the development of shared beliefs have received a lot of attention in the strategic cognition literature, there is little known about the process itself of how shared beliefs evolve over time. This research suggests that the emergence of "invisible" groups, the reinforcement and change of individual beliefs followed by the formation of "visible" group, may provide one explanation for the process of shared belief formation.

The strategic literature acknowledges that the strategic decision process can occur in the form of debates and discussions (Eden and Ackermann, 1998; Schwarz and Nandhakumar, 1999; von der Heijden, 1996). The literature also recognizes that during the strategy development process organizational learning occurs through individuals (Fiol and Lyles, 1985; Hedberg, 1981; Shrivastva, 1983) and between organizations and communities (Lucas and Ogilvie, 1999; Parkhe, 1991). This study supports the claim that during the strategic decision process strategic debates occur which involve organizational learning process on individual and organizational/group level. In addition, this research confirms the importance of knowledge sharing during the strategic decision process (e.g. Nonaka and Takeuchi, 1995; Sanchez and Mahoney, 1996; Spender and Grant, 1996; von Krogh et al., 1997).

Furthermore, this research would like to elaborate the concept of strategic debate and discussion by emphasizing the different occurrence of strategic debates amongst "like-minded" and between "different believers." These two type of strategic debates have a different impact on the organizational learning and knowledge-sharing process.

The findings of this research have several implications for practitioners ensuring creativity during the strategic decision process. First, the findings imply a need for a strong role for leadership in creating an open atmosphere for discussing and recognizing controversial views and managing participants' contribution and communication efficiently. Second, the findings imply a need for practitioners to participate in training "how to carry out strategic debates amongst different believers." This would help to acknowledge and raise the awareness of different views and beliefs as well as provide techniques for carrying out discussions more efficiently. Third, managers may consider the different intellectual, functional, social and cultural background of organisational members involved in strategic debates. This understanding may support the management in forming an adequate group of organisational members participating in the strategic decision process. In addition, this understanding may help to lead and manage the participants' contributions and communication more efficiently. More empirical work in this area is necessary to elaborate and verify these suggestions.

The literature acknowledges that a group sharing similar beliefs leads to group bonding (Gilbert, 1989; Kelly, 1955; Kuhn, 1970; Haas, 1992). This research suggests enhancing this view with the concept of the CMS related to senior managers participating in the strategic decision process. These decision-makers share a similar degree of trust and attitude to risk-taking (Hitt and Tyler, 1991). This research suggests that the risk attitude among these decision-makers increases with the growth of the CMS with similar beliefs and interests.

Finally, this research suggests that the development of shared belief is part of the strategic decision process and is the *emotional dimension* of the strategic decision process. These two processes take place in an iterative, reciprocal and to some extent sequential fashion. The two processes may contribute to changes in strategy such as changes in product and services, market and customers, organizational structure and finally, the future direction of the organization. The shared beliefs among the key decision-makers provide an emotional dimension for the successful development of strategy and implementation.

Understanding the emergence of different belief patterns and the relationship between the development of shared beliefs and the strategic decision process may provide additional insights into why organizations experience such different strategy development processes with regard to response time, quality of the decision processes and chosen strategic responses.

Conclusions

Previous research has explored and acknowledged the important influence of beliefs on the strategic decision process (e.g. Barr and Huff, 1997; Day and Lord, 1992; Hitt and Tyler, 1991; Melone, 1994; Priem, 1994; Schwenk, 1984; Walsh, 1988). In order to gain more insights into this area, this study aimed to explore the relationship between the development of shared beliefs and the strategic decision process, which has not yet been explored in the literature.

This research presents a theoretical framework explaining the reciprocal relationship between these two processes. The development of shared beliefs is presented in three major phases: the emergence of "invisible" groups, the reinforcement and change of individual beliefs and the formation of "visible" groups sharing similar beliefs. The strategic decision process involves two major types of strategic discussions: strategic debates under "like-minded" and strategic debates between "different believers." The reciprocal relationship between these two processes results in the evolution of a *critical mass of supporters* (CMS), the main theme of the framework.

This single in-depth field study provides a theoretical framework and general insights into the complex dynamic process of the strategic decision process and the development of shared beliefs. The findings have to be treated carefully in terms of generalizing from this single study (Yin, 1989; Scapens, 1990). The research provides a basis for understanding similar phenomena in other settings rather than enabling the predication of behavior in other contexts. Further empirical field studies in other settings would enrich the concepts developed in this study. Additional research into beliefs and their relationship to strategy development by, for example, focusing on strategy content and activities, timing and language related to the different subphases of the development of shared beliefs, and the strategic decision process, may provide a clearer picture of this reciprocal relationship and suggests an interesting avenue for future research.

Note

The author would like to thank the organizational members involved in this study for their time and cooperation during this project.
1   In this paper the meaning of executives and senior managers include chief administrative officer, the chief operating officer and managers who report directly to both of them.

References

Bantel, K. A. and Jackson, S. E. 1989: Top management and innovations in banking: does the composition of the top team make a difference? *Strategic Management Journal*, summer special issue, 10, 107–24.

Barnes, J. H. 1984: Cognitive biases and their impact on strategic planning. *Strategic Management Journal*, 5 (2), 129–39.

Barr, P. S. and Huff, A. S. 1997: Seeing isn't believing: understanding diversity in the timing of strategic response. *Journal of Management Studies*, 34 (3), 337–70.

Bazerman, M. H. 1998: *Judgement in managerial decision making*. 4th edn, New York: Wiley.

Beyer, J., Chattopadhyay, P., George, E., Glick, W. H., Ogilvie, D., and Pugliese, D. 1997: The selective perception of managers revisited. *Academy of Management Journal*, 40, 716–37.

Bougon, M., Weick, K. E., and Binkhorst, D. 1977: Cognition in organizations: analysis of the Utrecht Jazz Orchestra. *Administrative Science Quarterly*, 22, 609–32.

Byrne, D. 1971: *The attraction paradigm*. New York: Academic Press.

Chaganti, R. and Sambharya, R. 1987: Strategic orientation and characteristics of upper management. *Strategic Management Journal*, 8 (4), 393–401.

Chattopadhyay, P., Glick, W. H., Miller, C. C., and Huber, G. P. 1999: Determinants of executive beliefs: comparing functional conditioning and social influence. *Strategic Management Journal*, 20, 763–89.

Daft, R. L. and Weick, K. E. 1984: Toward a model of organizations as interpretation systems. *Academy of Management Review*, 9, 284–95.

D'Aveni, R. A. and MacMillan, I. C. 1990: Crisis and the content of managerial communications: a study of the focus of attention of top managers in surviving and failing firms. *Administrative Science Quarterly*, 35, 634–57.

Day, D. and Lord, R. 1992: Expertise and problem categorization: the role of expert processing in organizational sense-making. *Journal of Management Studies*, 29, 35–47.

Dearborn, D. and Simon, H. A. 1958: Selective perceptions: a note on the departmental identification of executives. *Sociometry*, 38, 140–4.

Eden, C. and Ackermann, F. 1998: *Making strategy: the journey of strategic management*. London: Sage.

Eisenhardt, K. M. and Zbaracki, M. J. 1992: Strategic decision making. *Strategic Management Journal*, 13, 17–37.

Falcione, R., Sussman, L., and Herden, R. 1987: Communication climate in organizations. In F. Jablin, L. Putnam, K. Roberts, and L. Porter (eds), *Handbook of Organizational Communication*, Newbury Park: Sage, 195–227.

Finkelstein, S. and Hambrick, D. C. 1990: Top management team tenure and organizational outcomes: the moderating role of managerial discretion. *Administrative Science Quarterly*, 35, 484–503.

Fiol, C. M. 1989: A semiotic analysis of corporate language: Organizational boundaries and joint venturing. *Administrative Science Quarterly*, 34, 277–303.

Fiol, C. M. and Lyles, M. A. 1985: Organizational learning. *Academy of Management Review*, 10, 803–13.

Fiske, S. T. and Taylor, S. E. 1991: *Social cognition*. New York: McGraw-Hill.

Frederickson, J. W. 1984: The comprehensiveness of strategic decision processes: extensions, observations, future directions. *Academy of Management Journal*, 27, 445–66.

Gilbert, M. 1989: *On social facts*. Princeton: Princeton University Press.

Gioia, D. 1986: Conclusion: the state of the art in organizational social cognition: a personal view. In H. Sims and D. Gioia (eds), *The thinking organization: dynamics of organizational social cognition*, San Francisco: Jossey-Bass, 336–56.

Gioia, D. and Chittipeddi, K. 1991: Sensemaking and sensegiving in strategic change initiation. *Strategic Management Journal*, 12 (6), 433–48.

Gioia, D. and Sims, H. 1986: Social cognition in organizations. In H. Sims and D. Gioia (eds), *The thinking organization*, San Francisco: Jossey-Bass, 1–19.

Glaser, B. G. and Strauss, A. L. 1967: *The discovery of grounded theory: strategies for qualitative research*. New York: Aldine Publishing.

Gray, B., Bougon, M. and Donnellon, A. 1985: Organizations as constructions and destruction of meaning. *Journal of Management*, 11, 83–98.

Grundy, T. and Johnson, G. 1993: Managers" perspectives on making major investment decisions: the problem of linking strategic and financial appraisal. *British Journal of Management*, 4, 253–67.

Haas, P. M. 1992: Introduction: epistemic communities and international policy coordination. *International Organization*, 46,1–35.

Hage, J. and Dewar, R. 1972: Elite values versus organizational structure predicting innovation. *Administrative Science Quarterly*, 17, 279–90.

Hambrick, D. C. 1988: *The executive effect: concepts and methods for studying top managers*. Greenwich: JAI Press.

Hambrick, D. C. and Mason, P. A. 1984: Upper echelons: The organization as a reflection of its top managers. *Academy of Management Review*, 9, 193–206.

Hambrick, D. C., Geletkanycz, M. A., and Frederickson, J. W. 1993: Top executive commitment to the status quo: some tests of its determinants. *Strategic Management Journal*, 14, 401–18.

Harris, S. G. 1994: Organizational culture and individual sensemaking: A schema based perspective. *Organization Science*, 5, 309–21.

Hauenstein, N. and Foti, R. 1989: From laboratory to practice: neglected issues in implementing frame-of-reference training. *Personnel Psychology*, 42, 359–78.

Hedberg, B. 1981: How organizations learn and unlearn. In P. C. Nystron and W. H. Starbuck (eds), *Handbook of organizational design*, New York: Oxford University Press, 3–27.

Hitt, M. A. and Tyler, B. 1991: Strategic decision models: integrating different perspectives. *Strategic Management Journal*, 12 (5), 327–51.

Hodgkinson, G. P. and Johnson, G. 1994: Exploring the mental models of competitive strategists. *Journal of Management Studies*, 31, 525–49.

Huff, A. S. 1982: Industry influences on strategy reformulation. *Strategic Management Journal*, 3, 119–31.

Huff, A. S. 1990: *Mapping strategic thought*. New York: Wiley.

Huff, A. S. and Reger, R. 1987: A review of strategic process research. *Journal of Management*, 13, 211–36.

Ireland, R., Hitt, M. A., Bettis, R., and de Porras, D. 1987: Strategy formulation processes: differences in perceptions of strength and weakness indications and environmental uncertainty by management level. *Strategic Management Journal*, 8 (5), 469–86.

Janis, I. L. and King, B. 1954: The influence of role playing on opinion change. *Journal of Abnormal and Social Psychology*, 49, 211–18.

Kelly, G. 1955: *The psychology of personal constructs*. Vols 1 and 2, New York: Norton.

Krackhardt, D. and Kilduff, M. 1991: Friendship patterns and culture: the control of organizational diversity. *American Anthropologist*, 92, 142–54.

Kuhn, T. 1970: *Structure of scientific revolutions*. 2nd edn, Chicago: University of Chicago Press.

Kulik, C. T. and Ambrose, M. C. 1992: Personal and situational determinants of referent choice. *Academy of Management Review*, 17, 212–38.

Lant, T., Milliken, F., and Batra, B. 1992: The role of managerial learning and interpretation in strategic persistence and reorientation: an empirical exploration. *Strategic Management Journal*, 13, 585–608.

Lawrence, P. R. and Lorsch, J. W. 1967: Differentiation and integration in complex organizations. *Administrative Science Quarterly*, 12, 1–47.

Lord, R. and Foti, R. 1986: Schema theories, information processing, and organizational behavior. In H. Sims and D. Gioia (eds), *The thinking organization: dynamics of organizational social cognition*, San Francisco: Jossey-Bass, 20–48.

Lucas, L. M. and Ogilvie, D. T. 1999: Inter-unit knowledge transfer in multinational corporations. In *Proceedings of Third International Conference on Organizational Learning*, Lancaster, 608–29.

March, J. 1991: Exploration and exploitation in organizational learning. *Organization Science*, 2, 71–87.

Markoczy, L. 1997: Measuring beliefs: accept no substitutes. *Academy of Management Journal*, 40, 1,128–42.

Martin, P. Y. and Turner, B. A. 1986: Grounded theory and organizational research. *Journal of Applied Behavioural Research*, 22 (2), 141–57.

Melone, N. P. 1994: Reasoning in the executive suite: The influence of role/experience-based expertise on decision processes of corporate executives. *Organization Science*, 5, 438–55.

Miller, C. C., Burke, L M. and Glick, W. H. 1998: Cognitive diversity among upper-echelon executives: implications for strategic decision processes. *Strategic Management Journal*, 19 (1), 39–58.

Minsky, M. 1975: A framework for representing knowledge. In P. H. Winston (ed.), *The psychology of computer vision*, New York: McGraw Hill.

Mintzberg, H., Raisinghani, D., and Theoret, A. 1976: The structure of unstructured decision processes. *Administrative Science Quarterly*, 21 (2), 246–75.

Nandhakumar, J. and Jones, M. 1997: Too close for comfort? Distance and engagement in interpretive information systems research. *Information Systems Journal*, 7, 109–31.

Narayanan, V. K. and Fahey, L. 1990: Evolution of revealed causal maps during decline: a case study of Admiral, In S. A. Huff (ed.), *Mapping strategic thought*, New York: Wiley, 109–33.

Nonaka, I. and Takeuchi, H. 1995: *The knowledge creating company: how Japanese companies create the dynamics of innovation*. London: Oxford University Press.

Norburn, D. and Birley, S. 1988: The top management team and corporate performance. *Strategic Management Journal*, 9 (3), 225–37.

Parkhe, A. 1991: Interfirm diversity, organizational learning, and longevity in global strategic alliances. *Journal of International Business Studies*, 22, 579–601.

Pettigrew, A. M. 1990: Longitudinal field research on change: theory and practice. *Organization Science*, 1 (3), 267–92.

Pettigrew, A. M. 1992: The character and significance of strategy process research. *Strategic Management Journal*, 13, 5–16.

Priem, P. I. 1994: Executive judgement, organizational congruence, and firm performance. *Organization Science*, 5, 421–37.

Rajagopalan, N., Rasheed, A. M., and Datta, D. K. 1993: Strategic decision processes: Critical review and future directions. *Journal of Management*, 19 (2), 349–84.

Rumelhart, D. 1980: Schemata: the building blocks of cognition. In Spiro et al., (eds), *Theoretical issues in reading comprehension*. Hillsdale: Erlbaum, 33–58.

Salancik, G. R. and Pfeffer, J. 1978: A social information processing approach to job attitudes and job design. *Administrative Science Quarterly*, 23, 224–52.

Sanchez, R. and Mahoney, J. T. 1996: Modularity, flexibility and knowledge management in product and organisation design. *Strategic Management Journal*, 17 (10), 63–7.

Scapens, R. W. 1990: Researching management accounting practice: the role of case study methods, *British Accounting Review*, 22, 259–81.

Schwarz, M. and Nandhakumar, J. 1999: The evolution of strategy in a newly transformed organization: the interplay between strategy development and corporate culture. In M. A. Hitt, P. G. Clifford, R. D. Nixon, and K. Coyne (eds), *Strategic management resources: development, diffusions and integration*, New York: Wiley, 97–128.

Schwenk, C. R. 1984: Cognitive simplification processes in strategic decision-making, *Strategic Management Journal*, 5, 11–128.

Schwenk, C. R. 1995: Strategic decision making. *Journal of Management*, 21 (3), 471–93.

Shrivastava, P. 1983: A typology of organizational learning systems. *Journal of Management Studies*, 20, 7–28.

Silverman, D. 1993: *Interpreting qualitative data: methods for analysing talk, text and interaction*. London: Sage.

Smith, K. G., Smith, K. A., Olian, J., Sims, H., O"Kannon, D., and Scully, J. 1994: Top management and demography and process: the role of social interaction and communication. *Administrative Science Quarterly*, 39, 412–38.

Song, I. 1982: Diversification strategies and the experience of top executives of large firms. *Strategic Management Journal*, 3 (4), 377–80.

Spender, J. C. and Grant, R. M. 1996: Knowledge and the firm: overview. *Strategic Management Journal*, 17 (winter special issue), 5–9.

Sproull, I. S. 1981: Belief in organizations. In P. G. Nystrom and W. H. Starbuck (eds), *Handbook of organizational design: remodeling organizations and their environments*, Vol. 2. London: Oxford University Press, 203–24.

Starbuck, W. H. and Milliken, F. 1988: Executives' perceptual filters: what they notice and how they make sense. In D. C. Hambrick (ed.), *The executive effect: concepts and methods for studying top managers*, Greenwich: JAI Press, 35–65.

Strauss, A. and Corbin, J. 1990: *Basics of qualitative research: grounded theory, procedures and techniques*. Newbury Park: Sage Publications.

Sworder, C. 1995: Hearing the baby's cry: its all in the thinking. In B. Garrett (ed.), *Developing strategic thought*. San Francisco, McGraw-Hill.

Tetlock, P. 1983: Accountability and complexity of thought. *Journal of Personality and Social Psychology*, 45, 74–83.

Thomas, J and McDaniel, R. 1990: Interpreting strategic issues: effects of strategy and top management team information processing structure. *Academy of Management Journal*, 33, 286–306.

Thomas, J., Clark, S., and Gioia, D. 1993: Strategic sensemaking and organizational performance: Linkages among scanning, interpretation, action, and outcomes. *Academy of Management Journal*, 36, 239–70.

Von der Heijden, K. 1996: *Scenarios: the art of strategic conversation*. Chichester: Wiley.

Von Krogh, G., Nonaka I., and Ichijo, K. 1997: Develop knowledge activists!. *European Management Journal*, 15 (5), 475–83.

Walker, G. 1985: Network position and cognition in a computer software firm. *Administrative Science Quarterly*, 30, 103–30.

Waller, M., Huber, G. P. and Glick, W. H. 1995: Functional background as a determinant of executives" selective perception. *Academy of Management Journal*, 38, 943–74.

Walsh, J. 1988: Selectivity and selective perception: an investigation of managers' belief structures and information processing. *Academy of Management Journal*, 31, 873–96.

Walsh, J. 1995: Managerial and organizational cognition: notes from a trip down memory lane. *Organization Science*, 6, 280–321.

Walsh, J., Henderson, C., and Deighton, J. 1988: Negotiated belief structures and decision performance: an empirical investigation. *Organizational Behavior and Human Decision Processes*, 42, 194–216.

Watts, W. 1967: Relative persistence of opinion change induced by active compared to passive participation, *Journal of Personality and Social Psychology*, 5, 4–15.

Weick, K. 1979: *The social psychology of organizing*. Reading: Addison-Wesley.

Weick, K. 1995: *Sensemaking in organizations*. Thousand Oaks: Sage.

Weick, K. and Bougon, M. 1986: Organizations as cognitive maps: Charting ways to success and failure. In D. Gioia and H. Jr Sims (eds), *The thinking organization*, San Francisco: Jossey-Bass.

Wiersema, M. F. and Bantel, K. A. 1992: Top management team demography and corporate strategic change. *Academy of Management Journal*, 35, 91–121.

Wortman, C. and Linsenmeier, J. 1977: Interpersonal attraction and techniques of ingratiation in organizational settings. In B. M. Staw and G. Salancik (eds), *New directions in organizational behavior*, Chicago: St. Clair's Press, 133–78.

Yin, R. 1989: *Case study research: design and methods*. Newbury Park: Sage.

CHAPTER SEVEN

The Social Construction of Organizational Capabilities: A Multilevel Analysis

V. K. Narayanan, Benedict Kemmerer, Frank L. Douglas, Brock Guernsey

Theory about organizational capability building remains underdeveloped in strategic management. Although attention to the origins of organizational capability is visible in prior works on internal corporate venturing (e.g., Burgelman, 1983; Garud and Van de Ven, 1992) or corporate entrepreneurship (e.g, Birkinshaw, 1997), and authors have recently begun to pay explicit attention to the evolution of firm capabilities (e.g., Chang, 1995; Kim, 1998), most studies conceptualize capability building processes at a relatively high level of abstraction, often based on secondary data (see Raff, 2000 and Tripsas and Gavetti, 2000 for notable exceptions). Thus the focus has been on issues such as product sequencing (Helfat and Raubitschek, 2000), entry into related markets (Klepper and Simons, 2000), and other macro-phenomena. Very little, however, is known about the managerial processes involved in capability building. A number of significant questions have not occupied the center stage of theory and empirical analysis: How do organizational members perceive and conceptualize a specific organizational capability? How do organizations go about building the capability? How is the organizational capability institutionalized as the organization-wide phenomenon its name implies?

This chapter constitutes one of the first empirical attempts to document the (internal) managerial processes involved in developing an organizational capability. Our conclusions are drawn from a three-year intensive study of the initial phases of a capability development initiative in a major pharmaceutical company. The development, which was initiated by senior management and was, hence, top-down, focused on embedding speed in the drug development process by creating autonomous, cross-functional project teams to work on high-priority projects. However, unlike the internal dynamics of project teams portrayed in the literature (e.g., Denison et al., 1996; Bennis and Biederman, 1997), we will document the managerial actions that truly rendered the initiative an exercise in building "organizational" capability.

In our portrayal of the capability building process, we highlight two themes.

1   We will chart the timing and patterns of coordination and structuring undertaken by management that shaped the behavioral and cultural context of operations of the project teams, and allowed for the inter-temporal replication of the fast-cycle mode of operation.
2   We will argue the utility of a social constructionist perspective in both the early and later phases of capability building, demonstrating, in particular, how the social construction processes hindered the institutionalization of the capability.

The scheme of the chapter is as follows. In the first section, we argue for a social constructivist perspective on the process of building organizational capability and summarize the three major theoretical assumptions that inform the study. Second, we outline the grounded theory approach employed in the study. Third, we provide, in some detail, the key findings from the study, both in terms of the stages of capability building and the ultimate outcome of the initiative. In the final section, we discuss the findings in light of the received theory, and present methodological and managerial implications.

Theoretical Background

The construct of organizational capability

Organizational capabilities represent a firm's ability to purposefully utilize an integrated set of resources in order to achieve a desired end (e.g., Hitt et al., 1999). The pursuit of organizational capabilities requires the development of management capabilities and difficult-to-imitate combinations of organizational, functional and technological skills (Teece et al., 1997). Thus, although some technical capabilities may be assembled through market mechanisms, organizational capabilities require managerial action (Teece et al., 1997: 510). In addition, organizational capabilities have consequences in the market. As emphasized by Leonard-Barton (1992), capabilities reflect an organization's ability to achieve new and innovative forms of competitive advantage given path dependencies and market positions.

For the purpose of this study, we underscore the *organizational* nature of the construct. It is true that capability can be viewed at different levels. For example, the mechanism for embedding speed in the organization in our case was through fast-cycle teams (Bower and Hout, 1988; Meyer, 1993). A significant, separate body of knowledge about managing the internal dynamics of project teams exists at this micro-level of analysis. In contrast, we focus on the processes and structures that elevate the skills and capabilities of individual teams to an *organization-level* capability:

1   At the (macro) *management* level, organizational capability involves the design of structures and systems that ensure and monitor the operation of project teams (i.e., micro levels). These structures and systems embed lower-level capability in the organization and create the context for their operation. Thus, according to Teece et al. (1997), organizational capabilities need to be understood mainly in terms of the organizational structures and managerial processes – coordinating/integration, learning, and reconfiguration – that support productive activity.

2   At the *inter-temporal* level, organizational capability is actualized through replication: The focus is not on the accomplishments of a specific team as in large parts of the project team literature (e.g., Ancona and Caldwell, 1990), but on the degree to which an organization can replicate certain performance features, in our case speed of execution.

These two criteria are of course related: Managers create the internal context (Noda and Bower, 1996; Ghoshal and Bartlett, 1997) that allows for the systematic creation, operation, and dissolution of fast-cycle project teams – that is, inter-temporal replication.

Social construction of capabilities

Understanding the process of building capabilities entails a focus on human interpretation and action: where do the concepts behind a capability originate? How are they interpreted? How do various actors in an organization interact to define and enact capabilities? Given this focus on human beings as active shapers of organizational capabilities, the social constructivist perspective – in both its cognitive and political aspects – provides a major platform to theorize about the process of capability development and evolution. A key feature of social constructivism is the attempt to understand how social actors recognize, produce, and reproduce social actions and meanings and how they come to negotiate a shared understanding of the world around them (Berger and Luckmann, 1966; Schwandt, 1997). This perspective also enables us to connect capability building to several strands of contemporary scholarship. First, given its focus on human agents and their interactions, it addresses the nature of managerial work (Mintzberg, 1973): just what do top level managers do? Second, by bringing interpretive processes to the center stage, it links to the emerging body of work in cognition and strategy (Narayanan and Kemmerer, 2001). Third, the social influence attempts that underlie the human interactions featured in this perspective allows us to create linkages to the behavioral theory of the firm (Cyert and March, 1963), logical incrementalism (Quinn, 1980), and the politics of organizations (Bower and Doz, 1979; Crozier and Friedberg, 1980; Pfeffer, 1981; Narayanan and Fahey, 1982).

Theoretical assumptions

Designed or emergent, the social construction of capabilities unfolds over time. This renders all the more useful, a process model of building organizational capabilities that focuses on the pathways by which an organization identifies, develops, and institutionalizes requisite capabilities. We anchor our discussion of the social construction of organizational capabilities in three major assumptions: (1) stages as theoretical units; (2) capability development as a multi-layered process; and (3) context dependence of organizational capabilities.

Stages as theoretical units
A process is a sequence of events over time (Van de Ven and Huber 1990); a process model identifies systematic regularities in the sequencing of events for a specific phe-

nomenon. We use the term *stages* to cluster events occurring in temporal proximity to identify regularities. At the theoretical level, stages are thus the relevant units in a process model, unlike at the phenomenal level, where the events that operationalize a stage are idiosyncratic and organization specific. Most process models are thus Janus-faced: they focus on generalizations at the level of stages, but are idiographic at the level of events.

Stages invoke the image of organizations as blueprinted growth systems (Boulding, 1956; Pondy and Mitroff, 1979). Two important ideas underlie this conceptualization:

1   The stages are linked over time in a normal developmental sequence. However, the temporal evolution over stages is contingent on both internal dynamics – the social construction process – and the existence of specific boundary conditions. Where these conditions are not met, the normal sequences may be disrupted by decay of development, cycling between stages, and reversion to previous stages.
2   Each stage deals with a set of specific developmental challenges. The methodological challenge is to document the developmental dilemmas, and to identify the mechanisms by which these dilemmas are resolved: what are the issues identified by organizational actors? How do they resolve those issues? What are the markers by which we can judge that a stage has concluded?

This process view has thus two major implications. First, given its focus on the unfolding of events, it underscores the temporal nature of capability development, and the faculty of emergence inherent in social construction processes. Second, on a pragmatic level, by identifying the transition points between two stages, it highlights the role of timing in action. Managers need to attend to differing challenges and levers of influence over time during the process of capability development.

Capability building as a multi-layered process

As pointed out by Teece et al. (1997), capabilities involve coordination across multiple organizational subsystems. Following other process works (Bower, 1970; Burgelman, 1983, 1994) we suggest that the capability building process involves both vertical (hierarchic levels) and horizontal (functional divisions) layers:

1   Both senior, middle and lower levels of an organization will be involved in the capability-building process. Capability development requires resources and coordination, and this implicates senior management. Since capabilities involve routines or skills in operation, lower levels will need to act as enactors of the capability. As an intermediary between senior and lower levels, middle managers often play crucial roles (Burgelman, 1994; Floyd and Wooldridge, 1997).
2   A second layering of the process is across various horizontal subsystems within an organization. Capability building entails the involvement of various sub-units within an organization, who may have different degrees of stakes and interests and who may be operating from different bases of power (Pfeffer, 1981).

Since the process of capability building involves multiple actors who differ in terms of power, authority, resources, and relevance to the capability, the elements of social construction developed here – human agents, interactions, resource flows, and information – are relevant to capturing the intricacy of the process. Who initiates the capability building? What cognitive beliefs drive the process? How do the negotiations get played out? How do actors collectively develop shared understandings of the action implications of a specific capability?

A key implication of the multi-layered process is the heterogeneity in the pathways by which capabilities are developed. It is likely that the sequencing and duration of stages and the pattern of linkages among the elements of social construction vary between emergent and purposefully designed capabilities. On a pragmatic level, the levers of influence available to senior managers may also be different. In emergent processes, they may serve as the legitimators of the capability toward the end of the process, unlike in top-down processes where they are likely to initiate the design process and may retain an active role over various stages.

Context dependence of organizational capabilities

Theoretical discussions often acknowledge the context dependence of organizational capabilities in a firm's search for competitive advantage. The value and scarcity of capabilities are judged in the context of the industry, and the imitability or substitutability is determined by competitors' capabilities (e.g., Grant, 1991; Barney, 1991). Thus for a specific capability to be discovered or developed, it should be deemed meaningful for the strategic context of the firm. Thus the history of the firm, its resources, and market position – the initial conditions – are a constraint on the beginning stages of capability development. The context dependence has two additional implications:

1   There are innumerable decision points over the entire process for human actors to shape the evolution of the capability, as well as for major organizational events (e.g., mergers) to alter the path of evolution. The process of social construction admits potentially innumerable ways in which a general capability can be conceptualized and implemented or its evolution disrupted. Thus, the various stages are deemed to be *sensitive to local conditions.* The initial conditions may trigger activation and foreshadow other stages, but as the process unfolds, the ensuing stages are susceptible to human actions undertaken in response to prevailing circumstances.

2   Although at the level of outcomes, specific organizational capabilities may be comparable, there is likely to be variation in the *means* by which firms construct the fast-cycle capability. For example, fast-cycle capability in the abstract refers to an organization's ability to enact and execute decisions with speed; however, firms may differ in terms of the resources they employ or the activities they focus on to enact fast-cycle capability (George and Narayanan, 1999).

Put another way, the resources and routines, which constitute a specific capability, and the pathways by which capabilities are built are likely to be determined by the firm's specific context. This is consistent with Teece et al.'s (1997) proposition that capabilities are assembled within an organization and not easily traded in the market.

Methodology

Organizational setting

This study is part of a larger project that tracked the evolution of the fast-cycle capability in a major pharmaceutical company, Marion Merrell Dow (MMD), headquartered in the midwestern United States. The firm's path towards building fast-cycle capability began in 1992. Internally, the company was still in the process of integrating differing cultures which had been inherited from the merger between the two predecessor companies. One predecessor company had been involved primarily in licensing drugs, performing late-stage development, and marketing them. The other company, while strong in basic research, had limited success in bringing drugs to market. The newly formed company inherited several senior managers from the firm's predecessors, but also brought in new key players, among them a new executive vice president of drug innovation and approval (DIA), who also chaired the senior management (research and development) team (RDMT) and had a seat on the board.

Externally, the company was facing the threat of significant future declines in sales and profitability. Several important patents were nearing their expiration and were expected to lose most of their market share to generic competitors. In addition, actions by the Food and Drug Administration (FDA) threatened to shorten the lifecycle of another product that contributed significantly to revenues and profits. Since speed to market was becoming a major competitive issue in the pharmaceutical industry, the management decided to build fast-cycle capability concurrently with its commitment to drug development.

The strategy of building the capability was to focus on a select set of fast-cycle projects, to learn from the experience, and to then embed the capability in the organization as a whole. As an outgrowth of this decision, the senior management designated several projects as "fast-cycle"; in terms of completing the milestones, these projects had to beat the best in class in the industry. These fast-cycle projects ran concurrently with "regular" projects that operated according to the accepted practices within the company. This strategy facilitated the research effort in two major ways. First, given the firm's explicit emphasis on organizational capability, the setting provided an occasion to examine the process of capability building as a multi-layered process rather than as merely a project team phenomenon. Second, the regular teams provided a baseline against which to assess any claims about the distinctiveness of fast-cycle teams made by the firm.

Research design

This research was based on a nested case study design within one corporate setting (e.g., Yin, 1984; Leonard-Barton, 1990; Burgelman, 1994). At the organizational level, focusing on the managerial processes, the data constituted the material for a single case: archival, interview, and survey data were collected on the evolution of fast-cycle capability from multiple levels within the firm over a period of two years. Nested within the organizational context, at the micro-level, case studies were created for six projects: four were fast-cycle projects, and the other two, labeled "regular," provided a basis for comparison. The fast-cycle projects represented a diverse array of compounds: (1) internally developed as well as in-licensed, and (2) completed as well as discontinued projects.[1] The regular projects served as a baseline for comparison; they also helped to discover the spillover effects from the fast-cycle project experience. The data sources and analysis are described in more detail in appendix 7.1.

Findings

Recall that the organizational capability building tracked in this study was designed by senior management, and followed an incremental strategy of first learning from the operation of a select set of projects and later institutionalizing the learning in the organization. Our interviews revealed that a six-stage process could best capture the experience. The first three stages – activation, articulation, and mobilization – resembled those identified by Narayanan and Fahey (1982). The fourth stage – implementation as project capability – was unique to this case whereas the last two stages – diffusion of routines, and retention of capability – were institutionalization processes akin to the retention stage in ecological models.

We will first outline the various stages and the outcomes of the initiative to provide the background for our discussion of findings and implications.

Stages of development of fast-cycle capability

Activation
This stage involved the decision to embark on fast-cycle capability building in the Drug Innovation and Approval division of the pharmaceutical company. The "vision" for embedding the capability in the organization originated with the head of DIA who came from another pharmaceutical company. The significant challenge at this stage was to get some degree of commitment from the senior management team to launch the initiative.

Activation was somewhat facilitated by the local conditions, e.g., the sense of urgency precipitated by the actions of the FDA. However, significant internal forces were arrayed against it. The development of fast-cycle capability could not be accomplished within the set of core beliefs and practices existing in the organization; instead, it required a significant shift in both the beliefs and the behavior of senior management. In addition, the new head of DIA, despite his credentials and track record in other firms, had not yet established a secure political base within the firm. Thus, it took significant political influence processes, both horizontally within the RDMT and upwards, towards the top management team, to achieve a tentative coalescence of senior and top management opinions around the vague idea of fast-cycle capability. However, some senior managers were persistent in their opposition and – while publicly supportive of the initiative – privately undermined the efforts.

The activation stage was *protracted*, and lasted over a year until the head of DIA decided to confront the issue directly. One of the undermining senior managers was asked to step down and, subsequently, left the company. The other was given an assignment elsewhere in the organization. After this realignment of upper management, the fast-cycle initiative proceeded towards a clearer definition. Two factors drove this process. One, the anticipated medium-term financial situation created a strong sense of urgency. Second, a consensus emerged that the concept of fast-cycle teams was *applicable* and *immediately relevant* to the strategic situation of MMD. Despite this general buy-in, lack of conviction remained a significant phenomenon at this stage and throughout later stages.

Articulation

This stage involved activities by senior management to tailor the fast-cycle initiative to their organization. Unlike activation, this stage was characterized less by political and more by analytical activities. The principles that emerged during that process were a result both of general fast-cycle principles as well as the specific organizational context and resource constraints of MMD. Thus, on the one hand MMD reaffirmed fast-cycle principles such as an emphasis on speedy decision-making, priority in resource access, and increased decision autonomy of project teams. On the other hand, MMD decided not to co-locate project teams, and kept fast-cycle project teams anchored in the traditional context of scientific functions which were the backbone of the MMD DIA organization. Similarly, resource constraints forced MMD to assign fast-cycle status only to a small number of research and development projects. Other basic principles articulated during this phase were the establishment of economic and scientific feasibility criteria for deciding which projects to designate as fast-cycle.

To shift power from functions to teams, a sponsor role was created within the RDMT, and the four fast-cycle project leaders reported to the sponsor. The sponsor was to advocate the cause of the project teams (i.e., help marshal resources) within the RDMT, to maintain priorities and transfer best practices among the fast-cycle projects, to serve as coach to project leaders, and to help them in their negotiations with functional heads (see also Meyer, 1993). At the same time that power was shifted from the functions, the functions also retained key roles in the capability building process: enforcing standards, maintaining quality, and facilitating the transfer of function-specific learning across teams.

Mobilization

Having achieved a sufficient degree of senior management consensus on the need and the emergent gestalt of the fast-cycle capability building initiative, senior management initiated an organization-wide intensive communication effort that particularly targeted the DIA organization which was most affected by the move towards fast-cycle.

Garnering support for the fast-cycle initiative among a wide range of DIA personnel was particularly challenging due to the long-held central premises of the organization that focused on "functional excellence." Functional excellence, that is the pursuit and preservation of the highest possible scientific and functional standards above all else, had been traditionally the key tenet that guided research and development operations at MMD. The idea of "fast-cycle" with its more pragmatic approach to R&D, emphasizing the need for speed, often conflicted with functional excellence.

Furthermore, the introduction of fast-cycle teams also created uncertainty for functional managers as well as project team members. Fast-cycle teams had more decision making power and direct access to senior management, partially circumventing traditional reporting relationships. Thus, the role of functional managers evolved from a control-oriented towards a more support-oriented role, creating a natural level of discomfort among some affected managers. Similarly, project team members of fast-cycle teams – while still anchored in their functions – left the traditional functional structure and way of operating, creating uncertainty in the areas of performance evaluation criteria, career progression, and required skill sets.

Thus, the mobilization phase was characterized by *sensemaking* (Weick, 1995) attempts of organization members, who tried to make sense of the fast-cycle initiative and to assess its impacts on their own positions. Corresponding to this sensemaking process were intensive *sensegiving* (Whetten, 1984; Gioia and Chittipeddi, 1991) attempts by senior managers trying to communicate the organizational benefits of the capability building process. The response in many cases may be more appropriately described as acquiescence rather than as an embracing of the initiative.

Both articulation and mobilization were of relatively short duration. And whereas articulation was primarily confined to the senior management of DIA, mobilization embraced the middle and functional levels. Temporally, the stages overlapped. The selection of four fast-cycle projects and their project team leaders marked the end of the mobilization phase.

Implementation as project-level capability

Once the specific compounds to be placed on the fast track were selected, the fast-cycle initiative moved to the implementation stage. The key challenge of this stage was managing the tension between fast-cycle principles and the established organizational standard operating procedures and tenets (such as functional excellence). The transition was difficult for the whole DIA organization, especially the scientific functions and for individual project team members.

As the fast-cycle experiment proceeded, the firm discovered the need to embed new organizational routines to leverage existing and developing resources. Embedding routines required compliance by different levels of the organization – senior management, middle management and project team levels. At the senior level, a structured process of portfolio planning, project leader selection, and organization-wide communication had to be implemented. Further, as new, more effective, routines emerged in one fast-cycle project team, the designated sponsor in the RDMT helped to disseminate them to other teams. Newer routines were also needed at the middle-management level. For example, during annual performance reviews of project team members, functional leaders had to incorporate the input from project leaders. The most visible organizational routines emerged at the project team level, which had been encouraged to do things differently in support of the project; these routines required both *cognitive* and *behavioral* learning. As one senior executive described it, fast-cycle team members had to migrate from relying on checklists to a problem-solving orientation for speedy execution.

While many project team members transitioned quickly into the fast-cycle way of operation and actually welcomed the increased autonomy, flexibility, and responsibility, others had difficulty resolving the cognitive conflict between the deeply rooted "ethos" of functional excellence and the more pragmatic and speed-oriented fast-cycle approach. In addition, not all members thrived in the hard-charging, unstructured, heavily team-oriented environment of fast-cycle projects. These issues were resolved by intensive training and group building efforts by project team leaders, but also through reassignment of personnel. The conflict for individual team members was exacerbated by the fact that many of them were not fully dedicated to the project team and thus were living in two worlds with two different belief systems at once. Also, pay and promotions were still largely under the control of the functions. Many functional leaders did not fully buy into the fast-cycle concepts and favored the status quo.

During the implementation phase, senior management played an active role in monitoring and empowering the fast-cycle projects both in terms of ensuring they received sufficient resources and also by using their power and political capital to insulate the project team from pressures to conform to standard functional procedures.

Forces from other parts of the organization also intruded into the implementation of the fast-cycle initiative. Although the board of directors understood the strategic value of the projects, and had approved the fast-cycle initiative, several top-level non-DIA executives in MMD had limited understanding of the logic of the framework and organizational architecture developed to support the initiative. Some top-level executives did not fully subscribe to the concepts from the beginning. Departures from normal organizational practices communicated through formal and more frequently through informal communication channels became occasions for discussion, and senior DIA managers often had to *buffer* the project teams from the intrusive pressures coming from outside the (DIA) division. Unlike the championing activities described by Burgelman (1983), these "buffering" activities involved protecting the fast-cycle experiment, and controlling the boundaries of the initiative.

This stage spanned the duration of the four fast-cycle projects, and culminated in their conclusion or discontinuance. The remaining stages were ongoing at the time of the research project, and were focused on the diffusion and institutionalization of the experience.

Diffusion of routines
Recall that the fast-cycle capability was initially implemented at the project level in four research and development projects.

As fast-cycle teams went into operation, they discovered newer, better, and faster ways of utilizing existing organizational resources. There were several attempts by various fast-cycle teams to capture their learning, once they were disbanded. These attempts at knowledge capture were fragmented and remained at the project team level. There was some recognition of the importance of organizational learning, but no systematic processes for accomplishing it.

Even so, there was spillover of best practices: members of some regular cycle teams mimicked the practices of the fast-cycle teams as they became aware of these practices; such regular teams – though not officially designated fast-cycle – operated in a fast-cycle manner and internally labeled their practices as such.

The process of codifying project-specific experience as capability was haphazard; serendipitous learning was common. There were several barriers to effective knowledge management. First, the turnover of fast-cycle team members, without appropriate human resource management practices to retain them, created great difficulty in capturing and retaining knowledge. During the study period, three of the fast-cycle project leaders left the company and one retired.

Second, short-term time and resource pressures sometimes inhibited codification of learning. Towards the end of fast-cycle projects, there was pressure for team members to be immediately reassigned to new projects as soon as they became available, leaving no time to reflect on the fast-cycle experience or to codify the lessons learned.

Third, turnover of senior management hindered the transfer of knowledge from one project team to another. Typically, senior managers acted as "information arbitrageurs," linking pockets of tacit knowledge and relevant problem-solving contexts. Senior management turnover diminished the effectiveness of the information arbitrage function in the organization.

Finally, the framing of experience into knowledge was idiosyncratic and was strongly influenced by the structural conditions and the occurrence of traumatic episodes in a project. For example, one discontinued project experienced difficulties in dealing with a licensing firm; partly as a result, the members concluded that it was inappropriate to designate in-licensed compounds as fast-cycle projects. In contrast, senior management, being closer to the strategic necessities of the firm, had realized the need to in-license compounds more frequently and had begun to explore ways by which they could strengthen the scientific scrutiny of compounds before entering into licensing agreements. From their perspective, the specific in-licensing agreement involved in the discontinued project was at fault; the difficulties were not generalizable to all in-licensed compounds.

Ultimately, the diffusion rested on the reassignment of fast-cycle team members to new projects or re-absorption within their functional areas. However, this made the knowledge diffusion process vulnerable to the inevitable employee turnover among fast-cycle project personnel. So, while some fast-cycle *practices* did spread across the organization, the diffusion of *capability* remained partial and fragmented.

Retention of capability
In order to ensure the inter-temporal replicability of fast-cycle capability, the capability has to be maintained and reinforced. This poses a particular challenge for fast-cycle capability in drug development: first, it is project-oriented, and, second, as a prioritization strategy, it will always apply only to some and never to all projects. As a consequence, there was a considerable danger of a significant decay in fast-cycle capability due to organizational inertia after the first round of fast-cycle projects neared completion. The key challenge for the organization at this stage was to focus the attention and efforts of organization members towards the maintenance of fast-cycle capability. While this process was only partially observable during the study period, some findings emerged.

A significant lever for senior management to underscore the importance of a capability was *framing the definitions of success* within the company. This was particularly important in the case of MMD where a long tradition of "functional excellence" was deeply ingrained in the culture of the DIA organization. This tradition had been bolstered by a corresponding reward system, which emphasized functional excellence as the basis for intangible (praise) as well as tangible (pay and promotion) rewards. However, fast-cycle principles often involved sacrificing, to some extent, tenets of functional excellence. Therefore, to sustain fast-cycle practices, the organization had to significantly and *visibly* reward fast-cycle team members. In this respect, MMD management was successful only to some extent. For example, discontinued projects were discontinued not necessarily due to project management failures, but due to scientific and commercial reasons. The senior management viewed discontinued projects as successful fast-cycle experience, since the project team quickly produced data to facilitate the decision to discontinue, unlike in the case of regular projects, where the decision to abandon emerges slower, consuming more resources.[2] However, some senior managers did not agree to significant rewards being given to these discontinued projects. While successful fast-cycle teams received significant financial rewards and – more importantly – ample public recognition, discontinued projects received no such recognition. Not surprisingly, our surveys indicate once the project team members returned to the functional unit, the middle and lower levels of the DIA organization generally ascribed greater status to them only if they had worked in completed fast-cycle projects in contradiction to the articulated principles, and to financial rationale. Thus, perceptions of success continued to focus on the outcome rather than the process of DIA and its associated fast-cycle principles.

In addition, fast-cycle projects required support from a wide range of personnel in functional and administrative departments interfacing with fast-cycle project teams. These people had to – among other things – adjust schedules and work overtime to ensure the smooth operation of fast-cycle teams. Initially, such people (which are essential for building an organization-level fast-cycle capability) were not explicitly included in either the financial rewards or the public recognition. This not only undermined the desired perception of fast-cycle as an *organizational* capability, but also created active resentment among such personnel. In later projects, management corrected this and very publicly included the organization in the symbolic rewards and recognizing the success of fast-cycle projects as the result of an organization-wide effort.

The process of building capability

Table 7.1 presents a summary of the stages of capability building documented in this study. As shown in the table, we have portrayed each stage in terms of triggers, major challenges, key actors, drivers, transition mechanisms, and the two facets of social construction – micro-politics and cognitive processes. *Triggers* and *transition mechanisms* bracketed each stage, with triggers initiating the stage, and the transition mechanisms signaling its conclusion. Each stage represented a set of issues – what we have labeled as *major challenges* – which needed to be resolved by the human actors. *Actors* from different levels featured prominently in different stages, thus rendering the capability building a multi-level phenomenon. *Key drivers* refer to the forces that enabled or retarded the resolution of the issues, they reflect the local conditions prevailing in the specific organization. The negotiations that led to resolution of the challenges hinged on *influence processes*, be they coercive (e.g., reassignment of people) or persuasive (e.g. analytical processes) as well as *cognitive processes* (e.g., sensemaking and sensegiving); of course these processes got played out across multiple levels.

Outcomes of the fast-cycle initiative

Recall that the four fast-cycle teams were initiated as a medium for embedding speed in the Drug Innovation and Approval processes of the firm – an "organizational capability." As in any top down process, the intentions behind the initiative were derived

Table 7.1 Overview of organizational capability building process stages (part I)

	Activation	Articulation	Mobilization	Implementation as project capability	Institutionalization	
					Diffusion or routines[b]	Retention of capability[b]
Characterization	Recognition of the need for augmenting the capability base and initiation of capability building process	Elaboration of the nature of the capability and the principles of implementation	Readying the organization for enacting the capability	First set of fast-cycle teams in operation	Organization-wide diffusion of learning from the fast-cycle initiative	Maintenance of organizational capability and prevention of unintentional decay
Triggers	Anticipated performance gap / Arrival of new head of DIA	Need for a specific action plan	Need for lower-level buy-in to execute action plan	Designation of fast-cycle projects	Recognized value of fast-cycle practices	N/A
Major challenges	Obtaining agreement on central premises behind the organizational capability	Framing the capability in terms of the specific organizational context	Garnering support for implementation of capability building	Managing the tension between fast-cycle principles and established operating procedures	Codifying and transmitting the tacit and explicit knowledge gained	Continued focusing of organizational attention on maintenance of capability
Drivers	Urgency / Applicability to organizational context	Interaction between nature of capability and the organizational context	Scale of the initial effort / Resource constraints	Project characteristics / Organizational inertia	Personnel reassignment / Personnel turnover / External events	Environmental pressure / Strategic relevance / Organizational inertia / Short term pressures
Transition mechanism	Coalescence of senior management[a] opinions	Agreement on action plan	Choice of projects / Choice of project team leaders	Completion or discontinuation of projects	Fast-cycle principles embedded in the organization (Only partially observable in our study)	N/A

[a] Senior Management refers to the senior management of DIA only. [b] Only partially observable in our study due to process decay.

Table 7.1 Overview of organizational capability building process stages (part II)

	Activation	Articulation	Mobilization	Implementation as project capability	Institutionalization	
					Diffusion or routines[b]	Retention of capability[b]
Key actors	Senior management[a] Top management team	Senior management Top management team	Senior management Functional DIA organization	Project team leaders Project teams Functional managers Interfacing organizational units	Senior management Fast-cycle team members DIA functional managers	(Insufficient data; only partially observable in study due to process decay)
Social construction processes						
Political processes	Upward influence senior management turnover Persuasion by new head of DIA	Horizontal influence operating principles	Intense top-down communication	Influence processes within project teams Influence processes between project teams and functional departments Senior management buffering of fast-cycle teams against organizational pressures	(No data due to partial decay of process) Allocation of financial	Influencing of definitions of success Allocation of rewards and human resources
Cognitive processes	Individual-level problem recognition Partial acceptance of premises behind organizational capability	Collective construction of core principles of action	Sensegiving by senior management Initial sensemaking by lower-level organization members	Altering of mental maps of functional managers Reframing of operational environment by project team members	Knowledge transfer	Cognitive construction of success definitions on a personal, project, and organizational level

[a] Senior Management refers to the senior management of DIA only. [b] Only partially observable in our study due to process decay.

from the interviews with the senior managers. But was the organization able to translate the intentions into reality? Several indicators available at the conclusion of the study helped to develop an answer to the question. At the project level, three outcomes were available:

1   Both of the projects that successfully won the FDA's approval were completed in the shortest time, relative to other projects in class previously completed by the company. Similarly, the duration of the relevant phases of both the projects was shorter than the industry benchmarks.
2   Economically, one of the complete projects rescued the company from a severe shortfall in sales that had been triggered by the actions of the FDA. The other project opened up a sizeable market for a new drug.
3   Both discontinued projects were shut down quickly, before even moving to the phase III trials that typically consume significant resources. This was unlike the traditional practice within the firm, where projects had continued to linger.

Thus there is evidence that the fast-cycle team initiative was successful.

Given the duration of the study, however, we are unable to document the replication of the accomplishment over later project teams. An examination of the evidence suggests that while there has been some replication (e.g., some of the regular project teams had begun to mimic the routines of fast-cycle teams), other elements necessary to institute an organizational capability (e.g., the definitions of success and the reward schemes) had not taken hold. Thus, although the four projects were "successful," the task of embedding the organization with the lessons from the experiment – building fast-cycle (organizational) capability – remained incomplete.

Link to competitive advantage
According to some resource-based theorists (Grant, 1991) capabilities are the bedrock on which organizational performance is built. The path from capabilities to performance and competitive advantage is, however, complex. First, capabilities are translated into performance only when they are deployed either in products or value chains (Grant, 1998; Narayanan, 2001). Second, not all capabilities yield competitive advantage. Some capabilities may be needed for a firm simply to "stay in the race"; these may not yield competitive advantages since many firms in an industry may possess these capabilities. In our case, the project teams worked on drug approval, thus joining the processes of development and deployment; to do so was the explicit strategy of the senior management. However, at the end of the study the process of capability building remained incomplete. Thus, the duration of the study does not permit us to draw conclusions about the link between the capability and competitive advantage.

Discussion

The study in context

Our study was oriented to understanding the process of capability building, rather than inferring the presence of capability from performance outcomes. Given the paucity of literature about capability building, we adopted a grounded theory approach, coupling case studies of six projects, based on archival sources and interviews with project leaders as well as senior and middle managers, to derive the history, intentions and logic of the whole initiative.

Grounded theory is oriented toward discovery of phenomena through description and interpretation, which are both contingent on access and validity of data. By concentrating on one organization, the researchers had access to sources with intimate knowledge of the details of the firm's efforts to build fast-cycle capability that made it possible to understand "the manager's temporal and contextual frame of reference" (Van de Ven, 1992: 181; see also Burgelman, 1994). Further, since the researchers had access to input from people in different levels of management involved in the process, this provided a basis for triangulation to ensure the validity of the data as well as to reduce the bias introduced by retrospective recall (e.g., Golden, 1992).

Grounded theory is not oriented toward generalizability, but we may identify three unique contextual features to place the findings in perspective:

1   *Industry characteristics.* The pharmaceutical industry is highly regulated (in drug development), and being first to market is crucial to gaining a strong competitive position. Unlike in many industries, the primary focus of drug approval – the "customer" – is the FDA or similar agencies in other countries. The role of ultimate customer – the patient – enters less into the drug development process, but more in terms of the market potential that drives the decisions to launch, continue or discontinue the development process.

2   *Top-down process.* The capability was initiated at the top levels, and hence top-down. This sets it apart from the emergent processes described by Burgelman (1994), or Pascale (1984). A fundamental feature of the top-down process is the *role of intentions* and the degree to which they are realized. In this study, the initiative was framed as an effort to build capability by the top manager of the R&D division; its realization remained incomplete.

3   *Strategy of capability building.* The firm adopted an experimental approach to capability building, by launching four projects, and operating them in parallel with other regular projects. The intention was to learn from the experiment. Other efforts, such as the quality initiative in Xerox (Kearns and Nadler, 1993), may reflect irreversible commitment by top managers.

The features set the limits to which the findings can be generalized; and as in any similar study, the features should serve as hypotheses to be (dis)confirmed in later endeavors of theory testing. The data presented enable us to showcase three major findings: (1) the key role of managerial processes in building organizational capability; (2) the fragility of transforming the learning from the experiment into an institutionalized capability; and (3) the prevalence of social construction throughout all stages of the capability building process. We take these up in turn.

Managerial processes in building organizational capability

The stages of capability building underscore the role that both senior and functional managers played during different time periods in the process, in addition to the project teams.

The *senior management team* performed six major functions: (1) realigning the team in congruence with the fast-cycle philosophy; (2) choosing the experimental mode for building the capability; (3) prioritizing the projects to fast track four of them; (4) articulating the structure for the teams; (5) defining the success criteria for the teams; and (6) managing the teams by choice of leaders, milestones, resources, rewards, empowerment, and oversight. These functions were time consuming, and indeed set the boundary conditions for the operation of the rest of the organization.

Functional managers were crucial for the implementation, since they allocated resources (people), and continued to be responsible for significant human resource management functions within the division. Further, they acted to maintain scientific standards in their respective functions during the progress of fast-cycle projects, and served as critical links in the transfer of learning from project to project.

As table 7.1 illustrates, the senior management roles were critical in the early phases, but continued throughout the process, whereas the functional manager's roles became more apparent during the operation of the teams. One of the fundamental insights from the study is that even when project teams are launched, the capability building is a multi-level process, and the roles played by senior managers and functional managers, by setting the internal context of the firm, are crucial to the success of the teams.

Thus our findings complement the work on project teams by highlighting the role of management: there is more to organizational capability than managing the internal dynamics of project teams. This is perhaps most apparent during the later stages which involved efforts at institutionalization, that is, efforts to imprint the learning on the organization.

Imprinting the learning on organization

Imprinting the learning or institutionalization is necessary to ensure *inter-temporal replicability* of processes to accomplish specified outcomes, in our case rapid drug development. At the project team level, the high visibility accorded the fast-cycle teams by senior management generated strong mimetic forces: other regular project teams mimicked the practices of fast-cycle teams, and even invited fast-cycle team leaders to conduct developmental sessions. The migration of individuals through reassignment after the disbanding of project teams and the information arbitrage function performed by some of the middle managers helped in the diffusion of learning. Deliberate actions to institutionalize the learning emanated from senior management levels in the form of codification of best practices and design of incentives and systems to support the capability. However, these remained incomplete at the end of the study.

The distinction between specific project accomplishments and broader organizational capability is crucial in our conceptualization of organizational capability. Put another way, organizational capability implies replication: success in an experiment does not by itself constitute a capability. Based on the senior and functional management roles identified above, we may capture the distinction as in table 7.2. As shown in the table, inter-temporal replication involves not merely project team functioning,

Table 7.2   Embedding speed: execution of individual processes vs. building organizational capability

	Executing fast-cycle projects	Building organizational capability
Project selection	Ad hoc selection based on specific strategic context	Selection is the outcome of a systematic and continuous review of prioritization and resource allocation, including fast-cycle team choice
Structural context	Ad hoc teams with idiosyncratic levels of empowerment	Fast-cycle teams have permanent role in structural context of the firm, including: 1 Permanent sponsor role at the senior management level 2 Structural empowerment of fast-cycle teams.
Role of functional managers	1 Control budgets, standards, people, and other resources 2 Timelines negotiated with project managers	1 Enforce quality standards 2 Facilitate knowledge transfer
Role of project managers	Task-related coordination	1 Control budgets, timelines, and people associated with the project 2 Task-related coordination
Human resource management systems	Ad hoc, idiosyncratic selection and reward mechanisms for each project	1 Identification and assignment of personnel to project teams is ongoing, critical tasks 2 Performance in the project team becomes primary basis for individual reward allocation
Socio-cognitive context	Temporary cognitive adaptation to new operating procedures	Cognitive shift congruent with core principles of the capability; shared conceptualization of organizational nature of fast-cycle capability
Role of senior managers	Monitoring of project team performance	1 Managing the internal behavioral and cultural context 2 Ensuring continuity through institution of enduring structures and systems

but also the stabilization of the structure, systems, processes, and organizational cognitions that set the behavioral context for the teams.

The process model developed from our data underscores the *fragility* of the capability during the early stages of institutionalization. For one, the capability is built up of several components – structural, systemic, and cognitive. The *structural components,* which included the shift of power from functions to project teams in this case, and the *systemic elements,* particularly those that involved reward and incentives were both sensitive to the micro-politics of the organization during the institutionalization stage.

The *cognitive elements* were arguably more insidious, requiring organizational participants to shift their frames of mind. Formal attempts at codifying practices that occurred during institutionalization failed to convey the logic of the decisions that linked various routines to the specific contexts in which they were incubated. Put another way, formal approaches, *by themselves*, were unable to transfer the contextual understanding that was needed to accomplish the cognitive shift. Informal human sensemaking and sensegiving activities were crucial, and the early phases of institutionalization were vulnerable to the exit of key individuals and the external events that shifted senior management focus.

What accounted for this difficulty in institutionalization? Our research suggests several clusters of reasons for this. The first can be traced to the conceptualization of the experience itself. The *capability was of a higher cognitive type than can be captured merely through organizational routines or standard operating procedures.* The senior managers and some middle managers envisioned the capability in terms of the *ends* achieved: to reduce the drug development time. They empowered project teams to alter the processes to accomplish the ends. This in turn required organizational members to "reframe" their thought process away from following organizational procedures, and toward inventing the means to reduce drug development time. The means themselves had to be seen in a contingent way, specifically tailored to the local conditions. Although importation of best practices proved useful, the fast-cycle teams had to "improvise on the spot"; this requirement was quite different from the injunction to follow "different" standard operating procedures. Even at the level of project teams, it was easier to create lists of specific action items (e.g., co-locate) – thus get fixated on specific means – than to arrive at a sense of the higher cognitive typing implied in the capability.

Second, the *strategic relevance* of the specific fast-cycle experience receded to the background once the teams were disbanded. First, the success of the teams took the profit pressure off the organization. Second, the firm undertook major mergers, causing the senior management to focus less on capability institutionalization and more on merger integration.

Third, the *external labor market* in the US was strong, the leaders and many members of the project teams were widely sought after, and out-migration of the individuals retarded the spontaneous spillover effects described earlier.

Fourth, the early stages of the *process of building the capability* itself contributed to the difficulties of institutionalization. The *only quasi-acceptance of the principles* of fast-cycle capability by middle managers sent confusing messages to the organization. For example, although the discontinued fast-cycle projects were a success according to the principles – the teams enabled the management to make the decision to discontinue very fast – the traditional labeling of success exerted itself in the later stages. Several managers explicitly withheld monetary rewards from members of discontinued teams. Also, survey data suggests that only the members who worked in successful teams were ascribed higher status in their functional groups once they returned "home."

Fifth, the *inertial forces* manifested themselves in political and structural forms. Politically, the sensitivity to local conditions, that was characteristic of the early stages, provided the rationale for some sectors of the organization to deny the success of the fast-cycle teams. The choice of one of the fast-cycle projects, involving a high revenue producer, was precipitated by FDA actions, but the science behind this drug was already in the advanced stages. It became easy for many scientists to argue that the success of this drug development team was attributable less to the fast-cycle practices than to the transparency and simplicity of the science involved. Structurally, the organizational capability required creation or evolution of organizational systems. A prioritization system to distinguish fast-cycle projects was necessary and human resource practices (including reward systems) had to evolve to accommodate the principles underlying fast-cycle capability. This was incomplete at best, and was susceptible to the inertial forces in the organization.

All five reasons identified in the study suggest the validity of social construction perspective in understanding the capability building process, a point we elaborate in the following section.

Social construction at work

Although economic considerations (such as market potential and scientific feasibility) weighed heavily in the decision to fast track specific projects, social construction may explain the logic of many decisions that led to the emergence of the specific organizational capability. First, why did MMD not focus merely on accelerating the development of the two successful drugs but instead engage in the elaborate fanfare of building organizational fast-cycle capability? Both options would have solved the short- and medium-term performance threats, the former probably much more cheaply and with less friction. The social construction processes described here provide one set of answers to the question. For one, the data suggests that the new head of Drug Innovation and Approval's push for fast-cycle capability is partially the outcome of his sensemaking of his previous experience in other, generally larger, pharmaceutical companies. In his mental model, fast-cycle capability was one of the cornerstones of building a competitive pharmaceutical company. This contrasted with the prevailing beliefs in the MMD organization he inherited. The ensuing social construction of the need for such a capability illustrates how political and cognitive processes are inextricably intertwined (Gioia et al., 1994), since – as shown above – significant political activity took place before a sufficient level of consensus (a form of cognitive homogeneity) was reached.

Second, why did MMD not implement a pure form of fast-cycle capability but instead opted for a compromise design characterized by some partially dedicated team members, a lack of co-location, and a continuing strong role of the scientific functions and their leaders? The decision did result in many difficulties for project team members (similar to those experienced in matrix organizations; Davis and Lawrence, 1977; Ford and Randolph, 1992), and was inconsistent with the idealizations (Meyer, 1993) that were presented to MMD during the planning stages. Clearly, some regulatory and industry-specific issues were a factor. However, our data suggest that it was also a result of the stark contrast between the existing organizational belief system built around "functional excellence" and the new set of meanings embodied by the concept of fast-cycle. Such tensions in meaning and identity decrease the probability of organization members accepting change initiatives, and thus MMD opted for a "tectonic change"

(Reger et al., 1994), that is, a level of change that was large enough to overcome cognitive inertia, but not so great as to overwhelm the organization. The baseline parameters of this intermediate form of fast-cycle were negotiated through a political process between senior management and functional leaders.

Third, in spite of strong inertial forces, many fast-cycle project team members did not revert to traditional practices and mindsets, once they returned to their functions. As the head of the Drug innovation put it: "those individuals will never be able to go back [to the old ways of doing things]." Despite strong normative pressures to revert to the standard operating procedures in their immediate environment, the actions of many individuals reflected a persistence of the new beliefs and meanings that resulted from their own fast-cycle experience. Some of them exited the organization rather than succumb to the inertial forces.

Finally, the only quasi-acceptance of specific fast-cycle principles (for example, meaning of success) suggests that few issues were ultimately settled, further organizational compromises would be necessary, and negotiations would persist into later stages of institutionalization. These negotiations crystallize in the emergent conceptualization and operation of the capability. Our data suggests that social construction processes underlie the organization specificity of the capability identified by Teece et al. (1997).

Unlike our study that documented the early stages of a top-down capability building effort, Burgelman's (1983, 1994) description of the emergence of a specific cluster of technical capabilities at Intel illustrated emergent processes. He showed how microprocessor expertise was nurtured at the middle ranks of the organization, and, in a fundamental strategy shift for Intel, the decision to exit DRAM market was legitimated at the highest levels of the organizational hierarchy. The initial phases were slow to evolve: time was being spent not merely on the development of the specific technology but also on political and cognitive realignment at the middle and lower ranks. The top managers adjudicated and rationalized the decision. In the top-down case we described, although the senior managers were the architects of the initiative, political and cognitive realignment at the middle and lower levels was needed during the institutionalization stage, which was slow to evolve. Indeed, a social construction perspective can accommodate both *emergent* and *purposefully designed* capabilities.

Implications

Methodological implications

Our study argued that organizational capabilities include managerial processes in addition to technical features (for example, product sequencing; Helfat and Raubitschek, 2000) or micro-level routines (such as project team dynamics). The challenge of examining the managerial processes involved in capability building underscores the unique contribution that process studies can make to our understanding. Since capabilities are not traded in the market, and are somewhat unique to the organization, these studies are perhaps better suited to profile the pathways to a capability. Large-scale empirical works, whose intent is to examine the role of a specific capability in competition, may rely on macro-indices such as average development time to operationalize the capability. But for those seeking to discover the pathways to implementation, process studies that couple multi-faceted operationalization with an understanding of the social construction processes may indeed be a more valid methodological choice. Specifically, the strategy of synchronic/diachronic analysis with its focus on time lines, specific actors, and their concerns helps us to triangulate interviews with archival data. This explicitness of triangulation, often lacking in grounded theory works, renders the resulting conclusions accessible to other scholars, and enables us to discover systematic differences.

Managerial implications

Our analysis suggests two major implications for senior managers embarking on capability building:

1 Significant attention to the later stages of development is warranted to ensure perpetuation of structures and systems (see table 7.2) that support the organizational capability. Especially when the initial efforts at building the capability are successful – in our case the success of two major projects – there is great pressure on senior managers to focus attention elsewhere, as we have seen here. Organizational fast-cycle capability is built only when requisite managerial processes are stabilized and a congruent culture has taken root.
2 Capability building is time consuming, and presents senior managers with a fundamental choice. One pathway is to accomplish the results with specific projects, without necessarily focusing on developing a capability that will alter the internal behavioral context. A second pathway is to view projects as a way of building organizational capability. An economic argument could be made for either in most cases. The choice will depend not merely on the economics, but on the senior manager's comfort level with that choice.

Unlike in an emergent process, where senior managers may play less active roles, top-down processes requires senior managers to commit their time and energy, in addition to money, throughout the process.

Conclusion

In this chapter, we charted the early stages of fast-cycle capability development in a pharmaceutical company. Our research yielded discernible patterns in the process that are consistent with other stage models featured in the literature (for example, Gioia and Chittipeddi, 1991). A major conclusion emerges from this work, however: there is significant process variation that should be captured in future process work. For example, as we proposed earlier, the nature of the capability, the locus of origin, and the strategy of building are likely determinants of the variation in the process. These three factors clearly distinguished our experience from that reported by Burgelman (1994). We expect future research to unearth other factors that differentiate among processes. We conclude with a call for additional intensive process work in other settings; cumulatively, the ensuing evidence may help us gain a clear understanding of the concept of capability and the processes of its implementation.

Notes

The authors thank Marion Merrell Dow for granting access and financial support. We also gratefully acknowledge the contributions of John Charnes, George Pinches, and Susan Mercer who not only helped with data collection, but also acted as project administrator. The data was gathered while the first author was head of the Center for the Management of Technology at the University of Kansas.

1   We use the terms *completed* and *discontinued* projects for two reasons. First, senior management discontinued projects due not necessarily to project management failures, but also for other reasons. Second, they viewed discontinued projects as successful fast-cycle experience, since the project team quickly produced data to facilitate the decision to discontinue, unlike in the case of regular projects, where the decision to abandon emerged slowly, consuming resources and time.
2   Economic rationale would dictate that discontinuing a failing project quickly is a value creating activity. See for example Pinches et al. (1996).

Appendix 7.1: Data Collection and Analysis

Data collection

Both archival and interview data were collected for the purpose of identifying the stages of developing fast-cycle capability.

Archival data
Four kinds of archival data were obtained from the firm, most of them prior to the beginning of the interviews:

1   DIA organizational data from 1990 to 1998: The formal structure, the names of the individuals in various positions, and so on
2   Written documentation, training materials, and presentation slides (where available) about the projects.
3   Project specific details: timelines, completion times, comparisons with industry benchmarks, and personnel allocation.
4   Financial data about projects, including sales projections and net present value (NPV) estimates, and their evolution over the project lifecycle were provided by the company.

The researchers also tracked published sources of data pertaining to best of class practices and performance figures in order to juxtapose the assessments derived from interviews and internal documentation.

Interview data
The interviews constituted the primary data for the purpose of this paper. They were conducted with (1) senior management regarding the logic of the introduction of fast-cycle teams and the challenges of implementation and transfer of learning, and (2) the six project leaders regarding their experience running the teams and the support and behavior of senior managers. Twenty-seven current and former managers were for-

Table A7.1   Interviewees

Position in 1996	Number of interviews
Executive VP (Head) of DIA, Chair of RDMT, and member of the Board of Directors	1
Senior VP of Operations, Technology, and Quality, and member of RDMT	1
Senior VP of Clinical, and member of RDMT	1
Senior VP of Development, and member of RDMT	1
VP of HR, and member of RDMT	1
VP of Clinical DIA, cardiovascular therapeutic area; and member of RDMT	1
VP; FCT projects sponsor; and member of RDMT	4
VP of Regulatory, and member of RDMT	1
Senior Director, Drug Safety	1
Senior Director, Pharmaceutics	1
Director, Portfolio and Project Management	2
Director, and North American Development Controller	2
Director, HR	1
Director, North American Pharmacokinetics	1
Director, Quality and Operations	3
Project Team Leader, Dolasetron	1
Project Team Leader, Rifapentine	1
Project Team Leader, Fexofenadine	3
Project Team Leader, Diabetes Agent	1
Project Team Leader, AntiAIDS/ Oncology Agent	1
Project Team Leader, Respiratory-Allergy Agent	2
Head, Clinical Research Operations	1
Head, Development–Operations Interface Team	1
Project Leader, Document Center	1
Project Manager, Fexofenadine	1
Manager, HR	1
Manager, Development Publishing	1

mally interviewed (some of them repeatedly) by two researchers during the first stage of the research (see table A7.1).

The interviews were open-ended and lasted between one and three hours. With the exception of two, all interviews were conducted in face-to-face sessions. One senior manager was located overseas, and a retired project leader had relocated; both preferred to do the interview on the phone. Most of the interviews were tape-recorded and transcribed; further, the researchers took notes and interpretive comments during the course of the interview. In a few cases technical difficulties rendered tape recording infeasible, and the researchers created written interview notes. Altogether, this resulted in five hundred transcribed pages, and nearly a hundred pages of handwritten notes. Both the interpretive comments and handwritten notes among the researchers showed consistent agreement on the substantive content of the interviews. This provided some confidence that the data were valid and reliable.

Six project teams were chosen for tracking: four fast-cycle teams and two regular teams, which provided a baseline for comparison. The chosen teams were diverse in terms of therapeutic areas as well as along several other criteria. Project leader interviews were summarized, and sent back to the project leaders for elaboration or modification, and redrafted based on their feedback. The revised interview summaries, together with the financial data about the projects, enabled the researchers to construct case briefs about each project, detailing the implementation challenges over its project lifecycle.

Validity checks

Two additional validation checks were built into the process. First, we created an internal steering board which also helped us to interpret the findings. Second, a group internal to the organization was asked to examine the report summarizing our data and conclusions. Their feedback served to further enhance the validity of the data.

Analysis

To construct *process stages from archival data and interviews,* the analysis adopted the logic of coupling synchronic and diachronic analyzes developed elsewhere (Narayanan, 1993). We created a set of timelines around the key events, identifying the key components of social construction for each stage. Narayanan and Fahey's (1982) stage model of micro-political processes (one aspect of social construction) served as a point of departure. As in all qualitative work, data analysis and conceptualization were iterative (Glaser and Strauss, 1967; Burgelman, 1994), and as the analysis progressed, a six-stage model emerged. We identified the elements of each phase in the model, highlighting in addition the political and cognitive processes to underscore the role of social construction in capability building.

References

Ancona, D. G. and Caldwell, D. 1990: Improving the performance of new product teams. *Research Technology Management,* 33, 25–9.

Barney, J. 1991: Firm resources and sustained competitive advantage. *Journal of Management,* 17(1), 99–120.

Bennis, W. G. and Biederman, P. W. 1997: *Organizing genius: the secrets of creative collaboration.* Reading, MA: Addison-Wesley.

Berger, P. L. and Luckmann, T. 1966: *The social construction of reality: a treatise in the sociology of knowledge.* Garden City, NY: Doubleday.

Birkinshaw, J. T. 1997: Entrepreneurship in multinational corporations: the characteristics of subsidiary initiatives. *Strategic Management Journal,* 18, 207–29.

Boulding, K. E. 1956: General systems theory: the skeleton of science. *Management Science,* 2(3), 197–208.

Bower, J. L. 1970: *Managing the resource allocation process.* Boston, MA: Division of Research, Graduate School of Business Administration, Harvard University.

Bower, J. L. and Doz, Y. 1979: Strategy formulation: a social and political process. In D. Schendel and C. Hofer (eds), *Strategic management: a new view of business policy and planning.*

Boston, MA: Little Brown, 152–66.

Bower, J. L. and Hout, T. M. 1988: Fast-cycle capability for competitive power. *Harvard Business Review,* 66 (6), 110–18.

Burgelman, R. A. 1983: A process model of internal corporate venturing in the diversified major firm. *Administrative Science Quarterly,* 28, 223–44.

Burgelman, R. A. 1994: Fading memories: a process theory of strategic business exit in dynamic environments. *Administrative Science Quarterly,* 39, 24–56.

Chang, S. J. 1995: International expansion strategy of Japanese firms: capability building through sequential entry. *Academy of Management Journal,* 38, 383–407.

Crozier, M. and Friedberg, E. 1980: *Actors and systems: the politics of collective action.* Chicago, IL: Chicago University Press.

Cyert, R. M. and March, J. G. 1963: *A behavioral theory of the firm.* Englewood Cliffs, NJ: Prentice-Hall.

Davis, S. M. and Lawrence, P. R. 1977: *Matrix.* Reading, MA: Addison-Wesley.

Denison, D. R., Hart, S. L., and Kahn, J. A. 1996: From chimneys to cross-functional teams: developing and validating a diagnostic model. *Academy of Management Journal,* 39, 1,005–23.

Floyd, S. W. and Wooldridge, B. 1997: Middle management's strategic influence and organizational performance. *Journal of Management Studies,* 34 (3), 465–85.

Ford, R. C. and Randolph, W. A. 1992: Cross-functional structures: a review and integration of matrix organization and project management. *Journal of Management,* 18 (2), 267–94.

Garud, R. and Van de Ven, A. H. 1992: An empirical evaluation of the internal corporate venturing process. *Strategic Management Journal,* 13 (summer), 93–109.

George, E. and Narayanan, V. K. 1999: Organizational speed: a conceptual integration. Paper presented at the Annual Meeting of the Academy of Management, Chicago, IL.

Ghoshal, S. and Bartlett, C. A. 1997: *The individualized corporation: a fundamentally new approach to management.* New York: Harper Business.

Gioia, D. A. and Chittipeddi, K. 1991: Sensemaking and sensegiving in strategic change initiation. *Strategic Management Journal,* 12, 433–48.

Gioia D. A., Thomas, J. B, Clark, S. M., and Chittipeddi, K. 1994: Symbolism and strategic change in academia: the dynamics of sensemaking and influence. *Organization Science,* 5, 363–83.

Glaser, B. and Strauss, A. 1967: *The discovery of grounded theory.* Chicago, IL: Adeline.

Golden, B. R. 1992: The past is the past: or is it? The use of retrospective accounts as indicators of past strategy. *Academy of Management Journal,* 35, 848–60.

Grant, R. M. 1991: The resource based theory of competitive advantage: Implication for strategy formulation. *California Management Review,* 33 (3), 114–35.

Grant, R. M. 1998: *Contemporary strategy analysis,* 3rd edn. Malden, MA: Blackwell Business.

Helfat, C. E. and Raubitschek, R. S. 2000: Product sequencing: co-evolution of knowledge, capabilities, and products. *Strategic Management Journal,* 21, 961–79.

Hitt, M. A., Ireland, R. D., and Hoskisson, R. E. 1999: *Strategic management: competitiveness and globalization,* 3rd edn. Cincinnati, OH: South-Western College Publishing.

Kearns, D. T. and Nadler, D. 1993: *Prophets in the dark: how Xerox reinvented itself and beat back the Japanese.* New York: Harper Business.

Kim, L. 1998: Crisis construction and organizational learning: capability building in catching-up at Hyundai Motor. *Organization Science,* 9, 506–21.

Klepper, S. and Simons, K. L. 2000: Dominance by birthright: entry of prior radio producers and competitive ramifications in the US television receiver industry. *Strategic Management Journal,* 21, 997–1016.

Leonard-Barton, D. 1990: A dual methodology for case studies: synergistic use of a longitudinal single site with replicated multiple sites. *Organization Science*, 1, 248–66.

Leonard-Barton, D. 1992: Core capabilities and core rigidities: a paradox in managing new product development. *Strategic Management Journal*, 13 (summer), 111–25.

Meyer, C. 1993: *Fast-cycle time: how to align purpose, strategy, and structure for speed*. New York: Free Press.

Mintzberg, H. 1973: *The nature of managerial work*. New York: Harper & Row.

Narayanan, V. K. 1993: Implementing high technology programs: the case of the space station. In P. Lorange et al. (eds), *Implementing strategic process*. London: Basil Blackwell, 71–90.

Narayanan, V. K. 2001: *Managing technology and innovation for competitive advantage*. Upper Saddle River, NJ: Prentice-Hall.

Narayanan, V. K. and Fahey, L. 1982: The micro-politics of strategy formulation. *Academy of Management Review*, 7, 25–34.

Narayanan, V. K and Kemmerer, B. 2001: A cognitive perspective on strategic management: contributions, challenges, and implications. Paper presented at the 2001 Annual Meeting of the Academy of Management, Washington, DC.

Noda, T. and Bower, J. L. 1996. Strategy making as iterated processes of resource allocation. *Strategic Management Journal*, 17 (summer), 159–92.

Pascale, R. T. 1984: Perspectives on strategy: the real story behind Honda's success. *California Management Review*, 26 (3), 47–72.

Pfeffer J., 1981: *Power in organizations*. Marshfield, MA: Pitman Publishing.

Pinches, G. E., Narayanan, V. K., and Kelm, K. M. 1996: How the market values the different stages of corporate R&D: initiation, progress and commercialization. *Journal of Applied Corporate Finance*, 9 (1), 60–70.

Pondy, L. R. and Mitroff, I. I. 1979: Beyond open system models of organization. *Research in Organizational Behavior*, 1, 3–39.

Quinn, J. B. 1980: *Strategies for change: logical incrementalism*. Homewood, IL: Irwin.

Raff, D. M. G. 2000: Superstores and the evolution of firm capabilities in American bookselling. *Strategic Management Journal*, 21, 1,043–59.

Reger, R. K., Gustafson, L. T., DeMarie, S. M., and Mullane, J. V. 1994. Reframing the organization: why implementing total quality is easier said than done. *Academy of Management Review*, 19, 565–84.

Schwandt, T. A. 1997: *Qualitative inquiry: a dictionary of terms*. Thousand Oaks, CA: Sage.

Teece, D. J., Pisano, G., and Shuen, A. 1997: Dynamic capabilities and strategic management. *Strategic Management Journal*, 18, 509–33.

Tripsas, M. and Gavetti, G. 2000: Capabilities, cognition, and inertia: evidence from digital imaging. *Strategic Management Journal*, 21, 1,147–61.

Van de Ven, A. H. 1992: Suggestions for studying strategy process. *Strategic Management Journal*, 13 (summer), 169–88.

Van de Ven, A. H. and Huber, G. P. 1990: Longitudinal field research methods for studying processes of organizational change. *Organizational Science*, 1 (3), 213–19.

Weick, K. E. 1995: *Sensemaking in organizations*. Thousand Oaks, CA: Sage.

Whetten, D. A. 1984: Effective administrators: good management on the college campus. *Change* (November–December), 38–43.

Yin, R. 1984: *Case study research: design and methods*. Beverly Hills, CA: Sage.

CHAPTER EIGHT

The Conditioning and Knowledge-creating View: Managing Strategic Initiatives in Large Firms

Martin W. Wielemaker, Henk W. Volberda, Tom Elfring, Charles Baden-Fuller

Introduction

Research context

Initiatives represent an important vehicle for firms to renew themselves. Firms must renew in order to co-evolve and maintain their fit with a changing environment. Many authors, such as Burgelman (1983) and Kanter (1989), have shown that initiatives can lead to the desired strategic renewal. Although the causal relation between initiatives and strategic renewal is still an object of research, the existence of a general relation between initiatives and strategic renewal is reasonably well established (Zahra, Nielsen, and Bogner, 1999). The study of initiatives therefore lies at the heart of strategic management and merits our attention.

With the relation between initiatives and renewal having been established to a certain extent, research efforts – specifically those based on strategy process research (Chakravarthy and Doz, 1992) – have also started to focus on the initiatives themselves (Birkenshaw, 1997; Kanzanjian and Rao, 1999; McGrath, MacMillan, and Venkataraman, 1995; Zahra, Nielsen, and Bogner, 1999; Floyd and Wooldridge, 1999): "how do initiatives occur and what facilitates them?" Initiative research did not start from scratch as it falls within the research on internal corporate venturing, which in turn is a subcategory of corporate entrepreneurship that belongs to the more general field of entrepreneurship; all these research areas have something to bear on initiatives.

Notwithstanding this large body of literature, initiatives remain an object of investigation as the literature shows conflicting findings, a lack of definitions, and unclarity about the conditions that facilitate initiatives. This study posits that part of the confusion is due to the existence of two perspectives that have barely been synthesized. One such perspective is the conditioning perspective that focuses on the conditions that facilitate or hinder initiatives (e.g. Bower, 1970; Burgelman, 1983). This stream of strategy process research has been accused of only looking at the organizational context or conditions that drive the selection of initiatives, failing to account for their creation. The other perspective, the knowledge-creating perspective, focuses on the processes that cause initiatives to be generated and developed (Nonaka and Takeuchi, 1995; Grant, 1996a, 1996b; Hargadon, 1998b). However, it fails to recognize that knowledge-creation is carried out in an organizational context that must also deal with knowledge-exploitation. Both perspectives focus on different aspects and therefore represent one-sided views of the initiative phenomenon (Kanzanjian and Rao, 1999; Zahra, Nielsen, and Bogner, 1999). What is called for is a synthesis of both, as organizational conditions not only impact the contextual development of an initiative, but also its content-wise development. Although there are recent studies that attempt to bridge the divide, they are either causal (Kanzanjian and Rao, 1999; Zahra, Nielsen, and Bogner, 1999), or conceptual (Crossan, Lane, and White, 1999; Floyd and Wooldridge, 1999) in nature. Process studies, certainly empirically based ones, that synthesize conditioning and knowledge-creating perspectives are lacking.

Research aim and questions

The aim of this study was to understand the impact that firms exert on the generation and development of initiatives by synthesizing the conditioning and knowledge-creating perspectives. In line with this research aim three research questions were formulated:

1 How can the conditioning and knowledge-creating views be synthesized?
2 How do the acquisition of resources (capital and assets) and knowledge interact in the initiative process?
3 How do firms impact the generation and development of initiatives?

Building on the work of many other researchers we define an initiative as a specific form of entrepreneurship that starts with the recognition of an opportunity and ends with a form of approval. During the process, the initiative seeks to acquire resources (capital and assets) and create knowledge.

In this study we differ between product and process *opportunities,* because such a difference has been known to lead to different findings (Abernathy and Utterback, 1975), and has been easy to detect in practice. Although other distinctions might have much theoretical value – such as between radical and incremental opportunities (Henderson and Clark, 1990), or between autonomous and induced opportunities (Burgelman, 1983), or between the locus of opportunity (Birkenshaw, 1997) – they are difficult to distinguish in practice (Lovas and Ghoshal, 2000) and laid aside in this investigation.

This study characterizes the *pursuit* both as a resource (capital and assets) acquisition and as a knowledge-creation pursuit. Although intrapreneurship researchers have pointed to learning effects (Burgelman, 1983; Kanter, 1988; Birkenshaw, 1997), it is nevertheless treated as a side-effect (Zahra, Nielsen, and Bogner, 1999). As we will point out later, the creation of knowledge is not just a side-effect of an initiative; it is partly what the initiative is all about. Hence, the pursuit involves both resource acquisition and knowledge-creation.

The "*approval*" refers to some form of sufficient approval, either in the form of resource commitment or approval of further knowledge creation. The commitment of resources alone does not constitute the end of the process, because these may very well be obtained outside the firm. We side with Birkenshaw's (1997) standpoint that the approval marks the end of the initiative process by an explicit or implicit approval, or by a rejection.

We also side with Birkenshaw in limiting the dependent variable to something called "*the outcome*." As said earlier, proving the causal relationship with strategic renewal is not the object of this study. The outcome is measured by asking the participants of an initiative what they consider the outcome of the initiative to be, which is in line with Birkenshaw.[1]

The crucial part of the definition is formed by the *facilitating conditions*. We want to know how these influence the trajectories of initiatives. Hence, we are really interested in the causality of these elements that are also considered to impact each other (Miller, 1986). The facilitating conditions can be divided into internal conditions, those that depend on the firm, and external ones, those that depend on the market. Although initiatives can use the market in pursuing their course, we shall not look at market conditions but only at the facilitating conditions as provided for by the firm, which is in line with Birkenshaw (1997). However, we shall show that the facilitating conditions differ when one takes a resource acquisition perspective or when one takes a knowledge-creation perspective. It is the purpose of this study to clarify the workings of these facilitating conditions.

Conditioning View of Initiatives

Initiative trajectories shaped by organizational conditions

Much of the literature that deals with initiatives, including the intrapreneurship or the more general entrepreneurship literature, agrees that organizational conditions impact the initiative process. Such conditions can be described as falling into four broad categories: strategy, structure, processes, and culture (Tushman, Newman, and Romanelli, 1986; Nohria and Ghoshal, 1997). Nevertheless, authors studying initiatives, such as Bower (1970), Burgelman (1983), Pinchott (1985), Bartlett and Ghoshal (1993), McGrath (1995), and Birkenshaw (1997), have also applied another, more operational, categorization for describing organizational conditions: organizational form, managerial roles, and administrative and incentive systems. Rather than stressing the content-wise development of initiatives, authors of the conditioning view tend to emphasize that the "main role of general managers lies in their role as shapers of an organization's context (Ghoshal and Bartlett, 1994: 108; based on Barnard, 1938)."

The first organizational condition, the *organizational form,* was considered to guide the general activities of the firm: not just initiatives. It was considered a given that management was not going to change the form for the sake of initiatives alone. Most authors generally agree (Burgelman, 1983; Bartlett and Ghoshal, 1993) that the hierarchical form is hostile to the necessities of the initiative because it is aimed at exploiting current knowledge and activities rather than exploring new territories. Solutions to its hostile nature were sought in hierarchical forms that allowed for the use of non-hierarchical teams, as was the case with the Matrix (Galbraith, 1973) or X-form (Williamson, 1975). However, the X-form remains in essence a hierarchical M-form (Chandler, 1962; Williamson, 1975) as the matrix structure is only carried through at the middle level. Others sought solutions in new business development structures (Burgelman, 1983) or skunk works (Peters and Waterman, 1982) that operated outside of the hierarchy often "illegally." But in all these cases the hierarchy remained essentially unquestioned, still leaving the initiative on its own to battle its way through. Only recently, have authors that investigate initiatives (Bartlett and Ghoshal, 1993) challenged the dominant assumptions about hierarchical modes of organization. This has encouraged the theorizing on new forms of organization such as the network N-Form whose main purpose is to encourage exploration rather than exploitation.

The *administrative and incentive mechanisms* are, similar to the organizational form, also often considered a given because they have been set up to deal with all activities of the firm. As such they are often inappropriate for the explorative and autonomous nature of initiatives. Simons (1994) describes these mechanisms[2] as diagnostic controls, boundary systems, and beliefs systems. The diagnostic control system is used to ensure effective implementation of intended strategy through the use of performance variables. Boundary and beliefs systems are used to ensure induced strategy through the specification of a search direction for new ideas and of what is out of bounds. However, initiatives seek the fulfillment of other sorts of performances than specified by the diagnostic control system, they neglect the beliefs system, and defy the boundary system. These control systems will therefore terminate such behavior. This leads to a situation that Hanan (1969: 44) describes as one in which "the [firm] has come to appear to many innovators as a hostile environment to change." Quelch, Farris, and Olver (1987) go even further and consider the reward system as punishing for those pursuing an initiative. Because of these problems authors have called for different administrative and incentive mechanisms for initiatives (McGrath, 1995; Kanter, 1986; Bartlett and Ghoshal, 1993). Some suggest the basic system is to remain intact and allow for exceptions (Burgelman, 1983). Others say it should be loosened to allow for slack and delegation of decision-making (Cyert and March, 1963). Others say it should change to a new system of measures and rewards, consisting of for example, discipline, stretch, trust, and support (Bartlett and Ghoshal, 1993). In the latter case it remains to be seen how such a system balances the mixture of intended and autonomous activities.

As opposed to the two previous organizational conditions, sets of *managerial roles* have been specifically proposed for initiatives. The roles have been related to managerial *levels*. Parson (1960) identifies three such levels, top management, middle management, and the bottom or front line. Even though in actual practice more hierarchical levels have been identified – Bower (1970) describes for example five levels – role differentiation has caused the grouping into three levels to become standard practice (Cauwenberg and Cool, 1982; Burgelman, 1983; Vaughn Blankenship and Miles,

1968). The *roles* have been characterized mostly in terms of the direction of strategy making. Originally the top was the entrepreneur with the other levels being implementers. When the idea took hold (Hunt, 1966: 89) that "planning and creative thinking [could no longer] be made the exclusive responsibility of a chosen few," the top was attributed a less autocratic but more guiding role, setting the general guidelines for decision-making at lower levels (Simon, 1947) in the form of standard operating procedures (Cyert and March, 1963). A bottom-up depiction of strategy-making was put forward by Bower (1970) who said, "planning is bottom-up; there is no division staff that prepares a plan that the subunits must then meet." People at the bottom were considered to "have the capacity to exercise [. . .] judgement" (Hunt, 1966: 86), because they have the necessary information as they are "closer to the markets (Bower, 1970: 21)." In such a bottom-up process, top management was attributed the role of judge (Bower, 1970) or, after the fact, retroactive legitimizer (Burgelman, 1983). Bartlett and Ghoshal (1993) have added a motivational role for top management as a creator of purpose. Burgelman corrected the one-sided views by depicting strategy making as consisting of both a top-down process, which he called induced behavior, and a bottom-up processes, which he called autonomous behavior. The role of the middle layer was merely to pass on information as a vertical integrator. Recently, the middle manager has received more attention (Floyd and Wooldridge, 1996), and his role has been described as that of a horizontal integrator (Bartlett and Ghoshal, 1993) as well.

The conditioning view takes for granted the internal development of initiatives and only attributes importance to the phases an initiative moves through, and to a lesser extent to the kind of idea. The *phases* the initiative moves through can all be related to the three basic stages of decision-making Simon described (1960): (1) problem identification, (2) development of alternatives, and (3) selection of the best alternative. Although the phases did not need to proceed as stated it was thought that they offered a good model for describing the process. The terminology of the phases has often been changed for various reasons. Aharoni (1966), for example, points out that proposals can be judged on their own merits rather than being selected against alternatives. The internal corporate literature (Burgelman, 1983) settles around three phases: definition, development, and implementation. The initiative literature, which regards the approval decision as the end of the process uses somewhat different terms: initiation, pursuit, and approval (Birkenshaw, 1997). Whilst the initiative phases will have mostly ended before the development or implementation stages have even commenced, this need not be the case. It might very well be that the approval is achieved after the development stage or even after it has been implemented. The *kind of idea* is thought to determine the trajectory it will follow. Much of the literature has used categorizations, such as radical, architectural, and incremental (Henderson and Clark, 1990), or as induced versus autonomous ideas, to illustrate the different trajectories followed by each type. However, in practice it is difficult to objectively determine the distinction, let alone that firms rarely make these distinctions. Aharoni (1966: 197) therefore concludes that "it would be very fallacious . . . to carry this dichotomy too far." The *development of the idea* is taken for granted in the conditioning view. Initiatives are considered stable particles that bounce back and forth between important actors. Although authors have pointed to aspects of learning (Cyert and March, 1963; Burgelman,

1983; Birkenshaw, 1997) this has served more as a side remark and has not been treated in a systematic and thorough manner (Zahra, Nielsen, and Bogner, 1999).

In the conditioning view the firm is capable of setting conditions because it supplies the *resources and legitimization* that the initiative needs Although resources can be defined quite broadly, it gradually became synonymous with capital and (complementary) assets. The idea that resources can also refer to knowledge has faded into the background. Lately, complementary assets have attracted much attention as something initiatives lack, but that large firms can provide very well. Legitimization is necessary to overcome resistance to change (Schon, 1963; Hanan, 1969). Venkataraman et al. (1992) mention various reasons for such resistance. The idea threatens the existing power and resource distribution. It can make knowledge and skills of powerful people obsolete. It may require large investments in, for example, training personnel. The people concerned do not wish to abandon their mode of thinking, as they are caught in competence traps (Levitt and March, 1988).

Whether firms are hostile or more supportive towards initiatives, the conditioning view tends to focus on the context- rather than the content-wise development of initiatives, focussing on resource allocation at the neglect of knowledge development issues.

Knowledge-creating View of Initiatives

Initiatives as knowledge-particles

Although there exists no body of literature that specifically deals with initiatives as knowledge particles, the contours of such a perspective are drawn by the knowledge, learning, and creativity literatures. Of these three the knowledge literature provides the notion of initiatives as knowledge-creating particles[3] (Nonaka, 1994; Zahra, Nielsen, and Bogner, 1999), particularly focusing on knowledge brokering (Hargadon, 1998a), transfer (Nonaka, 1991), and integration (Grant, 1996b). The creativity literature focuses on the interpretation or sense making of knowledge as a means of creating new knowledge (Amabile, 1988; Woodman, Sawyer and Griffin, 1993; Ford, 1996; Drazin, Glynn, and Kanzanjian, 1999). Recent creativity articles (Drazin et al., 1999) show a large resemblance to recent articles in the learning literature (Crossan, Lane, and White, 1999) that try to offer integrated frameworks of the entire knowledge-creating process.

Knowledge-creating process

A well-known representation of the knowledge-creating process (Nonaka, 1994) is the transformation process of tacit to explicit knowledge (Polanyi, 1966). Such a bipolar view has been critiqued as being overly simplistic (Tsoukas, 1996), in part because ideas can stem from a mixture of both tacit and explicit knowledge. Information-processing views of firms, extraction, processing, and acting (Miller, 1972; Simon, 1973; Galbraith, 1973), as well as learning views, acquisition, processing, storage, and application (Cyert and March, 1963; Argyris and Schon, 1978), have in turn been criticized for being too stimulus-response oriented (Levitt and March, 1988; Huber,

1991; Weick, 1991). Yet, recently these have been adapted towards more proactive representations of knowledge creation involving sensemaking (Drazin et al., 1999). Such a model by Crossan, Lane, and White (1999) depicts the knowledge creating process as intuiting, interpreting, integrating, and institutionalizing. Because the institutionalizing process describes the transfer of already created knowledge to the rest of the organization and comes after the approval stage of an initiative, it is laid aside in this chapter.

The initial stage of knowledge creating has also been termed *linking* (Clark and Fujimoto, 1991; Hedlund, 1994) instead of intuiting (Crossan, Lane, and White, 1999), because the former accentuates the need to come into contact with other knowledge, whereas the latter refers more to the "subconscious recognition of the pattern and/or possibilities" of that other knowledge (Crossan et al., 1999). Although both are relevant, the linking to other knowledge is a precondition for the second and facilitates the personal stream of experience (Weick, 1991) that is needed to get the knowledge creating process going. Social or informal networks have been found crucial in linking different knowledge domains (Granovetter, 1985). According to Granovetter (1974) it is weak ties, the non-dominant social network people have, such as acquaintances, which are particularly useful for idea generation. In a similar vein, according to DiMaggio (1992) and Burt (1992) it is the bridging of structural holes between social networks that constitutes the key to new ideas.

Interpretation refers to the bisociative process in which sense is made of the relation between previously unrelated knowledge domains (Koestler, 1981) and which often leads to innovative ideas (Baden-Fuller and Stopford, 1994). Such activity has been called "lateral thinking" (DeBono, 1970) or "kaleidoscopic thinking" (Kanter, 1986). Interpretation often involves experimenting because knowledge needs to be utilized for creative ideas to emerge (Venkataraman, Van de Ven, Buckeye, and Hudson, 1990; Moorman, 1995). The interpretation stage is the stage in which the basic idea or insight comes about.

Integration refers to the actual detailing of the basic idea and involves the combining of specialist knowledge (Demsetz, 1991; Kogut and Zander, 1992; Grant, 1996b) often through the use of teams. Of course, integration of knowledge domains has already occurred at a general level during the interpretation stage; such integrative knowledge is often conceived of individually. In this thesis the term integration is reserved for the combining of specialist knowledge, a process that often involves the use of teams.

The processes of linking, interpreting, and integrating are considered to move from the individual to the group and finally to the organization (Nonaka, 1991; Crossan et al., 1999). Yet, this is all with the understanding that (Nonaka, 1991: 15), "although ideas are formed in the minds of individuals, interaction between individuals typically plays a critical role in developing these ideas." Knowledge creation is thus an activity that involves both the individual and the organization (Tsoukas, 1996). Because the organization plays an important role in the process, much of the knowledge-creating literature has come to focus on the organizational conditions that support the linking, interpretation, and integration of knowledge.

Much less consideration is given to the control systems that relate to these supporting conditions. Teams, for example, are considered appropriate for integrating specialist knowledge, but how they are installed and by whom, is an issue often neglected (Kanter, 1988). By taking the initiative viewpoint the knowledge-creation view overlooks the point that organizational conditions are aimed at all firm activities, not just merely at the initiative. As such it fails to answer how knowledge-creation is to fit in an organization that is also aimed at knowledge implementation. Whereas it takes the content-wise development into account it fails to consider the context in which this takes place.

A Synthesizing Framework

The need for a synthesis

Although both the conditioning and knowledge-creating view analyze the same phenomenon, the initiative, they differ significantly in their focus. The knowledge-creating view concentrates on how the initiative is developed content-wise, whereas the conditioning view explains how it develops context-wise. The knowledge-creation view deals more with the initial stages, whereas the conditioning view deals more with the final stages of the initiative. They are therefore not just different perspectives (Allison, 1969); they also complement each other, suggesting a synthesis.[4] A synthesis would not only offer a more complete picture, but also managerial implications by explaining the impact of organizational conditions on the knowledge-creating process.

Various attempts at synthesizing have been made by various authors. Within the conditioning view Bartlett and Ghoshal (1993) have proposed organizational conditions that are more supportive of knowledge sharing. Yet, how these conditions impact the content-wise development of initiatives remains unraveled, as well as how they relate to the other activities of the firm. Within the knowledge-creating view we see similar attempts to cross the divide. Recent knowledge-creating research focuses on how individual knowledge or ideas reach the organizational level, using a sensemaking or issue-selling perspective (Woodman, Sawyer, and Griffin, 1993; Glynn, 1996; Crossan, Lane, and White, 1999; Drazin, Glynn, and Kanzanjian, 1999) or a causal perspective in which knowledge-creation results in new firm capabilities (Zahra, Nielsen, and Bogner, 1999; Floyd and Wooldridge, 1999). Although these contributions relate knowledge-creation to entrepreneurship, and thus to initiatives, they do not explain how organizational conditions relate to the knowledge-creating process. Hence, an explanation that synthesizes the conditioning and knowledge-creating perspectives is required.

Framework

The integrative framework (see figure 8.1) consists of various elements that are based on the two perspectives. The initiative starts with the identification of an opportunity (Nonaka, 1991; Birkenshaw, 1997), often referred to as an *idea*. Ideas can be considered particles of knowledge (Nonaka, 1991; Spender, 1996) that need to increase their knowledge base and legitimacy in order to become viable. In order for this to occur they require the involvement of *people*, such as the individuals that perceive the opportunity, the people who pursue the initiative, and those who supply the required knowledge and resources. Such *knowledge and resources* are required because the idea needs to be developed beyond the stage that it had when it was conceived. We limit resources to capital and assets, to distinguish it from knowledge that is sometimes considered a specific kind of resource. Knowledge is necessary to build the still-limited knowledge base of the initiative. Resources (capital and assets) are necessary ingredients for the development of that knowledge. The *approval* of the initiative is marked by being a sufficient form of go-ahead (or the negative thereof) or a sufficient level of knowledge developed (meaning that the idea knows no major uncertainties any more).[5] Before the idea reaches that level it needs to go through various *stages*: linking, interpreting, and integrating. The previous elements, which constitute the initiative, are then impacted by the *organizational conditions* consisting of the organizational form, the administrative and incentive mechanisms, and the managerial roles. These conditions can range between those focused at control and support, and can therefore be represented as a *control and support system*.

The framework relates the stages of development to the organizational conditions by suggesting that the balance between knowledge and resources shifts during the

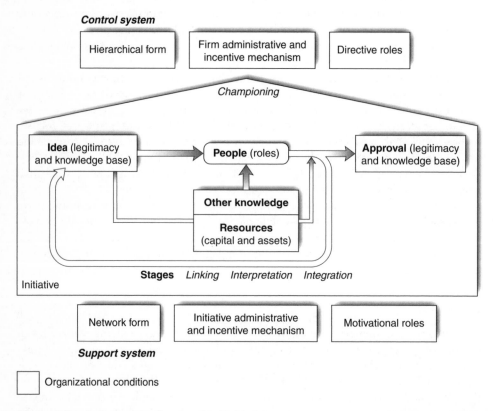

Figure 8.1 An integrative framework of initiatives

course of development and that this is accompanied by a shift from a support to a control system (see figure 8.2). Of course initiatives need not necessarily proceed according to the sequence put forward, but such a depiction serves describing a general picture.

The initiative pursues knowledge and resources, but the amount of each it needs differs per development stage. The further an idea develops the more its knowledge base increases and the less necessary other new knowledge becomes (Wheelwright and Clark, 1992). This trend is accompanied by an increase in the demand for resources (Gluck and Foster, 1975) in order to test, integrate, and implement ideas. Put more specifically, in the linking stage an insight is born through linking with other relevant knowledge. During the interpretation stage the matter becomes more forcefully pursued, now not just in terms of other knowledge but more so in terms of resources. The latter is possible because of the already built up knowledge base: it is becoming clear what resources are needed. Once the interpretation stage is over the search for other knowledge decreases drastically as the entire knowledge base has almost been built up. A detailing and integration of all the knowledge represents the next stage, which requires vast amounts of resources that are now actively pursued. The actual approval of the resources is often needed before the detailing can take place in order to set up a team of specialists. In other instances, this approval of resources can be partially delayed until the implementation phase.

The supply of knowledge and resources that the initiative requires is strongly influenced by the organizational conditions. As such, knowledge and resources tie the initiative to the firm's conditions. Consequently, a shift in the need for knowledge and resources over the development stages is accompanied in a shift in the kinds of organizational conditions. Such a shift can generally speaking be described as a move from a support system to a control system. The support system tends to focus on stimulating

Organizational conditions

	Organizational form	Administrative and incentive systems	Managerial roles
Development stagers — Linking	Network weak ties	Limited impact	T: Motivator M: Horizontal linker B: Entrepreneur
Development stagers — Integrating	Network strong ties	Strong impact	T: Selector M: Vertical linker B: Product expert
Development stagers — Integrating	Team	Moderate impact	T: Director M: Controller B: Specialists

Figure 8.2 The relation between the resource approval and development processes

knowledge creation, and as such is important in the initial stages of development. The control system deals particularly with the supply of resources and is therefore more important towards the final stages.

We can specify the organizational conditions per stage of development and thus obtain a more accurate picture of the changes across the stages. In the *linking* stage ideas are born mainly by being confronted with other knowledge. The resource requirements remain fairly small in this stage as the ideas are not materialized yet, nor are there a lot of people involved. As for the organizational form, a network of weak ties (Granovetter, 1974) is most appropriate for achieving a large number of links to sources of potentially interesting knowledge. The managerial roles have been arranged accordingly. The frontline, because of its specialist knowledge, is considered to be the idea generator (Nonaka and Takeuchi, 1995). Top management's role is that of a motivator stimulating variation. The crucial horizontal broker role (Gould and Fernandez, 1989; Hargadon, 1998a, 1998b) is reserved for middle management (Bartlett and Ghoshal, 1993; Floyd and Wooldridge, 1999). *The question is whether all middle managers in general perform such a brokerage role or whether this is tied to certain individuals.* We would expect that certain people within strategic business development units or R&D departments function as knowledge brokers as is suggested by Hargadon's studies (Hargadon, 1998a, 1998b) and studies pointing to product champions (Burgelman, 1983). The fact that middle managers are often resource allocators (for the later stages) causes conflicts of interests with a brokerage role. Moreover, one would expect strategic business units and R&D departments to cut across boundaries to a larger extent than middle managers that are tied to the hierarchy. The administrative and incentive mechanisms have only a limited effect on the generation of ideas because idea generators are in general intrinsically motivated (Amabile, 1988). *This also raises the question whether strategy sets the direction for variation.*

During the *interpretation* stage the basic hunch or insight is refined and elaborated until an appropriate understanding of how the idea works out is gained. It is during this stage that it becomes clear what specialist knowledge is to be integrated. For this understanding to emerge, linking and thus brokerage behavior remain essential, but so do interpretation (sensemaking) and experimenting. Because of the increased activity the amount of resources needed has increased. As for the organizational form a network is still required, but this time one of strong ties (Granovetter, 1974) in order to obtain the required resources and more detailed knowledge. This new form is accompanied by a shift in managerial roles. The frontliners become concept experts, which are often referred to as product champions (Schon, 1963). The middle managers become vertical linkers in the sense that they need to influence top management for the increased amounts of resources, as such becoming initiative sellers. Top management becomes a selector. Because the necessary resources are allocated in accordance with the formal strategy, initiatives are either repositioned to correspond with the strategy or the strategy is reinterpreted to fit the initiative. The administrative and incentive mechanisms function at their strongest level through rewarding or punishing entrepreneurial behavior in this stage.

The *integration* stage requires the actual integration of specialist knowledge. At this stage the knowledge base of the initiative is such that it seeks no other knowledge but merely to put together in a detailed fashion the knowledge it has already acquired.

Hence, whilst the need for knowledge has decreased, the need for resources has further increased as specialists must be made available to work in a team to carry out the detailing. Note that it has already become clear, through the linkage behavior of the previous stages, who these team members are to be; in most cases these "future" members have already contributed largely to the concept, thus having become "strong ties." As for the organizational form, the team is the structure used for integrating specialist knowledge. The managerial roles are accordingly arranged with the frontline being implementers, the middle manager being the controller, and the top being the director. The administrative and incentive mechanisms have a lessened impact as those involved have already made up their mind with respect to their participation. Often firms have set up separate venture funds and structures to facilitate this stage. In some cases resources necessary for integrating have been acquired from outside the firm's resource allocation system, such as from a customer. Burgelman (1983) has described instances in which approval is delayed further until the implementation stage, in some cases even after it was implemented. Notwithstanding that such trajectories are possible, in most cases initiatives depend on the firm to supply the necessary resources forcing them to obtain a go-ahead for the integration stage.

One should note that the three processes merely serve descriptive purposes and therefore will in reality often not occur in the linear fashion in which they have been treated above. As previous discussions of stage and phase models have clarified before (Simon, 1960; Aharoni, 1966; Burgelman, 1983), the process is very iterative in nature involving feed forward and feedback loops (Crossan, Lane, and White, 1999). Although the three processes – linking, interpreting, and integrating – have been treated in a universal manner in the knowledge creation literature, in our model we limit them to initiatives in large firms and to ideas that are considered to have the potential to impact the firm strategically.

Matching conditioning with knowledge creating

The integrative framework ties in the conditioning view with the knowledge-creating view, by pointing out how the two interact over time. It shows how organizational form shifts from weak network ties, via strong ties, to the team form over the consecutive stages because of a change in knowledge and resource demands. Similarly, new managerial roles have been suggested that shift across the various stages. Administrative and incentive mechanisms – as an offspring of strategy – have been shown to act on the selection rather than the variation of ideas.

Methodology

Process study

Notwithstanding its subjective limitations (Numagami, 1998), a qualitative case study was chosen as a research design for investigating initiatives (Pinfield, 1986; Anderson, 1983) because the study sought to answer *how* questions, because we had no control over events, and because it concerned dynamic and contemporary events (Yin, 1984).

The case study used a process study format similar to that of Burgelman (1983) in his internal corporate venture study.[6] However, as the field is now at a stage where quite some research has been conducted we took an interpretative (Eisenhardt, 1989) rather than a grounded approach as Burgelman (1983) had done. We selected multiple cases because we were not so much interested in a single initiative but in the general pattern of a multitude of initiatives, allowing a comparative analysis as well as an equifinality check. The case study was of an embedded nature. Specifically, rather than selecting a single firm various firms were chosen in order to differentiate between types of facilitating conditions. This allowed for comparison of initiative trajectories across firms that represented different sets of facilitating conditions.

Case selection

Firms were chosen on the basis of theoretical sampling (Glaser and Strauss, 1967; Eisenhardt, 1989). This was based on them possessing different sets of organizational conditions. As an approximation for these different sets of organizational conditions Volberda's (1996; 1998) typology of forms (rigid, planned, flexible, and chaotic) was used. We did not select a firm representing the rigid form, as that was uninteresting from an initiative viewpoint. We chose to select firms in different industries to further ensure differentiation of facilitating conditions. Other selection criteria used were that they had to be large firms that (1) had a presence in the Netherlands for reasons of access, (2) sales revenues of over 100 million guilders, and (3) participated in a global industry (similar to Birkenshaw, 1997). In this way, in what could be called planned opportunism (Pettigrew, 1990), we selected three firms. KLM Cargo was selected because it categorized as a form in-between the flexible and chaotic. Ericsson was selected as a form because it categorized as lying inbetween the planned and flexible, but leaning toward the flexible form. Van Ommeren was selected because it also categorized as lying in between the planned and flexible, but in this case leaning toward the planned form.

In each firm initiatives were then selected in a manner similar to Birkenshaw's (1997) selection method. First, senior management suggested about six initiatives that they considered particularly interesting from their viewpoint. Second, in order to offset the selection bias of the top managers somewhat, in each firm a smaller set of about three initiatives was analyzed that had been serendipitously encountered during our investigation. In this way we arrived at around 9 initiatives per company leading to a total of 25 initiatives (see table 8.1).

Data collection

The initiatives were analyzed by interviewing the key actors involved. This was done through semi-structured interviews that contained both general and more specific questions and were used as a general guideline. The initial questions focused, as Pettigrew suggested (1987), on the content (what was the initiative about) and context of the initiative (why did it come about). From there on the questions focused on the process (how did it take place). Mostly a single question, "describe how the project developed during the course of time," was enough to trigger the main process story. This in turn

Table 8.1   The initiatives investigated

	KLM Cargo	Ericsson the Netherlands	Van Ommeren
Location	Amsterdam	Gilze-Rijen	Rotterdam
Industry	Air freight	Telecommunications	Tank Storage
Initiatives	9	10	6
Interviews	27	20	20

led to questions of clarification or to questions on interesting aspects that had arisen. The semi-structured interview was mainly used as a back up to ensure that a broad range of topics covering all aspects of the framework was covered. Because the interviewees were the key players in an initiative, we managed to cover a large amount of aspects related to the initiative with a limited amount of key informants. Sometimes notes were taken and in all cases the interviews were taped and then transcribed in English.

Company reports, strategic plans, copies of transparencies, letters and memos, and in-company newsletters complemented the interviews. Similar to Pettigrew (1990), we also collected observational and ethnographic material, consisting of planned site visits for meeting staff and facilities, informal chance meetings and conversations, participation in formal meetings, sessions, and workshops.

Data analysis

The qualitative data was analyzed and visualized through tables and diagrams, which is in line with the recommendations of Miles and Huberman (1984). The analysis was undertaken by the three team members and differences were resolved through discussion.

Initially the analysis focused on understanding each initiative separately. The transcripts pertaining to a single initiative were read several times to grasp what the interviewees were saying. Then a case description was made and the general trajectory plotted into a process diagram similar to that used by Burgelman for describing his internal corporate ventures (1983). These case histories were then sent to the key informer of each initiative to verify that the case description was a fair representation.

Based on the case study database, tables that contained various parameters of the framework were filled in for each initiative. This was done separately and independently by three researchers, of which two had not carried out any data collection on that initiative (Pettigrew, 1990). Differences in the filling in of the tables were resolved through discussion. The initiatives were then compared with each other to detect general patterns. First, the initiatives of a single firm were compared by comparing the process diagrams and summaries of the separate initiatives and grouping them into similar categories. A table with initiatives of a single firm was composed of the individual initiative tables. As a final check the transcripts of each initiative were read again to check more thoroughly for the different aspects plotted in the table, and to see whether any important information regarding the facilitating conditions was over-looked. After having compared within a firm, a single table was then put together from the three separate firm tables. This table was then used to detect more general patterns and to detect differences between the firms.

Validity

Although some have suggested otherwise (Denzin and Lincoln, 1994), validity criteria remain accepted criteria for judging qualitative case research. More specifically, Yin (1984) stresses internal, external, and construct validity. The *internal validity*, which concerns the verification of the causality between key constructs (Leonard-Barton, 1990), appeared to be significant as all initiatives displayed a search for knowledge and resources that was impacted by conditions of the firms in which they were active. The *external validity*, which concerns the generalizability of findings, can be considered limited as only 25 initiatives in 3 companies were studied. Nevertheless, the findings are generally consistent with previous research (Bartlett and Goshal, 1993; Burgelman, 1983; Hargadon, 1998a, 1998b) suggesting that they are more generalizable than merely the three firms. The *construct validity*, which relates to whether the evidence truly supports its findings (Eisenhardt, 1989), was high for various reasons. First, constructs were specified a priori (Eisenhardt, 1989). Second, multiple sources of evidence were used: interviews, meetings, workshops, and documentary and archive data. In addition, the interviews were subject to triangulation as various people were interviewed on a single initiative. Moreover, the key informers reviewed the case descriptions (Yin, 1984). Various investigators analyzed the same data separately and then came together to discuss a consensus (Eisenhardt, 1989). And last but not least, a workshop was also organized for the management of the three firms in which the findings were presented.

Cases and Findings

The trajectories

The data collection and analysis have led to 25 lengthy case descriptions as well as various tables that have been used to detect patterns in the trajectories of the initiatives that rest with the authors. If we compare the trajectories across the 3 firms we see a clear pattern. At KLM most projects are top-down (7 top-down; 2 bottom-up) initiated by a single source, with bottom-up projects failing to get past the middle. There are lots of ideas but there isn't any mechanism in place to get them implemented. There is also a lot of misunderstanding present that hinders the initiative's progress.

At Ericsson, The Netherlands, we see a more balanced mixture of bottom-up and top-down ideas (4 top-down; 5 bottom-up, 1 middle through), from various sources. Most projects are client driven, and there is a frustration that radical projects cannot occur owing to a consensus model of operating. For bottom-up initiatives this implies oscillating back and forth between levels, because higher levels first want commitment from lower levels before signing on. This leads to a lengthy process. There is also a feeling that projects are fragmented because resources are tied to the divisions, instead of allocated at a higher level. There is quite some technological expertise in R&D, with a few inventors present in business development units that function as brokers for initiators. Compared to KLM the projects are less radical, are more diverse, and get implemented much better owing to the consensus model.

At Van Ommeren the pattern is different again. There we see that only one out of the six initiatives was bottom-up and exactly that one was terminated. Most projects are initiated by top or middle levels. All decision-making regarding initiatives is centralized – no consensus model – and projects get a clear go or no go signal. In summary we can conclude that Van Ommeren is experiencing the least amount of initiative activity, that KLM experiences most initiative activity, but from a limited range of sources, but fails to implement it, and that Ericsson is most successful in terms of variety and implementation

Organizational form

The data provides strong evidence that basic ideas predate the team formation. In other words, teams are formed in the later, not initial stages, of initiatives. Of the 21 projects in which a team was formed, the basic idea predated the team formation in all but two cases. In the two cases that didn't, the SDH-lower exit project and Telfort (B), the team happened to have been installed for an earlier project during which the new initiatives emerged. Perhaps the inappropriateness of teams for the initial stages is explained by the following quote.

> C3. "If a project team had been put on the Splitter project it wouldn't have worked. Project teams have the tendency to become bureaucratic and people start pulling at the project from different directions, whilst there is only one clear direction necessary."

We also found that of the 19 projects in which a team was formed after an idea had arisen, in 13 cases the people selected for the team had already been involved in the initiative beforehand. As expected, in all initiatives most of these candidates were from different hierarchical units. Together with the finding that most ideas were supplied by others not involved in the initiative (see next paragraph), this supports a depiction of the initiative process as a sequence of ideas-candidates-team formation. In terms of organizational form, this represents a shift from a network of weak ties to of one strong ties, in most cases culminating in a team form.

Administrative and incentive systems

The data strongly suggests that unless firms deliberately choose to do so strategy does not steer the birth and commencement of initiatives. If we leave out the top-down initiated strategies then 9 of the 12 initiatives were not initiated on the basis of a formal strategy. Many ideas were supplied by others not involved in the initiative, in most case clients. This is certainly true for Van Ommeren and Ericsson where clients suggested 6 of the 16 projects, and 3 were maybe not so much suggested by clients but clearly market driven. This underscores the opportunistic rather than strategy driven search for ideas. Notable is that KLM Cargo forms the exception. Not a single project was suggested by a client, all projects fell into the strategy from the onset. This can be explained by the important role of corporate business development in the initiative process at KLM leading to a lack of bottom-up initiatives that might not be based on formal strategy.

The data also suggests that formal strategy is only used in gaining legitimacy after the fact. Of the 25 initiatives only 3 projects were not considered to fit with formal strategy at the time the key actors where interviewed. Two of these were conflicting with formal strategy. The Tallin project had found out the hard way: it was terminated. The Unax project knew it was conflicting with interests of the American subsidiary. The Internet billing project worked on something that was not in the current strategy of Ericsson, but which the initiator himself firmly believed would be in the future. That means that all other 22 projects were considered to fit into formal strategy, whilst we know that of these 22 projects, 6 initiatives had not been originated on the basis of formal strategy. Because these 6 projects were considered to fit with strategy before they had been fully implemented, it suggests that proactive legitimization occurred.

Bypassing the administrative system by using existing customers worked very effectively at Ericsson, but not at KLM Cargo and Van Ommeren. The data could not reveal anything about new customers, because there weren't any such initiatives. At KLM Cargo initiatives were not aimed at customers and as such they couldn't function as sponsors. At Van Ommeren initiatives aimed at customers were still subject to formal approval, and customer sponsorship had little impact on the decision-making process. This is in contrast to Ericsson where sponsorship by a client was considered almost a guarantee for success, as is evident form the following:

> A4. "[if this option doesn't work] then I'll tie it into an . . . offer which I have lying here worth tens of millions of guilders, and if the client says 'yes do it,' then I'll have the space to give it hands and feet . . . So I think I need a customer to get things going."
> A5. "How can we do something in a firm with a limited budget? Well, besides garage work it also means that you have to do a lot together with clients."

The above findings support the notion that the administrative and incentive mechanisms had little influence on the initial stages, but a large influence on the interpretation stage of the initiative process. Strategy was found to have barely any impact on the generation of ideas. However, strategy, through the administrative and incentive mechanisms, was found to have a large impact on the interpretation stage in which legitimacy and resources were sought for the already conceived ideas. The impact was so large that bypassing tactics, such as the use of customer sponsorship, were found to exist in this second stage.

Managerial roles

The data is quite clear on the important role of people that work within autonomous venture units, business development units, or R&D departments. They were found to function both as idea generators and brokers. That they function as idea generators is not surprising given their job description. In KLM Cargo a single individual at corporate business development initiated 6 out of the 9 projects, and he was also heavily involved in the other 3. At Ericsson 5 out of the 9 projects were initiated by someone from the business development unit, by people from the strategic business development unit, and by people from R&D. At Van Ommeren this was irrelevant because there were no such units. However, they not only generated many ideas, but functioned as brokers for others as well. For example, at KLM Cargo all initiatives were in some way or another linked to the head of corporate business development. At Ericsson three projects involved a specific person from a business development unit, where he was functioning as a broker for others. Here's how others thought of him:

Q1. "Why did you go to Jacques [the business developer]?"
A1. "Well, because Jacques is always interested in novel things. It is also to sharpen your own teeth. At the time he was also busy with a couple of other things for the Internet."

These findings suggest that even though a role differentiation exists between the various organizational levels, role differentiation is also tied strongly to the task people carry out, irrespective of their level. Certainly idea generation and brokering was found to be tied strongly to people that could be typified as "inventors" within the firm.

Knowledge versus resources

As for knowledge it was clear that new ideas were related to the existing knowledge base. Of the 25 initiatives researched only in 5 instances did the knowledge have no bearing on the existing knowledge base. Outside knowledge was only crucial in two cases, Cable Dect, and Telfort, because it would've been almost impossible to develop the knowledge internally. In many cases outside knowledge was used to speed up certain parts of the initiative process. So the relevance of outside knowledge seems less than was expected. Knowledge is often supplied for free as is demonstrated by the previously discussed free handing over of ideas. In case the idea was already conceived and other knowledge was necessary the data is mixed as to whether such – more specialist knowledge – was supplied free, even by externals. About half the time return favors were counted on, other times it was supplied freely. As for knowledge search there was not a single case where brokering or the search for knowledge was prohibited. In that sense power does not seem to be used to conflict with the initial linking stages of initiatives.

There is limited evidence that the amount of resources needed increases during the course of an initiative. Of the 25 projects 12 showed an increase in the amounts of resources desired. These resource demands generally increased along the way, mainly because of the increasing amount of people involved. It is particularly notable that at Van Ommeren projects didn't seem to demand more resources along the way: only two of the six did. The reason is probably that at Van Ommeren most projects were really investment proposals, with the investment itself not being part of the initiative either because a client carried it out or because the initiative hadn't reached the investment stage yet. At Ericsson, people could often use slack but because of the increasing amount of resources needed this proved insufficient:

> A1. "When it started to get more body we said we ought to ensure that other divisions start contributing because our budget is very limited. I mean, we can give some money but as soon as it exceeds the fl. 50.000 – you want commitment, otherwise you just can't manage."

Control versus support

As for the balancing of the control and support systems by the firms we see the following picture. At Ericsson and Van Ommeren you see the simultaneous use of both a control and support system, with Van Ommeren wanting to strengthen its control and support system. At Ericsson the desire seems to be to want to strengthen their support system. At KLM there seems an absence of both a control and support system. This probably explains the lack of bottom-up ideas and of implementation. The projects show a picture of misunderstanding, absence of formalization, and so on. The following quotes of people interviewed at KLM Cargo serve to underline this point.

> B1. "People are not accustomed to explicating knowledge or updating it. And the disciplinary handing over of such knowledge was also a problem."
> B2. "Projects in Cargo are never formal, because project-based work is not common at Cargo. There is a lot of teamwork, but it is more ad hoc. And we don't need any formal team here either."
> B3. "The strategy is conceptually very good, but it is so complex that nobody can fully grasp how it is to be implemented."
> B4. "There is a hole that exists between the strategic thinking on the one hand, and the operational thinking on the other hand. There is too little in-between."

At Ericsson there is a balancing of both control systems that doesn't cause mixed signals. On the one hand people are forced in the control system through the consensus model, yet on the other hand there are all sorts of support mechanisms. What people generally found a problem was that resources and decision-making was located at the divisions causing fragmentation of plans, and the difficulty in carrying out experiments. The following quote is typical of what happens when someone is sent back by top management to the control system.

> A1. "[The business developer] invited me to [the director of the firm]. I had prepared a long story about this sort of stuff [the idea]. And what was the weird thing, he himself came with that story. The ideas that [the director of the firm] had were in fact the same ideas that I had. So it was funny and we left each other with an assignment. So I left the room with the task to carry things on. That was nice because such an assignment is always very useful."
> Q1. "How formal was that assignment? Did it include budget or time?"
> A1. "Normally you might say what it means in terms of money and time, but . . .

you shouldn't see it this way. I think his support, the fact that he also wants this, that is enough to convince people."

Yet the balance at Ericsson is tipped in favor of the control system. The consensus model is so strong that it hinders initiatives that are more radical.

> A2. "The closer the idea is to the current frame of mind of people, and let's say you can do it, then a lot can happen. But if you talk about totally different areas where we are not a player yet, then it is really a painful way in this organization."
> A3. "I would say that Ericsson's culture for consensus has its disadvantages . . . Basically because everyone has their own budget . . . See, you have to have consensus and that takes a lot of time."
> A4. "In this stage where [our firm] is now, you can only do that by behaving like a fool, by sticking yourself in the story. And that is only possible if you yourself have a certain attitude and insight. If a person doesn't have that and tries to mention it according to the official way and he gets along the first steps, at a certain moment he gets into a surrounding where the climate isn't good and then you have to continue on your own power and you have to continue no matter what. If you can't handle that, then it will terminate."

The support system is considered somewhat weak on other points

> A7. "What you would really like is a kind of free lab where you can say, 'ok, let us try if this works and if it is something worthwhile'."

At Van Ommeren the control and support system were considered weak, and in need of strengthening. The failure of the Tallin project, which was terminated by top management, was attributed to top management being involved too late, that is, a weak control system. The support system was also considered weak, which was attributed to a recent transformation process. Here is description of the support system at Van Ommeren.

> C1. "Everything that is new is kind of suspect; there is no entrepreneurial culture present. The current older generation are not the most entrepreneurial people."

Reflections

This study aimed to integrate the conditioning and knowledge-creating view in order to understand the initiative phenomenon. This study has particularly pointed to the role organizational form, administrative and incentive mechanisms, and managerial roles have on both the creation of knowledge and pursuit of resources of initiatives. The study has implications for various discussions that exist in the literature.

First, it demonstrated the importance of single individuals in business development units in the generation of ideas, in brokering and championing them. Whilst those of the hostile conditioning view (Burgelman, 1983; Block and MacMillan, 1993) have particularly stressed the use of organizational champions for acquiring resources, others have stressed the role of managerial levels (Ghoshal and Bartlett, 1994). Yet this study has shown in line with Hargadon (1998a, 1998b) that single individuals play an important role not just in the generation of ideas, known as product champions (Schon, 1963), but also in the brokering or linking of ideas. It suggests that managerial roles should therefore not just be set at the general level, but at the individual person.

Second, the study shows strategy to function as a selection, not as a variation mechanism (Campbell, 1969). People came up with ideas irrespective of strategy and only later on repositioned them to fit with the existing strategy, which is in line with the intrinsic motivation found in creative people (Amabile, 1988). This questions the relevance of strategic intent or guided evolution (Prahalad and Doz, 1987; Lovas and Ghoshal, 2000) as far as it concerns the generation of ideas. Yet, simultaneously it supports Lovas and Ghoshal (2000) in their questioning of the relevance of Burgelman's (1983) autonomous versus induced distinction for the generation of ideas. When people generated ideas they were found not to be influenced by strategy at all, often even unaware of the formal strategy, and thus ignorant of whether their ideas were autonomous or induced. However, when it came to the selection stage, strategy did play an important role. Initiatives took the strategic intent into consideration by repositioning themselves, but were then retroactively legitimized as well. The study therefore sheds new light on evolutionary views (Burgelman, 1991; Quinn, 1985) of the strategy process. It should, however, be said that even though the study shows strategy to have no effect on the direction of variation, it doesn't say anything about the impact of administrative and incentive mechanisms on the intensity of variation because such mechanisms were absent in the firms studied.

Variation was found to be tied to the knowledge base rather than to strategic initiatives. If initiatives managed to make the link to other knowledge areas and thus increase their knowledge base, that rather than the existence of a formal strategy enabled the onset of an idea and thus variation. Although administrative and incentive systems have been proposed for increasing rates of variation (like the use of time slots), this study points to the knowledge-base and to linking mechanisms as essential for variation. Hence, in order to increase variation firms should not only look at administrative and incentive systems, but also at enabling brokering and linking processes for an increased knowledge base. Although the literature has emphasized brokerage behavior it has done so more from a knowledge refinement point of view (Bartlett and Ghoshal, 1993), than from an idea generation point of view (Hargadon, 1998a,b).

The study also shows that as opposed to resources, knowledge knows no boundaries. In most cases the knowledge that generated a new idea originated in part from outside the firm. Although this is in line with much of the network literature (Hedlund, 1994), it poses a problem for the organizational conditions that have generally been set up for guiding initiatives within the boundaries of the firm, not least because resources are supplied through the hierarchy. But since variation is tied to the knowledge base and linkages to other knowledge organizational conditions need to allow for extra hierarchical behavior even before there is any talk of initiative.

The study also has a number of limitations. First, top management suggested a large portion of the initiatives to be researched which might have caused a selection bias towards, for example, top-down, turnaround, and successful initiatives. Second, the firms were chosen from a single country, limiting their external validity (Birkenshaw, 1997). Third, the firms chosen were not judged on their level of innovativeness within their respective industry. Fourth, with respect to the generation of ideas the accounts were retrospective. Nevertheless, notwithstanding these limitations, the setup of the research served to underline the differing impact of organizational conditions on knowledge-creating processes.

As for further research, we suggest various ways ahead. First, future research could try to tie in the findings at the intrafirm or firm level to that of the industry level. Current research is either at the microlevel (Burgelman, 1983; Birkenshaw, 1997; Bartlett and Ghoshal, 1993) or at the macrolevel (Rosenberg, 1972; Schmalensee, 1985). Second, strategic renewal from an internal perspective, such as intrapreneurship, and from an external perspective, such as alliances, are separated too much because the boundaries of the firm diffuse when it comes to knowledge creating and networking. Studies that take an intra- and extrafirm perspective have thus much light to shed on the initiative process. Third, notwithstanding that this study has shed considerable light on the origin of ideas it remains to be discovered what it is that ignites the creative spark. Although it is hard as an investigator to locate someone who is in the process of obtaining an idea – that is why such accounts are mostly retrospective – participant observation seems the method for future studies in order to unravel how ideas are ignited: an issue that, even in the creativity literature, remains a black box to this day.

Notes

1 Birkenshaw measured three kinds of outcomes: (1) average new investment in subsidiary as a result of approval, (2) average new sales for subsidiary within two years, (3) subjective long-term outcomes as stated by respondents. We do not use the first two because we feel that initiatives with high average investment and sales are not necessarily successful. The third option, asking the participants, is more appropriate because they can judge the status of the initiative when it hasn't yet reached the implementation stage. As opposed to Birkenshaw we measure the short-term outcome, because we want to relate the outcome to the initiative rather than to consecutive stages.

2 Simons actually describes a fourth one, interactive control systems, that he considers appropriate for emergent strategy. However, when he describes this system as "senior managers determine where participants should focus attention" it is clear that he is not referring to emergent but to induced strategy. Because emergent strategy cannot be controlled by definition, his fourth category is problematic and therefore not treated.

3 Although both author's didn't talk about initiatives specifically, they did talk about the more general categories of innovation (Nonaka, 1991) and corporate entrepreneurship (Zahra, Nielsen, and Bogner, 1999).

4 Both knowledge creation and resource acquisition (the focus of the conditioning view) are always involved, even though in some instances it might seem that only one of the two is involved. For example, the instance where no further knowledge creation is necessary beyond a first insight represents a case of knowledge creation, but one in which this is limited or compressed to the initial phase. As such, even though both perspectives can be associated per initiative, the value of either may differ per initiative.

5 Approval is always a sign of knowledge having been created. To obtain approval the initia-

tive had to legitimize itself, which it could only have done so if it developed its idea to a certain level, i.e. developed a certain level of knowledge.

6   Van de Ven (1992) explains that there are three types of process designs: (1) a variance theory explaining the causal relation between dependent and independent variables, (2) fixed variables that are operationalized as constructs, and (3) a "sequence of events or activities that describes how things change over time (170)." This study is of the third type.

References

Abernathy, W. J. and Utterback J. M. 1975: A dynamic model of process and product innovation. *Omega*, 3 (6), 639–56.

Aharoni, Y. 1966: *The foreign investment decision process*. Boston: Harvard University.

Allison, G. 1969: Conceptual models and the Cuban missile crisis. *The American Political Science Review*, 63 (3), 689–718.

Amabile, T. M. 1988: A model of creativity and innovation in organizations. In B. M. Staw (ed.), *Research in organizational behavior*, 10. Greenwich, CN: JAI Press, 123–67.

Amit, R., Glosten, L., and Muller, E. 1993: Challenges to theory development in entrepreneurship research. *Journal of Management Studies*, 30 (5), 815–34.

Anderson, P. 1983: Decision making by objection and the Cuban missile crisis. *Administrative Science Quarterly*, 28 (2), 201–22.

Argyris, C. and Schön, D. A. 1978: *Organizational learning: a theory of action perspective*. Reading, MA: Addison-Wesley.

Baden-Fuller, C. W. F. and Stopford, J. M. 1994: *Rejuvenating the mature business*. Boston: Harvard Business School Press.

Bartlett, C. A. and Ghoshal, S. 1993: Beyond the M-form: toward a managerial theory of the firm. *Strategic Management Journal*, 14 (winter special issue), 23–46.

Birkenshaw, J. 1997: Entrepreneurship in multinational corporations: the characteristics of subsidiary initiatives. *Strategic Management Journal*, 18 (3), 207–29.

Block, Z. and MacMillan, I. 1993: *Corporate venturing: creating new businesses within the firm*. Boston, MA: Harvard Business School Press.

Bower, J. L. 1970: *Managing the resource allocation process*. Boston, MA: Harvard Business School Press.

Burgelman, R. A. 1983: A model of internal corporate venturing in the diversified major firm. *Administrative Science Quarterly*, 28 (2), 223–44.

Burgelman, R. A. 1991: Intraorganizational ecology of strategy-making and organizational adaptation: theory and field research. *Organization Science*, 2, 239–62.

Burt, R. S. 1992: *Structural holes: the social structure of competition*. Cambridge, MA: Harvard University Press.

Campbell, D. 1969: Variation and selective retention in socio-cultural evolution. In J. A. C. Baum and J. Singh (eds), *Evolutionary dynamics of organizations*, New York: Oxford University Press, 23–38.

Cauwenberg, A. Van, and Cool, K. 1982: Strategic management in a new framework. *Strategic Management Journal*, 3, 245–64.

Chakravarthy, B. S., and Doz, Y. 1992: Strategy process research: focusing on corporate self-renewal. *Strategic Management Journal*, 13 (summer special issue), 5–14.

Chandler, A. D. Jr 1962: *Strategy and structure*. Cambridge: MIT Press.

Christensen, C. M. 2000: Will disruptive innovations cure health care? *Harvard Business Review*, 78 (5), 102–12.

Clark, K. B. and Fujimoto, T. 1991: *Product development performance*. Boston: Harvard

Business School Press.

Clayton, J., Gambill, B., and Harned, D. 1999: The curse of too much capital: building new businesses in large corporations. *McKinsey Quarterly*, 3, 48–59.

Crossan, M. M., Lane, H. W., and White, R. E. 1999: An organizational learning framework: from intuition to institution. *Academy of Management Review*, 24 (3), 522–37.

Cyert, R. M. and March, J. G. 1963: *A behavioral theory of the firm*. Englewood Cliffs, NJ: Prentice-Hall: The Free Press.

Day, D. L. 1994: Raising radicals: different processes for championing innovative corporate ventures. *Organization Science*, 5 (2), 148–72.

DeBono, E. 1970: *Lateral thinking: a textbook of creativity*. London: Ward Lock Educational.

Dees, J. G. and Starr, J. A. 1992: Entrepreneurship through an ethical lens: dilemmas and issues for research and practice. In D. L. Sexton and J. D. Kasarda (eds), *The State of the Art of Entrepreneurship*, Boston: PWS-Kent, 89–116.

Demsetz, H. 1991: The theory of the firm revisited. In O. E. Williamson and S. G. Winter (eds), *The nature of the firm*, New York: Oxford University Press, 159–78.

Denzin, N. K. and Lincoln, Y. S. 1994: Introduction: entering the field of qualitative research. In N. Y. Denzin and Y. S. Lincoln (eds), *The handbook of qualitative research*, Thousand Oaks, CA: Sage Publications.

DiMaggio, P. 1992: Nadel's paradox revisited and vultural aspects of organizational structure. In N. Nohria and R.G. Eccles (eds), *Networks and organizations: structure, form, and action*, Boston: Harvard Business School Press, 118–42.

Drazin, R., Glynn, M. A. and Kanzanjian, R. K. 1999: Multilevel theorizing about Creativity in Organizations: A sense-making perspective. *Academy of Management Review*, 24 (2), 286–307.

Drucker, P. F. 1985: The discipline of innovation, *Harvard Business Review*, 63 (3), 95–104.

Eisenhardt, K. M. 1989: Building theories from case study research. *Academy of Management Review*, 14 (4), 532–50.

Floyd, S. W. and Wooldridge, B. 1996: *The strategic middle-manager: how to create and sustain competitive advantage*, San Francisco, CA: Jossey-Bass.

Floyd, S. W. and Wooldridge, B. 1999: Knowledge creation and social networks in corporate entrepreneurship: the renewal of organizational capability. *Entrepreneurship Theory and Practice*, 23 (3), 123–43.

Ford, C. M. 1996: A theory of individual creativity in multiple social domains. *Academy of Management Review*, 21 (4), 1,112–34.

Galbraith, J. R. 1973: *Designing complex organizations*. Reading, MA: Addison-Wesley.

Galbraith, J. R. 1982: Designing the innovating organization. *Organizational Dynamics*, 10 (4), 3–24.

Ghoshal, S. and Bartlett, C. A. 1994: Linking organizational context and managerial action: the dimensions of quality of management. *Strategic Management Journal*, 15 (summer special issue), 91–112.

Glaser, B. and Strauss, A. 1967: *The discovery of grounded theory: strategies of qualitative research*. London: Wiedenfeld and Nicholson.

Gluck, F. W. and Foster, R. N. 1975: Managing technological change: a box of cigars for Brad. *Harvard Business Review*, 53 (5), 139–50.

Glynn, M. A. 1996: Innovative genius: a framework for relating individual and organizational intelligences to innovation. *Academy of Management Review*, 21 (4), 1,081–111.

Gould, R. V. and Fernandez, R. M. 1989: Structures of mediation: a formal approach to brokerage in transaction networks. *Sociological Methodology*, 89–126.

Granovetter, M. 1974: The strength of weak ties. *American Journal of Sociology*, 78 (6), 1,360–80.

Granovetter, M. 1985: Economic action and social structure: the problem of embeddedness. *American Journal of Sociology*, 91 (3), 481–510.

Grant, R. M. 1996a: Prospering in dynamically-competitive environments: organizational capability as knowledge integration. *Organization Science*, 7 (4), 375–86.

Grant, R. M. 1996b: Towards a knowledge-based theory of the firm. *Strategic Management Journal*, 17 (winter special issue), 109–22.

Hanan, M. 1969: Corporate growth through venture management. *Harvard Business Review*, January–February, 43–61.

Hargadon, A. B. 1998a: Knowledge brokers: A field study of organizational learning and innovation. *Best Paper Proceedings for the 1998 Academy of Management Conference*.

Hargadon, A. B. 1998b: Firms as knowledge brokers: lessons in pursuing continuous innovation. *California Management Review*, 40 (3), 209–27.

Hedlund, G. 1994: A model of knowledge management and the N-Form Corporation. *Strategic Management Journal*, 15 (summer special issue), 73–90.

Henderson, R. M. and Clark, K. B. 1990: Architectural innovation: the reconfiguration of existing product technologies and the failure of established firms. *Administrative Science Quarterly*, 35 (1), 9–30.

Hinnings, C. R., Hickson, D. J., Pennings, J. M., and Schneck, R. E. 1974: Structural conditions of intraorganizational power. *Administrative Science Quarterly*, 19, 22–44.

Huber, G. P. 1991: Organizational learning: the contributing processes and literatures. *Organization Science*, 2 (1), 88–115.

Hunt, P. 1966: The fallacy of the one big brain. *Harvard Business Review*, July–August, 84–90.

Kanter, R. M. 1985: Supporting innovation and venture development in established companies. *Journal of Business Venturing*, 1 (1), 47–60.

Kanter, R. M. 1986: Creating the creative environment. *Management Review*, 75 (February), 11–12.

Kanter, R. M. 1988: When a thousand flowers bloom: structural, collective, and social conditions for innovation in organization. *Research in Organizational Behavior*, 10, 169–211.

Kanter, R. M. 1989: *When giants learn to dance*. New York: Simon & Schuster.

Kanzanjian, R. K. and Rao, H. 1999: Research notes: the creation of capabilities in new ventures: a longitudinal study. *Organization Studies*, 20 (1), 125–42.

Koestler, A. 1981: *The art of creation*. London: Picador.

Kogut, B. and Zander, U. 1992: Knowledge of the firm, combinative capabilities, and the replication of technology. *Organization Studies*, 3, 383–97.

Leonard-Barton, D. 1990: A dual methodology for case studies: synergistic use of a longitudinal single site with replicated multiple sites. *Organization Science*, 1 (3), 248–66.

Levitt, B. and March, J. G. 1988: Organizational learning. In W. R. Scott (ed.), *Annual review of sociology xiv*, Palo Alto, CA: Annual Reviews, 319–40.

Lovas and Ghoshal, S. 2000: Strategy as guided evolution. *Strategic Management Journal*, 21 (9), 875–96.

Maidique, M. A. 1980: Entrepreneurs, champions, and technological innovation. *Sloan Management Review*, 21 (2), 56–76.

March, J. G. 1962: The business firm as a political coalition. *The Journal of Politics*, 24, 662–78.

March, J. G. 1991: Exploration and exploitation in organizational learning. *Organization Science*, 2 (1), 71–87.

McGrath, R. G. 1995: Advantage from adversity: learning form disappointment in internal corporate ventures. *Journal of Business Venturing*, 10 (2), 121–42.

McGrath, R. G., MacMillan, I. C., and Venkataraman, S. 1995: Defining and developing competence: a strategic process paradigm. *Strategic Management Journal*, 16, 251–75.

Miles, M. and Huberman, A. M. 1984: *Qualitative data analysis*, Beverly Hills, CA: Sage Publications.

Miller, D. 1986: Configurations of strategy and structure. *Strategic Management Journal*, 7 (3), 233–49.

Miller, J. G. 1972: Living systems: the organization. *Behavioral Science*, 17, 1–82.

Moorman, C. 1995: Organizational market information processes: cultural antecedents and new product outcomes. *Journal of Marketing Research*, xxxii (August), 318–35.

Morrison, E. W. and Phelps, C. C. 1999: Taking charge at work: extrarole efforts to initiate workplace change. *Academy of Management Journal*, 42 (4), 403–19.

Nohria, N. and Ghoshal, S. 1997: *The differentiated network: organizing multinational corporations for value creation*. San Francisco, CA: Jossey-Bass.

Nonaka, I. 1991: The knowledge-creating company. *Harvard Business Review*, 69 (6), 96–104.

Nonaka, I. 1994: Dynamic theory of organizational knowledge creation. *Organization Science*, 5 (1), 14–37.

Nonaka, I., and Takeuchi, H. 1995: *The knowledge-creating company*. New York: Oxford University Press.

Numagami, T. 1985: The infeasability of invariant laws in management studies: a reflective dialogue in defense of case studies, *Organization Science*, 9 (1), 2–15.

Osborn, A. F. 1963: *Applied imagination: principles and procedures of creative thinking*. New York: Scribner.

Parson, T. 1960: *Structure and process in modern societies*. Glencoe, IL: The Free Press of Glencoe.

Peters, T. J., and Waterman, R. H., Jr 1982: *In search of excellence*. New York: Warner Books.

Pettigrew, A. M. 1973: *Politics of organizational decision-making*. London: Tavistock.

Pettigrew, A. M. 1987: Context and action in the transformation of the firm. *Journal of Management Studies*, 24 (6), 649–70.

Pettigrew, A. M. 1990: Longitudinal field research on change: theory and practice. *Organization Science*, 1 (3), 267–70.

Pfeffer, J. 1981: *Power in organizations*. Marshfield, MA: Pitman Publishing.

Pinchott, G., III 1985: *Intrapreneuring*. New York: Harper & Row.

Pinfield, L. 1986: A field evaluation of perspectives on organizational decision making. *Administrative Science Quarterly*, 31 (3), 365–88.

Polanyi, M. 1966; 1983: *The tacit dimension*. New York: Doubleday & Company, Inc.

Prahalad, C. K. and Doz, Y. 1987: *The multinational mission: balancing local demands and global vision*. New York: Free Press.

Quelch, J., Farris, P., and Olver, J. 1987: The product management audit: design and survey findings. *Journal of Consumer Marketing*, 4 (3), 45–58.

Quinn, J. B. 1985: Managing innovation: controlled chaos. *Harvard Business Review*, 63 (3), 73–85.

Rosenberg, N. 1972: *Technology and American economic growth*. New York: Harper Torch Books.

Sapolsky, H. M. 1972: *The Polaris system development*. Cambridge, MA: Harvard University Press.

Sathe, V. 1985: Managing an entrepreneurial dilemma: nurturing entrepreneurship and control in large corporations. In J. A. Hornaday, E. B. Shils, J. A. Timmons, and K. H. Vesper (eds), *Frontiers of entrepreneurship research*, Babson College, Wellesley, MA, 636–57.

Schamlensee, R. 1985: Do markets differ much? *American Economic Review*, 75 (3), 341–51.

Schon, D. 1963: Champions for radical new inventions. *Harvard Business Review*, 84–91.

Simon, H. A. 1947: *Administrative behavior*. New York: Macmillan.

Simon, H. A. 1960: *The new science of management decision*. New York: Harper & Row.

Simon, H. A. 1973: Applying information technology to organization design. *Public Administration Review*, 33, 268–78.

Simons, R. 1994: How new top managers use control systems as levers of strategic renewal. *Strategic Management Journal*, 15 (3), 169–90.

Spender, J. C. 1996: Making knowledge the basis of a dynamic theory of the firm. *Strategic Management Journal*, 17 (winter special issue), 45–62.

Tsoukas, H. 1996: The firm as a distributed knowledge system: a constructionist approach. *Strategic Management Journal*, 17 (winter special issue), 11–25.

Tushman, M. L., Newman, W., and Romanelli, E. 1986: Convergence and upheaval: managing the unsteady pace of organizational evolution. *California Management Review*, 29 (1), 29–44.

Van de Ven, A. H. 1986: Central problems in the management of innovation. *Management Science*, 32 (5), 590–607.

Van de Ven, A. H. 1992: Suggestions for studying strategy process: a research note. *Strategic Management Journal*, 13 (summer special issue), 169–88.

Vaughn Blankenship, L. and Miles R.E. 1968: Organizational structure and managerial decision behavior. *Administrative Science Quarterly*, 13 (1), 106–20.

Venkataraman, S., Macmillan, I. C., and McGrath, R. G. 1992: Progress in research on corporate venturing. In D. L. Sexton and J. D. Kasarda (eds), *The State of the Art of Entrepreneurship*, Boston: PWS–Ket Publishing Company, 487–519.

Venkataraman, S., van de Ven, A. H., Buckeye, J., and Hudson, R. 1990: Starting up in a turbulent environment: a process model of failure among firms with high customer dependence. *Journal of Business Venturing*, 5 (5), 277–95.

Volberda, H. W. 1996: Toward a flexible form: how to remain vital in hypercompetitive environments, *Organization Science*, 7 (4), 359–74.

Volberda, H. W. 1998: *Building the flexible firm: how to remain competitive*. Oxford, UK: Oxford University Press.

Watson, A. K. 1962: Address to the international congress of accountants. In *Proceedings of the Eighth International congress of Accountants*. September 23–7, 22–5.

Weick, K. E. 1991: The nontraditional quality of organizational learning. *Organization Science*, 2 (1), 116–24.

Wheelwright, S., and Clark, K. B. 1992: *Revolutionizing product development*. New York: Free Press.

Williamson, O. E. 1975: *Markets and hierarchies: analysis and antitrust implications*. New York: Free Press.

Woodman, R. W., Sawyer, J. E., and Griffin, R. W. 1993: Toward a theory of organizational creativity. *Academy of Management Review*, 18, 293–321.

Yin, R. K. 1984: *Case study research: design and methods*. Thousand Oaks, CA: Sage.

Zahra, S. A., Nielsen, A. P., and Bogner, W. C. 1999: Corporate entrepreneurship, knowledge, and competence development. *Entrepreneurship Theory and Practice*, Spring, 169–89.

CHAPTER NINE

A Longitudinal Study of Organizational Learning, Unlearning, and Innovation Among IJVs in a Transitional Economy

Marjorie A. Lyles, Katalin Szabo, Eva Kocsis, Jeff Barden, Charles Dhanaraj, Kevin Steensma, Laszlo Tihanyi

Introduction

Researchers agree that organizational learning is a process, not an event (Fiol and Lyles, 1985). Many theorists describe the process as being comprised of three stages: understanding new external knowledge, assimilating it, and applying it to commercial ends (Cohen and Levinthal, 1990; Lyles, 1998). Despite the aptness of this description, little is known about the details associated with each stage, the transitions between the stages, or the impact on performance and survival.

This is particularly critical in transitional economies since organizational learning capabilities may affect survival rates, performance, and the economic health of the region. Private firms such as international joint ventures (IJVs) may develop competitive advantages by learning from external sources such as their foreign parents and by creating processes for learning internally (Antal-Mokos, 1998). Foreign firms in their roles as parents, suppliers, and customers bring knowledge of the market economy and of management practices. Our project will elucidate the concepts of learning processes within a transitional economy.

There are two phases to our project that occur simultaneously. Phase I involves the collection of survey data from 335 IJVs and private firms through structured interviews and builds upon data collected in 1993 and 1996 by the senior author that assess learning and absorptive capacity. This phase I builds on the two prior survey research studies and therefore, incorporates many of the same measures as the previous studies to allow for comparisons. Simultaneous to phase I, phase II makes important contributions by adding detailed case studies that assess the learning, unlearning and innovation processes. In phase II we conduct in-depth interviews with ten Hungarian international joint ventures and develop comparative case studies. The focus is to examine differences in what is learned, and in the way a firm learns and constructs its knowledge base. This chapter will cover the rationale for the project, the preliminary results of phase I indicating the factors affecting the survival and current form of the IJVs that participated in the 1996 survey, and the preliminary results of the results of in-depth interviews with four firms from phase II.

The Hungarian Project

Rationale and Objectives of the Project

Given the goal to assess the organizational learning, unlearning and innovation of firms in Hungary, the objectives of the present study are four-fold:

1   To determine what knowledge is being learned; whether knowledge is being transferred from foreign partners or parents; whether management styles remaining from the Soviet-style economy are being unlearned, and whether these firms are building new learning, competitive and innovation capabilities for the future;
2   To assess the relationship of learning, unlearning and innovation to the performance of the IJVs and private businesses;
3   To form general models that help to explain and to evaluate the process of organizational learning, unlearning, innovation, and performance; and
4   To identify successful strategies and public policy issues that will improve the competitive position of these firms.

Hungarian Context
Many theorists think that Hungary is an ideal country in which to examine the impact of the transition (Ernst, Alexeev, and Marer, 1996). It started the transitional process early and proceeded through a more gradual approach than other countries. Hungary exhibited characteristics typical of the former socialist economies such as an informal economy, inaccurate reporting, slow decision-making, socialist-type management skills, and little marketing knowledge.

The Hungarian enterprises studied by Lyles and Salk (1996) and Lane, Salk and Lyles (2001) are a particularly appropriate context for testing the model we propose. The domestic firms were formed shortly after the beginning of the transition to a market economy. Our assumption was that not all the firms would have the capabilities needed to compete in a market-based economy. The development of these capabilities may make acquiring knowledge from the foreign partners critical to the survival of transitional economy enterprises. In addition, the survival of the enterprises is a prerequisite for the domestic and foreign partners to achieve their goals. It is also a prerequisite for the domestic government to achieve its goals (Child and Markoczy, 1993). The common interest of all stakeholders in the survival of transitional economy private enterprises creates strong incentives to focus on learning capabilities.

Hypotheses

Empirically, we extend the research by resurveying the Hungarian enterprises studied by Lyles and Salk (1996) and by Lane, Salk, and Lyles (2001). This permits us to examine learning processes, that is, to assess learning from foreign partners over time, and to control for prior performance, two issues not addressed by previous research. Note that our sample is a subset of theirs, those IJVs that participated in the 1993 and 1996 surveys. Thus, where Lyles and Salk (1996) and Lane, Salk, and Lyles (2001) tested their predictions using a relatively young sample, we test ours using a sample of firms most of which were established at the time of the transition. Most of the firms were at least eight years old when the data for the current project was collected. Below are hypotheses for the current paper:

◆ *H1*:   Learning structures and mechanisms, including organizational flexibility and adaptability and managerial involvement by foreign partners will be positively associated with survival and learning capabilities.

◆ *H2*:   There will be a positive association between the degree to which an enterprise unlearns and its performance.

◆ *H3*:   Changes in institutional influences such as government controls, risk capital availability, and accounting practices will be positively associated with its survival.

● *H4*:   The knowledge an enterprise acquires or creates will be positively associated with its survival.

Relevance

When we look at the radically expanding demand for learning in Central-Eastern European companies, the significance of interfirm learning is of critical importance to new enterprises due to the transition into a market economy. Private enterprises not only enlarge the learning capacity and knowledge of their immediate participants, but also have a significant external effect on the learning activity of their outside actors (suppliers, clients, services companies, state bureaucrats, and so on). Foreign firms in their roles as parents, suppliers, and customers bring knowledge of the market economy and of management practices.

Phase I: Survival, Form, and Knowledge Transfer

Phase I involves the collection of empirical data from approximately 135 IJVs in Hungary in 2001. It builds upon two prior data collection periods (1993 and 1996). An analysis of results of the earlier data collection is reported in Lyles and Salk (1996), Steensma and Lyles (2000), and Lane, Salk, and Lyles (2001). This chapter reports on the first steps of the 2001 data collection that documents whether the IJVs surveyed in 1996 survived until 2001, in what governance form, and what factors influenced their survival. We assess whether prior performance and learning influence the survival. Because the performance and survival of these IJVs are vital for the ongoing development of the local private sector in transitional economies, the importance of these assessments cannot be overstated. Thus, the transitional economies rely on foreign direct investment to provide not only capital, but also the transfer and assimilation of know-how and resources (Child and Yan, 1998; Pearce and Branyiczki, 1997).

We start by contacting the firms that participated in the 1996 survey in order to determine their status. Do they still exist? Are they still IJVs? We find that we have 159 IJVs from the 1996 data collection for which we have full data. Here we will report the factors that influence the IJV performance and survival. The 159 IJVs are categorized into those that have filed bankruptcy, those that have become 100% foreign owned, those that have become 100% Hungarian owned, and those that have remained a joint venture. Moreover, we consider the possible interaction effects of IJV learning, institutional factors, and performance on these outcomes.

We consider IJVs from a knowledge-based perspective and assess how the foreign parent support provided to the IJV plays a role in the survival of these IJVs. This knowledge-based perspective considers the resources and capabilities of the IJV and, in particular, the transfer of critical knowhow from the foreign parent to the IJV (Mowery et al., 1996). This perspective presents the view that an organization's idiosyncratic knowhow and its ability to exploit and replicate knowledge are fundamentally responsible for organizational success. Cohen and Levinthal (1990) would describe this as the assimilation and utilization of the knowledge.

In addition to the knowledge perspective, we utilize institutional theory. In this study we draw from Scott (1995) to examine the role of institutional elements in studies on transition economies. Scott (1995) suggests that institutions are multifaceted systems and neoinstitutional researchers focus on different institutional elements or pillars in their studies. By emphasizing the distinct pillars of institutional settings, i.e., regulative, normative, or cognitive, researchers conceptualize different institutional arguments and mechanisms.

Phase I: Sample for Assessing Survival and Form

The sample used to test the factors that impact survival and form was limited to those IJVs which participated in the 1996 survey. The original approach to the sampling technique generated a stratified sample that is comprised of representative small- or medium-sized joint ventures, based on industry and the foreign partner's country-of-origin. The initial sampling criteria and sample were developed with the assistance of a Hungarian government agency, and then the sample stratification was based on statistics provided by Hungary's Central Statistical Office. These statistics furnished the percentage of IJVs in each industry as well as the percentage involving firms from the various foreign locales. The firms that participated were identified through directories, contacts, and the 1996 Hungarian database. Thus, the current analysis is based on 159 IJVs from the 1996 survey for which we have full data. Ninety-three percent of the firms were started between the years 1988 and 1991, and in 2001, we were able to ascertain their current status.

Data Procurement And Administration

In phase I, we report on the survival of the firms from 1996. See Steensma and Lyles (2000) for a detailed analysis of the factors affecting the survival of the IJVs from 1993 to 1996. Personal interviews were conducted to obtain the survey data. Care was taken to minimize the chance of interviewer bias by using a structured and standardized interview process. The complete interview process for each IJV entailed two distinct phases separated by a three-year time period. In brief, the structured interviews resulted in the accumulation of data for each IJV, detailing its founding, management, control and ownership, competitive strategy, parental relationship, and performance. This was first done in 1993 and was repeated in 1996 and in 2001. Management of the project involved cooperation between one of the authors, an institute in Hungary, and a group of carefully selected and trained Hungarian interviewers. The interviewers were bilingual and could conduct the interviews in the language most comfortable to the IJV manager. The informants were the presidents, general managers, or managers of the IJVs. Ideally, multiple informants would have been used but given the size and nature of the study, this was prohibitive. There is, however, previous support for relying on the IJV general manager (GM) for subjective data. Lyles and Salk (1996) and Geringer and Hebert (1991) find a significant correlation between the parent's assessment of IJV performance and the GM of the IJV. Moreover, Child, et al. (1997) found significant inter-rater reliability among IJV management for the assessment of parental influence.

Variables
With the exception of IJV survival, the measures were gathered from the 1996 contact with the IJV. For those measures comprising scales constructed from multiple questionnaire items, consistency was assessed using confirmatory factor analysis.

- *Institutional effects.* Institutional effects is a three-item scale that summarizes changes in government control, risk capital availability, and accounting practices
- *Absorptive capabilities.* This scale was adopted from Lyles and Salk (1996) who used it as a scale of capacity. It was measured using a three-item scale of Likert-type items based on the extent to which the IJV is flexible and adapting to change, is creative, and rewards performance (alpha = 0.67).
- *Foreign parental support.* Support is a seven-item scale that summarizes the extent to which the foreign parent contributes to the IJV in the following areas: managerial resources, administrative support, emotional support, product-related technology, manufacturing-related technology, on-going manufacturing support and time (1 = little, 5 = extensive; alpha= 0.84).
- *IJV learning from the foreign parent.* This scale summarizes the extent to which the IJV learned from the foreign parent (Lyles and Salk, 1996; Lane, Salk, and Lyles, 2001), and is a six-item scale summarizing Likert-type responses to the question. To what extent have you learned from your foreign parent: (a) new technological expertise, (b) new marketing expertise, (c) product development, (d) knowledge about foreign cultures and tastes, (e) managerial techniques, and (f) manufacturing processes (1 = little, 5 = to a great extent; alpha = 0.78).
- *Performance.* Performance is related to firm failure and has typically been included in mortality studies. Past research has indicated a correlation between objective and perceptual measures of performance (Geringer and Hebert, 1991; Hansen and Wernerfelt, 1989). Thus, performance was measured by asking the respondents to rate their IJV performance at time one on a scale of (1) poor to (5) excellent for a fifteen-item Likert-type scale, including increasing business volume, increasing market share, achieving planned goals, and making profits (alpha = 0.81).
- *IJV survival categories.* Survival is indicated by categorizing the 1996 IJVs by their

governance status in 2001, thus: bankruptcy, 100% foreign owned, 100% domestic owned, and continuing as a joint venture.

Control Variables
The sample selection process controlled for size and location. All of the IJVs were SMEs and were started around the time of economic liberalization. Thus, we consider three control variables: industry, age, and whether the foreign partner had majority ownership. To facilitate the estimation of a manageable model relative to our sample size, we initially examined the relationship between the control variables and IJV outcomes. Preliminary cross-tabs analysis indicated that firms from one industry, construction, had outcome rates that significantly differed from the outcome rate of the overall sample. Thus, this dummy variable (0 = not in construction industry, 1 = member of industry) was integrated into the overall model. Likewise, foreign partner majority ownership also significantly influenced outcome based on a cross-tabs analysis and was included in the overall model. An ANOVA indicated that there were no statistical differences in the average age of those IJVs that survived as a JV, became a foreign subsidiary, became a Hungarian subsidiary, or went bankrupt.

Phase I: Analysis
To test the hypotheses, a multinomial logit statistical framework was utilized. This technique has been used extensively when analyzing qualitative choice. With multinomial logit modeling, the continuous variables associated with the hypotheses and the control variables compose the independent variables, while the dependent variable is the differential odds of choosing one alternative relative to another. The specification of the model is as follows:

$$\log_e (P_{ij} / P_{i1}) = X_i B_j$$

where P_{ij} is the probability that the procurement i is of the method j; P_{i1} is the probability that procurement i is of the procurement method 1, where method 1 is a baseline method; X_i is a vector of the independent variables for the ith procurement observation; and B_j is a vector of coefficients of the independent variables for the jth procurement method. The parameters can then be estimated by setting the B's of one of the alternatives to 0. The choice of baseline category is irrelevant for the overall estimation of the model and can be set according to the desired comparisons (Liao, 1994). Multinomial logit allows for the simultaneous estimation of parameters when there are more than two categories in the dependent variable.

Phase I: Results of Longitudinal Analysis of Survival and Form
Table 9.1 displays the means, standard deviations, and correlation between the independent and control variables. We generated three models in a hierarchical fashion, such that the change in the likelihood ratio test statistic (χ^2) between two hierarchical steps and the significance of the change could be determined (table 9.2). The likelihood ratio test statistic is defined as $\chi2$ times the difference between the loglikelihood of the estimated model and the loglikelihood of a model containing only the intercept. This statistic is distributed as χ^2 and the degrees of freedom are equal to the number of

Table 9.1   Intercorrelation matrix for independent and control variables

Variables	Mean	SD	1	2	3	4	5	6
1 Construction	0.12	0.32	–					
2 Foreign majority equity	0.55	0.50	0.00	–				
3 Performance	44.21	7.55	–0.05	0.16*	–			
4 Institutional influences	8.13	2.68	0.00	–0.20*	–0.18*	–		
5 Assimilation capabilities	12.92	2.17	0.04	0.11	0.37**	–0.02	–	
6 Learning from foreign partner	17.21	6.44	–0.09	0.10	0.15	0.15	0.16*	–
7 Foreign partner support	30.75	7.67	–0.06	0.16*	0.33**	–0.01	0.20*	0.29**

* $p < 0.05$; ** $p < 0.01$.

independent variables in the model. Our results indicate that each additional set of variables (direct effects, interaction effects) significantly improve the model over and above the more restricted model.

Because of the nature of the hypotheses, three separate multinomial logit models were created, allowing for a complete comparison of any two outcomes. In one instance, the category of bankruptcy was used as the baseline. The derived coefficients are those comparing the likelihood of foreign-owned, Hungarian-owned, and joint venture to bankruptcy. Second and third models were created, with Hungarian-owned and foreign-owned as the baseline, to allow for the determination of the statistical significance of the remaining coefficients. Each model was created with the inclusion of a constant term.

The results are given in a contrast table (table 9.3). The coefficients for each contrast (for example, JV versus bankruptcy) can be interpreted as the marginal influence that a particular variable has on the likelihood that the given outcome occurs versus a given alternative. Thus, a positive and significant coefficient suggests that an increase of the respective variable increases the likelihood that the given outcome will occur over the alternative. Conversely, a negative sign suggests a decreasing likelihood.

Phase I: Implications of Survival Analysis
Our results help to distinguish between those IJVs that survived as an IJV, a 100% owned foreign subsidiary, or a 100% owned domestic company, and those that went

Table 9.2   Significance of the overall models

	Model 1: control variables	Model 2: direct effects	Model 3: interactions
Chi square	27.44***	67.90***	98.07***
Change in chi square		40.46***	30.17***
Pseudo R squared	0.17	0.38	0.50

Table 9.3 Coefficients for the models

	JV vs. bankruptcy	Foreign-owned vs. bankruptcy	Hungarian-owned vs. bankruptcy	JV vs. foreign-owned	JV vs. Hungarian-owned	Foreign-owned vs. Hungarian-owned
Control variables						
Construction	1.23	−.43	2.22*	1.66	−1.00	−2.66*
Majority foreign equity owned	.34	1.07*	−1.11*	−.73	1.44**	2.18***
Direct effects						
Performance	.17***	.12*	.14**	.05	.03	−.02
Institutional influences	.13	.01	.18	.12	−.05	−.17
Assimilation capabilities	.24t	−.04	.22	.27*	.02	−.26t
Learning from foreign parent	.00	.03	.03	−.03	.03	.06
Foreign parent support	−.06	.02	.07t	−.08*	.02	.10*
Interaction effects						
Institutional influences X performance	.04*	.01	.05*	.03t	.01	−.04*
Assimilation capabilities X performance	−.04	.03	−.02	.00	.02	−.01
Learn from foreign parent X performance	.00	−.02*	−.01	.02**	−.01	−.01
Support from foreign parent X performance	.00	.00	.00	.00	.00	.00

All models include an intercept term. Coefficients are listed according to model (control model, direct effects model, interaction model).

bankrupt. Few studies have been able to make these distinctions. From our results, inequity in ownership levels between partners does appear to influence its future such that a majority foreign equity position is less likely to convert to a Hungarian subsidiary. We also show that strong performance in 1996 significantly increased the probability that the venture would continue to exist as a viable business. Although this is intuitively obvious, it does confirm the validity of the data. In addition, we show that the institutional influences did not directly affect the outcomes. We do find that when the IJV recognizes significant changes in its institutional environment and it is performing well, it is more likely to convert to a subsidiary of the Hungarian parent as opposed to the foreign parent.

Our results also suggest a dilemma for foreign multinationals that want to establish stable IJVs in transitional economies in terms of encouraging the absorptive capacity of the IJV. The more flexible and creative the IJV, the more likely it would become 100% Hungarian owned or remain as an IJV. This suggests that it would be harder for a flexible, creative IJV to be integrated into the foreign parent firm because it was characterized as being independent.

Learning from the foreign parent had no direct affect on the survival categories; however, it did show an interaction effect with performance. When the IJV is performing well and learning from the foreign parent, the Hungarian parent is more likely to stay engaged, that is, the IJV would remain a joint venture. Indeed, our results suggest that when the IJV learns from the foreign parent and is performing relatively well, it is more likely to dissolve than to become a foreign subsidiary. This may be a further indication of the Hungarian parent's reluctance to relinquish control over a learning and high performing venture.

We also found that strong foreign parent support is conducive to IJV survival, and it increases the likelihood that the venture would become 100% foreign-owned rather than remaining a JV or becoming Hungarian-owned. It is interesting to note that while foreign parent support appears to lead to eventual control over the IJV by the foreign parent, high degrees of learning from the foreign parent by the IJV appears to keep the foreign parent from gaining complete control.

Phase II: In-Depth Interviews with IJVs

In phase II, we provide insight into the nature of learning, unlearning and innovation processes. Many Hungarian companies shortcut the development of new knowledge by partnering with foreign firms who bring tangible assets as well as intangible knowledge assets to the joint venture. Our analysis presented here includes interviews with four companies: Pharma, House Products, Software, and Auto Parts. Pharma is a joint venture partially owned by a French pharmaceutical company. House Products makes products for the building construction industry and is partially owned by an Austrian firm. Software was a Hungarian–British joint venture later purchased by an American software company. Auto Parts was a joint venture with a Hungarian–Austrian joint venture. We use statements by the people who were interviewed as supporting evidence for the insights from the interviews. These are not treated as direct quotations because of the translation issues.

*Phase 2: Transformation of Business Processes as a Necessary Precondition for
Organizational Learning in Emerging Economies*

Transformation of the Physical Plant. The state-owned enterprises were highly ineffi-
cient operations. The mountains of garbage and production waste surrounding many
factories and buildings made the onsite conditions desperate. More than symbolic, the
reorganization of the old industrial mammoths often began with a "big cleaning."
Several tons of waste, corroded machines, and rubbish were carried out from the factory yards. Other empirical researchers also underline the importance of "big cleaning" (Voszka, 1997). Initially this seems irrelevant to the reshaping of learning
capabilities, but in reality, physical order in the plant was a necessary precondition for
order at the organizational level. It also represents an unfreezing process that opens
the door to other changes and to new ways of thinking.

> One manager described literally the same situation. Beyond the big disorder in the plants,
> as in other Hungarian firms, the signs of the lack of environmental protection were obvi-
> ous. Production flow was poorly controlled and very large inventories of raw materials
> were allowed to accumulate. This common practice under the long planning cycles of the
> communist system was designed to protect against unexpected shortages.

Transforming the physical plant was often the first step in staging the conditions for
future knowledge transfer.

> Soon after the foreign investment, Pharma's Hungarian-dominated board of directors
> launched an important initiative. A *site reconstruction manager* was hired to renovate the
> buildings and clean up the land. This gesture had an extremely important psychological
> impact on the employees such that it encouraged them to take pride in Pharma. By build-
> ing on the success of creating order in the plants, senior management opened the minds
> of employees to new ways of doing their everyday business.

Transformation of the Organization Structure. The organizational chart of many companies seemed to be irrational. The bulk of some companies consisted of obsolete
small factories. This original "historical" structure had been kept for many decades.
Under Soviet management, no one re-thought the historically given structure on the
basis of efficiency.

> That was the case at Pharma as well. Its operations were largely fragmented so that each of
> its factories was responsible for its own functional requirements, including purchasing
> and human resources. Although some of the accounting and financial functions were
> automated at that time, information systems were also very fragmented and many operat-
> ing functions, such as production planning, were completely manual. At the time Hun-
> gary opened up to foreign investment and competition, Pharma was in desperate need of
> critical operational knowledge in order to stay competitive.

The foreign partners recognized early the ultimate need to reshape the organizational
chart and reorganize the whole business process. In many cases consultants were involved in rebuilding the company structure and the business processes.

In one IJV, Coopers-Lybrand undertook this task. As expected, the Coopers-Lybrand report identified several operations and production flow changes that would show the quickest returns to the bottom line. An industrial engineer from the foreign parent was brought in to update machinery and reorganize the physical layout of the plants. In addition, an ERP was introduced.

Transformation of the Core Business Systems. Implementation of the most modern and most effective manufacturing processes demanded very intensive, rapid and effective adoption. A surprising appraisal for many foreign firms was that the essence of the most current systems that were found in western firms was also present in Hungary at the point of transformation.

In the Pharma case, the ERP system was implemented to automate production planning, purchasing and manufacturing. Because the software mandated the implementation of certain inventory and production routines, it effectively provided a structured means of grafting new operational knowledge into the Pharma culture. One of the first changes that resulted from the ERP implementation was that logistics and production became two separate functions. Pharma also began centralizing other redundant functions.

To ensure that the knowledge inherent in the ERP system translated into effectiveness, Coopers-Lybrand placed Hungarian managers in charge of the implementation project, but their activities and performance were monitored very closely. Every two weeks, an executive from France would fly to Budapest to monitor the changes and plan the next steps.

At this point, the foreign investors mandated the transformation of systems. Little attempt was made to involve the local managers in these decisions. The foreign firms came in with their own ideas of how to make things work.

Transformation of the Managerial Processes. In many firms the transformation has been a time-consuming procedure, but even so, it has been much easier than the "recoding" of the managerial patterns. The imprinting of "Homo Sovieticus" survived the many systemic changes on the company level. The foreign managers often faced local managers who continued the old ways of doing things such as authoritarianism, inaccessibility, bureaucratic behavioral patterns, constant self-defensive tactics, and self-justification. The depressing heritage of the planned economy included these attitudes and more: servility, lack of initiative, opportunistic defenses, dependent behaviors, and herd spirit.

Punctuality and observance of performance criteria were previously not of critical importance in Hungary. For the successful adaptation in the IJVs, this needed to be transformed.

The changes in Pharma, including the new ERP system, were difficult for many of the Hungarian managers, especially the production managers. Suddenly, they were asked to make significant changes in their work habits and take on new responsibilities. In addition, weekly, even daily, performance assessments were suddenly possible and raw materials could be tracked down to the gram. This was very disturbing for the production managers who were accustomed to being able to hide productivity variances. On multiple occasions, production managers informally approached their Hungarian bosses and asked if they could be exempt from this new system and the informal response was always, "Of course, but if you choose to be exempt, then you must find another job." Given that Pharma paid significantly higher than average Hungarian salaries, this strategy proved successful.

Serious impeding factors to inter-firm knowledge flow were the cultural differences between the foreign and the local managers. A serious challenge for the Hungarian managers was working with foreign managers, whom the Hungarians really only knew from media stereotypes. But on the other side, the foreign managers had prejudices and knew quite little about Hungary and the Hungarians. As Pharma's communications director put it:

> Before the transition, many Hungarians knew little about French culture outside of France's reputation for producing good wine and romantic lifestyles. Senior managers knew that if the two sides were going to successfully interact and bring new ways of doings things to Pharma, these cultural barriers would have to be reduced in order to foster mutual trust. Relational capital and trust would be critical prerequisites to significant knowledge transfer from the foreign parent. One of the most important steps they took to achieve this was to send several managers from Pharma on a tour of the plants and operations sites in France. To promote a better understanding of French culture for the other employees, Pharma sponsored several educational programs about the country, including organizing a "France day" gathering during one weekend.

Phase II: Assimilation, Unlearning, and Discrimination

Assimilation is the process of recognizing new knowledge and of beginning to incorporate it into new ways of doing things. As the transformation processes took hold and the unfreezing process evolved, the Hungarian managers became open to new knowledge. In many companies the institution of "doubling the managers" was introduced to encourage learning the systems and to avoid major mistakes in business operations.

> In the case of Pharma introducing the ERP, each Hungarian manager was assigned to a "shadow manager" from Coopers & Lybrand. Weekly feedback and regular performance appraisals for the Hungarians took place. At first, the shadow manager system was very difficult for many of the Hungarians, especially the production line managers, because it severely limited their freedom to operate at will. It conveyed a message that they were not fully trusted. But over time, as they began to accept the organizational changes and to realize the difficulties of implementing the ERP system, the Hungarian managers began to appreciate the shadow managers as an important source of tacit knowledge.

Unlearning involves reassessing the current way of doing things such that the old ways may need to be "unlearned" and replaced with new ways. Learning and obtaining new knowledge supposes intensive *unlearning*. Unlearning may sound easy but it is no simple matter to change the conditioning of many decades and to break with managerial routines acquired at socialist large enterprises. Discrimination is also an important learning process in which the organization needs to make judgments regarding the appropriateness of utilizing other firms' ways of doing things and applying that unchanged to their own firm (Lyles, 1998). At Housing Products, the general manager said:

At the beginning of the IJV, there was a core staff (about 30%) who had spent 15 years in the Hungarian plant and who started to cooperate with the western firm from the first moment. Important attributes such as quick reaction time, problem solving, and loyalty to the firm were new. In the socialist systems, these three attributes were often difficult to learn. Even now in Hungary, the first reaction under socialism is a very complicated explanation of "Why doesn't it work?" This is followed by an explanation of how it is unsolvable and too complicated.

At first the Hungarian managers also accepted the superiority of foreigners. As Housing Products put it:

At first, the attitude of the local firm was that everything coming from the west or head-quarters was superior and that there was no need to change any of it. There was a general attitude in the country, not just in Housing Products, that anything from the west was the right way and wonderful. Over time, there was a change in attitude, questions were raised and everything was not simply accepted in unchanged form.

Western working style had a major impact. The Hungarians who went to the western firms and saw how western plants operated copied their style. As a Hungarian manager put it:

There is a continuous flow of knowledge from the international network of Housing Products into the local firm. They get new products from the international headquarters or from the network of the other local subsidiaries of Housing Products International. One of the technology licenses came from us. But nowadays there is a definite need to use all experiences locally and to orient ourselves toward the direction of development and innovation.

Phase II: Learning Capabilities and Mutual Teaching

Short-term interests drove the initial foreign investment in the transition countries, and this strengthened the use of bureaucratic operations. Independent, responsible action and flexibility of the local managers were seen as being beneficial only in the long run. Thus, paradoxically, some foreign partners have contributed to the survival of the "Homo Sovieticus" in the sense that they have centralized their affiliated firms. This centralization was particularly strong in the first years after establishing the IJVs. The foreign partners were operating in an unknown area, and they did not have confidence in the loyalty and knowledge of their East European partners and employees. Consequently, they preferred to direct them from New York or Vienna. So the majority of the foreign partners started with extremely hierarchical organizations and, initially, the autonomy of the local managers was limited.

Not everything, however, from the accumulated experiences of the socialist time needed to be unlearned. Interestingly enough, besides the bad genes of Socialist industrial dinosaurs, the JVs could inherit, through the Hungarian partner, viable genes as well. As an Auto Parts manager stated:

The success of (Auto Parts) is based on its long history, its knowledge capital and the very highly skilled workers. The workers had a lot of experience and were well trained. The manager's opinion is that green field investments, because they are new and have no history, deeply routed culture, knowledge or skills to build upon, would not be as successful, especially in the automobile industry.

The manager of Software reported about the turn taken from one-way learning to a kind of two-way learning.

> Software has adapted the foreign systems step-by-step. But the Americans also have adapted several methods used by Software. The time is already over when the Hungarians were the only ones who had to learn from others. Recently the partners learn from each other.

One of the Housing Products managers identified the importance of local knowledge. The share of local and of international elements could be very different in the different fields of business operations.

> Production is more standardized and the general methods are good for production across all eight plants. Marketing is on a national basis and local firms know better how to sell locally. Multinationals wanted to standardize everything, but there are some fields where local circumstances are more different than others. The production managers were always Austrian. Marketing was local. The Austrians understood this relatively early. There were two managing directors: one for production and one for marketing. This made an impact on knowledge flow, which was west to east for production, and east to west for marketing. The Hungarians who were marketing people could make decisions and have a greater impact and much earlier than the Hungarian production people.

Thus, at a certain phase of the IJV's development, the one-way learning becomes two-way learning.

> When Pharma began its transition, the lessons it needed to learn about operating in a free market were well understood by its parent. Implementing efficient production control procedures, altering financial practices and even training sales people were within the foreign parent's realm of understanding and capabilities. The relevant knowledge could be readily transferred to Pharma with the help of some consultants.
>
> But now Pharma began facing some obstacles with which the foreign parent had less experience. Russia's transition was unprecedented, and Pharma would have to respond to its economic fluctuations without the aid of a truly knowledgeable parent.

The problems were quite unique and unprecedented, and the Hungarians were more familiar with this type of crisis than were the foreign parents. The Hungarian expertise proved to be quite useful.

Phase II: Innovation and Creativity
It appears that the initial factor affecting organizational learning was the transformation of the business processes and structures. These transformations created an awareness of the need for change and an introduction to the foreign ways of operating. The transformation processes required new approaches to reporting and making decisions. The transformation was initially accepted without question, but after a time period, the local managers began to discriminate between what needed to be unlearned and what needed to be retained. The final phase involved both the recognition of the

foreign firms that two-way learning was possible and that the local firms had expertise and innovative capabilities. In Pharma there were early traditions of innovation:

> Throughout the 1920s and 1930s, Pharma rapidly developed several new compounds, products, and production techniques. After the politically turbulent 1950s settled down, Pharma went back to innovating by releasing a very popular painkiller among many other drugs, compounds and agrochemicals. As political and economic reforms began to accelerate in Hungary in 1989, Pharma registered its first pharmaceutical drug in the United States since World War II.

As the Housing Products CEO put it:

> Housing Products Hungary wanted to develop, not just to copy, something (products and ideas) and also new ways of doing things. It was an evolution. In the first 10 years, flow of knowledge was one way: from abroad to here. Later on came the chance to invent something here.

In some circumstances, based on the innovative capacity of the Hungarian employees in the IJVs, the western mother companies changed their strategy to allow some R&D and innovations in the local firms. In particular, the innovative attitude of Hungarian managers and experts could be considered as a positive inheritance from the history. For some of the interviewed Hungarian companies, innovation is not just one of the newly developed activities, but seems to be the core activity. For example "Software" runs as an R&D unit:

> Innovation is permanently going on. If the firm did not do that, the firm would disappear (would go bankrupt) soon. The recent situation is that the firm is highly profitable. Out of 75 employees, 60 persons are engineers. Software does not deal with any other enterprise function. Software has some common projects with its American counterpart. They cooperate with each other via Internet.

Phase II: Implications of In-depth Interviews
Transitional economy IJVs seek to acquire managerial, marketing, and manufacturing knowledge and skills that a foreign parent developed through its unique experience and that are premised on the assumptions and priorities of market-based organizations. Thus, the IJV first needs to become familiar with operating in a market economy before it can begin to learn its foreign parent's skills. This is a "dual" learning dilemma for the local IJVs. Our initial Phase II results show the importance of the transformation processes. These are critical to overcome the inertia and difficulties of the dual learning process.

Implications for Managers and Researchers

Prior research on facilitating IJV learning from foreign parents has focused on the structures and processes needed. Lyles and Salk (1996) found that an IJV's capacity to learn is associated with the IJV flexibility and its use of mechanisms like articulated goals and objectives to focus both IJV and foreign-parent managers on the knowledge to be transferred. They further found that active involvement by the foreign parent was significantly associated with learning and performance. Conflicts identified as cultural in nature had a negative impact on learning from the foreign parent, but only significantly in the case of 50/50 equity arrangements. We suggest that multinationals are being presented with an inherently conflicting situation. Although they may be able to maintain high levels of control over the IJV given their resource and knowledge contribution, a dominance in management control may lead to parental conflict and IJV mortality. The current study adds to these findings.

We find that the Shumpeterian term "creative destruction" seems applicable not just in the production of goods, but in the production of knowledge as well. The learning and the unlearning are in all of the investigated cases indissolubly intertwined. Most of the JVs are established on the ruins of an old socialist company and must go through a transformation process before new learning occurs. Development is also commonly determined by *"recombinant system elements"* of previous configurations reorganized in a new form. The knowledge capital of Hungarian parent organizations could not be considered as fully out of date and yet, it was difficult for foreign firms to determine how well prepared the Hungarian firms were. Thus the inheritance of Hungarian companies and managers consisted of some malfunctioning processes, but also of capabilities for development, learning, and adaptation.

One of the most important implications to managers of foreign firms investing in the transitional economies is to recognize the inherent knowledge and capabilities of the local management. There is a tremendous danger of the local managers becoming marginalized and uninvolved. Furthermore there is a need to develop loyalty to the local company by the local employees, and the foreign managers need to see this as appropriate and helpful to the total relationship. The transference of knowledge from the foreign parent to the IJV signifies to the local management that there is active involvement of the foreign parent, and this is viewed as a reason to continue the relationship. Foreign managers can be a source of knowledge and can serve as teachers. On the other hand, foreign managers can also serve as students and gain from the knowledge of the local managers and from innovations created locally.

Note

We would like to thank the US National Science Foundation (Grant SES-0080152), Budapest University of Economics and Public Policy, BB Foundation, and Indiana University for their support.

References

Antal-Mokos, Z. 1998: *Privatization, politics, and economic performance in Hungary*. Cambridge: Cambridge University Press.

Child, J. and Markoczy, L. 1993: Host country managerial behavior and learning in Chinese and Hungarian joint ventures. *Journal of Management Studies*, 30, 611–31.

Child, J. and Yan, Y. 1998: Predicting the performance of Sino-foreign joint ventures. Paper presented at the Research Conference on Management and Organizations in China, Hong Kong University of Science and Technology, January 15–17.

Child, J., Yan, Y. and Lu, Y. 1997: Ownership and control in Sino-foreign joint ventures. In P. W. Beamish and J. P. Killing (eds), *Cooperative strategies: Asian Pacific perspectives,* San Francisco: New Lexington Press, 181–226.

Cohen, W. M. and Levinthal, D. A. 1990: Absorptive capacity: a new perspective on learning and innovation. *Administrative Science Quarterly,* 35, 128–52.

Ernst, M., Alexeev, M. and Marer, P. 1996: *Transforming the core: restructuring industrial enterprises in Russia and Central Europe.* Boulder: Westview Press.

Fiol, F. M. and Lyles, M. A. 1985: Organizational learning. *Academy of Management Review,* 10, 803–13.

Geringer, J. M. and Hebert, L. 1991: Measuring performance of international joint ventures. *Journal of International Business Studies,* 22 (2), 249–64.

Hanson, G. and Wernerfelt, B. 1989: Determinants of firm performance: the relative importance of economic and organizational factors. *Strategic Management Journal,* 10, 399–411.

Kogut, B. and Zander, U. 1993: Knowledge of the firm and the evolutionary theory of the multinational corporation. *Journal of International Business Studies,* 24, 625–45.

Lane, P., Salk, J. and Lyles, M. A. 2001: Knowledge acquisition and performance in transitional economy international joint ventures. *Strategic Management Journal,* 22 (12), 1,139–62.

Liao, T. F. 1994: *Interpreting probability models: logit, probit, and other generalized linear models.* Thousand Oaks: Sage Publications.

Lyles, M. A. and Salk, J. E. 1996: Knowledge acquisition from foreign parents in international joint ventures: An empirical examination in the Hungarian context. *Journal of International Business Studies,* 27 (5), 877–904.

Lyles, M. A. 1998: Learning among joint venture sophisticated firms. *Management International Review,* 28, 85–98.

Lyles, M. A., von Krogh, G. and Aadne, J. H. 2003, forthcoming: The making of high knowledge acquirers: Understanding the nature of knowledge catalysts in international joint ventures and their foreign parents. *Management International Review.*

Mowery, D. C., Oxley, J. E. and Silverman, B. S. 1996: Strategic alliances and interfirm knowledge transfer. *Strategic Management Journal,* 17, 77–92.

Pearce, J. L. and Branyiczki, I. 1997: Legitimacy: an analysis of three Hungarian–Western European collaborations. In P. W. Beamish and J. P. Killing (eds), *Cooperative Strategies: European perspectives,* San Francisco: New Lexington Press, 300–22.

Scott, W. R. 1995: *Institutions and organizations.* Thousand Oaks: Sage Publications.

Steensma, K. and Lyles, M. A. 2000: Explaining IJV survival in a transitional economy through social exchange and knowledge-based perspectives. *Strategic Management Journal,* 21 (8), 831–52.

United Nations 1997: *World Economic and Social Survey.* New York: United Nations.

Voszka, C. 1997: The transformation of hearts and minds in Eastern Europe. *Cato Journal,* 17, 229–34.

World Bank 1997: *World development indicators.* Washington, DC: World Bank.

CHAPTER TEN

Strategic Renewal Processes in Multi-Unit Firms: Generic Journeys of Change

Henk W. Volberda, Charles Baden-Fuller

How do large multiunit firms renew? How do they reconcile the conflicting forces for change and stability? How do they promote order and control among their different units, while having to respond and learn? Past work has focused on issues of the interaction between the firm seen as a business and its industry, examining different processes and journeys. In this vast canvas, a new theme has emerged, that of co-evolution (cf. Lewin and Volberda, 1999). This approach has examined the two-way dynamics of the influence of the firm on its environment. We wish to extend and build on that work to look at multiunit firms so commonly found in today's landscape. The large multiunit firm has layers of management that modify industry forces of competition, and so permit its units to undertake journeys that differ from their stand-alone counterparts. In the multiunit firm, not only can the firm influence the environment, but there may be multiple levels of effects within the firm.

How will we approach the topic? On the basis of co-evolutionary theory, we begin by showing that there are three generic journeys that a successful multiunit firm can adopt. Moreover, we adopt the trick of examining a limited number of ideal types to highlight how firms could achieve these journeys: naive selection, managed selection, hierarchical renewal, and holistic renewal. Each ideal type contains mechanisms of variation and selection influencing learning and evolutionary journeys. Our ideal types can be seen as "engines" that resolve the many tensions that have been variously described in the strategy and organization literature. These include change versus preservation (cf. Poole and Van de Ven, 1989; Volberda 1996), adaptation versus selection (cf. Baum, 1996; Lewin and Volberda, 1999) and exploration versus exploitation (cf. March, 1991; Levinthal and March, 1993). Although March (1991) and Levinthal (1997) have used simulations to suggest that the optimal path for the firm is one of balanced exploitation and exploration, theories on processes of renewal are still limited. In this chapter, using a co-evolutionary perspective we examine how multiunit firms deal with these tensions over time. In doing so, we want to provide answers to the following questions: When is renewal a selection or an adaptation process? Are there generic patterns of renewal or is each renewal journey rather idiosyncratic? And what roles do managers at the corporate and unit level play in renewal journeys?

A Nested Micro-co-evolutionary Perspective

Considering paths or trajectories of renewal is not new in organization science and is implicit in many theories of adaptation and selection. Most work is at the level of the industry, some is at the level of the firm but little is directed specifically to multiunit firms. For this reason, we need to go back to the basics of evolutionary ideas in strategy. They stress how organizations and their units accumulate knowhow in the course of their existence and become repositories of skills that are unique and often difficult to alienate.

According to *population-ecology theory*, these skills are the source of both inertia and distinctive competence (Hannan and Freeman, 1977, 1984; Miller and Chen, 1994 p. 1). In a similar vein, *institutional theories* stress the coercive, normative and mimetic behavior of organizations in the face of environmental forces for change. They too stress how difficult it is for existing firms to create the requisite variety (DiMaggio and Powell, 1983; Greenwood and Hinings, 1996).

In *Evolutionary Theory of Economic Change*, Nelson and Winter (1982) present firms as repositories of routines which endow them with a capacity to search. Yet the same routines suppress attention span and the capacity to absorb new information by spelling out behavior that permits search only for new ideas that are consistent with prior learning. According to this theory, renewal journeys are contingent on the proximity to tacit knowledge and to prior and commensurate skills (Cohen and Levinthal, 1990; Henderson and Clark, 1990; Rosenberg, 1972). In a similar way, in the *resource-based theory* the firm is seen as a bundle of tangible and intangible resources and tacit knowhow that must be identified, selected, developed, and deployed to generate superior performance (Penrose, 1959; Learned et al., 1969; Wernerfelt, 1984). These scarce, firm-specific assets lead to a focused renewal trajectory with a limited capacity to change; firms are stuck with what they have and have to live with what they lack (Teece et al., 1997).

In the above selection and path dependent theories on renewal, firms do best by not trying to counter their history, but rather by allowing evolution to take place (see table 10.1). By contrast, other theories focusing more on adaptation and managerial intentions argue that renewal journeys are more versatile and less determined. It suggests that organizations can and do change, overcoming their own rigidities. For instance, Teece et al. (1997) have suggested it is not only the bundle of resources that matter, but also the mechanisms by which firms accumulate and dissipate new skills and new capabilities. They propose that *dynamic capabilities* represent the firm's latent abilities to renew its core competence over time. The *behavioral theory of the firm* (Cyert and March, 1963) argues that firm ability to renew is determined primarily by availability and control of organization slack and by the strategic intent to allocate slack to renewal. Their theory provides a process description of structural inertia and a justification for periodic renewal through restructuring and rationalization (Lewin and Volberda, 1999). The *strategic choice* perspective (Child, 1972, 1997; Miles & Snow, 1978,

Table 10.1   Selection and adaptation

Selection	Adaptation
Population ecology: procedural and structural baggage	*Dynamic capability theory*: latent abilities to renew core competences
Institutional theory: industry norms and shared logic	*Behavioral theory*: slack and strategic intent
Evolutionary theory: proliferation of routines	*Learning theory*: alignment based on learning, unlearning, relearning
Resource based theory: exploitation of core competencies	*Strategic choice theory*: dynamic process subject to managerial action

Source: Adapted from Lewin and Volberda 1999

1994; Thompson, 1967) argues that organizations are not always passive recipients of environmental influence but also have the opportunity and power to reshape the environment. In the contingency perspective, many theorists assert that renewal is a dynamic process subject to both managerial action and environmental forces (Hrebiniak and Joyce 1985; Khandwalla 1977; Mintzberg 1979). Finally, *learning theories* assume that renewal journeys are both adaptive and manipulative, in the sense that organizations adjust defensively to reality and use the resulting knowledge offensively to improve the fits between organization and environment (Fiol and Lyles, 1985; Hedberg, 1981, p. 3).

The theories shortly discussed above seem to describe renewal journeys as processes of either selection or adaptation (see table 10.1). Certain theoretical lenses, such as the behavioral theory of the firm, strategic choice, and learning perspectives attempt to further elaborate the role of managerial intentionality. Other theoretical lenses, such as population-ecology, institutionalism, and, to some extent, evolutionary theories discount the ability of organizations to self-consciously renew themselves significantly or repeatedly. Using variables such as resource scarcity, industry norms and shared logics, static routines, and structural inertia, these selection perspectives argue that journeys of renewal are highly restricted. While these theoretical lenses have shown us adaptive and selective renewal journeys, we think there is much more pluralism (Lewin and Volberda, 1999).

In this connection, ideas of *macro-co-evolution* have extended the evolutionary concept. They have focused on the joint outcomes of interactions at the level of the industry with that of the (typically) single-unit firm; (for example, Baum and Singh, 1994; Bruderer and Singh, 1996; Lant and Mezias, 1990; Levinthal, 1997; Teece et al., 1994). In this framework, adaptation and selection are not opposing forces but fundamentally interrelated. Firms can influence their environment just as the environment can influence firms. Such a macro-co-evolutionary approach assumes that renewal is not an outcome of managerial adaptation or environmental selection but, rather, the joint outcome of managerial intentions and environmental effects.

Macro-co-evolution is not the only kind of co-evolution which can exist, for co-evolutionary effects take place at multiple levels within firms as well as between firms

(McKelvey, 1997; Lewin and Volberda, 1999). *Micro-co-evolution* is the name for the process of interaction between levels within firms, the co-evolution of intrafirm resources, dynamic capabilities and competencies in an intrafirm competitive context (Barnett, et al. 1994; Galunic and Eisenhardt, 1996; Burgelman, 1991, 1994, 1996).

In our approach, we develop and extend past ideas on micro-co-evolution. Our contribution is to both examine and calibrate evolutionary journeys. We focus on the role of two key groups: top management and front line managers, and we pose different behaviors in the contexts of ideal types of firms. For example, in one ideal type we will have a reactive group that believes its units will have focused unchanging trajectories. In another ideal type, we have top management that appears to take the view of the adaptation theorists that the journey can be manipulated by a cognitive and holistic process operating at all levels of the enterprise. Likewise, we examine different possible behaviors of middle and frontline managers. Before we examine our ideal types, we begin by considering metrics for the possible journeys that a successful firm may undertake.

Generic Journeys

Most modern complex organizations can be seen as a combination of individual units, which are more or less integrated together (Chandler, 1962). This is equally valid for the multinational firm, and for the diversified single-country enterprise. We define units of multiunit firms as consisting of underlying resources (that is, skills, knowledge, routines, and competencies) and product-market or functional areas where these are utilized (cf. Galunic and Eisenhardt, 1996). Individual units may trade or relate to other units to a greater or lesser extent, but each may have its own path of evolution that can be different from its neighbors.

What is the objective of the ideal firm, and what are its overall goals? Economists are concerned with issues of profit maximization, but from an evolutionary perspective clearly survival is the objective. Survival is a complex issue; multiunit firms operate in complex environments where simple issues of profit have to be balanced with other issues such as conformity to regulatory concerns, especially where financial markets exercise at best a moderating influence. For some, survival is best achieved when there is a balance in the firm's activities from an evolutionary perspective (Poole and Van de Ven, 1989). We agree, and our definition of balance comes from March (1991), who defined exploration and exploitation as the two opposing states. According to Levinthal and March (1993), a firm needs to balance exploration with exploitation if it is to survive. Survival equates to balance over the longer term.

For the single business unit, balance over time is near impossible. Let us take the usual assumption that a business unit starts its life trying to define its purpose and develop a viable business model and over time eventually matures to the position where current practices drive out new ideas. In this scenario we can say that in early life, units begin with exploration in ascendancy, in mid-life they develop to a balanced state, and finally they degenerate to one where exploitation is dominant before death sets in. Thus in terms of Levinthal and March (1993), balance is only a transitory state (unless a unit can reverse its history which is rare). However, what is true for the unit need not be true for the firm. A firm can be balanced even when its individual units are travelling the lifecycle.

We take it as axiomatic that the journey of renewal of a multiunit firm can be summarized as the aggregate of the trajectories of the individual units. Because individual units have separate paths, the combinations can follow many possible evolving patterns, every one of which will result in some form of resolution of the tension between exploitation and exploration. For the multiunit firm, balance can be achieved in *three* ways, and these are shown diagrammatically in figure 10.1.

The first way of achieving balance (pattern A in figure 10.1) is by having all units alike, each at a constant state of exploration–exploitation balance. This very static view of balance can be achieved by the firm in several ways, one of which is by buying units which are balanced and selling units which are not. The second (pattern B in figure 10.1) is for the multiunit firm to have a portfolio of units that range along the explore–exploit continuum, and which together represent a balanced state. Since the firm's overall position is the average of its units, it is a trivial mathematical problem, but a seriously difficult one managerially. Over time, each unit will be changing, and in line with our initial assumption they will be tending to exploitation. The firm as a whole can present a picture of stability (like the swan that moves gracefully over the water whilst it paddles vigorously with its feet) providing there is a constant stream of new businesses being added that are in a state of exploration to match those in stasis.

Our assumption that individual units have an inevitable lifecycle can be challenged, and in the last part of our chapter we examine what happens if they can reverse their trajectories. Because we will recognize that individual units can engage in renewal themselves, and that the lifecycle of the evolutionary process can be reversed, other kinds of balance are possible. The number of possibilities multiplies, so we focus on one that is of considerable interest. This is where balance is achieved not at each point in time, but rather looked at historically over a long period (see pattern C in figure 10.1). Such a firm consists of a portfolio of units marching together, each of which is evolving between exploration and exploitation and each of which is engaging in a process of reversing the lifecycle of the evolutionary trajectory when too much exploitation threatens to destroy the unit. Thus, in pattern C the portfolio is not in balance at every moment in time, but is mostly unbalanced, oscillating between extremes.

The three patterns in figure 10.1 are important in the sense that they represent the fundamental categories by which balance may be achieved. These categories are balanced by means of stability, balanced by mixing the portfolio at each point of time for equilibrium, and lastly (pseudo) balanced by retrospective aggregation. Clearly, the first two categories fulfil the criteria laid down by Levinthal and March (1993), but the third only survives if the extremes do not become too great, resulting in breakdown (Volberda, 1998).

We should be clear from whose perspective we describe balance. Clearly, the initiative or unit can be new to the firm but not new to the industry (Baden-Fuller and Stopford, 1994). Such will typically be the case where the firm engages in mimetic behavior. Our perspective is that of co-evolution, and for us the concept of balance is the wider perspective of the industry. For the firm to be found engaging in exploration, in this chapter it has to meet the double hurdle of being new to both the industry and the enterprise.

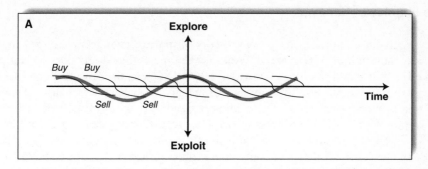

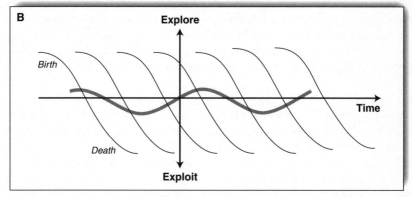

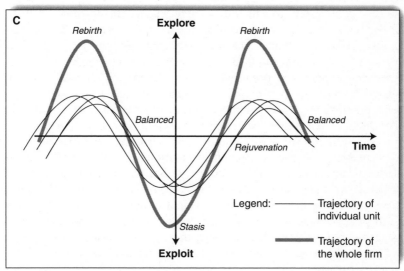

Figure 10.1   Generic renewal journeys of multiunit firms

The Engines of Renewal

There is no one comprehensive process theory of strategic change able to explain how and why multiunit firms renew and develop over time as they do (cf. Dooley and Van de Ven, 1999; Van de Ven and Grazman, 1999: 186; Van de Ven and Poole, 1995). In this section we propose four engines of managerial behavior that drive distinctly different processes of renewal. These engines are ideal types for make-believe firms, a sort of pure form rooted in process theories of organizations (Van de Ven and Poole, 1995). These in turn drive the mechanisms of variation and selection, the key mechanisms of the journeys that map onto the generic journeys described above and in figure 10.1. In table 10.2, we highlight for each renewal engine the role of managerial intentions; the complementary roles played by the different management levels (top, middle, and frontline); the mechanisms of variation and selection; and the particular renewal outcome (journey). Moreover, we describe the implications for learning and knowledge-sharing and under what environmental conditions these engines are most appropriate.

It is top management that ultimately decides the *selection mechanism* in the multiunit firm. The top management team faces many choices, and we highlight two dimensions. The first is whether management is reactive or proactive towards the industry's evolution. Reactive management takes the industry as given, and sees its role as interpreting market signals. Proactive management attempts to guess or influence the market's evolution, and so undertake selection mechanisms that influence the evolution of the industry. Top managers also face another choice that is even more central to our concerns, that is the extent to which they try to balance the portfolio of the firm in a static or dynamic manner. These mechanisms, we will explain, achieve effective balance by *either* insisting each unit is balanced (the naive journey), *or* juggling the portfolio to have a balanced collection (managed selection and hierarchical renewal), *or* by a retrospective-prospective sense of balance inter-temporally (holistic renewal). Each approach will be related to a different journey and gives rise to different processes.

Whilst top management can set the selection mechanism, they are not wholly in control of the mechanism that governs the variation process that generates new ideas. This process is often labeled as "blind" in the sense that it is "random," yet self-evidently managers at all levels in organizations attempt to influence the process. One particularly influential group in this respect is that of the frontline managers. Our engines identify several processes, essentially based on concepts of knowledge deployment. First, there are processes that allow business units to undertake their own variations, perhaps encouraged or discouraged by the incentives handed down from the top management and the market. Second, there are processes of variation that are influenced by top management in a deliberate fashion. Knowledge from outside of the unit is fed to managers in the unit in an attempt to alter the kinds of innovations that front line managers undertake. In the multiunit firm there is also the need to transfer knowledge between units. This gives rise to more effective organization learning. We touch briefly on this issue, in so far as it relates to our central concern of the evolutionary patterns of development.

It is clear that we could have a wide variety of potential engines corresponding to different possible sets of behaviors and incentives. In this chapter we explore four ideal

Table 10.2 An inquiry into journeys of strategic renewal in multiunit firms

Co-evolutionary paths	Motor of selection	Source of variation	Renewal journey	Intra-unit learning and sharing	Environmental conditions
Naive selection Denial of co-evolution; no pluralistic management roles	Top management chooses all units to be balanced between explore-exploit	Internal units only engage in local search. Purchase and sale of units from other firms represents the true source of variation	*Passive but purposefully balanced*	*Ignored by top management*	Slow-moving mature environments
Managed selection Facilitative micro co-evolution	Top management has a portfolio of units ranged over the spectrum of explore–exploit	Top management creates a strategic context for nurturing and selecting promising initiatives that come from the front line	*Balanced purposefully*	*Encouraged by top management* It provides the context	Fast-moving, unpredictable environments
Hierarchical renewal Directed macro- to micro co-evolution	Top management selects those units that fit with its own foresight or vision of the future	Top management creates clear strategic intent for the process of variation, and assists in its stimulation	*Top management's objectives are to align and influence environment, journey is usually balanced*	*Facilitated by top management* It provides considerable resources to support sharing	Moderately paced environments, especially those driven by regulatory processes or by clearly defined technologies requiring tight process integration
Holistic renewal Transformational cognitive processes that are macro to micro co-evolutionary	Collective sense-making determines fitness to the landscape	Variations are created by dualistic processes organized by top and frontline managers	*Cyclical* Radical processes of system-wide change are followed by incremental processes of consolidation	*Part of the philosophy and purpose of top management* Supported by extensive cultural, social, organization wide resources.	Not obviously restricted to any particular environment

types, which we believe reflect interesting extremes of behavior giving rise to different kinds of trajectories.

Naive Selection

In our first engine of renewal, top management takes a reactive stance towards the industry. They typically believe that their role is to interpret and amplify market forces and market signals for the benefit of the unit managers. In a sense they espouse the view that *the market knows best*. Of particular interest is the case where top management tries to keep all its individual units in a constant state between exploration and exploitation, usually by telling each unit that it should achieve a certain level of shareholder return by criteria such as return-on-assets (pattern A in figure 10.1). This overall objective sets in train a clear set of mechanisms for the co-evolutionary process.

This attitude and objective function of top management makes a conceptually simple selection mechanism for units to follow. Each unit is judged in isolation as to whether it fulfils the criteria handed down to all, profitability and balance. Units will be selected "in" or "out" by a process that sets them against this benchmark, and units that do not reach the standard will be either sold or closed.

How does variation take place in this environment? Clearly, individual units will engage in variation, because of the competitive forces for survival. However, the incentives for variation are strongly favoring narrowly based search close to the core competence. It is only these kinds of variation that are likely to yield the fast track rewards that top management desires. Ideas that are more distant from the core are unlikely to be funded, or if funded they will only be developed to the state that allows them to be sold. The units cannot afford to take big risks.

If the top management were to rely solely on such minimal variations within the firm, the organization would die. However, variation takes place not just inside the firm, but also outside. In this reactive journey top management will typically scan the environment to look for new units that fulfil the criterion of balance between exploration and exploitation to replace the units that are being closed or sold. These new units may well have started life in an embryonic form perhaps in another multiunit firm, or in a venture capital incubator or as an independent organization. For our ideal firm, trading units is the key lever that achieves its long-term survival. Obviously, long-run success in this ideal type depends on there being an active market for the purchase and sale of vibrant units. This is only possible if the industry contains many players and there are active markets for the purchase and sale of units.

How do top managers in our firm react to the search for synergies so often viewed as the hallmark of success of multiunit enterprises? The philosophy of our ideal type – *the market knows best* – suggests that they do not look to create synergies intentionally. Although it is widely accepted that effective coordination across functional and organizational boundaries cannot take place without managerial permission or active managerial support (Liebeskind et al., 1996) this ideal type typically believes that top management intervention will degenerate into meddling and disruption (Weick, 1979, p. 8). Although knowledge transfer is a process of horizontal linking between units, in this journey top management denies its role in the process. Knowledge sharing between units will be no greater or less inside the firm than within the market.

The naive selection journey has low administrative costs. Goold and Campbell (1987) noted that these selection processes are common among many high-performing conglomerates, and they labeled the style *financial control*. Units often perform very well in the short term, selecting carefully among their capabilities to achieve maximal returns. Failure has clear sanctions, when a division or unit is "selected-out," it is closed, sold, or finds resources withdrawn.

The story of ICI illustrates our theme. The UK bulk-chemical giant appointed a new top management team. This team felt that the portfolio was overweight in declining cyclical business in the bulk-chemicals sector. The board therefore proceeded to sell the majority of the old businesses and purchase new businesses in more emerging sectors. Most of these new businesses were balanced in their own right. (The success of the strategy has yet to be proved.)

The argument for the ideal naive journey cited above is usually couched in terms of its suitability to dealing with mature slow-moving environments, with little evidence of synergies between units that cannot be done through the market. The benefits of the naive balanced approach is in avoiding the myopia of being wedded to particular ideas or notions (see for instance Goold and Campbell, 1987, and their description of Lord Hanson's management of Hanson Trust), a trap that mature firms can fall into in even mature environments. This probably explains why historically some firms developed this approach for the decades when the industry was stable. It is doubtful if this journey should be applied to volatile environments where there is a need to build synergies.

How does the reactive view map onto the past literature that we reviewed at the outset? We suggest that the managers of these firms behave as if the evolutionary process was extremely deterministic. For them, individual units are highly path dependent as was noted by the population ecologists. Survival of the firm requires a distancing of the top management of the multiunit enterprise from the constituent components.

Managed Selection: Intended variation processes driving facilitated renewal journeys

Our next ideal type that we call managed selection is characterized by a more co-evolutionary journey. Whilst top management still takes a reactive stance towards its ability to shift the industry forces, it responds by trying to be prepared for the changes that may come about. It still seeks to maintain a portfolio that is balanced overall, but that balance is achieved by a spread of units some of which are mature and others of which are in the early exploration stages (see pattern B in figure 10.1). "Be prepared," the scouts' motto, appears to represent the attitude of top management. This ideal type of managed selection fits closely with the thinking of strong evolutionary theorists who are not at the extreme of population ecology, but take a more balanced view of the possibilities open to management.

The process of *managed selection* uses more elaborate processes to select its units than the naive ideal type. In this ideal type, top management has an image of both the requirements for success today and a perspective on the requirements for success tomorrow. This is not foresight, a situation that we discuss in our next ideal type, but something more generic, a capability to adjust. The top management weeds out units with inferior match-ups that do not fit the now or the future. In this process, it not only protects units that perform well at present, but also nurtures potential growth units that it believes will be appropriate for the future. In this selection process top management deliberately encourages internal units to come up with exploratory moves. Units that create new possibilities will be rewarded.

There are well-documented examples of nested co-evolutionary journeys in firms that appear to emulate our ideal type. Galunic and Eisenhardt's study (1996) of inter-corporate domains reveals that selection occurs among competing units but charter losses involve purposive action by group executives and major adaptive shifts by divisions. Burgelman (1994) in his study of Intel shows that it was not the corporate strategy but the "internal selection environment" that caused a shift from memory chips towards microprocessor business. He conjectures that the higher the correspondence between the vicarious selection criteria and external selection pressures, then the better the selection mechanism guarantees the co-evolution of a multiunit firm's competencies with the sources of competitive advantage of the industry. Campbell (1994) warns that the validity of this selection mechanism may decline over time when these internal selectors become more isolated from the external selection environment. Barnett et al. (1994) found in their comparison of single-unit versus multiunit firms in retail banking that multiunit firms were able to buffer their sub-units from the external selection environment by seeking positional advantages in the market. Internal selection mechanisms replaced the external selection mechanism by "soft" incentives that were weaker than those that act on a population of single firms. In this case, they appeared to inhibit variety inducing learning processes that generate distinctive competencies, but they were immune from dysfunctional learning effects such as core rigidities or competence traps.

The process of variation inside the managed firm is different from that within the naive (reactive) firm. Top management now focuses on initiatives within rather than from without. It does this through originating, developing and promoting strategic initiatives from the frontline managers (cf. Kimberly, 1979; Burgelman, 1983; Quinn, 1985). Frontline managers, it is argued, typically have the most current knowledge and expertise and are closer to the routines and sources of information critical to innovative outcomes. Top management's roles is to create a strategic context for nurturing and selecting promising renewal initiatives ensuring the maximum incentives for frontline renewal. Its role is often described as retrospective legitimizer (Burgelman, 1983) or judge and arbiter (Angle & Van de Ven, 1989) and supporter of lower-level initiatives. This is not a unidirectional vision process; rather, it is something much more flexible and open.

The studies noted above suggest that in managed selection journeys top managers need *variety generators* to facilitate venture creation that parallels or anticipates the selection out of older more mature activities. (In terms of the pattern B in figure 10.1, those units that are the extreme of exploitation are matched by those that are at the extreme of exploration.) We can distinguish variety generation by top management intervention in different degrees, ranging from the creation of skunk works (Peters and Waterman, 1982), corporate ventures (Fast, 1979, Burgelman, 1983) to even completely new venture departments. Some variety generation can be achieved by isolating a flexible unit from the rigid operating core. This principle was applied at IBM when the IBM PC was developed, as the mainframe logic was strongly preserved in IBM's culture and prevented entry into the new PC market. Similarly, Eastman Kodak, Philips, and Xerox have tried internal venturing and new business development programs. Although the creation of a separate flexible unit accelerates progress in new areas of opportunity, it often leads to problems of morale disruption, and reassimilation difficulties. Consequently, exploiting the new opportunities (i.e. forcing units along the trajectory towards exploitation) can be slow and frustrating (cf. MacMillan, 1985; Burgelman, 1983).

Stronger variety generators involve the continuous splitting of groups into separate units. Hewlett Packard, Johnson & Johnson, and Origin are examples of such multiunit firms that have developed new unit generation mechanisms that encourages entrepreneurs to pursue their ideas in new separate divisions, while the older, more established units provide continuity and stability. Overall, these organizations appear to be in a perpetual stage of adaptation, never really rigid or planned as long as new units are being regularly created from within (Mintzberg and Westley, 1992). Their variety generation mechanisms (for example, 70 percent of HP's sales have to be represented by products introduced or substantially modified in the previous two years) bring costs, such as the difficulty of integrating the new ideas back into the old organization. But they also bring some benefits; the new ideas are typically insulated from the inertia of the center, and have the possibility to flourish without being suffocated.

In *managed selection*, there is considerable potential for learning across the units of the firm. Bartlett and Ghoshal (1993), in their careful analysis of ABB and comparison with the traditional Chandler type of hierarchical renewal, suggest that top management sets the context and provides the challenge for encouraging sharing. Yet the thinness of the top management group and the lack of significant resources devoted to moving knowledge will still make intra-corporate learning limited. Managed selection is congruent to the network view, where trade in knowledge takes place principally by horizontal interaction between separate units. Although co-owned, the connections between the parties is mutual and voluntary, and typically one party is the center or broker (Miles and Snow, 1986).

The process of the facilitated or managed journey is difficult to handle for top management, but has the potential to yield great results when the environment is turbulent and where it is hard to predict or influence industry evolution. Be prepared is not just a metaphor in such cases. Teece et al. (1994) argue that organizations driven by managed selection are typically narrowly diversified and effective for operating in rapidly moving trajectories. With narrow diversification, technological interdependence will encourage units into knowledge sharing without the need for direction from top management (Hart, 1992: 344). Managed selection is ideal in highly complex and dynamic markets where a deliberate strategy of any kind is risky. Such an ideal type neatly fits the "ambidextrous organization" of Tushman and O'Reilly (1996) and the thinking of "the edge of chaos" of Brown and Eisenhardt (1998).

Hierarchical Renewal: Administrative processes driving directed renewal journeys

In naive selection and managed selection journeys, the role of top management was mainly passive, first in a negative manner and second in a more positive mode. In our next two ideal types, we shift to top management having a much more proactive stance. This renewal journey is more closely akin to the kinds of paths envisaged by the strategic choice theorists outlined in our opening section. In directed renewal journeys, top managers believe they have some power over their environment and that strategy making in large complex firms involves multiple levels of management in a co-evolving manner (cf.. Van Cauwenberg and Cool, 1982). In this perspective, renewal journeys are driven by a priori top-managerial intentions that develop cascade-down and frontline managers are not seen as the source of inspiration. The source of renewal is not selection or quasi-selection, but ex ante managerial purpose. As a result of top-down strategy-making processes, multiunit firms can and do make changes in their strategy deliberately, adapting to changes in their competitive environment. In this mainly teleological journey it is assumed that the multiunit firm is purposeful and adaptive; it sets goals, scans the environments, searches for alternatives, chooses one, and monitors the process (Van de Ven and Poole, 1995: 316). This ideal type is not so much in the vein of "be prepared" but that of "take control."

The emerging journey of renewal may be balanced (see pattern B in Figure 1) for the desire to control extends to everything that is strategic. More important, the journey is characterized as a highly rational, proactive process that involves activities such as establishing goals, monitoring the units, assessing unit capabilities, searching for and evaluating alternative actions, and developing plans to achieve organizational goals (Ansoff, 1965; Hofer and Schendel, 1978; Lorange and Vancil, 1977). In this ongoing sequential process, "strategy formulation" precedes "strategy implementation". Ideally, the role of the management is that of a "rational actor" issuing directives from the seat of power. It requires that an exhaustive analysis can be undertaken before action is taken, and that management holds a considerable amount of power and has access to complete information. Regarding implementation, the role of management is to orchestrate local rejuvenation, diffusion among units and to push the units towards goal achievement.

For *hierarchical renewal,* the top management team takes an approach that fits with classical administrative theorists such as Barnard (1938), Selznick (1957), and Chandler (1962). This perspective also matches Prahalad and Hamel (1990), who argue that strategic renewal depends on the strategic intent (Hamel and Prahalad, 1989) of the CEO or corporate management, and that it should be based on superior industry foresight. O'Dell and Grayson (1998) point out that with these situations, senior management has to commit resources to make things happen, and to actively become involved in the process.

In hierarchical renewal, selection processes are based on foresight by the top management team, fitting the points made above. Variation, in turn, is a process that is directed by the top, aimed at creating units that fit with the vision. This does not mean that top management undertakes the variation, but they give a steer. Typically there is a unit near to the apex of the firm called the strategy department that is very powerful, and filled with specialists in creating new ideas. This group may undertake its work in close connection with the frontline. Top managers reinforce their foresight by employing consultants, and by engaging in the buying and selling of units to achieve their strategic purpose. Unlike our first case of passive journeys, the criteria for a sale or a purchase will not be that the unit is in balance. Rather the opposite may hold; the new units will be typically embryonic and have the capability of stimulating and provoking other units into changing direction.

For *hierarchical renewal,* the top management team takes a very directive approach, and we argue that the underlying administrative engine gives greater opportunities for knowledge sharing. Nonaka argues that to share knowledge a directive approach is necessary, and that top management needs to foster the spirit of *Ba* (Nonaka et al., 2000). It can facilitate the processes by setting up special units to facilitate knowledge movement, accepting lower profits from units which provide knowledge to other units, and in investing in specific programs within units. O'Dell and Grayson (1998) point out that senior management can direct resources to make sharing better, and they cite Chevron and Rank Xerox, both associated with a hierarchical style. The typically tightly controlled multinational also falls into this category. There is a very large literature here on what firms can and ought to do, with key contributions from Prahalad and Doz (1987).

It is clear that hierarchical renewal processes are ideal for environments where managers can influence and predict industry change. We focus attention on two environmental circumstances, those of politicized environments such as regulated industries and those populated by vertically integrated firms.

In recently privatized utilities in Europe, directed journeys of hierarchical renewal have been very evident. Top management has typically hired outside consultants to teach the multiunit firm the new competitive rules set by the industry regulator. Top management can clearly see the regulatory mechanism, and is charged by the regulator for conveying the information relating to the competitive rules. In regulated industries, top management can also influence the regulator. Often an individual, he or she typically calls for new ideas and responses to regulatory proposals to maintain a politicized process. Whereas top management can influence the dynamics of regulation and competition, there is little opportunity for middle management to have much impact. Rather, they have to conform to new imposed rules rather than create them (Baden-Fuller and Dean, 1999). Grant (1996) and Grant and Cibin (1996) argue that most oil companies are hierarchically managed with respect to knowledge flows, because of the politicized nature of their environments and the need for centralized information processing.

Apart from the politicized sector, there are industries whose technologies demand tight integration between successive stages of the value chain: highly integrated firms that need direction and hierarchy for regulation of internal change, for it is not effective if the different units go off in different directions. Typically, such firms face a high degree of technological interdependence between the units, where careful coordination is vital. Because of the great demands placed upon top management by hierarchical renewal, the risk of "paralysis by analysis" is always present, making this journey difficult in dynamic, rapidly changing environments.

Holistic Renewal: Shared sensemaking processes propelling transformational renewal journeys

The first three ideal types are neatly mapped onto trajectories A and B in figure 10.1. What of trajectory C? This trajectory is not so much a question of balance at a point of time, but rather a perspective that sees journeys as unfolding paths that oscillate, and where perspective and retrospection are important. This kind of journey does not map neatly into the patterns of thought in our opening review. Rather we will draw on a new stream of thinking that is also consistent with our arguments about journeys. In the transformational holistic journey, top management believes that it should try to influence the world by working closely with the lower levels creating an effective engine for renewal. In this ideal firm, the question of what drives renewal thus depends on the socially constructed reality of organizational participants (Barr, 1998; Barr, Stimpert, and Huff, 1992). Reality is defined through collective sensemaking in which perceptions are affirmed, modified, or replaced according to their apparent congruence with the perceptions of others and other levels. Weick (1979) described this sensemaking as enactment where the journey is driven by the development of shared strategic schemata or collective frames of reference (Bettis and Prahalad, 1995; Chaffee, 1985: 93; Prahalad and Bettis, 1986). The process is not just one of micro co-evolution within the firm, but also (cognitively) macro co-evolution to the environment. New schemata may stimulate novel and interesting environments that can in turn preface novel and interesting strategic initiatives (Dijksterhuis et al., 1999). For top management, the belief is not in concepts such as "the market knows best," "be prepared," or "take control" but "total involvement of all in the challenge"!

The journey of holistic renewal is transparent when applied to the small unit, especially the start-up. There, a single entrepreneur is seen as the driving force of the innovation process. Typically, he or she imbues a spirit in the whole enterprise collecting and motivating like-minded individuals. For such small entrepreneurial units, there is typically a dynamic alternation between exploitation and exploration because of the rising and falling energy levels of the founders. Variation and selection take place together, perhaps in the same individual. The lack of tight commitments and relatively low sunk costs enables these smaller start-ups to change radically and easily. The role of these new units in changing industries is not only a central tenet of economics thinking, but is also self-evident in the emerging new e-economy. Firms such as Amazon and AOL have changed the industry landscape.

In the larger, multi-unit established firm, shared strategic schemata are difficult to change. It is important to understand that a strategic schema is not purely a system of beliefs and assumptions, but that it is preserved and legitimized in a 'cultural web' of organizational actions in terms of myths, rituals, and symbols (Johnson, 1988). Recently, considerable attention has been paid to the regeneration of mature units, or whole complex organizations, especially those which are in a crisis or facing decline (see for instance Grinyer et al., 1988; Beer et al., 1990, Kotter and Hesketh, 1992). These studies show that the underlying cognitive changes begin with incremental changes in causal concepts and linkages, then exhibit a more significant and dramatic change, followed by incremental adjustments that further specify the new interpretation (cf. Barr, 1998). These underlying cognitive changes give rise to cyclical renewal journeys. Periods of incremental change paths will alternate with radical change paths that are associated with significant unlearning (Argyris and Schön, 1978), new ways of thinking and new mindsets (Spender, 1980), different paths of technology (Clark, 1985; Tushman and Anderson, 1986), and particular kinds of corporate entrepreneurship (Schumpeter, 1934; Guth & Ginsberg, 1990). Not all organizations will be able to sustain the oscillations – some will over react with too much exploration and disintegrate into chaos; others will get stuck in exploitation and degenerate into rigidity and failure (Volberda, 1996, 1998).

What is the process of variation and selection in the holistic ideal firm? We suggest it is a shared conception driven from the top. There are profound differences between this process and that of hierarchical renewal. In holistic paths, the top management team, typically led by the chief executive, is much more than an administrator, he or she is a transformational leader who drives the process from the front but involves others and brings them along too. Although this is not a sustainable process over long periods of time, it is a well-recognized journey for the moments of radical upheaval. Here the literature has generally pointed to the dualistic roles of many in the organization. "Variation" and "selection" cannot be separated simply by level or by time; rather, it is integrated as Calori et al. (2000) show in their study of change at Novotel. This is not the case of one level driving another, but of team-working among levels and functions, as is pointed out by Kanter (1983), Hurst et al. (1986), and Wooldridge and Floyd (1990).

Collective sensemaking which drives both variation and selection is the result of the participation of all levels and is an important requirement for knowledge integration processes as highlighted by Grant (1996). Collective sensemaking is a key component of the integrative processes that seek to maximize organization learning. Of course, top management does have a special role. As a group, they are primarily involved in the promotion and protection of values; the institutional leaders (Selznick, 1957), the heroes (Deal and Kennedy, 1982), the change masters (Kanter, 1983), or the purposing leaders (Vaill, 1982).

It is known that to achieve knowledge transfer between units horizontally it is necessary to have extensive and intense knowledge sharing between units as well as across levels, all of which is associated with double loop learning (Senge, 1990; Argyris and Schön, 1978). Holistic renewal provides the best context in all our firms for this to happen. It combines the effectiveness of the hierarchical system coupled with the motivation for front line managers to create and use the knowledge. In holistic renewal, the cognitive processes ensure that there is a high degree of knowledge integration, of both the tacit and explicit kind. This creates the right conditions for effective interactions between top management and front line managers, unpacking tacit knowledge, managing intellectual property rights and dealing with issues of exploiting knowledge domains. We know that such processes are observed in highly integrated multiunit knowledge-based firms such as leading-edge management consultants and some multinational product firms.

Baden-Fuller and Stopford (1994) confirm the importance of complete organizational transformation in cases of mature firms renewing to achieve not only radical change for themselves, but also change for their sectors, thus linking corporate renewal to industry renewal. They point out, using examples such as Richardson in knives, and Edwards in high-vacuum pumps, that although triggers for change may have come from many quarters and may take time to gather speed, in the end the whole state of the organization can change from maturity to dynamism. In addition, case histories show how holistic journeys of renewal can take a cyclical form. In Unilever, for instance, since the early 1980s there have been three periods of sharp upheaval followed by periods of comparative stability (see Maljers, Baden-Fuller, and Van den Bosch, 1996).

Holistic managerial journeys are often associated with narrowly defined technological trajectories, but wide dispersion in other dimensions. For example, large multinational firms, where all the divisions are in a closely related business and where the environment is evolutionary but punctuated by occasional radical shifts. In such cases the importance of intra-organization learning is often high (transmitting best practice from one country to another) (Prahalad and Doz, 1987; Birkinshaw and Hood, 1998; Hedlund, 1986). Radical shifts are occasionally necessary, and the firm can on occasion rise to the challenge.

Drawing Connections

It is important to draw connections between our highly stylized modeling and the reality of large firms. We have not formally mapped existing organizations onto our ideal types. We have hinted at examples, and in doing so we may have given the (false) impression that it is possible to fit firms one by one to a box. Some firms may fit into classification boxes, as Goold and Campbell have found; others may defy such classification as they try to manage different parts of their portfolios differently. For example, top management could be trying to operate a naive selection journey in one part of their portfolio and a managed selection process in another. Whether this is a sustainable strategy is an open question, and a possible avenue for empirical work. Our reasoning, based on ideal types, suggests that few will have the managerial capacity to sustain such paradoxical tensions over time. Indeed, the normative implication of our work (and hence the potentially testable) implication is that firms would do better to be consistent in their behaviors and that a stable trajectory can be an outcome of that consistency.

A second question is whether one kind of renewal process is intrinsically superior to another and if so, whether firms can actually make a transition from one style to another. Put another way, for those firms that do fit an ideal type and follow an engine of renewal, can they move to a different ideal type, characterized by a different renewal engine? Such meta or development journeys of renewal could form part of the portfolio of strategic choice.

There is limited evidence that meta-development journeys are possible. Such journeys require changes in behavior of both top management and frontline managers. Consider GE's corporate revitalization guided by its CEO Jack Welch, Philips' corporate change initiated by Jan Timmer and further accelerated by Cor Boonstra, or Novotel's renewal led by Pellison. The starting point of these companies seemed to be a period of stasis where both top and frontline managers had been reactive and where the financial community was threatening to impose its own form of selection through

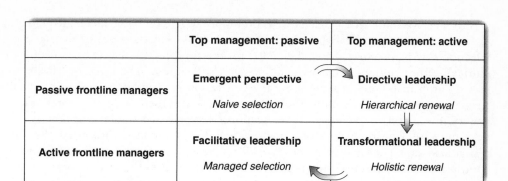

Figure 10.2   One example of a development journey of strategic renewal
Source: Adapted from Volberda et al., 2001a

breakup. New CEOs arrived and drove a development journey. Typically they began with a process of competence development led by the CEO, which introduced new concepts, communicated them in an understandable manner through the use of meta-phors and analogies, and reiterated them repeatedly. Consequently, new capabilities such as speed, simplicity, and market responsiveness were passed down the organiza-tion almost as an order or instruction to be followed (cf. Nonaka and Takeuchi, 1995). Following these periods of top-down hierarchical renewal, the organizations have moved onto another period, where top management shows more transformational leadership and other management levels are involved in order to create system-wide change (ho-listic renewal). Finally, top management becomes more of an orchestrator, facilitating decentralized entrepreneurship, and the journey is more like that of managed selec-tion. We show one possible sequence of development journeys in figure 10.2, which is meant to illustrate rather than analyze possibilities. It is clear that our journeys have not only implications for managerial roles but also for styles of leadership. A fruitful avenue for empirical research is the extent to which meta journeys are possible and lead to survival. We leave open to other researchers the question of how often firms can make such transitions, noting only that many claim to do so, but most fail.

Our exposition does not allude to a single best way. Brown and Eisenhardt (1998), Anderson (1999a), Tushman and O'Reilly (1996) and many other scholars special-ized on complexity theory (cf. Anderson, 1999b), loosely coupled systems, and co-evolution (cf. Lewin and Volberda, 1999) provide valuable evidence that managed selection may be very effective, and could dominate the future landscape. Renewal proceeds most rapidly, they argue, when top management effects small probes in a characteristic rhythm, recombining the elements of a portfolio of modular units, so that novelty is deliberately generated without destroying the best elements of past experience. Top management operates on unit managers indirectly, taking advantage of the tendency for myriad local interactions to self-organize into a coherent pattern. Rather than shaping the pattern that constitutes strategic renewal (hierarchical re-newal), managers shape the context within which it emerges, speeding up co-evolu-tionary processes. Moreover, in this perspective, holistic renewal is a signal of missed inflection points. Managed selection journeys are ongoing and relentless.

Although we think that managed selection journeys are probably most adequate in fast-moving, unpredictable environments, we think that the case for managed selection may be overplayed (see table 10.2 for the appropriate environmental conditions). Other engines could be equifinal, and still prevail. The three questions, how do firms map onto ideal types, are there meta-journeys and is there equifinality raises important questions about empirical work. To date there is a paucity of good empirical work on co-evolution. Cross-sectional survey-based studies and time-series simulation (for instance, Mollona and Noda, 2001) dominate the empirical research landscape (Lewin and Volberda, 1999). Both these carriers have important contributions, but the first suffers from a lack of dynamics; the second lacks real data. We need more long-term studies of how industries and firms co-evolve and emerge over very long periods of time where several of the engines of renewal can be compared, not just two at a time. Until now, there have been few very long-run analyses, yet they often yield valuable results. For instance, Barr et al. (1992) showed great insight in their study of railroads, Van de Ven and Grazman (1999) in comparing twin cities' healthcare organizations, and Huygens et al. (2001) showed that dominant firms in the music industry have survived for a very long time despite major technological upheavals. Large-scale longitudinal international research programs such as the NOFIA (New Organization Forms in the Information Age) or INNFORM (Innovative Forms of Organizing in the Twenty-first century) may be helpful vehicles to create data sources for studying journeys of strategic renewal, the underlying engines as well as the micro- and macro-coevolution.

We mention one piece of our own work (Volberda et al., 2001b) that examined the trajectories of renewal of UK and Dutch financial service firms. We used the metric of exploration exploitation to track the journeys of eight firms over an eight-year period. We found that many firms had indeed maintained a fairly constant balance overall, even though individual initiatives had varied widely between exploration and exploitation. This work has not yet identified clear engines, but hinted at their existence. Such work has been time consuming but because it used a common metric and approach it has been able to compare firms across time and so provide a starting point for further work.

Limitations and Conclusions

Organizations are not static, and often resist attempts at simple categorization. While journeys of renewal are highly idiosyncratic, we used in line with McKelvey (1997) idealized models to approach the problem of idiosyncrasy. These idealized engines compartmentalize phenomena of renewal into three types of balance as outlined in figure 10.1 earlier. Our four models represent distinct combinations of managerial behaviors that are compatible with balance. There is the proactive or reactive mode of behavior of top management with respect to the environment, and the differing behaviors of the frontline. Each engine crudely maps onto one of the strands of thinking in the theories of selection and adaptation outlined at the start of the chapter. In simple terms they represent the four modes of thinking: "the market knows best," "be prepared," "take control of your destiny by directing from the top," and "get control by total involvement of everyone."

Our analysis has many limitations, and we identify only some of them here. To begin, we take no account of the potential pluralism that exists *within* the top management group and *within* middle managers. Yet obviously, such differences are important, especially as firms globalize. Global companies are increasingly experiencing mixed cultural teams. French middle managers are different from those in the UK (cf. Calori et al., 1997), and from those in emerging Asian economies. All multinational firms must take cognizance of these differences, and cope with the consequence both between countries and within decision-making units. Yet, as we begin the Twenty-first century more managers will receive American-style management education (albeit from different schools around the world). This education will not harmonize but keep distinctive the separate roles of middle and top managers. These differences remain a key dimension of managerial pluralism, and a driving force for the continued importance of our four different engines.

Another major limitation of our analysis is its lack of attention to new organization forms that are replacing the multiunit firm. We did not discuss the internal network firm, nor the constellation of partnerships into which many firms are evolving. These will be important features of the landscape because they offset the problems of horizontal knowledge sharing experienced in naive as well as managed selection journeys of traditional multiunit firms (mostly M-firms) in which strong internal walls exist between units. We believe that a challenge to researchers is to see that these forms are not all alike, any more than the multiunit firm is a singular institution. We suggest that in these new forms there are different engines for change and development, as hinted by Miles and Snow (1986) and Lorenzoni and Baden-Fuller (1995). These engines could also yield differing paths for renewal and differing capacities for dealing with macro-coevolution, and this is obviously a subject for further research.

Of equal significance is the need for further theory building which bridges finance and strategy. According to finance theory, longevity is not the only test of success; a successful firm may run its course and be broken up, a less successful one may live on for a long time. Survivor studies could be misleading. Finance theory tells us we must compute the returns to the stakeholders, and that firms that break up may be more valuable to stakeholders and society than those which survive. The problem we face is made more complex because each engine has a different risk return profile and different profiles of income streams, so simple comparisons may be misleading. Consider for example trying to measure the effectiveness of the managed selection engine. The process of generating new ventures by deliberate variation and vicarious selection will create many units which are spun out. These units are not necessarily failures, they may have high option value (Dixit and Pindyck, 1997). This value may be captured by the firm or its stakeholders, and its effect needs to be modeled by the researcher. The effectiveness of this engine may be under-recorded. For different reasons, holistic renewal may also appear worse than it really is. In this journey, there is the roller coaster of exploration–exploitation so the income streams at any point in time could be unrepresentative. During periods of upheaval, stock market valuations and financial results are likely to be depressed; during periods of sustained exploitation the reverse may be true. The full flow of returns needs to be modeled over long periods of time, and its effects computed.

Finally, our themes point to important managerial lessons for strategists and those who teach them. By setting up the benchmark of "selection" where managers are seen as passive actors driven by path dependency in a biological game, we point out that there are real choices that managers can make (explicitly or implicitly). These choices include at least four different engines driving different journeys for running the multiunit firm. Each of these is distinctive from the other, having different benefits and costs. Each may respond differently to different environmental stimuli. Each implies differences in managerial pluralism between top and frontline management. We offer potential insights into some of the consequences of these choices. For example, surprisingly our analysis suggests that trying to maximize the amount of learning is perhaps highly risky for firms, especially those in high-velocity environments, and we provide a sound theoretical explanation for this view. Exploiting pluralism has both costs and benefits.

Note

We thank participants from the SMS Mini-Conference "Shaping, Implementing and Changing Strategies" in St Gallen, Switzerland, for their helpful comments. We particularly note the help of Bala Chakravarthy. All errors are the authors' responsibility.

References

Anderson, P. 1999a: The role of the manager in a self-organizing enterprise. In J. Clippinger (ed.), *The biology of business: decoding the natural laws of enterprise,* San Francisco: Jossey-Bass.

Anderson, P. 1999b: Complexity theory and organization science. *Organization Science,* 10 (3), 216–32.

Angle, H. L. and Van de Ven, A. H. 1989: Suggestions for managing the innovation journey. In A. H. van de Ven, H. L. Angle, and M. S. Poole (eds), *Research on the management of innovation,* New York: Harper and Row, 663–97.

Ansoff, H. I. 1965: *Corporate strategy: an analytic approach to business policy for growth and expansion.* New York: McGraw-Hill.

Argyris, C. and Schön, D. 1978: *Organizational learning.* Reading, MA: Addison-Wesley.

Baden-Fuller, C. and Dean A. 1999: *Punctuated and incremental change: the U.K. water industry.* Best Papers: Proceedings of Academy of Management, Chicago.

Baden-Fuller, C. and Stopford, J. M. 1994: *Rejuvenating the mature business.* Cambridge, MA: Harvard Business School Press.

Barnard, C. I. 1938: *The functions of the executive.* Cambridge, MA: Harvard University Press.

Barnett, W. P., Greve, H. R. and Park, D. Y. 1994: An evolutionary model of organizational performance. *Strategic Management Journal,* 15, 11–28.

Barr, P. S. 1998: Adapting to unfamiliar environmental events: a look at the evolution of interpretation and its role in strategic change. *Organization Science,* 9(6), 644–69.

Barr P. S., Stimpert, J. L. and Huff, A. S. 1992: Cognitive change, strategic action, and organizational renewal. *Strategic Management Journal,* 13, 15–36.

Bartlett, C. A. and Ghoshal, S. 1993: Beyond the M-form: toward a managerial theory of the firm. *Strategic Management Journal,* 14, 23–46.

Baum, J. A. C. 1996: Organizational ecology. In S. R. Clegg, C. Hardy, and W. R. Nord (eds), *Handbook of organization studies,* London: Sage, 77–114.

Baum, J. A. C. and Singh, J. V. 1994: *Evolutionary dynamics of organizations.* New York: Oxford University Press.

Beer, M. R., Eisenstat, R., and Spector, B. 1990: *The critical path to corporate renewal*. Cambridge, MA: Harvard Business School Press.

Bettis, R. A. and Prahalad, C. K. 1995: The dominant logic: retrospective and extension. *Strategic Management Journal*, 16 (1), 5–14.

Birkinshaw, J. and Hood, N. 1998: Multinational subsidiary evolution: capability and charter change in foreign-owned subsidiary companies. *Academy of Management Review*, 23(4), 773–95.

Brown, S. L. and Eisenhardt, K. M. 1998: *Competing on the edge: strategy as structured chaos*. Boston: Garvard Business School Press.

Bruderer, E. and Singh, J. V. 1996: Organizational evolution, learning and selection: a genetic-algorithm-based model. *Academy of Management Journal*, 39 (5), 1,322–49.

Burgelman, R. A. 1983: A process model of internal corporate venturing in the diversified major firm. *Administrative Science Quarterly*, 28, 223–44.

Burgelman, R. A. 1991: Intraorganizational ecology of strategy making and organizational adaption: theory and field research. *Organization Science*, 2, 239–62.

Burgelman, R. A. 1994: Fading memories: a process theory of strategic business exit in dynamic environments. *Administrative Science Quarterly*, 39 (1), 24–56.

Burgelman, R. A. 1996: A process model of strategic business exit: implications for an evolutionary perspective on strategy. *Strategic Management Journal*, 17, 193–214.

Calori, R., Badden-Fuller, C., and Hunt, B. 2000: Managing change at Novotel: back to the future. *Long Range Planning*, 33 (6), 779–804.

Calori, R., Lubhatkin, M., Very, P., and Veiga, J. F. 1997: Modelling the origins of nationally bound administrative heritages: a historical institutional analysis of French and British firms. *Organization Science*, 8 (6), 681–96.

Campbell, D. T. 1994: How individual and face-to-face-group selection undermine firm selection in organizational evolution. In J. A. C. Baum and J. V. Singh (eds), *Evolutionary dynamics of organizations*, New York: Oxford University Press, 23–38.

Chaffee, E. E. 1985: Three models of strategy. *Academy of Management Review*, 10 (1), 89–98.

Chandler, A. D. 1962: *Strategy and structure: chapters in the history of the American industrial enterprise*. Cambridge, MA: MIT Press.

Child, J. 1972: Organization structure, environment and performance: the role of strategic choice. *Sociology*, 6 (1), 1–22.

Child, J. 1997: Strategic choice in the analysis of action, structure, organisations and environment: retrospect and prospect. *Organization Studies*, 18 (1), 43–76.

Clark, K. B. 1985: The interaction of design hierarchies and market concepts in technological evolution. *Research Policy*, 14, 235–51.

Cohen, W. M. and Levinthal, D. A. 1990: Absortive capacity: a new perspective on learning and innovation. *Administrative Science Quarterly*, 35 (1), 128–52.

Cyert, R. and March, J. 1963: *A behavioral theory of the firm*. Englewood Cliffs, NJ: Prentice-Hall.

Deal, T. E. and Kennedt, A. A. 1982: *Corporate cultures*. Reading, MA: Addison-Wesley.

Dijksterhuis, M., Van den Bosch, F., and Volberda, H. W. 1999: Where do new organizational forms come from? Management logics as a source of co-evolution. *Organization Science*, 10 (5), 569–82.

DiMaggio, P. and Powell, W. 1983: The iron cage revisited: institutional, ismorphism, and collective raftionality in organization fields. *American Sociological Review*, 48, 147–60.

Dixit, A. K. and Pindyck, R. S. 1997: The options approach to capital investment. In J. S. Brown (ed.), *Seeing things differently: insights on innovation*. Cambridge, MA: Harvard Business School Press, 85–104.

Dooley, K. J. and Van de Ven, A. H. 1999: Explaining complex organizational dynamics. *Orgtanization Science*, 10 (3), 358–72.

Fast, N. D. 1979: The future of industrial new venture departments. *Industrial Marketing Management*, 8, 264–73.

Fiol, C. M. and Lyles, M. A. 1985: Organizational learning. *Academy of Management Review*, 10 (4), 803–13.

Galunic, D. C. and Eisenhardt, K. M. 1996: The evolution of intracorporate domains: divisional charter losses in high-technology, multidivisional corporations. *Organization Science*, 7 (3), 255–82.

Goold, M. and Campbell, A. 1987: *Strategies and styles.* Oxford: Blackwell.

Grant, R. M. 1996: Toward a knowledge based theory of the firm. *Strategic Management Journal* 17 (winter special issue), 109–22.

Grant, R. M. and Cibin, R. 1996: Strategy, structure and market turbulence: the international oil majors 1970–1991. *Scandinavian Journal of Management*, 12, 165–88.

Greenwood, R. and Hinings, C. R. 1996: Understanding radical organizational change: bringing together the old and the new institutionalism. *Academy of Management Review*, 21 (4), 1,022–54.

Grinyer, P. H., Mayes, D. G., and McKiernan, P. 1988: *Sharpbenders: the secrets of unleashing corporate potential.* Oxford: Blackwell.

Guth, W. D. and Ginsberg, A. 1990: Guest editors introduction: corporate entrepreneurship. *Strategic Management Journal*, 11, 5–15.

Hamel, G. and Prahalad, C. K. 1989: Strategic intent. *Harvard Business Review*, May–June, 63–76.

Hannan, M. T. and Freeman, J. H. 1977: The population ecology of organizations. *American Journal of Sociology*, 82 (5), 929–63.

Hannan, M. T. and Freeman, J. H. 1984: Structural inertia and organizational change. *American Sociological Review*, 49, 149–64.

Hart, S. L. 1992: An integrative framework for strategy-making processes. *Academy of Management Review*, 17 (2), 327–51.

Hedberg, B. 1981: How organizations learn and unlearn. In N. Nystrom and W. Starbuck (eds.), *Handbook of organizational design*, Oxford: Oxford University Press, 3–27.

Hedlund, G. 1986: The hypermodern MNC: a hierarchy. *Human Resource Management*, 25 (1), 9–35.

Henderson, R. and Clark, K. 1990: Architectural innovation: the reconfiguration of existing product technologies and the failure of existing firms. *Administrative Science Quarterly*, 35, 9–30.

Hofer, C. W. and Schendel, D. 1978: *Strategy formulation: analytical concepts.* St Paul: West.

Hrebhiniak, L. G. and Joyce, W. F. 1985: Organizational adaptation: strategic choice and environmental determinism. *Administrative Science Quarterly*, 30 (Sept.), 336–49.

Hurst, D. K. Rush, J. C., and White, R. E. 1986: Top management teams and organizational renewal. *Strategic Management Journal*, 10, 87–105.

Huygens, M., Baden-Fuller, C. Van den Bosch, F. A. J. and Volberda, H. W. 2001: Coevolution of firm capabilities and industry competition: investigating the music industry 1877–1997. *Organization Studies*, 22 (6), 971–1,011.

Johnson, G. 1988: Rethinking incrementalism. *Strategic Management Journal*, 9, 75–91.

Kanter, R. M. 1983: *The change masters: innovation and entrepreneurship in the American corporation.* New York: Simon & Schuster.

Khandwalla, P. N. 1977: *The design of organizations.* New York: Harcourt Brtace Jovanovich.

Kimberley, J. R. 1979: Issues in the creation of organizations: initiation, innovation, and institutionalization. *Academy of Management Journal*, 22, 437–57.

Kotter, J. P. and Heskett, J. L. 1992: *Corporate culture and performance.* New York: Free Press.

Lant, T. K. and Mezias, S. 1990: Managing discontinuous change: a simulation study of organizational learning and entrepreneurship. *Strategic Management Journal*, 11, 147–79.

Learned, E., Christensen, C., Andrews, K., and Guth, W. 1969: *Business policy: text and cases.* Homewood, IL: R. Irwin.

Levinthal, D. A. 1997: Adaptation on rugged landscapes. *Management Science,* 43 (7), 934–50.

Levinthal, D. A. and March, J. G. 1993: The myopia of learning. *Strategic Management Journal* 14, 95–112.

Lewin, A. Y. and Volberda, H. W. 1999: Prolegomena on coevolution: a framework for research on strategy and new organizational forms. *Organization Science,* 10 (5), 519–34.

Liebeskind, J. P., Lumerman Oliver, A., Zucker, L., and Brewer, M. 1996: Social networks, learning and flexibility: sourcing scientific knowledge in new biotechnology firms. *Organization Science,* 7 (4), 428–43.

Lorange, P. and Vancil, R. F. 1977: *Strategic Planning Systems.* Englewood Cliffs, NJ: Prentice-Hall.

Lorenzoni, G. and Baden-Fuller, C. 1995: Creating a strategic centre to manage a web of partners. *California Management Review,* 37 (3), 146–63.

MacMillan, I. G. 1985: *Progress in research on corporate venturing.* Working Paper, NY University, Center for Entrepreneurial Studies.

Maljers, F., Baden-Fuller, C. and Van den Bosch, F. 1996: Maintaining strategic momentum: the CEO's agenda. *European Management Journal,* 14 (6), 555–61.

March, J. G. 1991: Exploration and Exploitation in organizational learning. *Organization Science,* 2 (1), 71–87.

McKelvey, B. 1997: Quasi-natural organization science. *Organization Science,* 8 (4), 352–80.

Miles, R. E. and Snow, C. 1978: *Organizational strategy, structure, and process.* New York: McGraw-Hill.

Miles, R. E. and Snow, C. 1986: Organizations: new concepts for new forms. *California Management Review,* 28 (3), 62–73.

Miles, R. E. and Snow, C. 1994: *Fit, failure, and the hall of fame: how companies succeed or fail.* New York: Free Press.

Miller, D. and Chen, M. 1994: Sources and consequences of competitive inertia: a study of the U.S. airline industry. *Administrative Science Quarterly,* 39, 1–23.

Mitzberg, H. 1979: *The structuring of organizations: a synthesis of the research.* Englewood Cliffs, NJ: Prentice-Hall.

Mintzberg, H. and Westley, F. 1992: Cycles of organizational change. *Strategic Management Journal,* 13, 39–59.

Mollona, E. and Noda, T. 2001: Revisiting the role of a visible hand in the intra-organizational ecology of organizational change. Paper presented at the SMS Mini-Conference "Shaping, Implementing and Changing Strategies," St Gallen: Switzerland.

Nelson, R. R. and Winter, S. G. 1982: *An evoluntionary theory of economic change.* Cambridge, MA: Harvard University Press.

Nonaka, I. and Takeuchi, H. 1995: *The Knowledge-creating company.* New York: Oxford University Press.

Nonaka, I., Toyama, R. and N. Konno, 2000: SECI, Ba and Leadership: a unified model of dynamic knowledge creation, *Long Range Planning,* 33, 5–34.

O'Dell, C. and Grayson, C. J. 1998: If only we knew what we know: the identification and transfer of internal best practice. *California Management Review,* 40 (3), 154–75.

Penrose, E. 1959: *The theory of the growth of the firm.* London: Basil Blackwell.

Peters, T. J. and Waterman, R. H., Jr 1982: *In search of excellence.* New York: Warner Books.

Poole, M. S. and Van de Ven, A. H. 1989: Using paradox to build management and organization theories. *Academy of Management Review,* 14 (4), 562–78.

Prahalad, C. K. and Bettis, R. A. 1986: The dominant logic: a new linkage between diversity and performance. *Strategic Management Journal,* 7 (6), 485–501.

Prahalad, C. K. and Doz, Y. L. 1987: *The multinational mission: balancing local demands and global vision*. New York: The Free Press.

Prahalad, C. K. and Hamel, G. 1990: The core competence of the corporation. *Harvard Business Review*, 68, 79–91.

Quinn, J. B. 1985: Managing innovation: Controlled chaos. *Harvard Business Review*, 63 (3), 78–84.

Rosenberg, N. 1972: *Technology and American economic growth*. New York: Harper Torch Books.

Schumpeter, J. A. 1934: *The theory of economic development*. Cambridge, MA: Harvard University Press.

Selznick, P. 1957: *Leadership in administration: a sociological interpretation*. New York: Harper and Row.

Senge, P. 1990: The leader's new work: building learning organizations. *Sloan Management Review*, 32(1), 7–23.

Spender, J. C. 1980: Strategy making in business. University of Manchester, doctoral dissertation.

Teece, D. J., Pisano, G., and Shuen, A. 1997: Dynamic capabilities and strategic management. *Strategic Management Journal*, 18 (7), 509–33.

Teece, D. J., Rumelt, R., Dosi, G., and Winter, S. 1994: Understanding corporate coherence: theory and evidence. *Journal of Economic Behavior and Organization*, 23 (1), 1–30.

Thompson, J. D. 1967: *Organizations in action: social science bases of administrative theory*. New York: McGraw-Hill.

Tushman, M. L. and Anderson, P. 1986: Technological discontinuities and organizational environments. *Administrative Science Quarterly*, 31, 439–65.

Tushman, M. L. and O'Reilly, C. A. 1996: The ambidextrous organization. *California Management Review*, 38 (4), 8–30.

Vaill, P. 1982: The purposing of high performing systems. *Organization Dynamics*, autumn, 23–40.

Van Cauwenberg, A. and Cool, K. 1982: Strategic management in a new framework. *Strategic Management Journal*, 3, 245–64.

Van de Ven, A. H. and Grazman, D. N. 1999: Evolution in a nested hierarchy: a genealogy of twin cities health care organizations, 1853–1995. In J. A. C. Baum and B. McKelvey (eds), *Variations in organization science: in honor of Donald T. Campbell*. London: Sage, 185–209.

Van de Ven, A. H. and Poole, M. S. 1995: Explaining development and change in organizations. *Academy of Management Review*, 20 (3), 510–40.

Volberda, H. W. 1996: Toward the flexible form: how to remain vital in hypercompetitive environments. *Organization Science*, 7 (4), 359–74.

Volberda, H. W. 1998: *Building the flexible firm: how to remain competitive*. Oxford: Oxford University Press.

Volberda, H. W., Baden-Fuller, C., and Van den Bosch, F. A. J. 2001a: Mastering strategic renewal: mobilizing renewal journeys in multi-unit Firms. *Long-Range Planning*, 34 (2), 159–78.

Volberda, H. W., Van den Bosch, F. A. J., Flier, B., and Gedajlovic, E. R. (2001b). Following the herd or not? Patterns of renewal in the Netherlands and the UK. *Long Range Planning*, 34 (2), 209–29.

Weick, K. E. 1979: *The social psychology of organizing*. Reading, MA: Addison-Wesley.

Wernerfelt, B. 1984: A Resource-based view of the firm. *Strategic Management Journal*, 5, 171–80.

Wooldridge, B. and Floyd, S. W. 1990: The strategy process, middle management involvement and organizational performance. *Strategic Management Journal*, 11, 231–41.

CHAPTER ELEVEN

Shaping, Implementing, and Changing Strategy: Opportunities and Challenges

Bala Chakravarthy, Guenter Mueller-Stewens, Peter Lorange, Christoph Lechner

In today's turbulent business environment, where the challenge for managers is to catch a "business reality that is in flight," this field devoted to the shaping, implementing and changing of strategy is central to business performance. Answering the fundamental questions of the field is essential to the growth and adaptation of firms, and for determining their success or failure over time. We have presented in chapter 1 a framework for structuring the many research questions in the field and for answering them more effectively. The chapters that followed have illustrated this more modular approach to research. In this concluding chapter, we step back from our journey and explore some of the fundamental shifts we will have to make as researchers in order to produce more useful knowledge for the practitioner.

The Central Tasks of Managers

The central tasks of managers are in the discovery or creation of new business opportunities, accumulation of distinctive resources, and the successful exploitation of the two. Each chapter in this book has tried to help in these tasks by describing how a firm's purpose, organizational context, decision/action/learning processes can help both in the *exploration* for new opportunities and resources and in their *exploitation*.

We have primarily focused our attention in this book on organic growth. Surely, alliances and mergers and acquisitions (M&A) can add to or strengthen a firm's competitive position and competence platform; and also help in their exploitation. We have only one paper on this theme in our book (chapter 9). Clearly, more work is needed in this area. But an external solution will be fruitful only if there are complementarities of interests with the external partner (Doz and Hamel, 1998) or if the proposed acquisition/merger can be consummated on favourable terms (Haspeslagh and Jemison, 1991). Regardless of whether a firm uses internal or external means, its top management will have to pay continuous attention to six activities (see figure 11.1):

1 scanning the firm's business context to reset its purpose proactively,
2 aligning the organizational context to its purpose,
3 ensuring a firm's organizational context does lead to the proper action and decision premises,
4 realizing the desired competitive positions and competence platforms so as to exploit the firm's business context effectively,
5 influencing the firm's financial valuation both by producing the desired performance and by managing the expectation around it,
6 learning from the firm's financial valuation what needs to be modified in its actions/decisions, organizational context and purpose.

We need a deeper understanding of how each activity can be managed better, and how each is linked to the overall process of shaping, implementing, and changing strategy. While this book illustrates how this effort can be undertaken, a lot more needs to be done.

As Volberda and Baden-Fuller argue in chapter 10, the relative roles in the strategy process for top management as well as all other managers in a firm can differ depending on the renewal path that is chosen. But by and large, senior executives in a multibusiness today are faced with the following recurring dilemmas:

1 How do you draw from the firm's legacy and yet not make it an obstacle in competing for the future?
2 How do you commit to specific strategies and resources, and yet retain the flexibility to walk away from them?
3 How do you manage to be both externally and internally fitted?
4 How do you work towards innovation and still enhance productivity?
5 How do you provide empowerment without abdicating control?
6 How do you compete and cooperate with your partners, at the same time?

Balance these and other related dilemmas requires new knowledge. The reductionism that has characterized our research to date on strategy process will not help in the building of this new knowledge. We need new theories and new methods.

New Theories

Recall from the preface to this book that practitioners complain not about too much theory but actually about the paucity of good (and therefore useful) theories in our field. Theory development is an urgent need.

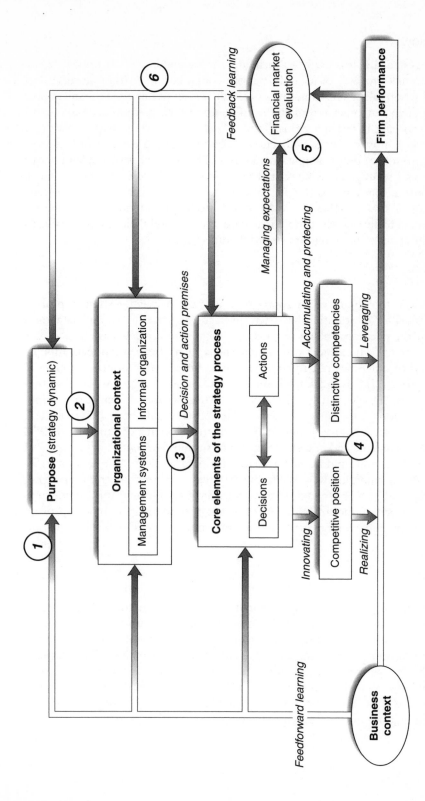

Figure 11.1 An integrative framework
Source: Adapted from Chakravarthy and White, 2001

What to Study?

We have suggested that it is useful to focus the theory building effort on the "every day organizational process" of idea generation, communication, learning, decision-making, and action taking and examining both the impact of this basic organizational process on strategy outcomes as well on the influence that a firm's purpose and organizational context have in reshaping this process. Such a focus would have at least two advantages. First, most decisions and actions follow routinized patterns of behavior, which are the result of past strategic orientations. The often-heard complaint about the failure of new strategies may be related to the inability of these strategies to move "beyond words and intents" and make a dent on the basic organizational process. Second, issues of strategic change would automatically get attention, since the researcher will have to answer why certain managerial actions and their timing are able to fundamentally alter the ongoing process, while others fail.

Unit of Analysis

A related issue is the choice of an appropriate unit of analysis for strategy process research. While a lot of attention has been given in the literature to understanding decisions and the decision-making process, the focus on decisions has also led to a narrowing of the field. It excludes other phenomena such as expost rationalization or the realization of outcomes not through decisions but through a more subtle and complicated process. It fails to acknowledge that actions often trigger decisions or that decisions are just one element in a long chain of organizational events, sometimes fizzling out without having any major impact. An alternative unit of analysis is needed. Focusing on strategic initiatives is one such productive approach (Birkinshaw, 1997). These initiatives launched in order to create or sustain competitive advantage and can originate in the top, middle or lower management levels of a firm, both in an intended or slowly emerging way. While the "strategy of a firm" is a rather general, difficult to observe concept, strategic initiatives are more easily observable. As concrete undertakings – such as the introduction of a new technology, the build-up of an e-business or entry into a foreign market – initiatives provide a well-defined focal point for research.

Perspective

Strategy process research is heavily dominated by the assumption of an existing *subject–objection–relation*. Researchers are mostly concerned with how an individual or a group – such as the top management team – communicated its intentions to the rest of the organization, or how, for example, middle management introduces its point of view to the top. Strategy formation is not considered a relational, collective phenomenon, but as a transparent process in which the source of input and the purpose connected to it is clear. Such methodological individualism leads to shortcomings in the understanding of how strategies are shaped.

Table 11.1 Overview of the chapters

	2 Cuervo-Cazurra	3 Siggelkow	4 Schnatterly/Maritan	5 Camillus	6 Schwarz	7 Narayanan et al.	8 Wielemaker et al.	9 Lyles et al.	10 Volberda/Baden-Fuller
Research stream	A Longitudinal content research		B Linking organizational context to firm performance		C Interaction between organizational context and process elements			D Interplay of Context/Process/Outcomes	
Research question	How do a firm's resources and activities (competitive position) co-evolve?	How is a firm's internal fit adapted to changes in its external environment?	How do features of a firm's organizational context and its resources impact its financial market valuation?	What are the few necessary features that all superior planning systems must have?	What is the impact of shared beliefs on strategic decision making?	What is the impact of managerial processes on capability formation?	How does the organizational context for an initiative vary with its development phase?	What is the relationship between learning/unlearning and the four survival taxonomies for an IJV?	How do large multiunit firms renew?
Methodology	Four cases, each in three different industries: paper, petroleum, and construction in Argentina and Spain. Language process method	A longitudinal case study of Liz Claiborne using archival data and field interviews	Thirty-eight matched pairs of companies with average and high M/B ratios. Qualitative data collection (SEC); discriminant analysis	Questionnaire and interviews in 22 high and 80 average performing companies	Longitudinal study of belief systems and decision-making in a European multinational firm	Longitudinal study of six projects in Marion Merrell Dow (MMD) on how fast-cycle capability was built in that firm	A field study on the conditioning and creation of 25 initiatives across three large Dutch companies with differing organizational contexts	A survey of 335 IJVs in Hungary, followed by multinomial logit analysis. Follow-up case studies on four IJVs in Hungary	Conceptual study
Study layout	Describes how resources (along 8 dimensions) and activities (along 3 dimensions) co-evolve	Addresses how a tight fit among a firm's activities affects its ability to react to external changes	Proposes three types of intangible assets: resources, management systems, and governance mechanisms	Suggests a four-phase process to study all planning systems	Examines the reciprocal relationship between shared beliefs and strategic decision process	Develops a six-stage model of capability formation	Proposes a three-phase development process and 4 context categories	Classifies four survival categories and measures their learning/unlearning characteristics	Describes three generic renewal journeys and four co-evolutionary paths
Link to firm performance	Adaptation	Market valuation	Market/book ratio	"Best practice" in the eyes of experts	—	—	—	Firm survival	Firm survival
Theoretical perspective	Resource- and activity-based	Activity-based view	Resource-based view	Normative theory	Social constructivist	Social constructivist	Contingency theory	Knowledge management	Evolutionary theory

Borrowing from Sister Disciplines

When it comes to analyzing collective phenomena, social science and organizational theories offer a rich repertoire of frameworks that are rarely applied in strategy process research. Recent approaches, using systems theory (Luhmann, 1991), structuration theory (Giddens, 1984), or discourse analyses (Foucault, 1971), are likely to be of particular relevance. They deal with issues essential to the field of strategy process research, such as complexity and ambiguity, the reciprocal relationship of structure and action, organizational practice, and mechanisms of discourse. Also, research on the role of trust, social and intellectual capital or the significance of intra- and inter-organizational networks are of great salience to strategy process research. The studies included in this book have applied different theoretical frames to study the phenomenon (See table 11.1). This is healthy, but more can be done to absorb ideas from other disciplines. For example, perhaps psychology can help us better understand the intra-personal creative process through which new opportunities are discovered, social psychology, how members within an organization share resources and forge a common strategy and philosophy, how leaders deal with dilemmas.

Core Questions

Chakravarthy and Doz (1992) noted that strategy process research was anchored in multiple disciplines. The purpose of providing an integrative framework here (see figure 11.1) is to invite scholars from these disciplines to work on *strategy* problems. It is the context in which they do their research, which should define their work as a contribution to the strategy process field. We consider the following questions to be particularly relevant in this regard:

◆ *Emergence and coherence*: What are the collective phenomena that shape strategy? How does coherence of cognition, communication, and action occur and evolve in the process of strategy formation? How do they interact? Where and why does friction between them occur? What effects does this have? When do situations occur where companies first act and in a second step retrospectively reflect and decide? What roles do timing and sequence play in this process?
◆ *Protagonists and observers*: Who are the major protagonists in the process of strategy formation and how do they interact? How do external observers (such as financial analysts or competitors) influence the process? What effects do professional service providers, such as consultants, have? How does the knowledge transfer from theory to practice take place? How are strategic manoeuvres dispersed in an industry?
◆ *Discourses*: Which discourses take place? Which modes of argumentation are allowed, which ones excluded? How do legitimizing- and justification-procedures change? Are there different "rationalities"? What happens when high ambiguity prevails? How is social reality constructed here? What happens in cases of crises or radical environmental changes?
◆ *Success standards*: What influence do success standards have on strategy formation? Which standards of success do protagonists focus on? How do these standards

change over time? What happens in case a firm's stakeholders differ on the standards of success?

New Methods

Patterns of Action and Decision: Illusion or Reality?

The distinction between "*deliberate*" and "*emergent*" aspects of strategy making raises an important methodological issue. While it is undoubtedly correct to say that the deliberate approach to strategy making, advocated by the classical process model, is rarely to be found, the sequential pattern of formulation and then implementation that it suggests is still followed by many firms. From our point of view, it is vital to integrate the observer's perspective in order to better understand the "who," "when," and "what" of a strategy, that is, who formulates, perceives, or describes a strategy and when does it take place? As Kirsch (1997) noted, what appears as an emergent strategy to a researcher may not be one at all, especially if the observed pattern exists only in the mind of the researcher. Also an "emergent" strategy may have been in essence "planned" by an individual, but he/she may have failed to forge an explicit consensus around it.

Recall the case, where a major consulting firm described the entry of the Japanese motorcycle firm Honda in the US as a deliberate strategy, aimed at harnessing the benefits of the experience curve. Subsequent investigation and interviewing of the involved managers painted a very different picture, viz. one of failure of the intended strategy, frustration, and incremental adaptation and muddling through to what eventually was a winning strategy (Pascale, 1984). Thus we have to be aware that observed strategy patterns are often a construction of managers, researchers or consultants of what they perceive, more a reflection of their conceptual lenses and less an accurate description of some ontological reality.

Getting closer to Reality

Providing valid data from the field is a particularly difficult challenge for strategy process researchers. The researchers whose work is reported in this book have relied on multiple sources of data to triangulate their observations. Several of them have also chosen to work as a research team for their study. Both of these approaches help in bringing greater validity to their observations. The other challenge for the researcher is the sheer complexity of the process. If our framework can be compartmentalized and the associated streams of research simplified, as we tried to do in our sorting of the nine studies reported in this book, we can research the process using a more modular approach. The six activity streams suggested earlier in this chapter (figure 11.1) are examples of what these modules or research sub-communities may look like.

But some of the researchers in this volume have suggested "co-evolution" as the proper theoretical anchor for studying strategy process. Will co-evolution negate the pursuit of a modular approach to research? If this were the case, research on strategy process can be very expensive, involving:

- ◆ multi-disciplinary teams,
- ◆ working together over long periods of time,
- ◆ interacting real time with the phenomenon, and
- ◆ using multi-disciplinary conceptual frames

We may have to look to new computer simulations and analytic modeling techniques to complement this mammoth field effort. But to build these models we would still need more robust theoretical building blocks.

Also, each process study must have a direct or indirect link to a strategy outcome and financial performance for it to be labeled strategy process research. The papers selected for this book are exemplary in this regard. Of course, it can be asked whether process cannot be a source of competitive advantage in and of itself. If we agree with Teece, Pisano, and Shuen (1997) then the only basis for sustainable competitive advantage is "dynamic capability" (for example, the ability to learn, to restructure a business, or to find a new strategic alignment). But unless this "dynamic capability" is shown to lead to sustained superior performance for the firm, it would be hard to argue that this is of any competitive advantage. Instead of concentrating only on financial outcome measures, more weight should be given to analysing which strategy processes lead to successful innovating, imitating, migrating or consolidating. By picking the appropriate intermediate performance variable, each study can contribute to the more complex causal link that ultimately leads to superior financial performance.

Conclusion

Recall we said that we were offering through this book a "living document" for progressively defining the strategy process field. The field focuses on one simple question: "*How are strategies shaped, implemented and changed?*" As Mintzberg and Waters (1985) have noted, realized strategy has both a planned and an emergent component; it covers both formulation and implementation. Of course, this envelopes a vast territory. We need subcommunities that can work on different aspects of the framework proposed here. But we must first agree on a framework. We would like active debates and discussions on how the framework proposed can be improved. The nine studies, which we present in this book, illustrate the framework; but they also provide the data with which to critique it. We now invite you to join us in revising this "living document."

References

Birkinshaw, J. (1997): Entrepreneurship in multinational corporations: the characteristics of subsidiary initiatives, *Strategic Management Journal*, 18 (3), 207–29.

Chakravarthy, B. and Doz, Y. 1992: Strategy process research: Focusing on corporate self-renewal, *Strategic Management Journal*, 13, 5–14.

Chakravarthy, B. and White, R. 2001: Strategy process: forming, implementing and changing strategies. In A. Pettigrew, H. Thomas, and R. Whittington (eds), *Handbook of Strategy and Management*. London: Sage, 182–205.

Doz, Y. L. and Hamel G. 1998: *Alliance advantage: the art of creating value through partnering*. Boston, MA: Harvard Business School Press.

Foucault, M. 1971: *L'ordre du discours*, Paris: Gallimard.

Giddens, A. 1984: *The constitution of society: outline of the theory of structuration*. Cambridge: Polity Press.

Haspeslagh, P. C. and Jemison, D. B. 1991: *Managing acquisitions: creating value through corporate renewal*. New York: Free Press.

Kirsch, W. 1997: *Wegweiser zur Konstruktion einer evolutionären Theorie der strategischen Führung*. Munich: Kirsch Verlag.

Luhmann, N. 1991: *Sociale Systeme: Grundriss einer allgemeinen Theorie*. Frankfurt am Main: Suhrkamp Verlag.

Mintzberg, H. and Waters, J. A. 1985: Of strategies, deliberate and emergent. *Strategic Management Journal*, 6, 257–72.

Pascale, R. T. 1984: Perspective on strategy: the real story behind Honda's success. *California Management Review*, May–June, 47–72.

Teece, D., Pisano, G., and Shuen, A. 1997: Dynamic capabilities and strategic management. *Strategic Management Journal*, 18 (7), 509–33.

Author Index

Page references for figures and tables are in italics; those within notes are followed by an n.

Abernathy, F. H.
  et al. (1995) 62
Abernathy, W. J.
  and Utterback (1975) 165
Agrawal, A. (2000) 79
  and Mandelker (1990) 82
Aharoni, Y. (1966) 17, 168
Alchian, A. A.
  and Demsetz (1972) 82
Almaney, A. (1974) 81
  and Lengal (1986) 81
  and Vishny (1986) 82
Amabile, T. M. (1988) 169, 174, 184
Ancona, D. G.
  and Caldwell (1990) 139
  and MacMillan (1990) 113
Anderson, D.
  et al. (1993) 82
Anderson, P.
  (1983) 175
  (1999a) 225
  (1999b) 225
Andrews, K. (1971) 1, 4
Angle, H. L.
  and Van de Ven (1989) 218
Ansoff, H. I.
  (1965) 18, 19, 43, 220
  (1991) 98, 104
Antal-Mokos, Z. (1998) 191
Argyris, C.
  and Schon (1978) 169, 223

Baden-Fuller, C. (1990) 82
  and Dean (1999) 221
  and Stopford (1991) 21
  and Stopford (1994) 170, 212, 223
Bain, J. (1956) 19
Bantel, K. A.
  and Jackson (1989) 110

Barnard, C. I. (1938) 220
Barnes, J. H. (1984) 113
Barnett, W. P.
  and Burgelman (1996) 22
  et al. (1994) 211, 218
Barney, J.
  (1986) 20, 77
  (1991) 20, 35, 43, 77, 140
Barr, P. S. (1998) 222
  et al. (1992) 222, 226
  and Huff (1997) 110, 112, 113, 114, 131
Bartlett, C. A.
  and Ghoshal (1989) 22
  and Ghoshal (1993) 166, 167, 168, 171, 174, 178, 184, 185, 219
Bartunek, J. M. (1984) 70
Baum, J. A. C. (1996) 208
  and Singh (1994) 40, 43, 210
Bazerman, M. H. (1998) 113
Beatty, R. P.
  and Zajac (1990) 82
Beer, M. R.
  et al. (1990) 222
Belkin, L. (1986) 54, 56
Bennis, W. G.
  and Biederman (1997) 137
Berger, P. L.
  and Luckmann (1966) 139
Better, N. (1992) 56, 57
Bettis, R. A.
  and Prahalad (1995) 222
Beyer, J.
  et al. (1997) 112
Bierly, P.
  and Chakrabarti (1996) 79
Birkenshaw, J. (1997) 138, 164, 165, 166, 168, 169, 171, 176, 185, 185n, 236
  and Hood (1998) 224

Birmingham, J. (1985)   56
Block, Z.
   and MacMillan (1993)   183
Bougon, M.
   et al. (1977)   111, 113
Boulding, K. E. (1956)   140
Boulton, R. E. S.
   et al. (2000)   77
Bower, J. L. (1970)   140, 165, 166, 167,
      168
   and Doz (1979)   139
   and Hout (1988)   138
Bratman, F. (1983)   55
Brown, S. L.
   and Eisenhardt (1998)   219, 225
Bruderer, E.
   and Singh (1996)   210
Burgelman, R. A.
   (1983)   137, 140, 146, 157, 164, 165,
      166, 167, 168, 174, 175, 176, 177,
      178, 183, 184, 185, 218, 219
   (1991)   184, 211
   (1994)   140, 142, 152, 157, 158, 161,
      211, 218
   (1996)   211
Burns, T.
   and Stalker (1961)   71, 89
Burt, R. S. (1992)   170
Byrne, D. (1971)   112
Byrne, J. (1982)   55

Calori, R.
   et al. (1997)   227
   et al. (2000)   223
Cameron, K. S.
   et al. (1987)   69
Camillus, J. C. (1982)   98
   et al. (1998)   97
Caminiti, S. (1994)   62
Campbell, A. (1999)   97
Campbell, D. (1969)   184
Campbell, D. T. (1994)   218
Cauwenberg, A. Van
   and Cool (1982)   167
Caves, R. E. (1977)   19
   and Porter, M. E. (1977)   19
Center for Quality of Management   28
Chaffee, E. E. (1985)   222
Chaganti, R.
   and Sambharya (1987)   110

Chakravarthy, B.
   and Doz (1992)   4, 4, 20, 97, 164, 238
   et al. (2002)   6
   and White (2001)   3, 4
   and White (2002)   71
Chandler, A.
   (1962)   6, 46, 167, 211, 220
   (1990)   18, 22
Chang, S. J. (1995)   137
Chatterjee, S.
   and Wernerfelt (1991)   32
Chattopadhyay, P.
   et al. (1999)   112, 114, 129
Chauvin, K. W.
   and Hirschey (1993)   77
Child, J.
   (1972)   209
   (1997)   209
   et al. (1997)   195
   and Markoczy (1993)   192
   and Yan (1998)   193
Clark, K. B. (1985)   223
   and Fujimoto (1991)   170
Cohen, W. M.
   and Levinthal (1990)   191, 194, 209
Collis, D. J.
   and Montgomery (1997)   23
Crossan, M. M.
   et al. (1999)   165, 169, 170, 171, 175
Crozier, M.
   and Friedberg (1980)   139
Cuervo-Cazurra, A.
   (1999)   28
   (2001)   29
Cyert, R. M.
   and March (1963)   139, 167, 168, 169,
      209

Daft, R. L.
   and Macintosh (1984)   81
   and Weick (1984)   112, 129
D'Aveni, R. A.
   and MacMillan (1990)   110
Davis, S. M.
   and Lawrence (1977)   156
Day, D.
   and Lord (1992)   110, 113, 127,
      131
Deal, T. E.
   and Kennedy (1982)   223

Dearborn, D.
  and Simon (1958) 111
DeBono, E. (1970) 170
DeCarolis, D. M.
  and Deeds (1999) 79
Demsetz, H. (1991) 170
  and Lehn (1985) 82
Deng, Z.
  et al. (1999) 79
Denison, D. R.
  et al. (1996) 137
Denzin, N. K.
  and Lincoln (1994) 178
Detert, J. R.
  et al. (2000) 28
Deveny, K. (1989) 57
Dierickx, I.
  and Cool (1989) 77
Dijksterhuis, M.
  et al. (1999) 222
DiMaggio, P. (1992) 170
  and Powell (1983) 209
D'Innocenzio, A. (1994) 62, 63
Dixit, A. K.
  and Pindyck (1997) 227
Dooley, K. J.
  and Van de Ven (1999) 214
Doz, Y. L.
  and Hamel (1998) 233
Drazin, R.
  et al. (1999) 169, 170, 171
  and Van de Ven (1985) 47

Eden, C.
  and Ackermann (1998) 113, 129
Eisenhardt, K. M. (1989) 18, 176, 178
  and Zbaracki (1992) 113
Ernst, M.
  et al. (1996) 192
Ettore, B. (1980) 55

Fahey, L. (1982) 139, 143
Falcione, R.
  et al. (1987) 112, 129
Fama, E. F. (1980) 82
  and Jensen (1983) 80, 82
Fast, N. D. (1979) 218
Ferris, S. P.
  et al. (1998) 82
Finkelstein, S.

  and Hambrick (1990) 110, 113
Fiol, C. M.
  (1989) 110, 113
  and Lyles (1985) 113, 130
Fiol, F. M.
  and Lyles (1985) 191, 210
Fiske, S. T.
  and Taylor (1991) 112
Floyd, S. W. (1996) 168
  and Wooldridge (1997) 140
  and Wooldridge (1999) 164, 165, 171, 174
Fombrun, C.
  and Shanley (1990) 80
Ford, C. M. (1996) 169
Ford, J. D.
  (1985) 62
Ford, R. C.
  and Randolph 156
Foucault, M. (1971) 238
Frederickson, J. W. (1984) 113
Freeman, J.
  Hannan and (1984) 52
  Crozier and (1980) 139
Fryxell, G. E.
  and Wand (1994) 80

Galbraith, J. R. (1973) 167, 169
Galunic, D. C.
  and Eisenhardt (1996) 211, 218
Garud, R.
  and Van de Ven (1992) 137
Garvin, D. A. (1998) 4
Gavetti, G.
  and Levinthal (2000) 70
George, E.
  and Narayanan (1999) 14
Geringer, J. M.
  and Hebert (1991) 195
Geroski, P.
  and Vlassopoulos (1991) 21
Gersick, C. J. G. (1991) 48
Ghoshal, S.
  and Bartlett (1994) 166, 184
  and Bartlett (1997) 139
  et al. (1994) 81
  and Nohria (1989) 81
Giddens, A. (1984) 238
Gilbert, M. (1989) 111, 130
Gilmore, W. S.
  and Camillus (1996) 98

Gioia, D. (1986) 112, 129
  and Chittipeddi (1991) 110, 114, 145, 158
  et al. (1994) 156
  and Sims (1986) 111
Glaser, B. G.
  and Strauss (1967) 114, 116, 161, 176
Glick, W. H.
  et al. (1990) 23
Gluck, F. W.
  and Foster (1975) 173
Glynn, M. A. (1996) 171
Golden, B. R. (1992) 152
Goold, M.
  and Campbell (1987) 217
Gould, R. V.
  and Fernandez (1989) 174
Granovetter, M.
  (1974) 170, 174
  (1985) 170
Grant, R. M.
  (1991) 141, 151
  (1995) 23
  (1996) 221, 223
  (1996a) 165
  (1996b) 165, 169, 170
  (1998) 151
  and Cibin (1996) 221
Gray, B.
  et al. (1985) 111
Grazman (1999) 43, 214
Greenwood, R.
  and Hinings (1996) 209
Greiner, L. E.
  and Bhambri (1989) 70
Griliches, Z. (1981) 79
Grinyer, P. H.
  et al. (1988) 222
Grundy, T.
  and Johnson (1993) 114
Gupta, A. K.
  and Govindarajan (1991) 81
Guth, W. D.
  and Ginsberg (1990) 223

Haas, P. M. (1992) 111
Hage, J.
  and Dewar (1972) 110
Hall, B.
  and Ziedonis (2001) 85

Hall, R. (1993) 80
Hambrick, D. C. (1988) 110
  et al. (1993) 111, 112
  and Mason (1984) 48, 110, 111, 112
Hammer, M.
  and Champy (1993) 7
Hammond, J. H. (1993) 63
Hannan, M. T.
  and Freeman (1984) 52
Harris, S. G. (1994) 111
Hart, S. (1992) 4
Hass, N. (1992) 54, 57
Haas, P. M. (1992) 130
Hage, J.
  and Dewar (1972) 113
Hambrick, D. C.
  and Mason (1984) 113
Hamel, G.
  and Prahalad (1989) 220
Hanan, M. (1969) 167, 169
Hannan, M. T.
  and Freeman (1977) 209
Hansen, G.
  and Wernerfelt (1989) 195
Hargadon, A. B.
  (1998a) 169, 174, 178, 184
  (1998b) 165, 174, 178, 184
Hart, S. L. (1992) 19
Haspeslagh, P. C.
  and Jemison (1991) 233
Hatcher, L.
  et al. (1989) 81
Hauenstein, N.
  and Foti (1989) 111
Hayes, R. H.
  and Jaikumar (1988) 52
Hedberg, B.
  (1981) 113, 130, 210
Hedlund, G.
  (1986) 224
  (1994) 170, 184
Helfat, C. E.
  and Raubitschek (2000) 137, 157
Henderson, R.
  and Cockburn (1994) 79
Henderson, R. M. (1993) 69
  and Clark (1990) 69, 165, 168, 209
Hill, C. W. L.
  and Snell (1989) 82

Hitt, M. A.
  et al. (1999)   138
  and Tyler (1991)   110, 113, 130, 131
Hodgkinson, G. P.
  and Johnson (1994)   111, 113
Hofer, C. W.
  and Schendel (1978)   220
Holderness, C. G.
  and Sheehan (1988)   82
Hoskisson, R. E.
  et al. (1993)   81
Hosmer, D. W. Jr
  (1997)   21
  and Lameshow (1989)   85
Hrebiniak, L. G.
  and Joyce (1985)   210
Huber, G. P. (1991)   169-70
Huff, A. S.
  (1982)   111
  (1990)   110
  and Reger (1987)   3, 4, 113
Hunt, P. (1966)   168
Hurst, D. K.
  et al. (1986)   223
Huygens, M.
  et al. (2001)   226

Inkpen, A.
  and Choudhury (1995)   1
Ireland, R.
  et al. (1987)   111
Itami, H. (1987)   23

Jaikumar, R. (1986)   46
Janis, I. L.
  and King (1954)   112
Johnson, G. (1988)   222
Johnson, R. A.
  et al. (1993)   82

Kanter, R. M.
  (1983)   223
  (1986)   167, 170
  (1988)   166, 171
  (1989)   164
Kanzanjian, R. K.
  and Rao (1999)   164, 165
Kauffman, S. A. (1993)   48
Kawakita, J. (1991)   28
Kearns, D. T.

  and Nadler (1993)   152
Kelly, G. (1955)   111, 130
Khandwalla, P. N.
  (1973)   47
  (1977)   210
Khun, T. (1970)   130
Kim, L. (1998)   137
Kimberly, J. R. (1979)   218
Kirsch, W. (1997)   2, 3, 239
Klepper, S.
  and Simons (2000)   137
Koestler, A. (1981)   170
Kogut, B.
  and Zander (1992)   170
Kosnik, R. D. (1990)   82
Kotter, J. P.
  and Hesketh (1992)   222
Krackhardt, D.
  and Kilduff (1991)   112
Kuhn, T. (1970)   111
Kulik, C. T.
  and Ambrose (1992)   112

Lane, P.
  et al. (2001)   192, 193, 195
Lant, T.
  et al. (1992)   70-1, 113
  and Mezias (1990)   210
  and Mezias (1992)   70
Lawrence, P. R.
  and Lorsch (1967)   46
Learned, E.
  et al. (1961)   46
  et al. (1969)   209
Lechner, C.
  and Mueller-Stewens (2000)   4
Leonard-Barton, D.
  (1990)   22, 142, 178
  (1992)   138
Lev, B.
  (1999)   77
  and Sougiannis (1996)   77
  and Sougiannis (1999)   77
  and Zarowin (1999)   77
Levinthal, D.
  (1992)   52
  (1997)   46, 48, 208, 210
  and March (1993)   208, 211, 212
  and Myatt (1994)   43
  and Siggelkow (2001)   50

Levitt, B.
  and March (1988)   52, 169
Lewin, A. Y.
  and Volberda (1999)   208, 209, 210,
    211, 225, 226
Liao, T. F. (1994)   196
Liebeskind, J. P.
  et al. (1996)   216
Lippman, S. A.
  and Rumelt (1982)   42
Lorange, P.
  and Vancil (1977)   220
Lord, R.
  and Foti (1986)   112
Lorenzoni, G.
  and Baden-Fuller (1995)   227
Lovas, B.
  and Ghoshal (2000)   40, 43, 165,
    184
Lucas, L. M.
  and Ogilvie (1999)   113, 130
Luhmann, N. (1991)   238
Lyles, M. A. (1998)   191, 202
  and Salk (1996)   192, 193, 195, 205

MacDuffie, J. P. (1995)   46
McGrath, R. G. (1995)   166, 167
  et al. (1995)   164
McKelvey, B. (1997)   211, 226
MacMillan, I. G. (1985)   219
McPhee, R. D. (1990)   22
Mahoney, J. T.
  and Pandian (1992)   79
Maljers, F.
  et al. (1996)   224
March, J. G. (1991)   111, 208, 211
Markoczy, L. (1997)   111
Martin, P. Y.
  and Turner (1986)   114
Martinez, J. I.
  and Jarillo (1989)   81
Melone, N. P. (1994)   110, 113, 131
Merton, R. K. (1958)   89
Meyer, C.
  (1993)   138, 144, 156
Miles, M.
  and Huberman (1984)   177
Miles, R. E.
  and Snow (1978)   71, 209
  and Snow (1986)   219, 227

  and Snow (1994)   210
Milgrom, P. R.
  and Roberts (1990)   46, 50, 58
  and Roberts (1995)   46
Miller, C. C.
  et al. (1998)   113
Miller, D.
  (1986)   47, 166
  (1993)   48
  (1994)   48, 62
  (1996)   50, 71
  and Chen (1994)   209
  and Friesen (1982)   52
  and Friesen (1984)   47, 52
  et al. (1996)   48
  and Shamsie (1996)   79
Miller, J. G. (1972)   169
Milliken, F. J. (1990)   48, 62
  and Lant (1991)   48, 63
Minsky, M. (1975)   111
Mintzberg, H.
  (1973)   139
  (1979)   71, 210
  (1994)   2
  et al. (1976)   113
  and Westley (1992)   219
Mizruchi, M. S. (1983)   82
Mollona, E.
  and Noda (2001)   226
Moorman, C. (1995)   170
Mowery, D. C.
  et al. (1996)   194
Murmann, J. P.
  and Tushman (1997)   48

Nadler, D. A.
  et al. (1994)   47
Nandhakumar, J.
  and Jones (1997)   115
Narayanan, V. K.
  (1993)   161
  (2001)   151
  and Fahey (1982)   139, 143, 161
  and Fahey (1990)   110, 113
  and Kemmerer (2001)   139
Narin, F. (2000)   83, 85
Nelson, R. R.
  and Winter (1982)   209
Noda, T.
  and Bower (1996)   139

Nohria, N.
  and Ghoshal (1997)   166
Nonaka, I.
  (1991)   169, 170, 171, 185n
  (1994)   169
  et al. (2000)   221
Nonaka, I. (*cont'd*)
  and Takeuchi (1994)   113
  and Takeuchi (1995)   165, 174,
    225
Norburn, D.
  and Birley (1988)   110
Numagami, T. (1998)   175
Nystrom, P. C.
  and Starbuck (1984)   48

O'Dell, C.
  and Grayson (1998)   220, 221

Pakes, A. (1985)   79
Park, C. S.
  and Srinivasan (1994)   77
Parkhe, A. (1991)   113, 130
Parson, T. (1960)   167
Pascale, R. T. (1984)   152, 239
Pennings, J. M. (1987)   46
Penrose, E. (1959)   18, 19, 32, 38, 42, 43,
    209
Peteraf, M. A. (1993)   20, 77, 79
Peters, T. J.
  and Waterman (1982)   167, 218
Pettigrew, A.
  (1987)   48, 176
  (1990)   114, 176, 177
  (1992)   4, 20, 115, 116
Pfeffer, J. (1981)   139, 140
Pierce, J. L.
  and Branyiczki (1997)   193
  et al. (1991)   81
Pinches, G. E.
  et al. (1996)   159
Pinchot, G. III (1985)   166
Pinfield, L. (1986)   175
Polanyi, M. (1966)   169
Pondy, I. R.
  and Mitroff (1979)   140
Poole, M. S.
  and Van de Ven (1989)   208, 211
Porter, M. E.
  (1980)   18, 19, 23, 43

  (1985)   18, 19
  (1991)   6, 19, 20
  (1995)   47
  (1996)   46
  and Rivkin (1998)   46
Prahalad, C. K.
  (1975)   8
  and Bettis (1986)   222
  and Doz (1987)   22, 184, 221, 224
  and Hamel (1990)   220
Press, S. J.
  and Wilson (1978)   85
Priem, P. I. (1994)   110, 113, 127, 131

Quelch, J.
  et al. (1987)   167
Quinn, J. B.
  (1980)   98, 139
  (1985)   184, 218

Raff, D. M. G. (2000)   137
Rajagopalan, N.
  et al. (1993)   97, 112
Reger, R.
  et al. (1994)   157
  and Huff (1987)   113
Rivkin, J. W. (2000)   46, 48
  and Siggelkow (2002)   71
Romanelli, E.
  and Tushman (1994)   48
Rosenberg, N. (1972)   209
Rosenkopf, L.
  and Tushman (1994)   35, 40, 43
Rumelhart, D. (1980)   111

Salancik, G. R.
  and Pfeffer (1978)   112, 129
Sanchez, R.
  and Mahoney (1996)   113, 130
Scapens, R. W. (1990)   131
Schmalensee, R. (1985)   185
Schon, D. (1963)   169, 174, 184
Schumpeter, J. A. (1934)   223
Schuster, M. (1984)   81
Schwandt, T. A. (1997)   139
Schwarz, M.
  and Nandhakumar (1999)   113, 115, 129
Schwenk C. R.
  (1984)   110, 113, 131
  (1995)   110, 113

Scott, W. R. (1995)   194
Selznick, P. (1957)   220, 223
Senge, P. (1990)   223
Sharma, S.
  and Vredenburg (1998)   21
Shiba, S.
  et al. (1993)   28
Shleifer, A.
  and Vishny (1986)   82
Shrivastva, P. (1983)   113, 130
Silverman, D. (1993)   115
Simon, H. A.
  (1947)   168
  (1960)   175
  (1973)   169
Simons, R.
  (1994)   167, 185n
Singh, J. V.
  et al. (1986)   52
Skolnik, R. (1985)   57
Smith, K. G.
  et al. (1994)   110, 112
Song, I. (1982)   110
Spender, J. C.
  (1980)   223
  (1996)   171
  and Grant (1996)   113, 130
Sproull, I. S. (1981)   111
Srinivasan, V. (1994)   77
Starbuck, W. H.
  and Milliken (1988)   110, 112
Steensma, K.
  and Lyles (2000)   193, 194
Steiner, G. A. (1969)   97
Straus, A.
  and Corbin (1990)   114, 116
Suchman, M. C. (1995)   52
Sworder, C. (1995)   113
Szwajkowski, E.
  and Figlewicz (1999)   80

Technology Review, (2001)   83
Teece, D. J.
  (1998)   77
  et al. (1994)   210, 219
  et al. (1997)   138, 140, 141, 157, 209
  et al. (1997)   42, 240
Tetlock, P. (1983)   112
Thomas, J.
  et al. (1993)   110, 113 , 127

and McDaniel (1990)   112
Thomson, J. D. (1967)   210
Tosi, H. L. Jr
  and Gomez-Mejia (1989)   82
Toulan, O. (1997)   26
Traub, J.
  and Newman (1985)   55
Tripsas, M.
  and Gavetti (2000)   137
Tsoukas, H. (1996)   169, 170
Tushman, M. L.
  and Anderson (1986)   223
  et al. (1986)   48, 166
  and O'Reilly (1996)   219, 225
  and Romanelli (1985)   47, 48
  and Rosenkopf (1996)   48

Vaill, P. (1982)   223
Van Cauwenberg, A.
  and Cool (1982)   220
Van de Ven, A. H.
  (1992)   18, 20, 152, 186n
  and Garud (1994)   40, 43
  and Grazman (1999)   226
  and Huber (1990)   139
  and Poole (1990)   23
  and Poole (1995)   71, 214, 220
Vaughan, D. (1996)   72
Vaughn Blankenship, L.
  and Miles (1968)   167–8
Venkataraman, S.
  et al. (1992)   169
Virany, B.
  et al. (1992)   71
Volberda, H. W.
  (1996)   176, 208, 223
  (1998)   176, 212, 223
  et al. (2001)   226
von der Heijden, K. (1996)   113, 129
von Krogh, G. et al. (1997)   113, 130
Voska, C. (1997)   200

Walker, G. (1985)   111, 112
Waller, M.
  et al. (1995)   112
Walsh, J.
  (1988)   111, 112, 113, 131
  (1995)   110, 111
  et al. (1988)   110

Warner, J. B.
 et al. (1988) 82
Watts, R. L.
 and Zimmerman (1990) 82
Watts, W. (1967) 112
Watzlawick
 et al. (1974) 70
Weick, K. (1995) 112, 129, 145
 and Bougon (1986) 111
Weick, K. E.
 (1976) 47
 (1979) 216, 222
 (1991) 170
 (1995) 3
Weisbach, M. S. (1988) 82
Welbourne, T. M.
 et al. (1995) 81
Wernerfelt, B. (1984) 18, 19, 43, 209
Westhoff, F. H.
 et al. (1996) 48
Wheelwright, S.
 and Clark (1992) 173
Whetten, D. A. (1984) 145

Wiersema, M. F.
 and Bantel (1992) 110
Williamson, O. E. (1975) 167
Willke, H. (1993) 3
Womack, J. P.
 et al. (1990) 51
Woodman, R. W.
 et al. (1993) 169, 171
Wooldridge, B.
 and Floyd (1990) 223
Wortman, C.
 and Linsenmeier (1977) 112
Wright, S. (1932) 48

Yin, R.
 (1984) 142, 175, 178
 (1989) 131
 (1994) 18

Zahra, S. A.
 et al. (1999) 164, 165, 166, 169, 171,
 185n
Zajac, E. J.
 and Bazerman (1991) 52

Subject Index

Page references for figures and tables are in italics.

actions
  and shared beliefs   113
  and strategic planning   107
actions (managerial) and organizational
    capability building   137
activities (management), integrative
    framework   235
activity choices   47
American Productivity and Quality Center
    (APQC)   98, 99
Argentina
  construction firms in   22, 28
  paper firms in   22, 26–8
  petroleum firms in   22, 26
Auto Parts   199, 203
axial coding   116

balance of firm
  and co-evolutionary perspective   212
  and managerial behavior   226
behavioral theory of the firm   209
belief patterns, emergence of   119–21, *120*
belief systems
  and fast-cycle capability   146, 156
  and initiatives   167
beliefs (executive) and strategic decision
    process   110–11, 112, 113–14
beliefs (individual)   111, 128–30
  see also shared beliefs; executive beliefs
Boxer, Leonard   55, 58

capabilities and competitive advantage   138
capability building   140–1, 148–51, *149–50*
  capability retention in   147–8
  and fast-cycle projects   142, 143–8
  social construction   140–1, 156–7
  temporal nature of   140
case studies
  construction firms in Argentina   22, 28
  construction firms in Spain   22, 28

firms in transitional economy   192–205
initiative development in three
    firms   176–83, *177*
Liz Claiborne   53–67
multinational (European)   114–16
paper firms in Argentina   22, 26–8
paper firms in Spain   22, 26–8
petroleum firms in Argentina   22, 26
petroleum firms in Spain   22, 26
pharmaceutical company (US)   142–51
Charron, Paul   54, 65, 66, 67, 73
Chazen, Jerome   55, 56, 57, 72
choices
  and competitive position   61
  and environmental change   62–5, 69–70
  and fit   46–7, 51–2, 61, 63, 69
  and management   52, 55–8, *59*, 65–7,
    68
  and performance of firm   46, 69
  and shared beliefs   113
CMS *see* critical mass of supporters
co-evolutionary perspective
  and balance of firm   212
  and competitive advantage   19–20, 41–2
  and environment of firm   21
  resources and scope   40–1, *42*, 42–3
  strategy process research   239–40
  see also macro-co-evolution; micro-co-
    evolution
co-evolutionary process   14, 19, 208
competitive advantage   18–19, 20, 21, 28,
    42
  and capabilities   151
  and environmental change   21–2, 46–7
  and fit   46
  and transformation process   20, 21, 28,
    38–42
  in transitional economy   192
  and multiunit firm   208
content–context analysis   84–5

control systems (management) in initiative
     development   170–1, 172, 182
creativity in organizational learning in
     transitional economy   204–5
critical mass of supporters (CMS)   117–18,
     124, 126, 127, 129, 131

"different believers" see shared belief system
     debates
diffusion of routines in fast-cycle
     capability   146–7
Eastman Kodak   219
environment   110, 117, 118–19, 210
   and competitive advantage   21–2, 46–7
   and executive beliefs   110, 112, 117
   and fit   164
   and issue identification   104
   and management in multiunit firms   226
   and resources   21, 35, 78–80
   and shared belief development   118–19
environmental change   21–2, 62, 69
   and competitive advantage   46–7
   and fit   48, 50–2, 51, 69–70
   at Liz Claiborne   47, 61–5, 69
   and performance landscape   50, 69, 71
environmental forces and inertia   48
Ericsson   176, 178, 179, 180, 181, 182–3
evolutionary theory of economic
     change   209
executive beliefs
   and environment   110, 112, 117
   and firm performance   110, 112
   influences on   112, 117
   and organizational processes   110
   and strategic choices   110
   and strategic decision process   110–11,
     112, 113–14
exploration/exploitation and survival of
     firm   211, 212, 214

fast-cycle capability building   142, 143–8
   and knowledge   147
   and learning   146–7, 153–5
   and sensegiving   145
   and sensemaking   145
fast-cycle process
   activation stage   143–4
   articulation stage   144
   and belief systems   146, 156
   cognitive elements   155

and diffusion of routines   146–7
   implementation stage   145–6
   mobilization stage   144–5
   project teams   139
   and senior management   144
FDA   142, 143, 151, 156
fit   46
   and competitive advantage   46
   and organizational inertia   47, 69, 70
   and value chain   59, 68
   see also fit (internal) and fit (external)
fit (external) and environmental
     conditions   47, 69
   at Liz Claiborne   60–1
fit (internal)   46, 47
   and activities   47
   and environment   69
   at Liz Claiborne   58–60, 67
Ford mass-production system   50, 52

governance (high-level)   80, 82, 84, 89–90
governance (operational-level)   80, 81, 84,
     87–9, 91
governance mechanisms   78, 80–2, 86,
     90–1
   and competitive advantage   80
grounded theory   114, 116, 152

Hewlett Packard   219
hierarchical renewal   208, 220–1
holistic renewal   208, 222–4
"Homo Sovieticus"   201, 203
Hong Kong Productivity Council
     (HKPC)   98, 99
Housing Products   199, 202–3, 204, 205

IBM   219
ICI   217
inertia   48
   and capability-building   155–6, 157
   and fit   48
initiative development
   and conditioning perspective   165,
     166–9, 171
   an integrative framework   171–5, 172
   and knowledge-creating perspective   165,
     169–71
   and knowledge-creation   165–6
initiatives, research   164–5
initiatives and organizational

conditions   166–9, 172, 173, *173*
innovation in organizational learning in
    transitional economy   204–5
institutional context *see* environment
intangible assets
    and competitive advantage   90
    and market-to-book value of firm   78
    and value creation   77–8, 90
Intel   218
issue evaluation in strategic planning
    process   104–5
issue generation in strategic planning
    process   104
issues and environment   104
issues (management) and strategic planning
    process   108

Japanese lean manufacturing system   50, 51,
    52, 63
Johnson & Johnson   219

KJ method   28
KLM Cargo   176, 178, 180, 181, 182
knowledge   234
    and fast-cycle capability building   147
    and initiative development   172, 173,
        174–5, 181–2, 184
    and naive selection   216
    in transitional economy   192, 202
    in multiunit firm   214
knowledge-creating process   169–71

language process method *see* KJ method
lean mass production system *see* Ford mass-
    production system
learning in transitional economies   192,
    193, 199, 203, 204
learning and fast-cycle capability
    building   146–7
learning and fast-cycle teams   153–5
learning in IJVs from foreign parent   205–6
learning and managed selection   219
"like-minded" believers *see* shared belief
    system debates
Liz Claiborne
    decline of   61–5
    design choices   55, 65
    historical overview   53–4
    presentation choices   55–6
    selling process   56–7, 60

macro-co-evolution   210, 222
managed selection   208, 217–19
management
    activities   233–4, *235*
    and capability development process   140,
        158
    and environmental changes   70
    and renewal process in multiunit
        firm   214
    and strategic renewal journeys: four ideal
        types   224–5
management actions and organizational
    capability building   137
managerial processes
    and capability building   137
    in transitional economy   201–2
managerial role in initiative process   167–8,
    174, 180–1, 183–4
Marion Merrell Dow (MMD)   142–51, 156
market-to-book value of firm   78, 83, *86*
market-to-book value and governance   81,
    82
micro-co-evolution   209, 211, 222

Naive selection   208, 216–17

open coding process   116
organizational capabilities
    context dependence of   141
    and environment   141
organizational capability   138–9
organizational capability building   137
    vs. execution of individual projects   *154*
    and managerial processes   152–3
    process model   139–40, 154
    from social constructivist
        perspective   139–41
organizational context and performance   *11*
organizational learning in transitional
    economy   192, 204–5
    transformation of business processes   200
organizational processes and executive
    beliefs   110
organizational success and strategic planning
    process   97
Origin (company)   219

patents   79–80, 84, 87
performance of firm and executive
    beliefs   110, 112

performance landscape   47, 48–9, *49*, 62–5,
    69, 70, 72n
  and environmental change   50, 69, 71
  and fit   49–50
personnel
  and capability building   140, 145–6, 148,
    153
  and strategic planning process   106
  in transitional economy   201–2
Pharma   199, 200, 201, 202, 205
Philips   219
population-ecology theory   209
positioning view of strategy *see* activity-based
    view of strategy

renewal theories
  and adaptation   *210*
  and selection   *210*
reputation as an intangible asset   80
resource accumulation   28
  in international competition   26
resource-based theory   18, 19–20, 78–9,
    209
resources   78–80, 83, *86*
  and activities   21, 28–9, 38–40, *42*
  and competitive advantage   35, 78–80
  and environment   21, 35, 78–80
  and initiative development   172, 173,
    181–2
  and market-to-book value   91
  and scope   28, 40–3
  and transformation actions   29–38
  and transformation process   23–6, 28–9,
    30, 31, 40–1

Sales & Marketing Management
    magazine   57
scope
  activities   26, 27
  and competitive positioning   *27*, 26–8,
    30,
  and resources   28, 40–3
  and transformational cycle   40–1
senior management and fast-cycle
    capability   144
sensegiving and fast-cycle capability
    building   145
sensemaking
  and fast-cycle capability building   145
  holistic renewal   223

  and knowledge-creation   170
shared belief system debates among "like-
    minded"   117, 121–2, 129, 130, 131
shared belief system debates between
    "different believers"   123–6, 129, 130,
    131
shared beliefs   110
  and actions   113
  and choices   113
  and cognitive consensuality   111
  and environment   118–19
  formation of groups sharing similar
    beliefs   122–3
  and shared strategic frames   111
  and shared understanding   111
  and strategic decision process   116–18,
    117, 119–21, 125, 128, 131
  see also beliefs; executive beliefs
Software (company)   199, 204
Spain
  construction firms in   22, 28
  paper firms in   22, 26–8
  petroleum firms in   22, 26
strategic choice perspective   209–10
strategic choices and executive beliefs   110
strategic decision process
  and belief patterns   119–21, *120*
  and cognitive biases   113–14
  and executive beliefs   110–11, 112,
    113–14
  and shared beliefs   116–18, *117*, 119–21,
    125, 128, 131
  theoretical framework   127–30, *128*, 131
strategic planning   97
  a process framework   101–3, *102*, 107
strategic planning process
  and communication   105–6
  elements   97, 101, 103–4
  evolution   97
  and financial performance   105, 107
  issue generation   104
  and management systems   106
  and reviews   107
strategic renewal journeys in multiunit firms,
    four ideal types   *215*
  see also naive selection; managed selection;
    hierarchical renewal; holistic renewal
strategy
  activity-based view   18, 19
  resource-based view   18, 19–20

strategy process research
  and co-evolution 239–40
  and sister disciplines 238
strategy process research development 236
supply and marketing 23–6, *24, 25,* 28–9,
  30, 33
support systems in initiative development *see*
  control systems
Systematic Updated Retail Feedback (SURF)
  System 57, 60

technological ability (as a resource) 79–80,
  83, 84, 87
theoretical saturation 116
transformation actions 6, 29–38
  activity entry 29–32, 38–9
  activity exit 33–4, 39
  activity (ongoing) development 34–5,
    39–40
  and competitive advantage 31–2, 34, 35,
    36–7
  and resources 28–9, *30*
transformation process 23, 42
  and activities 28–32, *30,* 33–5, *36–7*
  and competitive advantage 20, 21, 28,
    38–42

  and processes 38–40
  and resources 23–6, 28–9, *30,* 31, 40–1
  and scope 40–1
transitional economies
  case studies of firms in 192–205
  competitive advantage in 192
  creativity in organizational learning
    in 204–5
  innovation in organizational learning
    in 204–5
  knowledge in 192, 202
  learning in 192, 193, 199, 203, 204
  managerial processes in 201–2
  organizational learning in 192, 204–5
  personnel in 201–2
  unlearning in 193, 202–3
  see also learning in transitional economies

value creation model *78*
value creation and market-to-book value 91
Van Ommeren 176, 179, 180, 181, 182
variables, measurement *86, 88*
Variety generators in managed selection
    process 218

Xerox 219